'THE CONSCIENCE OF THE WORLD'

'The Conscience of the World'

The Influence of Non-Governmental Organisations in the UN System

edited by
PETER WILLETTS

a publication of
the David Davies Memorial Institute
of International Studies, London

THE BROOKINGS INSTITUTION,
WASHINGTON, D.C.

About Brookings

The Brookings Institution is a private nonprofit organization devoted to research, education, and publication on important issues of domestic and foreign policy. Its principal purpose is to bring knowledge to bear on current and emerging policy problems. The Institution was founded on December 8, 1927, to merge the activities of the Institute for Government Research, founded in 1916, the Institute of Economics, founded in 1922, and the Robert Brookings Graduate School of Economics, founded in 1924.

The Institution maintains a position of neutrality on issues of public policy. Interpretations or conclusions in Brookings publications should be understood to be solely those of the authors.

Published in North America
by The Brookings Institution
1775 Massachusetts Avenue, N.W.
Washington, D.C. 20036

Library of Congress Cataloging-in-Publication Data

"The conscience of the world"; the influence of non-governmental
organisations in the UN system / edited by Peter Willetts.
    p. cm.
Includes bibliographical references and index.
ISBN 0-8157-9420-7 — ISBN 0-8157-9419-3 (pbk.) (alk. paper)
    1. United Nations — Non-governmental advisory organizations.
2. Non-governmental organizations. I. Willetts, Peter.
JX1977.3.A2C66 1996
361.7'7-dc20
                                                  96-33353
                                                        CIP

Printed in Hong Kong

CONTENTS

CONTENTS

PREFACE

The genesis of this book lies in a 1987 study on the specialised agencies and the United Nations initiated by the David Davies Memorial Institute of International Studies.[1] That book was only able to address the subject of the relationship between non-governmental organisations and the United Nations in a short Appendix and it noted the need for a more comprehensive study. As it said,

> NGOs have established a role for themselves as sources of organised criticism of the imperfections of international society, as a stimulant to progress, as promoters of new ideas and programmes, as sources of additional voluntary funds for development, and as channels of publicity for the United Nations and its Agencies. These are valuable functions. NGOs deserve help in performing them more effectively.

This book *inter alia* provides that help.

I was pleased to be asked to chair the Study Group assembled by the Director of the David Davies Memorial Institute, Sheila Harden, to examine the effectiveness of some NGOs in specific areas as displayed by their work at the UN. Thanks to a formula developed by the Institute, the book is more than a collection of essays. Each chapter is the product of the individual researches of the separate authors, but all were submitted for discussion and criticism by the members of the Study Group in a series of meetings in late 1993 and 1994. All the chapters were revised as a result of these discussions, but the individual chapters remain the sole responsibility of the authors and not of the Study Group or Institute.

The Group, whose composition is given below, consisted of both academics and people active in NGOs. The final responsibility, as editor, for ensuring coherence between the different contributions fell to Peter Willetts to whom we owe a large debt of thanks.

Finally, members of the Group received a great deal of help and encouragement in their researches from friends and colleagues in Britain and elsewhere, to whom we are all very grateful. Particular thanks go to Alexandra McLeod and Elizabeth Lee of the London UN Information Centre.

JOHN SANKEY

1. Douglas Williams, *The Specialized Agencies and the United Nations* (London: C. Hurst & Co., 1987).

ABBREVIATIONS

ACC	Administrative Committee on Coordination
ADG	Assistant Director-General
AFL	American Federation of Labour
AVARD	Association of Voluntary Agencies for Rural Development (India)
CAME	Conference of Allied Ministers of Education
CEDAW	Committee on the Elimination of the Discrimination Against Women
CFA	Committee on Food Aid Policy
Cidse	Coopération Internationale pour le Développement et la Solidarité
CRDU	Children's Rights Development Unit
CSD	Commission on Sustainable Development
CSW	Commission on the Status of Women
DCI	Defence for Children International
DG	Director-General
ECOSOC	Economic and Social Council of the UN
ELC	Environment Liaison Centre
FAO	UN Food and Agricultural Organisation
FOE	Friends of the Earth
G7	Group of Seven
GATT	General Agreement on Tariffs and Trade
GNP	Gross National Product
HABITAT	UN Centre for Human Settlements
IADL	International Association of Democratic Lawyers
IAEA	International Atomic Energy Agency
IATA	International Air Transport Association
IBRD	International Bank for Reconstruction and Development
ICAO	International Civil Aviation Organisation
ICFTU	International Confederation of Free Trade Unions
ICOM	International Council of Museums
ICOMOS	International Council on Monuments and Sites
ICPD	International Conference on Population and Development
ICRC	International Committee of the Red Cross
ICSDW	International Council of Social Democrat Women
ICSU	International Council of Scientific Unions
ICSW	International Council on Social Welfare
ICVA	International Council of Voluntary Agencies
IDA	International Development Association
IDP	Internally Displaced Population
IEFR	International Emergency Food Reserve
IFAD	International Fund for Agricultural Development
IFC	International Finance Corporation

IGY	International Geophysical Year
IIED	International Institute for Environment and Development
ILO	International Labour Organisation
IMF	International Monetary Fund
IMO	International Maritime Organisation
IPPF	International Planned Parenthood Federation
ISBA	International Sea-Bed Authority
ISCA	International Save the Children Alliance
ISO	International Organisation for Standardisation
ITU	International Telecommunication Union
IUCN	International Union for the Conservation of Nature and Natural Resources (*also known as* World Conservation Union)
IWRAW	International Women's Rights Action Watch
LDC	London Dumping Convention
MAB	Man and the Biosphere
NORAD	Norwegian Agency for Development Cooperation
ODA	Overseas Development Administration *or* Official Development Assistance
OECD	Organisation for Economic Cooperation and Development
ONUSAL	UN Observer Mission in El Salvador
PP	Participation Programme
SCF	The Save the Children Fund
SCOPE	Special, later Scientific, Committee on Problems of the Environment
UIA	Union of International Associations
UN	United Nations
UNCED	UN Conference on Environment and Development
UNCTAD	UN Conference on Trade and Development
UNDCP	UN International Drug Control Programme
UNDP	UN Development Programme
UNESCO	UN Educational, Scientific and Cultural Organisation
UNEP	UN Environment Programme
UNFPA	UN Population Fund
UNHCR	Office of the UN High Commissioner for Refugees
UNICEF	UN Children's Fund
UNIDO	UN Industrial Development Organisation
UNIFEM	UN Voluntary Fund for Women
UNTAC	UN Transnational Authority in Cambodia
UPU	Universal Postal Union
WFP	World Food Programme
WFTU	World Federation of Trade Unions
WHO	World Health Organisation
WIDF	Women's International Democratic Federation
WILP	Women in the Law Project
WILPF	Women's International League for Peace and Freedom
WIPO	World Intellectual Property Organisation
WMO	World Meterological Organisation

WRI	World Resources Institute
WTO	World Trade Organisation (previously GATT)
WWF	World Wide Fund for Nature
YWCA	Young Women's Christian Association

THE CONTRIBUTORS

John Sankey (chairman) British High Commissioner to Tanzania, from 1982–5, and Permanent Representative to the UN in Geneva, 1985–90. In Tanzania he was able to see many NGOs at work in a developing country, while in Geneva he represented Britain in the Executive Committee of the UN High Commission for Refugees, various Human Rights bodies, the UN specialised agencies (WHO, ILO, ITU, WMO, WIPO) and UNCTAD. He led the British government delegation to the International Red Cross Conference in Geneva in 1987. He contributed the chapter on 'Decolonisation' in Eric Jensen and Mark Fisher (eds), *The United Kingdom – the United Nations* (Macmillan, 1990).

Peter Willetts (editor) Reader in International Relations, City University, London. He is the editor of *Pressure Groups in the Global System: The Transnational Relations of Issue-Orientated Non-Governmental Organisations*, a study of how NGOs enter world politics. He has been commissioned to work on this subject for a United Nations University conference, for an Open University course and for the Ford Foundation. He has also published two books on the Non-Aligned Movement and one on global interdependence.

Seamus Cleary Freelance overseas development consultant, specialising in the identification, monitoring and evaluation of development projects and the activities of the international financial institutions. His clients include academic institutions, multilateral development organisations and NGOs; he advises a number of the latter on relations with the World Bank and its activities. Before establishing his consultancy business in 1991, he was senior policy researcher at the London-based Catholic Fund for Overseas Development and president of the Policy Advisory Group of the 14-member Brussels-based international Catholic development NGO network, Coopération internationale pour le développement et la solidarité (CIDSE).

Jane Connors Senior Lecturer in Law at the School of Oriental and African Studies, University of London, specialising in human rights and family law. Her research interests are concerned with the human rights of women and the particular issue of violence against women. She has written widely on both these topics, acting as a consultant to the UN and the Commonwealth Secretariat. She is the author of a major UN study on domestic violence and is often called upon by governments to act as a consultant on this and other issues related to the concerns of women.

Helena Cook Head of the Legal and Intergovernmental Organizations office, Amnesty International, 1990–4. She is currently lecturing and working as a freelance consultant in international human rights law and related fields. She practised as a solicitor in 1979–82 and then as staff attorney with the New York-based Lawyers Committee for Human Rights in 1984–87, with a special focus on Africa, particularly South Africa. She joined Amnesty International (International Secretariat) in 1987 as a legal adviser. She has written widely on human rights issues.

Richard Hoggart Assistant Director-General of Unesco, 1970–5. Professor of Modern English Literature, Birmingham University, 1962–73; director, Centre for Contemporary Cultural Studies, Birmingham University, 1964–73; Warden, Goldsmiths' College, University of London, 1976–84. Author of numerous books, articles, pamphlets, reviews including *The Uses of Literacy, Speaking to Each Other, Only Connect, Life and Times* (3 vols).

Michael Longford Retired British civil servant. His last posting was in the International Relations Division of the Department of Health and Social Security. He represented the United Kingdom on several international organisations, and in 1983–8 was the British delegate on the Working Group which drafted the UN Convention on the Rights of the Child. Before entering the civil service in 1967 he was a District Commissioner in East Africa and later worked as the Deputy General Superintendent of Dr Barnardo's, the child care organisation. He is now the International Relations Attaché of the European Centre for Social Welfare Policy and Research and the Chairman of the Children's Rights Publications Foundation. He is a member of the UK Committee of UNICEF.

Sally Morphet Has worked in the Research and Analysis Department of the Foreign and Commonwealth Office since 1966, specialising first in South and South East Asia and from 1974 in general international and UN questions. She has published material on the non-aligned, the Security Council and human rights. Her last contribution to a book was a chapter on Peacekeeping and Election Monitoring in Adam Roberts and Benedict Kingsbury (eds) *United Nations, Divided World* (2nd edn, 1993).

Angela Penrose Senior overseas information officer with The Save the Children Fund (UK). She has worked in Ethiopia, Libya, Nigeria, Burundi and Zambia as a writer, teacher and journalist, and was the administrator of a relief and rehabilitation programme run by staff and students of Addis Ababa University during the Ethiopian famine in the 1970s. She is co-author with Kurt Jansson and Michael Harris of *The Ethiopian Famine* (Zed, 1987) the story of the 1980s famine.

John Seaman Head of the Policy Development Unit of The Save the Children Fund with responsibility for the technical content of projects in twenty-five countries concerned with the development of health care systems, food and nutrition planning, early warning systems for drought and relief programmes. He qualified as a medical practitioner in 1967 and has worked in Nigeria, India, Bangladesh, Ethiopia and other developing countries. He is Honorary Senior Lecturer in Nutrition at the London School of Hygiene and Tropical Medicine.

Bill Seary A freelance consultant on European matters advising national and international organisations on their responses to European developments and acting as an organiser and facilitator of meetings and training courses. He is currently working with the European Council on Refugees and Exiles on its programme in Central and Eastern Europe, and has previously worked with the European Social Action Network, the European Anti-Poverty Programme, the Euro Citizen Action Service and numerous UK-based organisations. He was previously head of International Affairs at the National Council for Voluntary Organisations and has been an office-holder in several international and European organisations.

Henry Steel Legal Adviser to the Foreign and Commonwealth Office (Colonial Office, CRO), 1955–80; to the British Mission to the UN, 1973–6; and to the Governor of Southern Rhodesia, 1979–80. Since 1987 he has been the leader of the British Delegation to UN Human Rights Commission, Geneva; a consultant on international, Commonwealth and constitutional law; and Legal Adviser to the governments of British Antarctic Territory and British Indian Ocean Territory.

Douglas Williams Retired as Deputy Secretary from the Ministry of Overseas Development, 1977. In 1968–73 he was Under-Secretary in charge of their International Division, and was also Co-Chairman of the Geneva Group in 1969. He was a member of the British delegation to UNCTAD III in 1973 and an alternate governor of the Asian Development Bank and African Development Fund. After retirement he was a member of the Economic and Social Committee of the European Community in 1978–82. He is the author of *The Specialized Agencies and the United Nations: The System in Crisis* (1987) and various studies of the relationship between Human Rights and Economic Development.

INTRODUCTION

Peter Willetts

When international relations are discussed by politicians, lawyers, diplomats, journalists and academics, it is usually in terms of the diplomatic interactions between governments. The activities of private, non-governmental groups in world politics are not seen as being worthy of attention. A few groups, such as Amnesty International, the Red Cross and Greenpeace, have managed to break through the barrier of invisibility. Other major global bodies, such as the World Council of Churches or the International Confederation of Free Trade Unions, seldom obtain news coverage. Thousands of smaller, more specialised organisations can be of major importance in their particular field, but are known only to those directly involved in their work. Full understanding of the complex dynamics of world politics requires knowledge of the influence achieved by the relevant private groups. In the United Nations these are known as non-governmental organisations or simply NGOs.

Governments expect to dominate disarmament negotiations, military alliances, armed conflicts and the international arms trade. On the other hand, they will usually be cautious about claiming any authority at all in sport and religious affairs. Apart from these extremes, day to-day international politics does include both governments and NGOs. It is generally taken for granted that domestic politics within countries involves interactions between politicians, civil servants and pressure groups. Because of belief in a common 'national interest' it is less often acknowledged that the same process affects foreign policy. This book moves on from politics within individual countries to the global level, where governments are generally assumed to be the only participants. Nevertheless, even at this level, on most issues there are regular intense interactions between diplomats, international civil servants and organised private groups. Those studying international relations will often distinguish the 'high politics' of diplomacy conducted by governments from the 'low politics' of economic and social questions involving non-governmental organisations. Such a distinction does not reflect the reality that drugs, unemployment, exchange rates, population problems or the debt crisis are the 'high politics' of many countries.

Do these interactions make any difference to political outcomes?

1

Can the general public influence decisions at the United Nations? Before the main chapters of the book respond to these questions, it is necessary first of all to consider what is a non-governmental organisation; which types can take part in UN politics; whether the NGOs are all independent from governments; and how many of them there are.

What is a non-governmental organisation?

There is no standard name for groups that are trying to influence world politics. In the study of single countries, discussion of 'interest groups' and 'pressure groups' is commonplace. The term 'interest groups' is unsatisfactory, as it tends to imply that only groups with substantial economic resources have an impact. 'Pressure groups' is more precise but has political overtones which many self-help and/or altruistic groups, such as Oxfam, dislike. The American term, 'private voluntary organisations' is also unsatisfactory since it carries connotations of charitable activity and does not readily bring to mind either the interest groups, such as industrial companies and trades unions, or the campaigning groups, such as Greenpeace and Amnesty International.

There is also an American literature on the 'new social movements', which mainly covers peace groups, women's groups, minority ethnic groups and the environmental movement. As Chapter 2 describes, at the UN Conference on Environment and Development 'major groups' was a popular term adopted to include women, youth, indigenous peoples, workers and farmers. At times there was a strong sense that 'major groups' was the sanitisation by the diplomats of 'new social movements'. There are anti-establishment, populist connotations to the idea of social movements and the literature tends to assume that all progressive and liberal people should support them. In reality small influential groups with good establishment credentials may also work for very progressive causes and some social movements, for example European neo-Nazi groups, may be considered by many to be evil. Some organisations appear both to be able to work as 'insiders' with the establishment and to appeal to a mass membership, for example the World Wide Fund for Nature. The study of NGOs should encompass all types of groups. The prime question is 'What groups influence decision-making?'

All the above terms tend to focus on what happens in a single country. In order to emphasise that such groups do operate across country boundaries and that they are not covered by the conventional study of international relations, academics now refer to 'transnational relations'. A 'transnational actor' is defined as being any participant in world politics operating outside the group's home country, independently of their home government.[1] It is a good, neutral, all-encompassing term, but outside the academic world it is predominantly applied to transnational corporations. This is not a problem as long as it is remembered that transnational corporations are but one among very many different types of transnational actors.

In the world of diplomacy, there is widespread agreement on the use of the term 'non-governmental organisations' (NGOs). These can vary greatly in their size and the type structure. They can be small, specialist groups based in a single country. For example, the South Atlantic Council is a British group of fifty individual experts promoting Argentine and British mutual understanding of the Falklands dispute. Some specialist groups are much bigger, because they recruit individuals from many countries as members, for example the International Bar Association has a membership of sixteen thousand lawyers. Large organisations, with a wide range of concerns and global coverage, usually have more complex two-tier structures, with individuals joining recognised country-based groups and those groups forming an international non-governmental organisation. Amnesty International is an example of a highly-centralised international NGO with 'Sections' in fifty-three countries. In contrast, the International Planned Parenthood Federation is a decentralised, global NGO with 109 'member family planning associations'.

The highest level of complexity arises when international NGOs themselves form umbrella groups, either to mobilise support as a coalition campaigning on a specific problem, such as the International Baby Foods Action Network, or for more general organisational cooperation, such as in the International Council of Voluntary Agencies.

Recognition of NGOs by intergovernmental organisations

Almost all intergovernmental organisations now accept, as a norm of world politics, that they must have working relationships with NGOs.[2] From the standard practice, four restrictions on what is considered a legitimate NGO can be identified. First, they cannot be commercial organisations. The Council of Europe explicitly defines an NGO as having a 'non-profit-making aim'[3] whereas the UN does so implicitly by specifying that the NGO's resources should come from its members or from voluntary contributions.[4] However, global and regional federations of manufacturers and of other commercial interests are recognised as NGOs, both by the Council of Europe and by the UN. For example the Oil Companies International Maritime Forum is an important participant in a UN agency, the International Maritime Organisation. These federations do meet the criteria of being non-profit-making, though their activities may include lobbying on behalf of the commercial interests of their members.

The second restriction is that recognised NGOs cannot be openly engaged in violence or advocate violence as a political tactic. Liberation movements and other guerrilla groups are never covered by the term non-governmental organisations. Groups that took up guerrilla warfare against colonial authorities and against the South African and Israeli governments were recognised as 'national liberation movements' by the Organisation of African Unity and in several cases became full members of the Non-Aligned Movement. At the United Nations two of them, the South West African Peoples Organisation (SWAPO) and the Palestine Liberation Organisation (PLO), were given observer status in the General Assembly and a standing invitation to attend all UN conferences.[5] Many other groups have been witnesses before UN committees or treated as parties to the conflicts being monitored by UN peace-keeping operations.

Thirdly, groups that want to replace existing governments, whether they are individual political parties or more broadly based coalitions of opposition groups, are not regarded as being NGOs. On the other hand, transnational groupings of political parties, such as the Liberal International, the Socialist International and the International Democrat Union, are widely recognised. The formal requirement is that an NGO should not be 'systematically engaging in unsubstantiated or politically motivated acts' against governments represented in the UN.[6] At times, individual governments have tried to use this restriction to prevent the recognition of NGOs who criticise them, particularly human rights NGOs, but in recent decades they have usually only been able to delay the granting of recognition.

Lastly, because the intergovernmental organisations want to see some benefit for themselves in the relationships, they insist that the NGO should support the goals and the activities of the organisation which recognises them. This restriction could have led to the stifling of debate and the suppression of criticism, but it has not done so. There has only been one recent case when an NGO was refused recognition at the UN, because it was hostile to a whole field of UN activity.[7] Overall only 4 per cent of the 495 applications received from 1970 to 1993 were rejected.[8]

It is worth noting that single-country NGOs are not automatically excluded and the range of issues on which they may be active is not limited. The UN prefers to deal with international NGOs 'covering, where possible, a substantial number of countries in different regions of the world'.[9] Nevertheless, as the phrase 'where possible' implies, this is not an essential requirement. Indeed, in recent years there has been a desire to increase the participation of single-country NGOs from developing countries. Although NGOs in the UN are accredited to the Economic and Social Council (ECOSOC), NGO consultative status has not been restricted to 'low politics' issues. The traditional 'high politics' issues also arise in the global NGO community. There are NGOs who support the Palestinian cause, and ones supporting Israel. Throughout the Cold War, some pro-Western and a few pro-communist NGOs were recognised by the UN.

From this review of terminology and practice, some definitions can be offered. 'Transnational relations' covers all activity by groups – including companies, guerrillas and political parties – who are seeking to communicate with other groups or governments in a foreign country. An NGO is any non-profit-making, non-violent, organised group of people who are not seeking government office. An international NGO has a less restrictive definition. It can be any non violent, organised group of individuals or organisations from more than one country. The members of an international NGO will usually be NGOs from different countries, but they can also have any mixture of individuals, companies, political parties, NGOs or other international NGOs as members.

While it would be convenient if 'NGOs' were used to cover groups based in a single-country and 'international NGOs' to cover groups based in more than one country, the term NGOs is also widely used to refer to international NGOs. The reader must assume that an NGO being discussed in this book could be either a single-country or a multi-country group.

Relations between NGOs and governments

It is also necessary to consider the extent to which non-governmental organisations are independent from governments. Again the situation is more complicated than might be expected. The UN has specified that an NGO may be 'any international organisation which is not established by intergovernmental agreement',[10] but this specification has not been strictly adhered to. The International Red Cross, which is governed by the Geneva Conventions, has had two of its components, the International Federation of Red Cross and Red Crescent Societies and the International Committee of the Red Cross (ICRC), recognised as NGOs at the UN by ECOSOC.[11] Two other prominent NGOs, the International Union of Local Authorities and the Inter-Parliamentary Union, although not composed of central government executives, are intergovernmental in a broader sense. Any legal interpretation of 'nongovernmental' is simply not maintained in political practice.

Questions of finance, the use of violence and seeking government office relate most obviously to a group in one country being independent from the government in its own country. Governments are also concerned that NGOs should be independent in a different sense. They should not be instruments of foreign governments. From this point of view, finance is the most sensitive question. In addition to being non-profit-making, there is concern that NGOs should obtain finance from their membership. As a result some NGOs such as Amnesty International are very cautious about accepting any money at all from governmental sources, for fear of suspicion that they have compromised their independence.[12]

On the other hand, development NGOs may receive substantial resources from governments, either in cash or supplies, to support their operational activities, particularly for disaster relief. The UN fully accepts this situation, provided that governmental contributions to NGOs are openly declared.[13] The development NGOs themselves are much more concerned that the NGO community is losing its integrity. The dangers include projects being tailored to the concerns of the donors, new NGOs being established solely to attract funds and NGO leaders being co-opted on to official bodies.[14] At the extreme, in a few countries an NGO may be established by the government to infiltrate and gather information on the NGO community. These 'government NGOs' are of particular concern in the field of human rights.

Single-country NGOs come together in international NGOs, and governments from different countries come together in a great variety of intergovernmental organisations. There is a logical possibility that a combination of single-country NGOs from various parts of the world and some governments could form a joint international organisation. The idea is so alien to traditional patterns of thought that there is not even an English word to describe this phenomenon.[15] The UN has explicitly accepted that such an organisation can be considered as an NGO: it includes in the consultative arrangements 'organisations which accept members designated by governmental authorities, provided that such membership does not interfere with the free expression of the views of the organisation'.[16] Such bodies are here called hybrid international organisations. They may be defined as international organisations that include in their membership both government departments (or other governmental institutions) and NGOs.

The table below lists eight categories of international organisations that span the spectrum from the pure intergovernmental organisation to the pure international NGO, with the hybrids as three of the middle categories. One important hybrid, the International Red Cross has already been mentioned. This is perhaps the best example there can be of an arrangement expressing full equality between NGOs and governments. The Red Cross is governed by an International Conference, which normally meets every four years: resolutions are passed, with each National Society and each 'State' having one vote, by a simple majority in a joint decision.[17] The work of the International Committee of the Red Cross, protecting prisoners of war, providing humanitarian assistance and acting as an intermediary in conflicts, is predominantly funded by governments, while the work of the International Federation, assisting refugees and providing disaster relief, is predominantly funded by the National Societies, although some of their funds can also come from governments. All the governments of the world in principle, if not always in practice, fully support the goals of the International Red Cross and are therefore content to take part in full institutional integration with NGOs (that is with the National Societies).

In other areas of policy the balance between governments and NGOs may be rather different and this is the basis for producing the eight categories of international organisations in the table. There are several areas of environmental and economic policy where NGOs and private companies take the main responsibility. In some countries, however, governmental bureaucracies or government-owned industries are also involved. Thus, some major organisations that are commonly seen as being NGOs are in fact hybrids. They include the World Conservation Union (IUCN), the International Council of Scientific Unions (ICSU), the International Organisation for Standardisation, the International Air Transport Association and the International Chamber of Shipping.[18]

There are not nearly as many hybrid international organisations as there are pure international NGOs without governmental membership. However, the hybrids are important within their own field of activity. They are also of significance for how we think about world politics, in demonstrating unambiguously that the international relations of governments cannot be separated from the international relations of NGOs. In hybrids, governments and NGOs recognise each other as having the right to take part in joint decision-making. Neither side automatically has a superior status; indeed they formally have equal status.

The sixth category in the table does not fit easily within the classification scheme. It consists of international organisations that are

Peter Willetts

Table 1.   CLASSIFICATION OF INTERNATIONAL
ORGANISATIONS

Intergovernmental Organisations

Only government members; NGO links not routine	North Atlantic Treaty Organisation
Only government members; NGO links routine	United Nations

Hybrid International Organisations

Government and NGO members; governments dominant status	International Labour Organisation*
Government and NGO members (the two with equal status)	International Red Cross
Government and NGO members; NGOs dominant status	Birdlife International

International Non-Governmental Organisations

Groups of government employees as members	International Union of Police Federations
Only NGO members; government funding welcomed	International Planned Parenthood Federation
Only NGO members; government funding not routinely welcomed	Amnesty International†

*Strictly speaking, in the ILO 'states' are members and the governments, employers and trades unions are all representatives of their states. However, the different types of delegates are free to cast their votes separately.

† Amnesty International is so cohesive that the separate Sections should not be seen as distinct NGOs.

composed solely of government employees or officials, either with individuals as members (the International Association of Chiefs of Police) or with country-based groups (the International Union of Police Federations). They could be seen as intergovernmental organisations. However, when they operate in these groups, the employees and officials are promoting their own interests and values rather than government policy. In this sense they are comparable to private professional bodies, such as the International Union of Architects. They are best seen as a special category of NGO, to which governments will usually expect to have easy access.[19]

The global coverage of NGOs

There is no authoritative source to provide a global picture of the number of NGOs, but some parts of the picture can be brought into clearer focus than others. At the UN, as of December 1993, there were 969 NGOs on the ECOSOC list,[20] and in July 1994, 552 environment and development NGOs were provisionally given Roster status. Many more NGOs have formal consultative status with at least one of the UN specialised agencies or operational programmes. The Union of International Associations (UIA) has been producing a *Yearbook of International Organisations* since the 1950s. The UIA grand total in the 1990s editions has been over 20,000 NGOs, but this includes inactive bodies and single country NGOs. The more reliable figures for 'Conventional International Bodies' show a steep increase from a thousand NGOs and hybrids in the late 1950s to two thousand in the early 1970s. For most of the following decade, a steady figure of around 4,600 is reported, with 4,830 NGOs and hybrids being identified in 1993.[21] Thus UN ECOSOC consultative status has been granted to about one-fifth of the possible organisations. However, the UN is involved with a greater proportion of the international NGO community than this, because many organisations do not seek consultative status. They confine themselves to lobbying the UN when issues of particular concern to them arise.[22]

It is sometimes assumed that NGOs will exist only in Western societies with a long tradition of a civic culture or in developed societies with a complex modern economy, but the situation is not so simple. The world's largest democracy, India, is a non-Western, developing country with a vibrant civic culture that generates much transnational activity. On the other hand, Western governments are not always tolerant of private groups.[23] In all societies, even the most authoritarian, there are a variety of religious, occupational, communal, co-operative, cultural and self-help groups, and thus some involvement in global NGO relationships. If the country is authoritarian, particular types of NGOs may be absent. Those that do exist may still keep a small window open to the outside world.[24] The size and the diversity of a country will interact with the level of authoritarianism and the level of development to affect the number and type of NGOs operating in the country.

There are three ways in which NGOs are actively promoting their spread to all regions of the world. Individual NGOs encourage the formation of comparable NGOs in other countries. The spread of Friends of the Earth from the United States, first to Western Europe, then to developing countries and finally to Eastern Europe, would be a good example. A somewhat different process occurs when one group encourages the formation of a partner group, rather than a replica of itself, in another country. Northern fund-raising NGOs will support cooperatives and community groups in the South, while those who are oppressed in one country often try to form campaign groups, such as the Anti-Apartheid Movement, working on their behalf in another country. Lastly, one NGO may be influenced to expand its activities into more countries. This can occur as an NGO increases the resources at its disposal or it can result from a changing perception of its role. For example, Oxfam had been operating for twenty years before it became predominantly oriented towards developing countries. The development process has also generated new NGOs in the South. As one study put it, 'From the middle of the 1970s, a trend of growing importance has been the emergence of indigenous NGOs in the South as active partners in development efforts. In the 1980s, conservative estimates put their number at 6,000–8,000.'[25] The collapse of communism in Eastern Europe and the Soviet Union has meant that in the 1990s global NGOs that were previously forbidden are also expanding into the region.

Conclusions

There is therefore, great variety among the transnational actors involved in world politics. Guerrilla groups may take part as observers at the UN or even as full members in other intergovernmental organisations, but they never have NGO status. Transnational corporations and political parties cannot on their own be treated as being non-governmental organisations, but they can gain access to the UN through wider federations that are recognised as NGOs. At the global level, NGOs may have individuals as members; they may be organisations of organisations; or they may have both individuals and organisations as members. NGOs may have a very small membership or have millions of members. They may represent privileged elites or the oppressed and the disadvantaged. They may be little-known lobbies, influencing governments behind the scenes, or they may be mass movements, gaining coverage in the global news media. NGOs may have members from one country, from a group of countries in a specified region or from all parts of the world. They may deal with 'high politics' or 'low politics', controversial issues or obscure issues: indeed it is reasonably safe to say that there are transnational NGOs dealing with virtually every issue that is of concern to more than a small local community. NGOs are not separate from the world of governments. A few have been established by intergovernmental treaties and many are channels for government finance. In some cases recognised NGOs have government-ment ministries and other governmental bodies as members and should be seen as belonging to a special category of hybrid international organisations. There is no such thing as a typical NGO.

There is a widespread attitude that NGOs consist of altruistic people campaigning in the general public interest, while governments consist of self-serving politicians. On some issues, such as human rights, this may generally be valid and NGOs are 'the Conscience of the World'. Even so, such an attitude should not be adopted as an unchallenged assumption and hence the title of the book is put in quotation marks. It is in the nature of NGOs that they will often be raising new issues and expressing public unease with the policies of governments. Changing the agenda for debate is their most important impact on politics. However, it is logically impossible to support all NGOs because they do not all pursue the same values. There are conflicts within the NGO community, both in specific terms such as pro-abortion versus anti-abortion NGOs and in general terms such as reformers versus advocates of radical change. NGOs do not automatically deserve support and governments are not necessarily in the wrong. This book is not designed to mobilise support for any of the NGOs it covers. Its aim is to demonstrate that UN politics cannot be understood without assessing the impact of NGOs on each issue.

The first two chapters of this book give the history of how NGOs won a place for themselves in world politics and explain what arrangements exist for them to take part in the United Nations. (For those less familiar with the UN, Appendix A outlines its basic structure and distinguishes between its various principal organs, subsidiary bodies, operational programmes and specialised agencies.) Seven chapters provide detailed case-studies from three different perspectives – UN agencies, policy-making and individual NGOs. The first two consider the role of NGOs in the World Bank and UNESCO. Two chapters approach the question of the overall impact of NGOs in two policy areas, the environment and women's rights; another covers the narrower activity of negotiating the text of the Convention on the Rights of the Child. Two chapters written by activists from Amnesty International and Save the Children show how their organisations have influenced UN decisions.

All the chapters to some extent show the NGOs involved in agenda-setting, policy-making and implementation of policy, but the balance between the three types of activities varies quite considerably. On women's rights, the NGOs are mainly agenda-setting, while the Save the Children study focuses on the effective implementation of policy. The other chapters are more mixed. In each case the NGOs tend to feel dissatisfied, because they have worked hard and long to achieve less than they would have wished. In each case the governments involved and outside observers tend to feel the NGOs have achieved more than would seem possible for relatively small organisations working with limited resources on complex problems.

NOTES

1. For more detailed academic discussion of transnational relations see R. O. Keohane and J. S. Nye (eds), *Transnational Relations and World Politics* (Cambridge, MA: Harvard University Press, 1970) and P. Willetts (ed.), *Pressure Groups in the Global System: The Transnational Relations of Issue-Orientated Non-Governmental Organisations* (London: Pinter, 1982).
2. While most intergovernmental organisations have relations with NGOs, practice varies considerably. The Council of Europe is similar to the UN (see notes 3 and 22 below). In contrast the European Community has no formal system, but has been accessible to about 3,000 special interest groups and 'intends to make these relations slightly more formal and thereby more transparent'. (Press Release IP 996, 2 December 1992). The International Tropical Timber Council has mixed formality and access, by granting formal observer status to any NGO that presents itself at the start of a session.
3. Quotation from Article 1 of the Convention, given in *Explanatory Report on the European Convention on the Recognition of the Legal Personality of International Non-Governmental Organisations* (Strasbourg: Council of Europe, 1986).
4. UN ECOSOC Resolution 1296(XLIV), para. 8. The full text of this resolution is given in Appendix B.
5. Two other liberation movements from South Africa, the African National Congress and the Pan-African Congress, were invited to many conferences before 1994.
6. UN ECOSOC Resolution 1296(XLIV), para. 36(b).
7. See Human Life International, p. 37 below.
8. See UN doc. E/AC.70/1994/5 of 26 May 1994, p. 26. The proportion 'rejected' has been calculated on the assumption that those 'deferred' or 'not considered' were handled in subsequent years.
9. UN ECOSOC Resolution 1296(XLIV), para. 4.
10. *Ibid.*, para. 7.
11. The organisation of the International Red Cross is highly complex. The basic international law is now given in the four Geneva Conventions of 1949, the two Additional Protocols of 1977 and the Statutes of the International Red Cross, but its foundation dates back to 1863. Until 1992 the International Federation of Red Cross and Red Crescent Societies was known as the League of Red Cross and Red Crescent Societies. The ICRC and the International Federation became the only NGOs to be granted Observer status with the UN General Assembly, by Resolution 45/6 of 16 October 1990 and Resolution 49/2 of 19 October 1994 respectively. The ICRC subsequently withdrew from its Category II status with ECOSOC.
12. Amnesty will not accept core funding from governments, but it does accept money from government lotteries or from the police in countries where those forced to submit to on-the-spot fines are able to nominate Amnesty as the recipient. Direct government funds are accepted for relief purposes. See

M. Ennals, 'Amnesty International and Human Rights' in P. Willetts (ed.), *op. cit.*, p. 69.

13. UN ECOSOC Resolution 1296(XLIV), para. 8.

14. J. Clark, *Democratizing Development: The Role of Voluntary Organizations* (London: Earthscan Publications, 1991). Clark shows particular concern about the danger of governments compromising the integrity of NGOs. see pp. 8–9, 45, 53, 64, 79 and 89–91.

15. In Britain, the word quango has been coined to refer to quasi-autonomous non governmental organisations, such as the Arts Council or the Sports Council, that may be funded and/or staffed by the government, but still are expected to act independently. The current author has suggested that a new word, *iquango*, should be used to cover international quasi-non-governmental organisations that are composed both of NGOs and of governmental bodies. See P. Willetts. 'Transactions, Networks and Systems' in A. J. R. Groom and P. Taylor (eds), *Frameworks for International Cooperation* (London: Pinter, 1990).

16. UN ECOSOC Resolution 1296(XLIV), para. 7.

17. *Rules of Procedure of the International Conference of the Red Cross*, Article 17. The ICRC and the International Federation also each have one vote.

18. In contrast to the International Chamber of Shipping, Intercargo (the International Association of Dry Cargo Shipowners) remains a pure NGO, because it specifies in Article 4 of its constitution that the members may not be government-owned.

19. Various other attempts have been made to classify NGOs on the basis of what brought the members together or the type of activities they pursue. See for example, P. Willetts (ed.), *Pressure Groups . . .*, pp. 2–8, and Clark, *op. cit.* pp. 40–1. Such empirical classifications are bound to be of limited value. The categories overlap, NGOs move in and out of categories as their activities change from year to year and there are special cases that defy classification. For the alternative argument that a variety of variables should be used to describe NGOs, see P. Willetts, *Transnational Actors and Changing World Order* (Yokohama: International Peace Research Institute Meigaku, Occasional Paper no. 17), pp. 15–16.

20. UN doc. E/1994/INF/5 of 13 May 1994. For full discussion of the ECOSOC system of consultative status for NGOs, see Chapter 2.

21. Union of International Associations, *Yearbook of International Organisations, 1993–1994, vol. I* (Munchen: K. G. Saur, 30th edn, June 1993). The data given is from Appendix 4 (Statistics), p. 1699.

22. The Organisation for Economic Cooperation and Development (OECD) has produced three directories of NGOs covering the twenty-four member countries and identifying 2,542 development NGOs, 649 environment NGOs and 591 concerned with human rights, refugees and migrants. This should not be taken as giving a total of 3,782, because there is overlap between the three directories. The figures are also exaggerated, because they include the national sections of an NGO along with the international NGO which brings them together. On the other hand, there can be at times a real sense that the international NGO and each of the country sections is a distinct organisation. A Council of Europe directory covers 232 of the 317 NGOs in consultative status as of 1 March 1989, while a Commonwealth directory covers 199 NGOs. See below, note 25, and the following: Development Centre of the OECD, *Directory of Non-Governmental Environment and Development Organisations in OECD Member Countries* (Paris: OECD, 1992); Development Centre of the OECD, *Human Rights, Refugees, Migrants and Development. Directory of NGOs in OECD*

Countries (Paris: OECD, 1993); *Directory of NGOs (International Non-Governmental Organisations) enjoying Consultative Status with the Council of Europe* (Strasbourg: Council of Europe, 1989); *Directory of Commonwealth Organisations* (London: Commonwealth Secretariat, 1991).

23. It should be remembered that the British MI5 has monitored the Campaign for Nuclear Disarmament and there is evidence suggesting other groups are also monitored. The French secret service in July 1985 actually blew up a Greenpeace boat, the *Rainbow Warrior*, in New Zealand, killing one person who was on board.

24. Even Romania under Ceauşescu was host to one global NGO, the International Federation of Beekeepers' Associations.

25. Development Centre of the Organisation for Economic Cooperation and Development, *Directory of Non-Governmental Organisations in OECD Member Countries* (Paris: OECD, 1990), p. 24. There is a wider literature on development NGOs. Most of it is more concerned with the impact of NGOs on development at the grass-roots in developing countries than their impact on international organisations. For examples of work that are more relevant to this study see Clark, *op. cit.*; *World Development*, supplement to vol. 15: 'Development Alternatives: The Challenge for NGOs' (Oxford: Pergamon, 1987); OECD, *Voluntary Aid for Development. The Role of Non-Governmental Organisations* (Paris: OECD, 1988); J. Farringdon *et al.*, *Reluctant Partners? Non-Governmental Organisations, the State and Sustainable Agricultural Development* (London: Routledge for the Overseas Development Institute, 1993) and three companion volumes on NGOs in Asia, Latin America and Africa; UNDP, *Human Development Report 1993* (Oxford University Press, 1993).

1

THE EARLY HISTORY

FROM THE CONGRESS OF VIENNA TO THE
SAN FRANCISCO CONFERENCE

Bill Seary

This chapter examines the coordinating structures that developed among international NGOs, largely in response to the growth of intergovernmental organisations, and discusses their relationship to those intergovernmental bodies up to and including the United Nations Conference on International Organisation held in San Francisco in April–June 1945.

Much of what follows concerns European-based organisations and activities. The only other continent with a significant number of independent states was Latin America. The United States, almost a continent by itself, saw the development of nation-wide NGOs, but its international activity in the field appears, from a European perspective anyway, to have been centred on Europe.[1] The same is true of NGOs in the British Dominions which, over the period, took an increasingly independent line in international matters.[2]

The growth of international non-governmental organisations

Leaving aside the religious and academic networks that date from the middle ages (and which, strictly speaking, were more cosmopolitan than international), NGOs first appear on the international scene in the nineteenth century. The date of the earliest of them is a matter of opinion. White[3] favours the World Alliance of YMCAs which was founded in 1855 with member associations in Belgium, England, France, Germany, the Netherlands, Scotland, Switzerland and the United States of America. Lyons[4] believes that four had already been established by 1849. The difference is probably due to varying ideas about what constitutes an international NGO. It is clear however that their numbers remained low until the last quarter of the nineteenth century.[5]

15

These new organisations covered a wide range of topics, such as the treatment of offenders, the slave trade, the traffic in women and children, organised labour, the opium trade, peace and humanitarian assistance. The Société internationale d'études, de correspondance et d'échanges, founded in Paris in 1895, had as its aim the development of international relations and the fostering of goodwill across national frontiers.

One organisation deserves special notice. In 1859 Henri Dunant, a Swiss national, had been profoundly affected by his experience of helping to care for the wounded from the battle of Solferino. He inspired the formation of a small committee in Geneva which developed into the International Committee of the Red Cross. In 1863 it convened an international conference which led to the formation of national committees. Within ten years there were twenty-two of these committees (later known as national Red Cross Societies). Up to this point the organisation had developed in a fairly typical way. One person had identified a need and had collected a small group to campaign for an organisation to answer that need. The group had inspired the establishment of similar ones in other countries. The International Committee of the Red Cross (the membership of which was, and still is, entirely Swiss) continued to act as the centre of the movement rather than encouraging the creation of an international non-governmental organisation. It was also able to persuade the Swiss government to convene a diplomatic conference which in 1864 drafted the first of the Geneva Conventions. It was not until 1919 that the needs of post-war societies and the vision of Henry P. Davison of the American Red Cross led to the formation of an international organisation – the League of Red Cross and Red Crescent Societies, now known as the International Federation of Red Cross and Red Crescent Societies.[6]

The 1914–18 World War did not completely stop the formation of new international NGOs. For example, the Fellowship of Reconciliation and the Women's International League for Peace and Freedom were both formed during the war. Lyons[7] estimates that fifty-one organisations were set up in the period 1915–19, but it is likely that most of these organisations were formed after the end of hostilities.

At much the same time, building on years of less formal contact through conferences and other international meetings, the International Chamber of Commerce and the International Federation of Trade Unions burst into life.[8] At the other end of the scale, individuals were coming together to give practical or intellectual effect to their concern for peace and reconciliation. The Save the

Children International Union was established in 1920 to prevent overlapping among the organisations caring for starving children in Europe and the Near East;[9] Service Civil International has its roots in a workcamp for reconciliation held near Verdun in 1920/1;[10] and the International Federation of League of Nations Societies was formed for the purpose of supporting the work of the League of Nations.

In the 1920s and 1930s, as the diplomatic situation was getting steadily more difficult, this seems, if anything, to have stimulated non-governmental efforts to maintain contact and understanding between countries. The Associated Country Women of the World was established in 1929[11] and in 1932 the International Youth Hostel Association was founded to enable young people to travel in other countries. By 1935 the World's Student Christian Federation was involved in 'the process of interchange and of deepening of our consciousness'.[12]

The total number of international NGOs is estimated to have risen from 400 in 1920 to 700 in 1939.[13]

Causes of the development of international non-governmental organisations

Why did international NGOs not appear before the nineteenth century? And why then rather than later?

Towards the end of the eighteenth century, more people became concerned about social conditions and believed that part of the answer to this lay in the formation of societies committed to action.[14] Committees, societies and associations have been a noticeable feature of English society since the mid-eighteenth century, related to the emergence of the polite society of gentry and nobility, and the increased mobility made possible by advances in the design of carriages and improvements in the road system.[15] In most continental European countries, associations of citizens only began to form in the first half of the nineteenth century. Even then, many had legal systems which were generally unhelpful for the formation of associations. However, the nineteenth century saw a dramatic growth in the middle classes and a consequent increase in the numbers of people with the time, education and resources to take part in associations. Many of today's cultural and scientific societies had their origins in this period.

Secondly, the world was growing smaller politically. Although the nineteenth century is noted for the rise of nationalism, this was not at the expense of internationalism. Indeed, internationalism depends upon the existence of national structures. The Congress of Vienna established an international approach to certain ethical and economic questions. The Central Commission on the Navigation of the Rhine is arguably the earliest of the international agencies.[16] In the same year as the Congress of Vienna, the Treaty of Paris established the first intergovernmental political structure in the sense of regular meetings with broad objectives and an open agenda:

> To ensure and facilitate the execution of the present Treaty and consolidate the close ties which today unite the four Sovereigns for the good of the world, the High Contracting Parties have agreed to renew at fixed intervals, either under the auspices of the Sovereigns or in the person of their respective Ministers, meetings devoted to their great common interests and to the examination of those measures which on each occasion may be judged the most salutary for the ease and prosperity of their peoples and for the maintenance of peace in Europe.[17]

Subsequent Congresses took place at Aix-la-Chapelle in 1818, Troppau (in Silesia) in 1820, Laibach (Ljubljana) in 1821 and Verona in 1822. The Aix-la-Chapelle Congress confirmed the structure which was to continue, with some modifications in mid-century, till 1914. Five great powers divided Europe into areas of influence and arranged, certainly as far as the three more eastern powers were concerned, for nationalist and democratic movements to be suppressed. The result was a Europe which saw a substantial degree of peace from 1815 until 1848 and again, if less securely, from 1878 to the end of the century. For much of the nineteenth century it was possible to think of Europe as a continent where issues were pan-European and could be addressed in pan-European ways.

The third factor is the logistical one. Postal reform in Britain in 1840 was followed swiftly in other countries and in 1874 the Conference of Berne established the Universal Postal Union, greatly facilitating the sending of mail from country to country. In the 1840s telegraph systems started to expand, following widespread acceptance of Morse's code. In 1851 a telegraph cable was laid between England and France, putting the London-Brussels-Paris carrier pigeon service out of business.[18] Similarly, national rail systems grew quickly; in 1860 Bavarian Railways hosted a conference involving Baden, Württemberg, Austria and France to agree international timetables. By 1873 sleeping cars were available for long journeys.[19] Such changes represented significant improvements in pan-European communications.

The relationship with early intergovernmental organisations

Until the nineteenth century, governmental congresses concerned themselves almost entirely with the diplomatic adjustments following a war. As we have seen, this changed early in the new century with the Congress of Vienna dealing, *inter alia*, with free naviga tion of international rivers and suppression of the slave trade. Thus economic and social questions became part of diplomacy, not least because economic interests on the one hand, and philanthropists on the other, had the ability and the inclination to direct the attention of governments towards these questions.

Later in the nineteenth century similar influences led to the convening of the intergovernmental conference on the 'Amelioration of the Condition of the Wounded in Armies in the Field'; and the Hague Peace Conferences of 1899 and 1907 were convened at least partly because of the pressure exerted by the Inter-Parliamentary Union.[20] The International Bureau for the Suppression of Traffic in Women and Children held a congress in Paris in 1902 which led in 1904 to the signature by the United States of America and several European governments of an international agreement on the subject.

Coordination among international non-governmental organisations

At the end of the nineteenth century, as the number of international organisations and international conferences grew, competition began to emerge between cities for the opportunity to host them. In 1889 and 1900, for example, the French government offered subsidies to NGOs to hold their conferences in Paris. Baldwin[21] records eleven conferences in 1889 (including accidents at work, transfer of real estate, dentistry, bimetallism, public charities, photography, women's affairs and peace) and ten in 1900 (including labour legislation, comparative legislation, assistance in time of war, chronometry and the teaching of social sciences) as meeting there. The real number of conferences in these years may be much higher – perhaps forty.[22] A high proportion of these conferences led to attempts, not always successful, to launch new international organisations, often with their headquarters in Paris.

Brussels also went out of its way to welcome international organisations. It has been estimated that between the Congress of Vienna and 1914, Brussels was host to between a quarter and a third of all the international conferences held.[23] This may be attributable in part to a desire to establish the identity of the new Belgian state. The value of these NGOs sharing their experiences across subject areas certainly occurred to Henri La Fontaine and Paul Otlet, Directors-General of the International Bibliographical Institute. In its original form their idea was to establish a world documentation centre.[24] Their initiative led in 1908 to the formation of the Central Bureau of International Organisations, bringing together twenty or so of the approximately one hundred international NGOs with their headquarters in Brussels. The Bureau cooperated with the International Bibliographical Institute and the International Peace Institute in the publication of the 1908–9 edition of *L'Annuaire de la Vie Internationale* which, with the 1910–11 edition, remains the key source of information on the international NGOs of the time.

The Central Bureau was involved in the organisation of a World Congress of International Associations which was held in Brussels in May 1910. This brought together representatives of 132 international NGOs and thirteen governments and led directly to the formation of the Union of International Associations (UIA), supported financially by the Belgian government and by the Carnegie Endowment for Peace. A second World Congress was held in 1913, involving 169 international NGOs and twenty-two governments.[25]

War led to the cancellation of the third world conference in San Francisco in 1915. The founders of the UIA however continued to work and, in particular, to campaign for the formation of a League of Nations. This work was later to be acknowledged by the Secretary-General of the League:

> The very nature of the work carried out by the Union of International Associations before the war rendered it indirectly and within the means at its disposal, one of the promoters of the League of Nations. It had already expressly declared at one of the Congresses that the principle of a League of Nations was the ultimate end of all international movements. During the war the leaders of the Union drew up drafts of a Covenant and of an international constitution.[26]

The development of the League of Nations during the 1920s had the effect of moving the focus of international NGOs from Brussels to Geneva.[27] In 1919, only three had their base in Geneva. This had risen to thirty by 1926 and to sixty by the end of the decade.[28] Geneva tended to attract those interested in the League or the International Labour Office, and organisations concerned with peace, religion, employment and health and humanitarian affairs. The

League of Red Cross Societies moved from Paris to Geneva when war broke out in September 1939.

The UIA remained a Brussels-based organisation and became isolated from many of the discussions in Geneva. This represented a failure to fulfil the role its leaders had in mind, namely that of a voice for the community of international NGOs. The Brussels base, which had been so appropriate before the 1914–18 war, became a liability after Geneva had been agreed as the headquarters of the League of Nations and the Belgian government failed to secure the presence of any other significant intergovernmental body. The other crucial factor is the failure of the UIA to renew its leadership. Henri La Fontaine and Paul Otlet were visionaries who do not seem to have realised that the respect that people undoubtedly had for their intellectual abilities did not guarantee that their ideas would be adopted. In the highly political world of the League of Nations, lobbying skills and willingness to settle for short-term gains on the way to longer-term visions might have served the UIA better.

The UIA was initially enthusiastic about the work of the League of Nations and enjoyed praise from the officials of the League (see the quotation above). It appears, however, to have been marginalised both in Geneva and, more hurtfully, in Paris where its own vision had been responsible for the formation of the International Institute of Intellectual Cooperation. A report to UIA organisations in 1923 by Paul Otlet[29] describes, with mounting incredulity, the acceptance of UIA's concept by the League of Nations, the decision to establish an International Committee on Intellectual Cooperation, the failure to invite anyone from UIA to serve on the Committee, the failure to persuade it to meet in Brussels and the omission of UIA from the organisations which were asked to present evidence to the Committee. Otlet notes bitterly that apart from a glowing tribute in the opening remarks, UIA had not even been mentioned in the minutes of the Committee, which at the time he wrote had not engaged in a discussion of any depth of the concept of an international organisation for intellectual work.

In 1929 the Federation of International Institutions came into being in Geneva,[30] and by 1938 it grouped together forty-two international NGOs. In contrast to the ambitious projects of the UIA, the Federation devoted its efforts to promoting the interests of its members in such practical matters as taxes, use of properties owned by the League and securing access by NGOs to League meetings.[31] This was assisted by the development of a procedure for determining the *bona fides* of NGOs.[32]

During these years international NGOs also began to organise themselves in broad subject areas. In 1932, for example, some thirty

peace and disarmament organisations formed an International
Consultative Group which 'promoted not only regular consultation,
but indirectly also cooperative action and coordinated policies'.[33]

The League of Nations

The formal recognition of NGOs by the League of Nations was
limited to a few specific cases. Article 25 of the Covenant of the
League read:

> The Members of the League agree to encourage and promote
> the establishment and cooperation of duly authorised voluntary
> national Red Cross organizations having as purposes the improve-
> ment of health, the prevention of disease and the mitigation of
> suffering throughout the world.

When it started its work, the League had thought of taking a wide
interpretation of Article 24 of the Covenant, which reads:

> 1. There shall be placed under the direction of the League all
> international bureaus already established by general treaties if
> the parties to such treaties consent. All such international
> bureaus and all commissions for the regulation of matters of
> international interest hereafter constituted shall be placed under
> the direction of the League.
> . . . . . .
> 3. The Council may include as part of the expenses of the
> Secretariat the expenses of any bureau or commission which is
> placed under the direction of the League.

In June 1921 the League of Nations Council decided to make it
possible for the patronage of the League to be given to all international organisations under certain conditions. This decision was
reversed two years later. The Council believed that 'it is not desir-
able to risk diminishing the activity of these voluntary organisations, the number of which is fortunately increasing, by even the
appearance of an official supervision'.[34]

At an informal level, the presence of NGOs was an established
fact. It was, for example, an annual event for the International
Federation of League of Nations Societies to present to the President of the Assembly the resolutions it had adopted at its conference. These resolutions were often published in the Journal of
the Assembly. International NGOs were invited to some League
meetings and from the time of the 1932 Disarmament Conference
bona fide unofficial agencies (sometimes national as well as inter-

national) were accorded special facilities as regards seating and documentation.[35]

In the earlier days of the League, many NGOs had 'assessors' on League committees. These had the rights and privileges of the government representatives, short of being able to vote. This arrangement became rarer in later years. The Committee on Social Questions was reorganised in 1936 and became entirely governmental. Although some international NGOs were invited to become 'Correspondent Members', and there was provision for assessors to be appointed *ad hoc*, the ability of NGOs to contribute to the discussions of the Committee was virtually eliminated.[36]

In general, the interaction between the League and international NGOs changed from one of NGOs supporting and contributing to the policy work of the League to one where the League was less interested in the opinions of NGOs but more willing to provide information for and about them. The League published a Quarterly Bulletin of Information on the Work of International Organisations from 1922 to 1938. It also published a *Handbook of International Organisations* and granted international NGOs limited access to its library.[37]

In 1921 the League set up a health organisation, the functions of which included:

> (*f*) to confer and to cooperate with International Red Cross Societies and other similar societies under the provisions of Article 25 of the Covenant;
> (*g*) to advise, when requested, other voluntary organisations in health matters of international concern.

The Health Committee was composed of a geographically balanced selection of public health officials with one representative from the International Labour Office and one from the League of Red Cross Societies (which had itself been formed only in 1919). At its third meeting Dr Santoliquido, the representative of the League of Red Cross Societies, made a statement about their relationship. He said that there should be a mutual exchange of documents and proposals; that the League of Red Cross Societies be entrusted with all that concerned popular instruction in matters of health; and that the League would extend to the Health Section of the League of Nations the cooperation which it was in a position to offer. In fact the League made a financial contribution to the work of the Health Organisation.[38] Later, however, the League of Nations seems to have felt that the League of Red Cross Societies had not lived up to expectations.[39]

Similarly, in other fields, the League of Nations started its work by cooperating closely with international NGOs. The International Chamber of Commerce, representing commercial interests from across the world, had three full places on the League's Economic Consultative Committee established in 1927.[40] It was represented at twenty-nine official conferences between 1927 and 1932, at times with full voting rights, and in 1928 it was one of the parties to the Final Act of the League Conference on export and import restrictions.[41]

The International Bureau for the Suppression of the Traffic in Women and Children was represented on the League of Nations Permanent Advisory Committee for the Suppression of Traffic in Women and Children. As we have seen, it had been instrumental in the signing of an international agreement in 1904 and continued to be active in ports and railway stations, maintaining close cooperation with the authorities.[42] The League was required by Article 23(c) to take over the supervision of the international agreements in this field. The International Federation for Aid to Young Women had an assessor's seat in the Permanent Consultative Committee for the Protection of Children and Young People and felt that this was an effective way of working. 'This Committee which, at the beginning, was favourable to the regulation of vice has so changed its point of view that the last international convention that it drew up to deal with the exploitation of the prostitution of others is strictly abolitionist.'[43]

Other intergovernmental organisations worked even more closely with the non-governmental sector, most noticeably the International Labour Office (ILO) set up in 1919. The tripartite ILO structure, where the national delegations to the annual conference consist of four delegates (two from government and one each from unions and employers), encouraged the International Federation of Trade Unions (IFTU) to take an active part in the organisation. Indeed it has been said that without the support of the IFTU, the ILO would not have been able to operate.[44]

The International Institute of Intellectual Cooperation, established in Paris in 1923, worked closely with international NGOs throughout its existence. It provided secretariat services for the Joint Committee of the Major International Associations and for the Committee of the International Students' Associations – a model which was to be followed by UNESCO. Indeed, the French government's first draft of the constitution for UNESCO provided for membership of international NGOs, if the Assembly voted in favour by a two-thirds majority.[45]

The formation of the United Nations

During the 1939–45 war international NGOs took virtually no part in the early discussions about the Atlantic Charter (1941), the Declaration of the United Nations (1942) or the Dumbarton Oaks conference (1944). National organisations maintained activities[46] and some, notably religious ones, pressed for the role of non-governmental action to be recognised. For example, the Archbishop of Canterbury, the Moderator of the Church of Scotland and the Moderator of the Free Church Federal Council issued a statement in March 1944 which discussed the future of Europe and made some practical suggestions including 'Common action to restore and revitalise the associations and institutions of every kind, local, national and international in which the cultural and social tradition of Europe is specially embodied'.[47] Other organisations which maintained pressure for an improved international system included the trade union movement,[48] the League of Nations Union and the Commission to Study the Organisation of Peace.[49]

The Dumbarton Oaks proposals for a new intergovernmental organisation were deliberately less aspirational than the Covenant of the League of Nations. The League committed itself to undertaking activities, whereas the Dumbarton Oaks proposal was for an organisation that coordinated and to some extent controlled other agencies which actually carried out activities. These agencies were not clearly defined but by implication they were to be intergovernmental ones on the model of the International Labour Office.

The Dumbarton Oaks proposals of the four main war-time Allies of the time (the United States, Britain, the Soviet Union and China) were based on the preparatory work of the US Department of State. They formed the basis of discussion for the United Nations Conference on International Organisation held in San Francisco in April–June 1945, where fifty governments were represented. Many of these governments had by then had the advantage of some public discussion of the issues raised. In addition, many NGOs concerned with such questions as racial inequality, religious discrimination or the status of women were in San Francisco to try to influence their governments. It was, naturally, easiest for American organisations to attend. Distance was not the only problem; one group from the United Kingdom was torpedoed in the Atlantic and had to return.[50]

The groups from the United States had another advantage. The US government invited forty-two of them to send representatives to San Francisco as consultants to the US delegation and a further 160 US NGOs attended the conference as observers. This worried

the United Kingdom government because 'all these people will
know precisely what is happening in committees, sub-committees
etc. and will not hesitate to use this knowledge for the purpose of
grinding their particular axes'.[51] Moreover, the group included the
American Jewish Conference and the American Jewish Committee,
which were felt to be capable of causing embarrassment over
Palestine.[52] The consultants urged that 'some orderly channel
should be established whereby national and international organisations of a non-governmental character could bring their views to
the attention of the Organisation'.[53]

Under the leadership of James Shotwell, who had participated
in the founding of the International Labour Organisation in 1919,
a working group of US representatives from agricultural, business,
labour and education NGOs was formed, calling themselves ABLE.
They suggested four changes to the draft UN Charter in respect of
the new Economic and Social Council (ECOSOC): it should hold
regular conferences to receive recommendations from NGOs; coordinate the activities of the specialised agencies; add education to
its functions and establish commissions for education and human
rights. However, other influences were also at work.[54]

In February 1945 a World Trade Union Conference (WTUC)
opened in London, bringing together major union confederations
from Britain, France, the United States, the Soviet Union and
Latin America, in order to draw up the constitution for a new
unified global trade union organisation. In the first week of the
San Francisco conference the WTUC leaders sent a memorandum
asking for participation rights at the conference. They also wanted
their new organisation, which in October 1945 became the World
Federation of Trade Unions (WFTU), to be granted a special status
in both the Security Council and ECOSOC. Initially a conference
committee invited the WTUC to send representatives, but US
and British opposition led to the invitation being rescinded. The
WTUC, with Soviet support, continued to press its demands, 'while
the American Federation of Labour went so far as to suggest
that the Council should be partly composed of representatives of
labour, agriculture and business'.[55] Other NGOs were stimulated
to ensure that unions would not be the only organisations granted
participation rights.

Many of the government delegations from smaller countries were
also seeking to strengthen the role of the General Assembly and
ECOSOC, and to widen the range of the UN's responsibilities.
Under the combined pressure of the US NGOs, the WTUC and the
small countries, the four major Allies accepted changes to the
Dumbarton Oaks proposals. The provisions for education, health

and human rights were added to the Charter. In practice the addition of education and health was not so important for the UN, because most work in these fields would be undertaken by the separate specialised agencies, UNESCO and WHO. Upgrading ECOSOC to a principal organ and specifying that it would set up a Commission on Human Rights was of fundamental importance, as otherwise there would have been a much slower development of human rights conventions and monitoring processes.

In the final version of the UN Charter, there was no hint of any role for NGOs in the affairs of the General Assembly or the Security Council. The US delegation at San Francisco also initially opposed any official role for NGOs in ECOSOC. When the drafting committee produced a compromise wording that provided for 'consultation' rather than 'participation without a vote', the US government gave in to pressure from the NGO consultants and accepted the idea. Until this point it had been widely assumed that only *international* NGOs would have a role in the UN system. However, at that time, the US trade union movement was split into two rival bodies, the Congress of Industrial Organisations (CIO) and the American Federation of Labour (AFL). The provision for international NGOs would cover the CIO, as a member of the WFTU, but not the AFL, which was not a member of any international federation. In order to avoid appearing to be taking sides between the CIO and the AFL, and to avoid the possibility of a major domestic lobby turning against the UN, the US delegation proposed an addition to the draft Article 71 to allow for 'national organisations' based in a single country, to be included. The wording that was approved and became part of the Charter was:

> The Economic and Social Council may make suitable arrangements for consultation with non-governmental organizations which are concerned with matters within its competence. Such arrangements may be made with international organizations and, where appropriate, with national organizations after consultation with the Member of the United Nations concerned.

At the time this was seen as a rather limited provision. It was assumed that, for example, peace organisations would need to find other channels for getting their views heard.[56] As we shall see in later chapters, it has in practice enabled a very wide range of organisations to make their views known to the government representatives assembled at various United Nations meetings.

NOTES

1. Many American authors were active in international organisations and, indeed, apart from the work connected with the Union of International Associations, much of the writing about international non-governmental organisations was done by American authors. The Carnegie Endowment for International Peace was an important source of funds. However, F. S. L. Lyon's *Internationalism in Europe 1815-1914* (Leiden: A. W. Sijthoff, 1963), p. 14, estimates that by 1914 out of 466 international non-governmental organisations, twenty had no connection with Europe.
2. Canada achieved dominion status in 1867, Australia in 1901, New Zealand in 1907 and South Africa in 1910.
3. L. C. White, *International Non-Governmental Organisations* (New Brunswick: Rutgers University Press, 1951), p. 4.
4. Lyons, *op. cit.*, p. 14.
5. Lyons gives the following estimates for the creation of international NGOs:

	International NGOs created
Before 1849	4
1850-4	1
1855-9	4
1860-4	6
1865-9	9
1870-4	8
1875-9	17
1880-4	11
1885-9	29
1890-4	35
1895-9	38
1900-4	61
1905-9	131
1910-4	112

Source: F. S. L. Lyons, *Internationalism in Europe, 1815-1914* (Leiden: A. W. Sijthoff, 1963), p. 14.

6. Paragraph based on material from Red Cross, *Red Cross and Red Crescent: Portrait of an International Movement* (Geneva: ICRC/LRCRCS, 1989).
7. *Ibid.*, p. 14.
8. White, *op. cit.*, p. 6.
9. *Ibid.*, p. 184.
10. Arthur Gillette, *One Million Volunteers* (London: Penguin, 1968), p. 16f.
11. White, *op. cit.*, p. 181.
12. W. A. Visser 't Hooft, *Students Find the Truth to Serve* (Geneva: World's Student Christian Federation, 1935), p. 64f, quoted in White, *op. cit.*, p. 7.
13. Bernard Pickard, informal paper for the International Secretariat on the arrangements to be made for international non-governmental organisations in the UN system; London, 1945. A copy is in the Public Record Office file FO371/50893, item U9333. White, *op. cit.*, p. 7, puts the 1939 figure as over a thousand, probably including many trade associations.
14. Francis Gladstone, *Charity, Law and Social Justice* (London: Bedford Square Press, 1982), p. 42.
15. Mark Girouard, *Life in the English Country House* (London and New Haven: Yale University Press, 1978), pp. 189-91.

16. White, *op. cit.*, p. 4.
17. Quoted in Jean-Baptiste Duroselle (ed.), *Europe: A History of its Peoples* (London: Viking, 1990), p. 315.
18. Note in *The Guardian* of 13 November 1993.
19. Lyon, *op. cit.*, p. 51, referring to Sir R. Wedgwood, *International Rail Transport*.
20. White, *op. cit.*, p. 13.
21. Simeon E. Baldwin, 'The International Congresses and Conferences of the Last Century as Forces Working Toward the Solidarity of the World', *American Journal of International Law*, vol. 1, pp. 817–29.
22. *Ibid.*, p. 572.
23. G. P. Speeckaert, 'A glance at sixty years of activity (1910–1970) of the Union of International Associations', in *Union of International Associations, 1910–1970: Past, Present, Future* (Brussels: UIA Document 17, 1970), p. 20.
24. *Ibid.*, p. 23.
25. This passage depends heavily on Speeckaert, *op. cit.*
26. Council document A43(B)1421 quoted in Speeckaert, *op. cit.*, p. 28.
27. It should be noted that Paris remained the largest centre for such bodies.
28. Bernard Pickard, 'The Greater League of Nations: a brief survey of the Nature and Development of unofficial international organisations', *Contemporary Review*, vol. CL, July–December 1936, pp. 460–6. Otlet, *op. cit.* states that in 1929 there were about fifty international non-governmental organisations in Geneva out of a world total of four or five hundred.
29. Paul Otlet, *La Société des Nations et l'Union des Associations Internationales: Rapport aux Associations sur les premiers actes de la Commission de Coopération Intellectuelle* (Brussels: UIA publication 107, 1923).
30. The official title of the FIIG is Fédération des Institutions Internationales Semi-Officielles et Privées Établies à Genève. By this time the Union of International Associations (UIA), apparently accepting that the centre of the international world had moved to Geneva, was proposing the establishment of a Cité Mondiale, based on plans by Le Corbusier, which would provide a physical and intellectual centre for international organisations. Otlet, *op. cit.*
31. White, *op. cit.*, p. 251.
32. Pickard: informal paper, *op. cit.* It is not clear what was the nature of this procedure.
33. Pickard, 'The Greater League of Nations', *op. cit.*, pp. 460–65.
34. Quoted in Pickard, *ibid.*
35. Pickard, informal paper, *op. cit.*
36. White, *op. cit.*, p. 254.
37. *Ibid.*, p. 251.
38. Public Record Office file FO371/8321, item 137.
39. Red Cross, *The League of Red Cross and Red Crescent Societies 1919–1989* (Geneva: League of Red Cross and Red Crescent Societies, 1989), p. 8.
40. White, *op. cit.*, p. 31. These appointments caused some comment from other interests, not least the International Cooperative Alliance.
41. *Ibid.*, p. 31.
42. *Ibid.*, p. 182.
43. Letter of 15 December 1937 from the Federation's President, quoted in White, *op. cit.*, p. 184.
44. *Ibid.*, p. 81.
45. *Ibid.*, p. 256.
46. For example The Save the Children Fund sent relief teams to help orphaned children behind the lines, starting in 1943 in Southern Europe. Oxfam was

established to provide civilian relief to Greece, against the British government's wishes, when Greece was still occupied by German forces.

47. Quotation taken from summary in *British Survey*, vol. V, no. 14, 1944.
48. See, for example, an informal paper by H. G. Gee of the British Ministry of Labour now in the Public Record Office file FO/371/50893, Item U9333.
49. Leland M. Goodrich and Edvard Hambro, *Charter of the United Nations* (London: Stevens, 1949), 2nd edn, p. 3.
50. *British Survey*, vol. VI, no. 16, August 1945, p. 3.
51. Unknown writer (from North America department) of an FO filenote in the Public Record Office – FO 371 50698, item U2673. The filenote goes on 'Our best hope is that the majority of these people will get bored and go away.'
52. Cable from British delegation to San Francisco to Foreign Office, dated 11 April 1945, now in Public Record Office in file FO 115/4192.
53. Pickard, informal paper, *op. cit.*
54. This account of the definition of ECOSOC's role and agreement on Article 71 draws on Chiang Pei-heng, *Non-Governmental Organisations in the United Nations: Identity, Role and Function* (New York: Praeger, 1981), pp. 39–49.
55. H. G. Gee, *op. cit.*
56. *Ibid.* and Pickard, informal paper, *op. cit.*

2

CONSULTATIVE STATUS FOR NGOs AT THE UNITED NATIONS

Peter Willetts

In 1945 the first significant success of non-governmental organisations (NGOs) in influencing the United Nations system was to obtain two major amendments to the proposed Charter. Article 71 was added to provide for consultation arrangements with the Economic and Social Council (ECOSOC) and the promotion of human rights was written in as one of the purposes of the UN. But NGOs failed to win any provision for their involvement in the work of the General Assembly or the Security Council; NGOs were seen as being 'non-political'. In practice, economic and social questions could not be separated from any aspect of politics. The ECOSOC arrangements for NGOs were to be greatly influenced by attitudes to fascism in the first years of the UN, the Cold War in the late 1940s and the 1950s, nationalism in developing countries from the 1960s onwards and environmental crises in the 1990s. At the same time NGOs have been able to navigate their way through the storms of these conflicts and establish the value of their knowledge, skills and distinct contributions to political debate. This chapter outlines how the consultative arrangements were established in the early years in ECOSOC; the formal rights of NGOs; their other activities; and how they now influence the political agenda and policy-making throughout the UN system.

Setting up the system in the early years

Although the United Nations came into being in October 1945, it was to take five years before the ECOSOC consultative arrangements were finalised. ECOSOC did not even exist until the first session of the General Assembly elected the members of the Council in January 1946. The Assembly itself quickly took up the question of consultations with NGOs and asked ECOSOC to act 'as soon as possible' to adopt 'suitable arrangements' for the World Federation of Trade Unions (WFTU), the International Co-operative Alliance and other NGOs.[1] In the early years, many of the UN's decisions about NGOs revolved around the changing status of the WFTU, which was seen as the largest and most prestigious of the NGOs. The initial expectation of the politicians seems to have been that a small number of high-status, global NGOs would make a significant input to the work of ECOSOC. Events, however, dictated otherwise. Many more NGOs than were expected applied for consultative status and the professional diplomats sought to allow only limited access to high-level decision-making.

The first session of ECOSOC established a committee to consider the arrangements for NGOs.[2] Its report was adopted by the Council in June 1946, thus determining many of the main features of the system as it still operates today. The first question was to define what type of organisation would be accepted into consultative status. The committee recommended that an NGO should be concerned with matters falling within the competence of ECOSOC, its aims should be in conformity with the UN Charter, it should represent a substantial proportion of the people in its field and it should speak for its members through authorised representatives. NGOs based in one country, referred to as 'national organisations', might be accepted if they were not members of an international NGO or had 'special experience' to offer.[3] Thus the American Federation of Labour (AFL) was one of the first three recognised NGOs, but it had to withdraw in March 1950 when the International Confederation of Free Trade Unions, of which it was a leading member, was given consultative status. Later, it was explicitly re-affirmed that single-country NGOs would only be accepted after consulting the relevant government.[4] While single-country NGOs have always been part of the system, until the mid-1990s they were few in number and the emphasis was on large international NGOs.

Three categories of NGOs

It was decided to divide the NGOs into three categories. Category A organisations had 'a basic interest in most of the activities of the Council'; Category B was for those with 'a special competence' in a few of the fields of activity; and Category C organisations were primarily concerned 'with the development of public opinion and with the dissemination of information'.[5] The Category C definition showed a failure to anticipate the political controversy surrounding NGOs which adopt a vigorous role as pressure groups. The Category was abolished in 1950 and replaced by a Register of organisations that were supposed to be very specialised and might be consulted on an *ad hoc* basis.[6] In 1968 at the end of a major review of NGO arrangements, the labels were changed to Category I, Category II

and the Roster, but the classifications remained essentially the same.
In principle, the categories are differentiated by objective, non-political criteria. In practice, there is a definite sense of the organisations being ranked by their status. The clearest illustration of this is the way in which the International Planned Parenthood Federation has been treated. The IPPF was formed in 1953 and applied for Category B status in 1955. It was rejected because of bitter opposition by Catholic governments. In August 1964 attitudes to population planning had changed sufficiently for the IPPF to be put on the Register and by 1969 it was promoted to Category II. Finally, in the run-up to the World Population Conference, it achieved Category I status in 1973. While the decisions are not normally so controversial, there has been a steady trickle of NGOs moving up the three ranks. Only half the organisations currently in Category I were accepted directly at that level. The other half first obtained consultative status with a lower rank and were promoted later. There is also a sense of the NGOs being ranked when organisations that fail to provide adequate information in their quadrennial reports are demoted from Category II to the Roster.[7]

The NGO Committee gains a permanent role

The NGO Committee was initially established on a temporary basis, but once the consultative system was in place it was made a permanent standing committee of the Council.[8] The NGO Committee is responsible for administering the system. Until 1978 it met annually to consider new applications for consultative status and requests for reclassification to a higher status. Since 1978 the Committee has met every two years and hence there has been dissatisfaction when some NGOs have had to wait two, or even four, years before their applications were considered. The Committee is also responsible for the first consideration of any general policy questions about the UN's relationship with NGOs. All its decisions are subject to the endorsement of the full Council.

The number of NGOs taking up consultative status

Only four organisations were accepted, all as Category A, in the first year. Initially, the NGO Committee took time to consider each application and many were controversial. Later the award of consultative status became a more routine bureaucratic process for most NGOs. Equally, when an NGO is inactive and fails to submit its quadrennial report, being struck off the list has become a routine matter. Decisions on what category an NGO should be in

or whether an NGO can be moved to a higher category cause more
debate. In the last two decades new applications for recognition
have averaged more than twenty per year, while applications for
promotion have averaged five per year.

Early controversy over relations with Spain

When the UN was formed, Spain, as a fascist country, was excluded
from UN membership even though it had not fought with the Axis
powers. This policy spilt over into differences in attitudes to NGOs
having relations with Spain. In October 1946 ECOSOC granted
Category A status to the International Chamber of Commerce,
even though it had a Spanish branch and one of its vice-presidents
was Spanish.[9] This led to a general decision in March 1947 that
NGOs with Spanish members could be accepted if the individual
members were not organised into a Spanish branch, if the branch
was independent of the Franco government or if the branch was
inactive.[10] Some international NGOs complied and expelled their
Spanish branches, but the International Bar Association and a few
others lost their Category B status because they failed to do so.[11]
When the General Assembly lifted its diplomatic boycott of Spain
in November 1950, ECOSOC followed suit and in March 1951
lifted the ban on NGOs with branches in Spain.[12]

The impact of the Cold War on NGO relations with ECOSOC

At the height of the Cold War, several international NGOs came
to be more sympathetic to the communists than Western opinion
could tolerate. As a result Western groups split from the world
organisations and formed their own rival international NGOs.
Thus the rump organisations came more firmly under communist
control. In ECOSOC the West used its voting majority against
these 'communist-front' NGOs. In July 1950, when the Soviet Union
was boycotting ECOSOC over the question of Chinese representation in the UN, the International Association of Democratic
Lawyers (IADL) and the International Organisation of Journalists
lost their consultative status, while the World Federation of Democratic Youth was demoted from Category B to the Register.[13] At
the following ECOSOC session in March 1951, the Soviet Union had
resumed its seat and tried to get these three NGOs reinstated in
Category B.[14] Not only did they fail, but the rival, pro-Western,
International Union of Socialist Youth was put in Category B and
the International Federation of Free Journalists was put on the

Register.[15] In April 1954 the Women's International Democratic Federation (WIDF) also lost its Category B status.[16]

There had been a similar split in the World Federation of Trade Unions, with the United States and British unions taking the lead in forming the International Confederation of Free Trade Unions. The WFTU remained strong enough to retain its place in Category A, even though the ICFTU was also admitted to Category A in March 1950.[17] The position of the communists improved after the NGO Committee was expanded in 1966 to allow for African and Asian representation. In June 1967 the IADL and WIDF regained their Category B status.[18]

This complex history of East-West rivalry in the NGO world shows how neither intergovernmental politics nor the specific interests of NGOs in their own activities can automatically be dominant. The two interact with each other in a balance that varies from case to case. Of the six communist-front organisations that have been mentioned, two were quickly expelled from the UN-NGO system, one was demoted, one was expelled after a delay and one had sufficient strength at the grass-roots to maintain its status.

Attempts to limit the numbers

There soon arose a feeling that too many NGOs were obtaining consultative status. Organisations that were seen as having overlapping interests were asked to have joint representation.[19] This was applied by ECOSOC to several pairs of organisations for some years, but ceased in the mid-1950s. Similarly, in a curious compromise, thirteen women's organisations were grouped in a Liaison Committee to act as the consultative body when they had the same views, but they were also allowed to operate separately when their views differed.[20] The Liaison Committee was eventually dropped from Category B in 1963. At current UN meetings and conferences, committees of NGOs quite often submit joint documents or make joint oral statements, but this is decided by the NGOs themselves, when they feel it is politically useful to form a broad coalition.

Attempts were also made to exclude organisations whose field of activity was the same as that of a UN specialised agency.[21] This continued until 1950, when the Register was explicitly opened to NGOs that had consultative status with an agency. However, the Register itself was designed as a means of cutting back NGO access. In 1946 the three categories of NGOs had all been seen as having consultative status. The abolition of Category C and its replacement by the Register was defined as taking away consultative status and depriving these NGOs of the right to put forward their views on their own initiative. The Register was constituted as a list of NGOs that ECOSOC might approach when it felt the need for their help.[22] As time has passed, efficient NGOs on the Register (now the Roster) have found they can in practice have as much impact as those in Category B.

Governmental opposition to particular NGOs

From 1950 until 1993 the official definition of the three categories of NGOs and the general practice in recognising NGOs was unchanged, but that did not mean the absence of controversy. Continual problems arose, and still do arise, with NGOs that criticise specific governments. This usually occurs in the field of human rights. The governments being criticised tend to respond by denying the right of any outsiders to interfere in their internal affairs and then by generalising their hostility to the activities of all NGOs in the UN system. While the conflict has been repeated over the years, the governments involved have changed. In the 1970s the Soviet Union and Argentina were the leading anti-NGO governments. In the 1990s it has been the Chinese and the Cubans. Even though objections are made to human rights NGOs and there may be delays, with persistence it is usually possible to find a majority of votes on the NGO Committee to accept them.

The Committee has been surprisingly liberal in according consultative status. There are many obscure NGOs (such as the International Federation of International Furniture Removers) or ones that may be important, but seem remote from the UN's work (such as the International Advertising Association). In addition some groups have been accepted when one might not have expected them to be. In a year when the nineteen members of the Committee could be classified as including eight strongly Catholic countries, four Orthodox countries, four Islamic countries and three others, the Islamic countries took the lead in expressing 'strong opposition to the ethical and moral values' represented by the International Lesbian and Gay Association. From a Committee of this composition, one would not have predicted a majority to grant Roster status to the Association by nine votes in favour to four against, with three abstentions.[23] Although the full Council endorsed the Committee's decision in July 1993, an intense reaction followed a year later, when it was suggested that the Association promoted or condoned paedophilia. In September 1994 the Council took the highly unusual step of holding a special session. This suspended the Association from the Roster and convened a special meeting of its NGO Committee to investigate the allegations.

It has already been mentioned that the IPPF was rejected in the 1950s as being too controversial, but it was accepted in 1964, at a point when Catholic and Muslim countries between them held a majority of the votes in the UN. Now the pendulum has swung so far on this issue that Human Life International, an anti-abortion group, has had its application rejected.[24]

Expansion of the NGO community

Despite the continual attempts by governments to limit the number of NGOs participating in the UN's work, they have grown in several ways. First, international NGOs that already existed when the UN was formed, or NGOs that were established in its early years, often only had branches in some Western countries. They have gradually expanded to become truly global, gained more resources and increased in legitimacy. Thus some are now in Category I or Category II, when initially it would not have been reasonable to give them so high a status. Secondly, groups that previously saw no reason to work with the UN, or were suspicious that their independence might be compromised, have seen how the system works and decided that they could benefit by obtaining consultative status. Thirdly, many new NGOs are being formed, as new areas of economic activity develop or new issues move onto the global agenda. Fourthly, as existing groups gain greater resources, experience and skills, they may expand the scope of their activities. Thus NGOs may move from having no concern with UN activities, or involvement with a single agency or programme, to a wider concern that leads them to seek consultative status.

As a result of these four factors, the numbers of NGOs with consultative status grew steadily, to the point that in the early 1990s ECOSOC was dealing with nearly 1,000 NGOs. The growth in numbers is depicted in the accompanying graph.

The formal rights of participation in ECOSOC

When the NGO Committee recommended in June 1946 that NGOs should be divided into three categories, it also recommended what rights of participation they should have. The Committee's starting point was that NGOs must have fewer rights in the Council than the observer delegations from specialised agencies or governments that were not Council members. All NGOs would be able to attend ECOSOC meetings. NGOs in Category A could circulate written

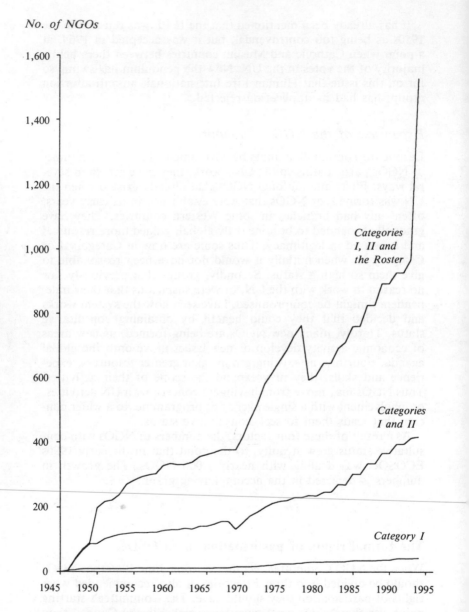

No. of NGOs

Categories
I, II and
the Roster

Categories
I and II

Category I

1945   1950   1955   1960   1965   1970   1975   1980   1985   1990   1995

Growth in the number of NGOs with ECOSOC
consultative status

Note The increase in 1994 was due to the inclusion of 552 environmental NGOs.

statements to the Council members. The other NGOs would have the titles of their statements put on a list, but the statements would only be circulated in full on the request of a member of the Council. NGOs in Category A could expect to address a Council committee or even the full Council if the NGO Committee so recommended. NGOs in Categories B and C could only expect to make oral presentations indirectly via the NGO Committee, which would then report their views to the full Council.[25]

The WFTU wins the right to put items on ECOSOC's agenda

The first use of the procedure came in October 1946, when the WFTU consulted the NGO Committee on the nature of the consultation arrangements.[26] The WFTU was clearly dissatisfied. As it had its headquarters in Paris, and as France had a left-wing coalition government, the French delegation in the following month put forward WFTU demands in the General Assembly. The Soviet delegation took up the demands and formally tabled a resolution to recommend ECOSOC to grant the WFTU the right to submit items for inclusion on the Council's agenda and the right to submit written and oral communications directly to the full Council on all agenda items. The first proposal was passed by the Assembly, the second was defeated.[27] The United States delegation, which had originally opposed granting any direct rights of participation to the WFTU, then changed its approach and tabled a resolution, which was passed, asserting the principle that all organisations in Category A should receive equal treatment.[28]

ECOSOC responded in March 1947 by setting up an Agenda Committee to act as a buffer between NGOs and the Council in deciding whether an NGO item should be accepted for its agenda. The WFTU came back in July with a letter to the Secretary-General asking the Assembly to endorse the WFTU having rights to convene special sessions of the Council, to participate in the Council when a decision is being taken on whether its suggested items should be on the agenda and to take part in Council debates on the substance of the items it has proposed. This time the Council pre-empted the Assembly and decided in August to reject any right for NGOs to convene ECOSOC, but accepted that all NGOs in Category A could introduce their own agenda items in the full Council and make a reply to the subsequent debate.[29]

Two decades of stability in the consultation procedures

In 1949 the UN Secretary-General was asked to prepare a report on how the consultative arrangements had been used and the NGO Committee was asked to review whether any improvements could be made. The Committee recommended unanimously in February 1950 that the right to submit items for the agenda should be withdrawn. The United States delegate argued that the right had been abused for propaganda purposes.[30] It is difficult to see that there had been serious problems. In the period 1947-9 only eight items had been placed on the Council's agenda by NGOs.[31] However, the US delegate also proposed an amendment to the report, retaining the right of NGOs to submit items, because all the NGOs in Category A had defended the right so strongly. Presumably it was also a factor that in an election year the Democrats would not wish to take away from the American Federation of Labour a right which they were actively using. The compromise outcome was to give the NGO Committee the decision on whether a proposal for an agenda item should be accepted and to make the Committee's decision final.[32]

The review process led to ECOSOC Resolution 288B(X) of 27 February 1950, which amended and consolidated all the previous decisions on the consultative arrangements. There were several significant changes. Increased emphasis was placed on consultations with ECOSOC commissions and committees rather than the full Council. The Secretariat was given a stronger role to try to make NGO activities more acceptable and the right to ask NGOs for help in producing studies or reports. As we have seen, Category C status was downgraded to listing on a Register, with reduced rights of participation. Finally, restrictions were put on the volume of documentation coming from NGOs. Previously all documents from NGOs in Category A were circulated in full, while summaries of documents from Category B groups were circulated. The changes put a limit of 2,000 words for NGOs in Category A and 500 words for those in Category B in statements to the Council and a limit of 2,000 words for both categories submitting statements to commissions.[33] For the next 18 years, Resolution 288B(X) remained the definitive statute, specifying the nature of the arrangements for consultative status.

NGOs made no further gains in their rights of participation in ECOSOC. The provisions for attendance, circulation of documents, hearings and proposing agenda items, though changed in some details, remain fundamentally the same to the present day.[34] Despite the fact that the WFTU was denied its more ambitious aims and that

Category II and Roster NGOs do not have full rights, in all its decision-making on economic and social questions the UN remains more open to pressure groups than do most governments. The major parliaments of the world do not allow NGOs to place items on their agendas or to make speeches from the floor of the house.

Turmoil and the 1968 review of the consultation system

In the early 1960s most committees within the UN system were restructured to allow for representation of the new African and Asian members that had joined the UN from 1955 onwards. Generally this restructuring was achieved by increasing the size of the committee and specifying a division of the seats between the Afro-Asians, the Latin Americans, the East Europeans (that is the communist countries) and the Western countries. This resulted in a substantial shift in the political balance of the UN, away from the long period of Western dominance. Because it required an amendment of the Charter, the composition of ECOSOC was not changed until September 1965. The next session of the Council expanded the NGO Committee from seven to thirteen members.[35] The Soviet Union also made a determined effort to reinstate the Women's International Democratic Federation (WIDF) and the International Association of Democratic Lawyers (IADL). With the more radical of the Afro-Asians supporting the argument that Western Cold War prejudices had distorted the universality of the UN, ECOSOC in June 1967 placed WIDF and IADL in Category B.[36]

In February 1967, just before the new enlarged NGO Committee started to consider whether to recommend the reinstatement of WIDF and IADL, a bombshell was thrown into the debate. The *New York Times* ran a series of stories on how the US Central Intelligence Agency had secretly financed several anti-communist NGOs, including the International Confederation of Free Trade Unions from ECOSOC Category A, and the International Commission of Jurists, Pax Romana and the World Assembly of Youth from Category B. This turned the consideration of the status of WIDF and IADL into a general debate about claims of Western domination of the ECOSOC-NGO system.[37]

The Tanzanian delegate led an onslaught in the Council. He successfully demanded a review of the criteria for admission to consultative status, redefinition of the precise requirements to distinguish between the three categories and review of NGO rights to participate in UN activities. Once the general principles had been reconsidered, the NGO Committee was then 'to review the nature and activities of each NGO'.[38] The general atmosphere of suspicion towards NGOs can be measured by the amount of support given at the end of the year to Afro-Asian attacks on NGOs in the General Assembly's debate on preparations for the International Conference on Human Rights. The Assembly's decision to invite ECOSOC NGOs to send observers to the conference was sustained by just one vote.[39]

Resolution 1296 and the re-emergence of consensus

After another year, including some acrimonious debate, consensus was finally achieved in the NGO Committee. A new resolution defining the consultation procedures was recommended to ECOSOC and adopted by the Council in May 1968 (the text of Resolution 1296(XLIV) is given in Appendix B). Despite all the contention, no fundamental changes were made. Categories A and B and the Register were relabelled Categories I and II and the Roster, but their definitions did not change, except to add 'scientific and technological' matters to the list of potential subject areas. It is interesting to note that in 1968 the environment was still not considered to be a subject requiring international attention and it was not mentioned in Resolution 1296. Only slight amendments were made to the participation rights.

The main changes concerned finance, the global coverage of NGOs, the introduction of regular NGO reports and provisions to withdraw consultative status. NGOs should be financed predominantly by their membership and should make public any contributions from governments. Several amendments were aimed at bringing NGOs from developing countries into the system. International NGOs were encouraged to cover 'the different regions of the world' and single-country NGOs would be more welcome if they 'help achieve a balanced and effective representation . . . of all regions'. All NGOs now have to submit reports on their activities every four years. Failure to declare government financing, engaging in 'politically motivated acts' against UN members or failure to make any effective contribution to the UN's work became the three grounds on which an NGO could lose its consultative status. In practice the third provision has been interpreted as failing to submit a quadrennial report and it has been the only ground on which NGOs have been struck off.

After Resolution 1296 had been passed, the review of individual NGOs caused emotional and divisive debate in both the NGO Committee and the full Council for a further year. Votes were forced on human rights NGOs and on Jewish and Catholic groups, on the grounds that they were 'politically motivated' against particular governments. However, while some NGOs had their category changed, none lost consultative status altogether.[40] It is a measure of the political strength of the NGOs collectively that, despite being tarred with the brush of CIA financing during a period of radical nationalism in the Third World, they emerged from the whole review process virtually unscathed. Indeed, the Tanzanian delegate who had initiated the process ended up apologising to the Council and became supportive of NGOs.[41]

The political behaviour of NGOs

There are three aspects of the formal arrangements which have a most important and direct effect on an NGO's political behaviour. First, NGOs have access to all UN documents, once these have been officially circulated. There may occasionally be a few documents classified as 'Restricted', which they are not supposed to receive, but in practice they may be able to obtain copies of these. Along with being able to attend the meetings and observe the proceedings, this means that the NGOs can gain high levels of information about the political process. They will not have perfect information, because there are always private meetings of caucus groups and private conversations between delegates, in which important decisions on tactics may be taken. In not being privy to these unofficial interactions, they are in the same position as most of the other diplomats who were not present.

Secondly, NGOs have security passes giving them access to all the buildings, including the lounges, bars and restaurants used by the diplomats. They therefore have access to the delegates. More information can be obtained by talking about the proceedings informally, including asking about what has been happening at the private meetings. Thirdly, being awarded consultative status gives the NGO a legitimate place within the political system. This means that the NGO activist is seen as having a right to be involved in the process. As a result, in the informal contacts with delegates, it is possible to express views about the issues on the agenda and to lobby for particular decisions to be taken. Again this compares very favourably to what pressure groups may expect in domestic legislatures. Many would be very pleased if they could gain immediate access to official papers, talk to members of their parliament and be seen as having a legitimate concern with the outcome of the proceedings.

NGO relations with Secretariat officials

As noted above, the UN Secretariat was given the task of making NGO behaviour more acceptable and it was allowed to work with NGOs to produce reports. These provisions legitimise any contacts that Secretariat officials and NGO activists may wish to have with each other. Contacts may well have been authorised on the basis that officials do not have a political role. Indeed NGOs are quite often described as being 'non-political'.[42] In practice the Secretariat and NGOs may wish to make common cause to oppose the policies of particular governments. There was obviously a political alliance when the Centre Against Apartheid, an office of the Secretariat, regularly supplied the Anti-Apartheid Movement, a Category II NGO, with multiple copies of UN reports and publicity materials that would provide arguments to counter Margaret Thatcher's unwillingness to apply sanctions against South Africa. The process is usually more subtle, with NGOs and Secretariat officials persuading a government to give higher priority to policy formulation on an issue or encouraging the commitment of greater resources, rather than seeking a change of direction in government policy. No less a person than the UN Secretary-General has welcomed the alliance of NGOs with the Secretariat. After referring to the difficulty of convincing governments that they should commit personnel, materials and money to the UN, he said 'I need the mobilising power of non-governmental organisations.'[43]

How NGOs gain prestige

The Introduction to this book emphasised the great diversity of NGOs. One must therefore be cautious in making generalisations about them. However, those which successfully gain the attention of government delegates and secretariat officials tend to have several important, closely-related features in common. Most possess specialised information or expertise; they will thus be influential if that information or expertise is seen as being relevant to the types of decisions that are to be taken. At the extreme, few politicians, bureaucrats or diplomats would dare argue with the considered conclusions of a professional scientific NGO on the nature of the scientific aspects of a policy problem. More generally, decision-makers will listen to NGO activists who appear to know more about a subject than they do, even when they disagree with the policy being advocated by the NGO. NGOs may also have a breadth of experience or range of contacts on a subject which surpasses that of government officials. NGO activists may devote a lifetime to one subject. In contrast, government officials are often moved around in their careers, particularly those dealing with the United Nations. Thus someone who has worked for many years in a small poorly-resourced NGO can possess more information and more experience than someone who has worked on the same subject for a short time in a large well-resourced government bureaucracy.

It is very important for an NGO to establish a reputation for reliability and integrity; Amnesty International has a policy of systematically checking from multiple sources of information.[44] There is no value in possessing information or experience if that information is not believed or the judgement of the NGO is not respected. On the other hand, when a reputation is well established, officials may take action solely in response to a word from the NGO. Finally, NGOs may also try to build up their prestige, for example by associating prestigious individuals with their work or by demonstrating widespread public support for their goals. These major assets of information, expertise, experience, reliability, integrity and prestige, once acquired, help to sustain each other and provide a formidable basis for exercising influence.

Agenda-setting, policy formulation and policy implementation

There are three distinct types of process through which an issue comes under contention in world politics. First, there may be problems in bringing an issue to the attention of the relevant decision-makers. This may be called the politics of agenda-setting. Secondly, there is debate over the formulation of the broad aims and specific objectives of policy. Thirdly, there is the problem of allocating sufficient resources in an appropriate manner, so that the agreed policy is implemented. Politicians in the home governments and diplomats at the UN tend to give the highest priority to policy formulation and are less subject to NGO influence in this process. On the other hand NGOs may dominate agenda-setting and be a major influence on policy implementation. The three processes may be clearly distinct in analytical terms, but in the world of day-to-day politics they interrelate quite closely. If an NGO publishes a report showing that insufficient resources are being allocated for a policy to be implemented successfully, they may be trying to seize media attention in order to establish an agenda for public debate about the need to formulate an alternative policy.

NGOs and agenda-setting

It is fundamental to the existence of NGOs and to the nature of governments that NGOs should dominate agenda-setting. A major reason for the existence of NGOs is that people come together in independent groups to promote some type of activity that is not currently being undertaken by governments. Alternatively, governments may already be involved in an issue, but groups are formed in order to challenge the way a government is handling the issue. Less often, the prospect of a change in government policy may result in a group being formed to resist any change. Even in the last case, the NGO is still trying to influence the content of the political agenda. Put simply, NGOs are often formed primarily to promote political change and new groups will usually aim to have some impact upon public opinion.

For their part, governments increasingly suffer from agenda overload. They are concerned about tackling short-term problems, in the immediate future. They are predominantly responding to events rather than setting the agenda. They usually try to define the tone and language of political debate. It is not so often that they are able to determine what issues are on or off the agenda.

There are two senses in which there is an agenda for politics. First, there is an agenda for public debate in the news media and, secondly, there is a formal agenda of items due for consideration by a legislature or the UN decision-making bodies. Clearly the public agenda and the formal agendas influence each other. NGOs mainly aim to influence the public agenda by activity within individual countries. The public agenda will vary substantially from one country to another, due to linguistic and cultural differences and varying structures for the media and for political debate. It is important for a global NGO to have distinct branches in as many countries as possible, in order to be able to maximise its ability to make its issues newsworthy in different ways for the different media. Different techniques are chosen according to the number and type of supporters, the skills of the permanent staff and the connections to the media that the NGO has built up.

UN meetings and conferences can be important to NGOs because they can be used as a focus for agenda-setting activities. UN occasions generate interactions between the public agendas in different countries, the formal agenda of the UN institution and the formal agendas of domestic legislatures. Holding a UN conference opens up the possibility of news media coverage in most countries, particularly if senior politicians attend. The need for governments to instruct their delegates generates attention, at least within the government bureaucracy and perhaps in the legislature as well. The outcome of the conference may well require financial commitments to be met, or treaties and other policy decisions to be ratified, and hence legislative action taken.

There are thus wide-ranging policy domains where the main issues have only been considered because of the work of NGOs. Environmental politics, women's rights and individual human rights have all been led by NGOs. Development politics was initiated within the UN system by the Bretton Woods institutions and by governments, but NGOs have substantially redefined the agenda. In the early 1960s, development was widely seen as increasing the average GNP *per capita*, whereas now most political actors accept the goal of human development, defined in terms of improving the quality of life of ordinary people. In other areas, such as East-West relations, Palestinian-Israeli relations and the attack upon apartheid, the main agenda has been defined by governments, but NGOs have often redefined aspects of that agenda, both in public debate and formally in international meetings. Most notably they have added a human rights dimension to these three domains. The chapters of this book on the World Bank, the environment, women's rights, the rights of the child and Amnesty International all document the ability of NGOs to change the agenda for governments.

NGOs and policy formulation

It was suggested earlier that the work of NGOs at the UN is less important in policy formulation. The main outline of policy for governments will be decided in capital cities prior to a UN meeting. Pressure from domestic NGOs or the output from earlier UN meetings can influence those decisions. Some NGO techniques at the UN are unlikely to have much impact on shaping the broad policy, though they can be used to mobilise support for a policy proposal that has already been drafted. For example, NGOs can put pressure on a government to sign or ratify a treaty at the end of a conference. Other techniques that generate policy debate at the early stages can be much more influential. Lobbying the UN Secretariat as soon as it takes up a new issue, or preparing an authoritative research report may help to establish the basic principles on which governments will form policy. (At this level, an NGO would be operating at the boundary where agenda-setting and policy formulation overlap.)[45] If the report is published under the name of the UN Secretariat, rather than solely under the NGO's own name, then the influence may be very great.

The main ability of NGOs to affect policy formulation lies not so much in the broad principles as in the details of policy, with committee work and lobbying. Here the NGO people involved must have not only the previously mentioned qualities of expertise, integrity and prestige, but also the ability to communicate and to assess whether there are opportunities for negotiation. In all committees that are not totally deadlocked there will come a point when the well-crafted proposal, which meets the basic requirements of most governments, will be gratefully accepted by tired delegates, even if it does come from an NGO. The best situation for an NGO can be to find a delegation which is already committed to the same policy objectives as the NGO, particularly if the delegation is under-resourced and prepared to receive assistance. They work together on drafting proposals which are tabled by the government. Intergovernmental negotiations will usually be dominated by the official delegations, but that does not exclude the possibility of significant NGO influence behind the scenes. The chapters on Amnesty International and the Convention on the Rights of the Child in this book show how NGOs can influence negotiations.

NGOs and policy implementation

It is not possible to generalise about the impact of NGOs on policy implementation. If governments are highly committed to a policy and have the required expertise and resources, NGO influence may be minimal. But if any of these factors is missing, NGO influence may be substantial. One process is to generate political embarrassment when governments have not achieved the policy goals to which they have officially committed themselves. Here one is back to the basic techniques of generating publicity and debate in the media. But whereas for agenda-setting the aim is to capture the imagination of the audience, for implementation the aim is to communicate specific information, to demonstrate that behaviour is not in accord with official policy. When policy has taken the form of making some practice illegal, then establishing proof that it is happening is effective in pushing governments to commit more resources to enforcement. Influencing implementation is mainly about influencing politics within each country. However, publicity in international organisations such as the UN is often an effective technique for generating pressure on the government back home.

The second major way in which NGOs are involved in policy implementation is that they can be commissioned as operational agents on behalf of the UN in the field. One reason for this may be to use NGO expertise and experience. Another is that governments and the UN may wish to distance themselves from the policy, either for political reasons or because NGOs are more trusted by those who are affected by the policy. A good example of governments maintaining their distance is work on sex education and family planning. NGOs are most likely to be commissioned for development projects, disaster relief and work with refugees.

NGO participation in UN conferences

The main reason for holding major UN specialised conferences is to shift a particular issue higher up public and formal agendas. The Stockholm and Rio environmental conferences, the Bucharest, Mexico City and Cairo population conferences and the series of women's conferences are among the best known. They generated widespread media coverage. Hundreds of other specialised UN conferences have been held.[46] Many have attracted little or no media attention, but they can still be highly important. Some engage in policy formulation at the global level. The conferences on the ozone layer and on high-seas fishing, for example, have been the forums for detailed intergovernmental negotiations to produce a common policy. NGOs are deeply involved in both types of conferences.

The main outcomes of broad-agenda, single-session conferences are largely determined in the pre-conference preparatory work. The more technical, multi-session conferences can move in unanticipated directions during the conference negotiations. Whatever the type of conference, it is standard practice to give rights of participation at UN conferences to NGOs with ECOSOC consultative status. It has also been common practice to give the same rights at conferences to a wider range of NGOs which apply to attend an individual conference. NGOs have learnt a variety of ways to exercise influence, both in the preparatory work and in conference negotiations.

Preparation of reports for conferences

In many cases, the General Assembly or ECOSOC resolution convening a UN conference will ask the UN Secretariat and governments to prepare reports on one or more of the main topics. Where a topic is a new one for intergovernmental action, or even perhaps for governmental action, Secretariat officials and government civil servants may have no choice but to turn to the relevant NGOs for assistance in compiling their reports. When NGOs are involved from the beginning in the preparation of such reports, they are participating in the most important aspect of agenda-setting: defining how political actors perceive the problem and the nature of what is, and what is not, to be discussed.

Participation in conference committees and plenary sessions

When there is committee work for a conference, either in the preparatory process or during the conference, NGOs are usually able to attend. NGOs which are oriented towards news media coverage or have not learnt the importance of committee work, or which simply do not have enough available personnel, may choose not to attend. Sometimes there may only be a small number of NGO representatives at the committee meetings. This can be an advantage, as they can be allowed to take part in the debate without the delegates being worried about their work being swamped by the NGOs.

Emphasis has been given to the exceptional nature of the participation rights of NGOs within ECOSOC. In practice these are used rather infrequently by a small number of NGOs. However, the existence of the rights in one of the central organs of the UN legitimises participation in other organs. The general pattern would appear to be that NGO participation is likely to be allowed on a more informal, less restricted basis when the meeting is not the subject of public attention, when the subject matter is fairly technical, when a small number of delegates is present, when few of the delegates are lawyers and when there is a general desire to reach agreement by consensus. All these factors tend to apply in conference committee work.

The orthodox view of the United Nations stresses that the members are states and that only government representatives have the right to vote. Increasingly the UN tries to operate by consensus and this is now the norm for specialised conferences. Thus voting is less important in formal terms than it used to be. The fact that NGOs do not have voting rights in the UN does not mean that they are unable to affect the decisions. Significant influence can be exercised through input to reports and committee work. In addition, it is now common for NGOs to be allowed to take part in the plenary debates. The time allowed is usually very limited, perhaps to a single short speech on behalf of all the NGOs, but occasionally several interventions are allowed. The work of NGOs inside and outside the conference hall can make it more difficult for the major governments to claim there is a consensus without making further concessions.

It has been pointed out that NGO representatives can lobby delegates and, when they find one sympathetic to their ideas, draft resolutions and have them tabled by one of the delegations. Because such actions violate the image of NGOs as 'non-political' consultants and the premise of diplomats obeying their government's instructions, they do not often come to light. Nevertheless, some illustrations can be quoted. The IPPF drafted the resolution on the right of access to family planning information passed by the 1968 International Conference on Human Rights and the International Baby Foods Action Network has drafted resolutions on baby foods passed by the World Health Organisation. A more complex story of the International Commission of Jurists being responsible for changing the Geneva Conventions on the laws of war has been fully documented.[47] The chapters in this book on the environment and on women's rights show the extent of NGO influence in agenda-setting conferences.

NGO forums and NGO newspapers

At some UN conferences, NGOs have two other important techniques for exercising influence: NGO forums and NGO newspapers. Alongside the official diplomatic conferences, there may be an unofficial NGO conference, which is usually called a forum. Neither 'conference' nor 'forum' conveys the full sense of the chaotic turmoil of the informal fermentation of ideas and debate. Many months before the conference opens, a leading NGO or a wider committee of NGOs will cooperate with the UN Secretariat in publicising the conference and arranging for NGOs to organise their own events in parallel with the diplomatic conference. Sometimes the forum is conveniently placed close to the conference hall, but sometimes it is in a different part of the city. In either situation, many diplomats make the effort to turn up to hear the talks, watch the street theatre, see the exhibitions, watch the films and attend the debates, which between them all raise a wider range of ideas than is discussed in the official conferences. The forums are also attended by journalists and hence widen the public agenda of media debate. Sometimes they will have a direct impact on the formal conference agenda, for example in Stockholm in 1972 when the demonstrations against whaling contributed to the decision of the environment conference to vote for a moratorium on commercial whaling.[48]

A conference with a forum usually also has an NGO newspaper. The first was organised as a relatively simple production by Friends of the Earth and the *Ecologist* magazine for the 1972 Stockholm conference, under the name *Eco*. The first fully professional newspaper was *Planet*, produced and funded by IPPF for the 1974

World Population Conference. These newspapers are printed on a daily basis and distributed free of charge first thing in the morning at the main hotels and the main conference buildings on each working day of the conference. They cover the full range of news reporting, cartoons and editorial columns and serve as information bulletins on forthcoming conference and forum events. A small team of experienced professional journalists produces better coverage of the conference than any ordinary newspaper could achieve. They make the diplomatic conferences more transparent in that the professional diplomats often may only learn what other delegations are doing from the NGO newspaper's reports. They also give public notice of NGO attitudes to the direction being taken by the official proceedings. As a general effect, the forums and newspapers provide a continuous reminder during the conference that the public agenda is much wider than the official agenda of the diplomatic proceedings.

NGO activists as insiders

When considering the full range of NGO activities, it can be seen that through involvement in report writing, committee work, lobbying, forums and their own newspapers, NGOs have a wide repertoire of activities from which to choose to influence conference proceedings from the outside. They can also exercise influence from the inside. The most prestigious NGOs experience a movement of personnel between their own secretariats and the UN secretariats and this occurs in both directions. Much more widespread is the practice of governments recruiting NGO activists as advisers on an *ad hoc* basis for the duration of a particular conference. When this happens the NGO individual officially becomes a government delegate and therefore has the maximum ability to lobby his own government's policy but he may lose some freedom to take part in the public debate or to lobby other governments. The most impressive example of NGO access was when Dr Sai, the President of the IPPF, was elected, in his role as head of the Ghanaian delegation, to chair the Preparatory Committee for the 1994 International Conference on Population and Development (ICPD).

NGO participation in other UN bodies

NGOs direct a great deal of time and effort to specialised conferences. As the outcomes are less rigidly defined by a long history of past decisions, they can usually achieve a greater impact here than at the regular meetings of established institutions. Nevertheless, input to reports, committee work and lobbying can occur in the same way to influence the decisions of the committees and commissions of ECOSOC and the decisions of the UN specialised agencies. As is shown in Chapters 5 and 6 of this book, a substantial impact is made by NGOs on the Commission on the Status of Women and the Commission on Human Rights. NGOs also have a special role in the new Commission on Sustainable Development as is discussed below.

With the exception of the Red Cross, recognised NGOs have not been allowed officially to participate in regular sessions of the General Assembly, but they have addressed special sessions on disarmament and on development and in November 1993 a curious new development occurred. The Assembly's Second Committee was debating the progress of the preparatory work for the ICPD when it suspended its discussions to hear from the head of the NGO Planning Committee, Billie Miller, and resumed when she had finished speaking: thus in reality an NGO addressed the Second Committee, while officially nothing happened.[49] It remains to be seen whether this was an isolated event or the first step down the road towards regular direct NGO involvement in the Assembly. For the time being, one access route is through working with specialised Assembly committees, outside the regular sessions. The second route to influence in the Assembly is through preliminary work in ECOSOC or specialised conferences, or sometimes through the agencies. Many of the General Assembly's resolutions come from recommendations by these other bodies and receive little time and attention in the Assembly itself. In practice an NGO that achieves success in a subsidiary body of ECOSOC may well be determining the text of an Assembly resolution. In addition, although they have no formal rights, NGOs engage extensively in informal lobbying in the corridors and the meeting rooms while the General Assembly is in session.

Very occasionally access has been gained to Security Council committees to report on violations of sanctions resolutions.[50] In general, direct influence on the agenda of the Security Council cannot be achieved. Indirect influence, via the public agenda, can occur. For example, reports in the world's media from the emergency relief NGOs in Somalia made a significant contribution to the Security Council decision to establish a UN peace-keeping operation. The distinction is not so much whether governments allow NGOs less access on questions of political conflict than on economic and social matters. The distinction is whether or not the meeting has procedures that legitimise NGO access and whether or not the particular NGOs seeking access have established a sound reputation for themselves.

In UN documents, and studies of UN politics based solely on the formal proceedings, the role of NGOs often seems insignificant. For example, a brief study by Kaufmann on the adoption of the UN declaration against torture talks in detail about the government proposals, speech-making and negotiations, but fails to mention Amnesty International or any other NGO.[51] Nevertheless, as Helena Cook outlines in Chapter 7, Amnesty was central to this whole process. Diplomats like to see NGOs as useful advisers, having 'consultative status', but definitely not as equal participants in diplomacy. Thus NGOs are usually very careful not to step beyond the bounds of accepted procedure. They have much less ability to take part in formal public UN meetings than in informal private meetings. Most of their influence is invisible except to the immediate participants, and it is therefore very easy to underestimate the impact of NGOs on UN proceedings. Recent resolutions have explicitly specified that 'non-governmental organisations shall not have any negotiating role'.[52] In terms of diplomatic norms, such a specification should be redundant. The fact that it has been thought necessary to assert this position is a warning to NGOs, but it is also a tribute to the prestige and the influence that NGOs have achieved.

The impact of the Earth Summit on the UN system

The relationship between the UN and NGOs went through another major period of change from 1992 to 1994, as a result of the UN Conference on Environment and Development (UNCED) – popularly known as the 'Earth Summit'. It is often asserted that the breadth of participation of NGOs at UNCED in Rio de Janeiro in June 1992 was unprecedented. In reality there has been a steady evolution in the role of NGOs, but many people only really became aware of it in 1992. The UN Conference on the Human Environment in Stockholm in June 1972 was a turning point. The Secretary-General of the conference, Maurice Strong, proposed that not only the ECOSOC NGOs but also 'other NGOs of genuinely international character' should be invited, provided that they were 'directly concerned with the subject matter of the Conference'.[53] In the 1980s the restriction that NGOs should be international was dropped and 'national NGOs' or even very local NGOs were able to attend. By 1987, at the International Conference on Drug Abuse and Illicit Trafficking, only 39 per cent of the 179 NGOs were on the ECOSOC list.[54] The participation in UNCED by many NGOs which had never before had any contact with the UN was simply an extension of existing practices. The result was to involve a much larger number of NGOs than at any previous UN conference. Of the 1,400 NGOs accredited beforehand, about 650 turned up and about 9,000 attended the unofficial Global Forum.

One understandable reason for the participation of NGOs in UNCED being seen to be so exceptional is that the outcome was unanticipated at the start of the process. In December 1989, when the General Assembly first decided to convene the conference, the developing countries were very suspicious of the environmental NGOs. The resolution that was adopted not only sought to restrict NGO participation to the established ECOSOC NGOs; it also implied that some would not be able to attend because they were not 'relevant'.[55] Many governments gave serious consideration to the role of NGOs for the first time in August 1990 at the first meeting of the Preparatory Committee, PrepCom I, with a 'sea change' in attitudes having occurred in the eight months since the Assembly decision.[56] The greatest shift was in the G-77 group of developing countries, which were now primarily concerned to ensure a balance between environmental and development NGOs and adequate participation by NGOs from developing countries. Even so some delegates still succeeded in imposing restrictive language in the agreed text.[57] Despite the wording of UNCED Decision 1/1 being *less* liberal than previous UN practice, it opened the door for any NGO to gain accreditation to the PrepCom meetings and the full conference.

The prestige of environmental NGOs

The media coverage of environmental issues and the diplomacy of the Earth Summit continued to generate an astonishing momentum to increasing the status of NGOs. Agenda 21, one of the five main documents produced by the Earth Summit, devoted one of its four sections, covering thirty-nine pages, to the proposition that 'the commitment and genuine involvement of all social groups' was critical to the effective implementation of sustainable development policies by governments.[58]

During the debates around the Earth Summit, the language about NGOs became very confused. Agenda 21 refers to 'social groups' and 'major groups'; some of the leading activists preferred 'independent sectors'; and the various documents were inconsistent on whether the term NGOs covered only the ECOSOC NGOs or all organisations.[59] Agenda 21 gave Section III the title *Strengthening the Role of Major Groups*, and devoted nine chapters to women, youth, 'indigenous people and their communities', non-governmental organisations, local authorities, workers and their trade unions, business and industry, the scientific and technological community and farmers. Maurice Strong, Secretary-General of the Rio conference, seems to have been trying to broaden the range of those involved in the conference, particularly by bringing in scientists and industrialists.[60] In this he was remarkably successful, with Agenda 21 carrying through to nothing less than the UN's first charter for democracy, in the call for all the 'major groups' to be involved in a 'real social partnership' with governments for the formulation and implementation of sustainable development policies both at the international level and within each country.

The new Commission on Sustainable Development

Chapter 38 of Agenda 21 called for the creation of a Commission on Sustainable Development (CSD) to ensure review and follow-up of the new commitments on environmental and development policy that had been made by all governments at Rio. Action by the General Assembly and by ECOSOC led to the creation of the CSD, election of its 53 members and the holding of its first meeting in February 1993.[61] Agenda 21 stated that in the follow-up process there should be 'an expanded role for non-governmental organisations, including those related to major groups, with accreditation based on the procedures used in the Conference' and this was endorsed in the resolutions establishing the CSD.[62]

When the time came to implement these decisions in New York, many divisions appeared within the Secretariat, among the governmental delegations and even among the NGOs. There were practical worries about security and about accommodating hundreds of new NGOs within the over-crowded headquarters facilities. Some delegates in New York were not as comfortable as those in Rio with the new ideas. Many of the new NGOs regarded the existing arrangements as too slow and cumbersome and the idea of 'consultative status' as being incompatible with 'social partnership'. On the other hand the established NGOs were satisfied with the existing procedures and were worried that their special position might be undermined by the new NGOs.[63]

On the same day as the CSD was created by ECOSOC, the Council approved an ambiguous, poorly-drafted Decision.[64] The new NGOs were placed on the Roster, solely for the purposes of consultation with the CSD. Because it was assumed that NGO requests to address the Commission would be too time-consuming, it was expected that NGOs would be asked to appoint a spokesperson.[65] In March 1993 the Secretariat wrote to all the non-ECOSOC NGOs accredited to UNCED and invited them to apply for a place on the CSD Roster by 15 April, in order to be in time for the first substantive meeting of the CSD. The Secretariat also went beyond the terms of the ECOSOC Decision and invited any other interested NGO to apply as well.[66] Although it had been estimated that up to a thousand new NGOs might apply, by the deadline only 479 UNCED NGOs and seventy-one other new NGOs had done so. They were all approved by the Council.[67] At the CSD session in June 1993 some 280 NGO representatives were present. This was a large number, but a far cry from the theoretical maximum of more than two thousand, combining the established NGOs and the potential new NGOs.[68]

After a year in which the new NGOs were denied full access to consultative status facilities, the first ECOSOC Decision was overturned and the environmental NGOs were brought in as another section of the Roster, operating by the established rules for consultation under the provisions of Resolution 1296.[69] The final result was that, following on from the UNCED precedent, from July 1994 single-country NGOs gained access to the UN system for the first time in large numbers, rather than as occasional exceptions to the norm that an NGO should be based in several countries.

Review of the arrangements under Resolution 1296

In the euphoria of the Earth Summit, provisions were written into Agenda 21 for a review of the 'formal procedures and mechanisms' for the involvement of NGOs in the United Nations system.[70] The pressures for such a review came from NGOs seeking a much greater role in ECOSOC than that provided by the existing consultative status, the need to consider whether special procedures were required on sustainable development questions and the desire of some to establish formal relationships in the General Assembly. The Secretariat wanted consideration of the resources allocated to their NGO Unit and the logistics of dealing with much greater numbers of NGOs. Some governments wished to give positive support to NGOs as part of the process of global democratisation, while others, which were antagonistic to human-rights NGOs and some environmental NGOs, no doubt hoped that the review process would provide opportunities for them to halt, or even reverse, the growth in the activities and the prestige of NGOs.

In February 1993 ECOSOC decided to establish a review. Rather than this encompassing all the activities of NGOs in the whole UN system it became simply 'a general review of current arrangements for consultation' under Resolution 1296.[71] The NGO Committee worked on the terms of reference for the review and recommended that an Open-Ended Working Group should consider the ECOSOC arrangements, the possibility of standardising the rules for participation in international conferences and improvement of the work of the NGO Committee and the Secretariat's NGO Unit. The preamble to their resolution prejudged the review by 'recognising the continued validity of its Resolution 1296(XLIV) as a useful framework'.[72]

At the time of writing, the review has not been completed. The Secretariat published a comprehensive report on how the arrangements have worked in the past[73] and in July 1994 the Open-Ended Working Group published an interim report, in which it was plain that the debate was again moving in a positive direction for the NGOs.[74] One weakness of NGOs is that they have an impatience with bureaucratic processes that seem irrelevant to their issue area, such as this review. Participation by the NGOs in the first stage of the review was predominantly by a small number of well-established traditional NGOs, mainly from ECOSOC Category I. The opportunity to push on an open door was not being taken.

The outcome will probably be a re-affirmation of the existing consultative arrangements that have worked successfully for more than thirty years, with only minor amendments being suggested. The really difficult question is whether any formal arrangements should be initiated for NGOs in the General Assembly. This is most improbable for the regular sessions, but a possible compromise is that standard procedures for international conferences should also apply to special sessions of the Assembly. There is a clear need for the Secretariat NGO Unit to be strengthened, but it may not be allocated the necessary resources. The events arising from the Earth Summit represented a significant change in the relationship between NGOs and the UN system, but they should be seen less as a dramatic turning point and more as part of a long evolutionary process.

Conclusions

This chapter has concentrated on the role of NGOs in the main UN policy-making bodies and not in the operational programmes or the specialised agencies. In these other parts of the wider UN system the role of NGOs has been much less controversial. In operational programmes, NGOs gain recognition through being effective partners in the field. In the specialised agencies, there is generally a formal consultative system similar to the ECOSOC one, but working with a smaller number of more specialised NGOs. Whenever governments are dealing with technical questions they are glad to deal with those who have technical expertise.

The extent to which NGOs are now recognised as being integral to the UN system was shown by the warmth of Boutros Boutros-Ghali's welcome in September 1994 to a conference of NGOs at the UN's headquarters.

I want you to consider this your home. Until recently these words might have caused astonishment. The United Nations was considered to be a forum of sovereign states alone. Within the space of a few short years, this attitude has changed. Non-governmental organisations are now considered full participants in international life.[75]

The following chapters offer case studies of how this participation by NGOs has made a significant difference to United Nations politics on a wide range of issues

NOTES

1. General Assembly Resolution of 16 February 1946 quoted in *Yearbook of the United Nations 1946–47* (New York: United Nations, 1947), p. 551.
2. For the purposes of simplification the main text has referred throughout to the NGO Committee. In practice the use of the term 'NGO Committee' covers what were officially five different mandates from February 1946 to May 1968.
3. *UN Yearbook 1946–47*, p. 552.
4. As early as August 1947 ECOSOC Resolution 95(V)II admitted four 'national' NGOs on the basis that their governments had approved, see *UN Yearbook 1947–48*, p. 687. This was incorporated as a general provision in Resolution 288B(X) of 27 February 1950, expressing the requirement in Article 71 of the Charter.
5. *UN Yearbook 1946–47*, p. 552.
6. Resolution 288B(X) and *UN Yearbook 1950*, p. 659.
7. Failure to produce a quadrennial report can lead either to demotion or to being struck off completely. For a recent example of demotions see *Report of the Committee on Non-Governmental Organisations*, UN doc. E/1993/63 of 7 June 1993, p. 18.
8. ECOSOC Resolution 1099(XL) of 4 March 1966 increased the size of the Committee on NGOs from seven to thirteen members and ECOSOC Resolution 1981/50 of 20 July 1981 increased it to nineteen members.
9. *UN Yearbook 1946–47*, p. 552.
10. *Ibid.*, p. 554 and ECOSOC Resolution 57(IV) of 28 March 1947. Further debate led to Resolution 214C(VIII) of 14 February 1949, which refined the details of Resolution 57(IV), see *UN Yearbook 1948–49*, p. 709–11.
11. *UN Yearbook 1947–48*, pp. 687, 689–90 and 694; *UN Yearbook 1948–49*, pp. 709–11.
12. General Assembly Resolution 386(V) of 4 November 1950; ECOSOC Resolution 366(XII) of 21 March 1951, repealing Resolution 214C(VIII) (see note 10

above); and *UN Yearbook 1951*, pp. 598–9.

13. ECOSOC Resolution 334A(XI) of 20 July 1950 and *UN Yearbook 1950*, p. 663. 598–9.
14. *UN Yearbook 1951*, pp. 597–8.
15. *Ibid.*, p. 597.
16. *UN Yearbook 1954*, p. 299.
17. ECOSOC Resolution 287(X) of 3 March 1950 and *UN Yearbook 1950*, pp. 661–2.
18. ECOSOC Resolution 1219(XLIII) of 5 June 1967 and *UN Yearbook 1967*, pp. 564, 570.
19. *UN Yearbook 1946–47*, pp. 552, 554. See also *UN Yearbook 1948–49*, pp. 713–4, for specification of the NGOs that had joint representation.
20. *UN Yearbook 1946–47*, p. 554, and *UN Yearbook 1948–49*, p. 714.
21. *UN Yearbook 1946–47*, p. 554.
22. *UN Yearbook 1950*, p. 659.
23. See *Report of the Committee on Non-Governmental Organisations*, UN doc. E/1993/63, pp. 12–13. This decision was endorsed by ECOSOC on 30 July 1993 in Decision 1993/329.
24. Human Life International was initially recommended in January 1991 by the NGO Committee for inclusion on the Roster (see UN doc. E/1991/20, p. 12). However, in May 1991 ECOSOC refused to endorse this decision and referred the application back to the Committee's 1993 session, (see ECOSOC Report, UN doc. A/46/3, p. 126 para. 63 and Decision 1991/216). Finally, in May 1993 the application was rejected (see UN doc. E/1993/63, p. 15). The factor that probably tipped the decision against Human Life International was that it had campaigned in the United States against children collecting money for UNICEF.
25. *UN Yearbook 1946–47*, pp. 551–2.
26. *Ibid.*, p. 553.
27. *Ibid.*, pp. 149–50, and General Assembly Resolution 49(I)B of 15 December 1946.
28. *Ibid.*, p. 151, and General Assembly Resolution 49(I)C of 15 December 1946.
29. *UN Yearbook 1947–48*, pp. 690–1 and ECOSOC Resolution 95(V)III of 16 August 1947.
30. *UN Yearbook 1950*, p. 657.
31. Of the eight ECOSOC agenda items proposed by NGOs, four originated with the WFTU (covering equal pay for men and women, freedom of association, trade union rights and full employment), while the AFL raised three items (the protection of migrant labour, forced labour and publication of information on development projects). In those days of Cold War antagonisms, some matters seemed more contentious than they do now. See *UN Yearbook 1947–48*, p. 693, and *UN Yearbook 1948–49*, p. 712.
32. *UN Yearbook 1950*, pp. 657–9.
33. *Ibid.*
34. All the practices were codified in ECOSOC Resolution 288(X) of 27 February 1950 and then reviewed and re-affirmed with some changes in Resolution 1296(XLIV) of 23 May 1968. The text of the latter resolution is given in Appendix B.
35. ECOSOC Resolution 1099(XL) of 4 March 1966.
36. ECOSOC Resolution 1219(XLII) of 5 June 1967.
37. Chiang Pei-heng, *Non-Governmental Organisations at the United Nations. Identity, Role and Function* (New York: Praeger, 1981). The references to the *New York Times* stories are given in pp. 120–1. The debates in early 1967 are covered in pp. 106–15. See also *UN Yearbook 1967*, pp. 563–4.

38. ECOSOC Resolution 1225(XLII) of 6 June 1967.
39. General Assembly Resolution 2339(XXII) of 18 December 1967, paragraph 10, invited NGOs 'that have a demonstrable interest' in the items on the agenda to send observers to the conference. The proposal in document A/L.542 to delete paragraph 10 was lost by a vote of 51 in favour to 51 against, with 11 abstentions. See *UN Yearbook 1967*, pp. 504–7.
40. Chiang, *op. cit.*, Chapter 6.
41. *Ibid.*, p. 184 and p. 211, note 48.
42. ECOSOC Resolution 366(XII) of 21 March 1951, passed by 11 votes to 5 with 2 abstentions, stated that relationships of NGOs with ECOSOC are 'technical and largely non-political in character'.
43. 'Statement by the Secretary-General on the Occasion of the Forty-Seventh Conference of Non-Governmental Organisations' (London: UN Information Centre, mimeo, 20 September 1994), p. 3. See Appendix C.
44. Martin Ennals, 'Amnesty International and Human Rights', in P. Willetts (ed.), *Pressure Groups in the Global System* (London: Pinter, 1982), p. 73.
45. At the extreme it is possible for NGOs to be fully credited, along with international secretariats, as joint authors of reports defining policy objectives. An important example would be the World Conservation Strategy.
46. See P. Willetts, 'The Pattern of Conferences' in A. J. R. Groom and P. Taylor (eds), *Global Issues in the United Nations Framework* (London: Macmillan, 1989), for a list of 147 global conferences from 1961 to 1985 and an analysis of their general features.
47. K. Suter, *An International Law of Guerrilla Warfare: The Global Politics of Law-Making* (London: Pinter, 1984).
48. T. Burke, 'Friends of the Earth and the Conservation of Resources', in Willetts, *op. cit.*, p. 121.
49. ICPD 94. Newsletter of the International Conference on Population and Development, no. 10, November–December 1993, p. 5.
50. A. Minty, 'The Anti-Apartheid Movement and Racism in Southern Africa' in Willetts, *op. cit.*, p. 40.
51. J. Kaufmann, *United Nations Decision Making*, (Alphen aan den Rijn: Sijthoff and Noordhoff, 1980), pp. 150–4.
52. See for example, Decision 1/1 in Appendix B; ECOSOC Resolution 1993/4 of 3 February 1993, and ECOSOC Decision 1993/215 of 12 February 1993.
53. UN doc. A/CONF.48/PC.11 of 30 July 1971.
54. *Report of the International Conference on Drug Abuse and Illicit Trafficking, Vienna, 17–26 June 1987*, UN doc. A/CONF.133/12, pp. 136–9.
55. General Assembly Resolution 44/228 of 22 December 1989, para. 12.
56. Stephen Collett, *Progress of UNCED, PrepCom I Nairobi, 6–31 August 1990* (Memo to NGO Development Committees, New York and Geneva, dated 15 August 1990), p. 3.
57. The key debate took place on 10 August 1990, at an 'open-ended meeting' to discuss amendments to the text of UN doc. A/CONF.151/PC/CRP.7.
58. *Report of the United Nations Conference on Environment and Development, Annex II, Agenda 21*, UN doc. A/CONF.151/26, quotation from the Preamble to Section III in vol. III, p. 4. See Appendix B.
59. For an illustration of the verbal confusion, note the five different meanings of the term NGOs implied in Agenda 21, paras 38.5, 38.8(d), 38.11, 38.13 and 38.14, in UN doc. A/CONF.151/26 vol. III, pp. 88–91.
60. Maurice Strong was responsible for the paper on NGOs (UN doc. A/CONF.151/PC/9) that led to Decision 1/1. In para. 8, he lists under 'groups in society' six of the nine groups covered by Agenda 21 Section III.
61. Much of the Agenda 21 text on the CSD was endorsed by the UN. See Agenda

21, Chapter 38, International Institutional Arrangements, A/CONF.151/26, vol. III, pp. 90–1; UN General Assembly Resolution 47/191 of 22 December 1992; ECOSOC Decision 1993/207 of 12 February 1993; and the elections of 16 February 1993 given in ECOSOC Decision 1993/201.

62. Agenda 21, para. 38.44 (see Appendix B) and General Assembly Resolution 47/191, para. 8.
63. For the debate on the role of NGOs in the CSD, see *The Independent Sectors' Network 92* published by The Centre For Our Common Future, Geneva, particularly August–September 1992, pp. 1 and 6, and January 1993, pp. 8–9. (From October 1992, '92' was dropped from the title of this newsletter.)
64. ECOSOC Decision 1993/215 of 12 February 1993, given in Appendix B of this book.
65. UN doc. E/1993/12 of 29 January 1993, paras. 18 and 20.
66. United Nations Secretariat ECOSOC/NGO Unit, *Notification*, 3 March 1993, given in Appendix B.
67. The applications for the CSD Roster are given in UN doc. E/1993/65 of 21 May 1993, with the UNCED NGOs and other new NGOs listed separately. The applications were approved by ECOSOC Decision 1993/220 of 26 May 1993. A single consolidated list of these two groups of NGOs is given in UN doc. E/CN.17/1994/INF/1 of 25 April 1994.
68. The UN documents do not record the level of NGO attendance at the first substantive session of the CSD, but *The Independent Sectors' Network* reports 'over 280 representatives of NGOs were in New York' (June, p. 1). As some NGOs would send more than one person, this means that probably less than 200 organisations were taking part.
69. See UN doc. E/1994/33 of 12 July 1994, para. 24, for the CSD recommendation that all the NGOs accredited to the Commission be placed on the Roster and ECOSOC Decision 1994/300 of 29 July 1994 giving provisional endorsement to the recommendation. See Appendix B.
70. Agenda 21, para. 27.6. See also paras 27.9(a) and 38.44.
71. ECOSOC Decision 1993/214 of 12 February 1993.
72. *Report of the Committee on Non-Governmental Organisations*, UN doc. E/1993/63 of 7 June 1993, endorsed with only minor amendments as ECOSOC Resolution 1993/80 of 30 July 1993.
73. UN doc. E/AC.70/1994/5 of 26 May 1994.
74. UN doc. A/49/215-E/1994/99 of 5 July 1994.
75. Statement by the Secretary-General . . ., *op. cit.*, p. 1, see note 43 above.

3

THE WORLD BANK AND NGOs

Seamus Cleary

As the Second World War drew to a close, the Allies turned their attention to the ordering of the post-war world. In the political and security fields, their deliberations led to the setting up of the United Nations. There were also serious economic problems to be addressed. The Allies met at the United Nations Monetary and Financial Conference held at Bretton Woods, New Hampshire, in 1944. There were proposals for three organisations – an international investment bank, an international monetary institution and an international trade organisation. The eventual outcome – the International Monetary Fund, the International Bank for Reconstruction and Development, and the General Agreement on Tariffs and Trade (finally agreed in 1947) – reflected US power and influence rather than the institutional requirements of the best working of the international economy.

The Bretton Woods institutions

The International Bank for Reconstruction and Development (IBRD) was established to act as an international investment bank. Early loans were to European countries, to rebuild their infrastructure and industry damaged by the war. By the mid-1950s, attention had turned to loans to promote economic growth in other parts of the world. Initially the IBRD made loans only for specific projects. It was thus concerned with micro-economic policy relevant to the success of its projects and not with government policy in general. The Bank has two sources for its loan capital. From its members, it receives subscriptions that are proportional to the size of each country's economy; but most of its funds come from borrowing on the international capital markets. Because the Bank's credit rating is the highest possible, AAA, its borrowings are at the cheapest rate commercially available. Loans are only made to member governments, although in recent years project funding may include grants to non-governmental organisations.

Towards the end of the 1950s, IBRD members agreed to establish

63

a soft-loan arm of the Bank. The International Development Association (IDA) was set up in 1960 for those developing countries that could not afford to pay market rates of interest on their borrowings. The IDA's resources come from profits made by the IBRD and a replenishment of its funds made every three years by the wealthier members. IDA's interest-free loans, known as 'credits', are for the poorest members (with a *per capita* GNP below $740 in 1990 US dollars). The IBRD and the IDA together constitute the World Bank.

The International Monetary Fund (IMF) oversees the working of the international financial system and provides currencies to fund short-term balance of payments deficits. Its resources come from the quotas paid in by each member, 25 per cent in internationally acceptable foreign exchange reserves and 75 per cent in the member's own currency. It does not engage in any investment or make any grants.Technically it does not provide loans, but makes currency swaps. Before obtaining funds from the various facilities, the member must agree to macro-economic policy changes and performance criteria that should eliminate the deficit. These conditions, which generally include cuts in government expenditure and liberalisation of markets, are known as structural adjustment programmes.

Since the early 1980s the distinctions between the activities of the IMF and the World Bank have become increasingly blurred. The IMF has moved from short-term to medium-term lending while the World Bank has moved from project to programme lending. Moreover, in order to improve the conditions for investment, a significant proportion of the Bank's loans have been to support sectoral adjustment, overall structural adjustment and economic reform programmes. Developments in the 1970s made it clear that it 'is virtually impossible to have a good project in a bad policy environment'.[1] Policy lending was maintained at levels between 20 per cent and 30 per cent of all lending throughout the latter part of the 1980s and into the 1990s.

Ultimate authority in both the World Bank and the IMF lies with their Boards of Governors, on which each member country is represented. The two Boards meet jointly in September/October every year. Each institution also has a smaller Executive Board, on which eight of the largest countries have their own representatives and the medium or smaller countries form themselves into constituencies represented by a single Director. The Executive Boards are based in Washington, meet several times a week for most of the year and are responsible for the detailed decision-making on approving projects and the terms and conditions for structural adjustment programmes.

Table 3.1. DISTRIBUTION OF THE VOTES IN THE BANK
AND THE FUND (%)

Group of Seven	IBRD	IDA	IMF
USA*	17.18	16.05	17.82
Japan*	6.64	10.16	5.55
Germany*	5.13	6.88	5.55
Britain*	4.92	5.30	4.99
France*	4.92	4.02	4.99
Italy	3.18	2.93	3.10
Canada	3.18	3.12	2.92
Total G7	45.15	48.46	44.92
Total G10	52.70	54.51	52.12
Other major members			
Saudi Arabia*	3.18	3.41	3.46
India	3.18	3.13	2.07
China*	3.18	1.99	2.29
Russia*	1.79	0.32	2.91
Total all others	35.97	36.64	37.15

* These eight countries are the only ones to have single-member seats on each of the Executive Boards.

The subscriptions to the Bank and the quotas in the Fund are determined mainly by formulae related to the size of a country's economy and this in turn determines the number of votes held by the Governors and the Directors.[2] This system of weighted voting and the predominance of US and West European personnel on the staff means that the Bank and the Fund are seen as being dominated by Western interests. The strength of the belief in the virtues of free markets also means the Bank and the Fund are seen as instruments of Western ideology.

In the 1950s and 1960s, conventional development theory was dominated by the assumption that developing countries should maximise economic growth and so reproduce Western democratic industrialised society. Over time, wealth would 'trickle down' to the poor through increased demand and new employment opportunities. Initially, real growth and improved living standards were achieved, as evidenced by reductions in infant mortality and improvements in life expectancy. From the 1970s onwards, however, the economies of developing countries were unable to cope with oil-price rises, population growth, the costs of arms supplies and the accumulation of wealth by the élites. In the 1980s the Western recession drastically reduced earnings from commodity exports,

while real interest rates rocketed, generating the debt crisis and the
'lost decade'. Public policy analysis continued to emphasise the
domestic political economy of developing countries and remained
determined to ignore the impact of the international market.
Unable or unwilling to question the value of economic growth,
trickle down, production for export and the market mechanism
itself, donor governments and the major aid institutions concluded
that internal public policy was the cause of development failures.

The impact of the debt crisis from the early 1980s hastened the
Bank's shift from project aid to broader programme or sector aid.
But the central advice remained the same: increase economic growth,
limit the government's interference in the economy, end restrictions
on international trade and increase production (mainly for export)
of goods in which the country has a comparative advantage. The
Bank and the Fund insisted that the market is more efficient and
government intervention causes inefficiencies and waste.

These beliefs did not survive the 1980s. By 1989, advocates of
private-sector pre-eminence were on the retreat within the Bank.
A report on Africa accepted that governments have a major role.
Sound macro-economic policy could provide an enabling environment for growth, but capacity building, in terms of health, education and effective government institutions, was also essential.[3]
The rethinking was completed in the 1991 World Development
Report: 'success in promoting economic growth is most likely when
governments complement markets'; they should 'concentrate their
interventions on areas in which markets prove inadequate'.[4] For
the World Bank in the 1990s, the government should provide the
basic infrastructure, such as communications networks, establish
the legal framework for economic activity, provide essential services, such as primary education and preventive health care, and
provide a safety net to protect the poorest people. NGO critics and
others assert that this means little real change. In World Bank practice the market is still brought to bear on those areas specifically
reserved for government responsibility. Action to build a base,
through education and health, to strengthen the *status quo* is
legitimate, but action intended to result in different forms of social
organisation and power relationships apparently is not.

Non-governmental development organisations

A report from the Organisation for Economic Cooperation and
Development (OECD) drawing on discussion by Sir Geoffrey

Wilson, a former Chairman of Oxfam-UK, characterised the relief and development NGOs:

> Most are concerned with development – agricultural, social, medical, educational, etc. – in both urban and rural environments. Of the wide variety of organisations operating internationally, church-related bodies still make up the largest number. The Red Cross societies, refugee relief bodies, the International Planned Parenthood Federation and its affiliated members and Save the Children Fund organisations account for another 'group' of specialised NGOs; followed by the specialist organisations concerned with leprosy, the blind, and other professional fields like adult literacy, agricultural development and vocational training. The remainder consist of private foundations like Rockefeller and Ford, which provide funding; organisations like Oxfam, which support a wide range of activities; some 'half-and-half' organisations that receive considerable government funding such as CARE and the volunteer-sending agencies and a larger number of small groups that fall into none of the above characteristics.
>
> A primary difference between NGOs and bilateral and multilateral government organisations is that NGOs are at the other end of the scale in terms of size. Except where they are financed by governments, their dependence on voluntary organisations keeps them small, by itself a pressure to do more with fewer resources. This means that NGOs can and must work with local groups and individuals: the competence and commitment, success or failure of these groups and individuals determined their own success or failure.[5]

The term 'NGO' achieved wide acceptance in Europe during the 1970s and 1980s. In the United States, private voluntary organisation is most commonly used to describe organisations which carry out such activities. More recently, both developing-country and European agencies appear to be moving away from the term NGO. Experiencing growing pressure from environmental organisations, development-oriented European NGOs perceived the need to clarify their identity still further; they now often term themselves non-governmental development organisations. African groups tend to refer to themselves as voluntary development organisations.

Environmental organisations, such as the US-based Environmental Defence Fund and the Sierra Club, or the more international membership organisations such as Friends of the Earth, Greenpeace or the World Wide Fund for Nature, won a significantly higher profile as NGOs in the course of the 1970s and 1980s.

Many support projects intended to defend the environment, both
in their own countries and in the developing world, as well as lobbying in support of environmentally friendly economic policies; the
focus of others is solely political.

The NGO community is very diverse. Its development-oriented
members probably share a common analysis of the necessary conditions for development to occur – an equitable global trading system
including just commodity prices, transparent political processes,
adequate external assistance, involving local people at all stages of
the development process and caring for the environment. It is by
no means evident that such an understanding is shared by all
environment-oriented NGOs. This has resulted in substantial conflicts within the NGO community. The outcome is often determined by two factors: access to resources, in particular money, and
proximity to the Bank's Washington headquarters. The NGO community's different analyses have resulted in the pursuit of two
distinct strategies being followed by the western NGO community.

NGOs and the World Bank

Bilateral and multilateral government organisations' interest in non-
governmental development organisations grew rapidly. Increasing
levels of donors' development assistance was channelled through
NGDOs which increasingly sought to influence the policies of
governments and the multilateral organisations. In 1988 Joseph
Wheeler, then Chairman of the OECD Development Assistance
Committee, paid the following tribute to NGOs:

> The voluntary sector has frequently articulated new policy
> insights reflecting changes which have been taking place in our
> societies. Ask an aid administrator why he or she has increased
> the emphasis on environmental concerns – or women in develop-
> ment, or population. Ask where the pressure comes from for
> more emphasis on reaching the poor, or on health and educa-
> tion. The answer is that these are concerns of our populations
> expressed through our political processes and usually pointed up
> by what we call our non-governmental organisations.
>
> But this dialogue works both ways. Official agencies are recog-
> nising that development is an enabling process – not primarily
> a welfare programme. They have encouraged the NGO commu-
> nity to go further in that direction and the NGOs have responded.
>   ... To us on the official side the NGO sector represents an
> educator of our publics, an aspect of our support, the origin of
> some of our policy, a welcome financial contribution, the source

of insights on methodology and a vehicle for administering a portion of our official assistance.

Today the DAC-country NGOs raise from their constituencies approximately [US] $3 billion for developmental activities in the developing countries. Our aid agencies channel another $1.5 billion through these organisations.[6]

The World Bank did not remain aloof from these developments; in many ways it was the earliest multilateral organisation to acknowledge the contribution to development which NGOs made.

Operational interaction with NGOs

Since the 1970s the Bank has sought to draw NGO experience and expertise into Bank-supported lending operations and, albeit more reluctantly, at the policy level. Since 1974, operational collaboration between the Bank and NGOs has shown a steady increase. According to the Bank's *Annual Report 1993*, this increase was continued in fiscal year 1993 when '30% of all new projects involved NGOs'.[7] While the majority of NGO involvement was still in the implementation stage, 'the involvement of relevant NGOs, and especially beneficiary groups, in the planning of Bank-

Table 3.2. REGIONAL AND SECTORAL PATTERNS IN WORLD BANK-NGO OPERATIONAL COLLABORATION, 1974–1993

	1974–89	1990	1991	1992	1993
Total number of projects	255	48	88	66	73
REGION	%	%	%	%	%
Africa	55	48	47	46	41
East Asia and Pacific	10	12	15	9	15
South Asia	13	23	8	14	10
Europe and Central Asia	1	–	3	4	3
Latin America and Caribbean	15	17	15	18	19
Middle East and North Africa	6	–	2	9	12
SECTOR					
Adjustment related	3	13	16	11	7
Agriculture/rural development	43	40	24	32	19
Education	10	12	11	9	8
Environment	2	6	6	15	18
Industry/energy	9	2	11	9	11
Infrastructure/urban	18	8	14	9	11
Population health and nutrition	13	19	16	12	22
Rehabilitation/reconstruction	2	–	2	3	4

Source: World Bank, *Annual Report 1993*, p. 95.

supported projects has been encouraged by the Bank's Executive
Directors and its senior management'.[8] Interaction at an early
stage is facilitated by the periodic distribution to NGOs of a list
of prospective Bank-supported activities in which 'Bank staff see
potential for NGO involvement'.[9] Table 3.2 above outlines Bank-
NGO collaboration on projects.

Policy dialogue with NGOs

Bank-NGO policy dialogue emerged from specialist workshops
involving NGOs which the Bank has organised since the mid-1970s.
Sector workshops are important forums for Bank-NGO interaction, with 'specialist' NGOs able to contribute to policy formulation. Over the past few years the topics covered have included
forestry, energy and water-resource management, popular participation and poverty reduction. At one such workshop in 1980, on
small-scale enterprise development, the idea of a formal World
Bank-NGO Committee emerged. This was established in 1981
and still exists. To a large degree, the story of World Bank-NGO
interaction and confrontation is the story of this Committee and
the reaction of the wider NGO community to it and to the Bank.

The Committee was aimed primarily at collaboration between
particular NGOs and the World Bank at the level of project operation. Its goals were to develop new approaches for NGO-World
Bank cooperation; review instances of NGO-World Bank cooperation with a view to replication and expansion; consider means of
improving information exchange and encouraging identification of
opportunities for cooperation; and examine the scope for, and
undertake the planning of, additional area and sector meetings
among the World Bank and NGO staffs.[10]

In 1982, arising from the experience of two sectoral seminars,
dealing with the urban sector and education, the Committee redefined its primary objective to be the organisation of regional and
sectoral seminars. Typically, having set its objectives, the Committee proceeded to ignore them (see below).

At the second Committee meeting, in Washington DC in 1982,
the Bank members of the Committee expressed their satisfaction
at the progress which the Committee had made. In their view, the
initial phase of NGO-World Bank dialogue had been successfully
concluded: the cooperation policy had been enunciated; an information and consultation network had been established; models for
country and sector reviews had been provided; and a mechanism
to monitor NGO-World Bank cooperation at project level had been
set up within the Bank itself. NGO Committee members proposed

Table 3.3. MEMBERS OF THE NGO WORKING GROUP
ON THE WORLD BANK, 1994

Region	NGO member
Africa	Fédération des Associations du Fouta pour le Développement (Senegal)
	Inter-Africa Group (Ethiopia)
	Islamic African Relief Agency (Sudan)
	Pan African Institute for Development (Cameroon)
	Organisation of Rural Associations for Progress (Zimbabwe)
Asia	Asian NGO Coalition for Agrarian Reform and Rural Development (Philippines)
	Society for Participatory Research in Asia (India)
	NGO Council of Sri Lanka (Sri Lanka)
	Rural Development Foundation of Pakistan (Pakistan)
	Third World Network/Consumers' Association of Penang (Malaysia)
Europe	Aga Khan Foundation (Switzerland)
	Association of Protestant Development Organisations in Europe (Belgium)
	Danish Coalition for North/South Cooperation (Denmark)
	EUROSTEP (Belgium)
Latin America and Caribbean	Carribbean Conference of Churches (Barbados)
	Centro de Estudios y Promoción del Desarrollo (Peru)
	Fundación Augusto Cesar Sandino (Nicaragua)
	Programa de Economía del Trabajo (Chile)
	Latin American Association of Development Organisations (Costa Rica)
North America and Pacific	Church World Service/Lutheran World Relief (USA)
	Institute for Development Research (USA)
	Interchurch Coalition on Africa (Canada)
	Community Aid Abroad (Australia)
International	Coopération internationale pour le développement et la solidarité (Belgium)
	International Save the Children Alliance (Switzerland)

that there should be in-depth discussions on policy issues, including operational links between the Bank and NGOs and the possibilities of co-financing, particularly in relation to the Bank's poverty-related programmes.

In pursuing this line, NGO members, particularly those based in Europe and North America, were responding to growing criticism of their role in the Committee. Such criticisms were twofold. On the one hand, they were criticised for their lack of accountability to the wider NGO community which the Committee members frequently claimed to represent. Such critics pointed to the failure of members to consult their NGO colleagues or even to inform them of the content of discussions within the Committee. As late as 1988 some NGO members still claimed that discussions and documents were 'confidential', effectively thwarting Bank efforts to use the Committee as a vehicle for communication with NGOs generally. The method of selecting NGO Committee members was also criticised strongly by NGOs which were neither Committee members nor members of one of the NGO networks, the Geneva-based International Council of Voluntary Agencies (ICVA) or the Brussels-based Coopération internationale pour le développement et la solidarité (Cidse).

Such criticism fed into the second charge: that the NGOs were serving the Bank as a fig-leaf of respectability by providing public relations cover through which the Bank would be able to dissipate criticism of its operations. These strands of criticism, which continue to the present day, saw the emergence of an NGO twin strategy *vis à vis* the Bank. On the one hand, some NGOs, e.g. Oxfam-UK, Misereor (Germany), Caritas Internationalis and the World Council of Churches pursued a 'reformist' policy from within the Committee; other NGOs, however, were far more critical of the Bretton Woods institutions, first calling for their root and branch reform and subsequently their closure. This latter group, the most prominent of which are US-based environment organisations, e.g. the Sierra Club, might best be categorised as 'revolutionaries'. While by no means mutually exclusive, the interaction of these two groupings with each other and with the Bank provided the dynamic for Bank-NGO relations during the 1980s.[11]

By the time of the fourth annual meeting of the Committee in 1984, this criticism had become more public and was recognised as having some legitimacy. NGO members perceived the need to meet with each other outside the joint Committee structure. With support from the Bank, the NGOs established an autonomous NGO Working Group on the World Bank. This meets once a year without the World Bank officials who are on the Committee, but its goals remained tied to those of the whole Committee. The Working Group has been serviced by a small staff housed at ICVA's headquarters in Geneva, with the ICVA Secretary-General having *ex-officio* rights to attend the meetings. ICVA was originally formed in 1962 as a forum for NGOs concerned with refugees but now covers nearly 100 NGOs concerned with humanitarian and/or development work. It has provided a wider context of collaboration and debate among NGOs upon which the Working Group could draw.[12] In 1995 this link will be weakened when the Working Group moves from Geneva to Washington, both in order to reduce its costs and to be nearer the Bank's headquarters.

Progress continued to be made. At the Committee's sixth meeting, in Santo Domingo in 1987, the Committee issued the breakthrough *Santo Domingo Consensus Conclusions*.[13] Five main points were agreed. First, it was necessary to draw upon the knowledge and experience of developing-country NGOs and grassroots organisations. Secondly, both the Bank and NGOs would ensure that the Bank's Resident Representatives in developing countries were aware of developing-country NGO initiatives and ask them to cooperate in organising systematic consultations. Thirdly, NGO participation in the design, implementation and monitoring of Bank-financed programmes was also agreed. Fourthly, in future the Committee would serve as a forum for dialogue on the Bank's and the NGOs' policies. Finally, it was agreed that NGOs and the Bank would exchange relevant research and experience on issues including debt, structural adjustment and popular participation in order to strengthen each other's analyses and policies. The major thrust of the conclusions was to increase the transparency of the Bank's activities at the national level.

In pursuit of greater transparency, one of the Committee members, AVARD (Association of Voluntary Agencies for Rural Development (India)), initiated a dialogue between the World Bank's Resident Representative in India and a cross-section of Indian NGOs. By mid-1988, a national World Bank Consultation Committee had been created to serve as a platform for regular discussion on Bank policies and projects between the two sides. Arising out of these consultation meetings, visiting Bank appraisal missions consult with Indian grassroots NGOs. Furthermore, consultations involving local NGOs on the basis of mid-term reviews of projects or issues raised by any member are now held at project level, and Washington-based Bank staff visiting India meet with relevant NGO representatives.

The Bank also supported developments in India with small annual grants: $10,000 for travel costs to facilitate participation by rural-based NGOs and $6,000 to meet the national Committee's secretarial expenses. Arising out of this experience, AVARD has recommended that the World Bank-NGO Committee should concentrate on facilitating and enhancing regional and national consultation between NGOs and the World Bank; and the World Bank should explore changes in staff orientation and training in order to avoid setbacks in work with NGOs which can result from normal staff transfers. While the Bank has made some efforts in this direction, the same cannot be said for NGOs, including most Committee members.

Public clashes

The publication of the Consensus Conclusions did nothing to dampen vociferous NGO criticism of the Bank and NGO members of the Committee. Since the early 1980s, European and US NGOs had focused on the deepening crisis in developing countries.

The 1980s saw increasing coordination of financial flows to developing countries by the aid donor community. Already experiencing economic problems, countries were refused development assistance (loans and grants) unless the government agreed 'an appropriate adjustment or economic reform programme'. In the overwhelming majority of cases, this means a programme which had received an (informal or formal) IMF-World Bank seal of approval. There were many examples of this. In 1985, Tanzania was forced to reverse a policy of almost twenty years standing and open negotiations with the IMF on an economic stabilisation package when all the country's bilateral aid donors refused to provide any further economic assistance until an acceptable programme had been agreed. Another instance was the withdrawal of $200 million worth of aid to Zambia following the abandonment of the country's adjustment programme in the wake of the 1986 food-price riots.

Aid donors also believed that developing countries' economic policies were wasting scarce aid resources. They saw aid pouring into bottomless pits, characterised by expanding budget and trade deficits, over-valued exchange rates, unsustainable subsidies of inefficient and unnecessary industries and inappropriate policies (e.g. underpriced agricultural commodities). There was near unanimity amongst official donors that developing countries' domestic policies were preventing development. NGOs were indignant, accusing the Bank of leading the 'recolonisation' of developing countries.

Putting NGO, and others', perceptions of 'neo-imperialist control' of developing countries aside, it is worth commenting on the rarity of such displays of common purpose amongst the donor community. It is only in this area that aid donors have managed to coordinate their actions so successfully. The continuing criticism of donors' responses to emergency situations, including African famine relief in 1984–6 and again during the Somali emergency (1991–3), is the lack of coordination.

Developing countries viewed matters very differently. By and large, their policies followed earlier advice from the donor community. Investment emphasis had been on industrial development, as it was believed that this would result in the greatest economic benefits; tariff barriers were raised to protect the infant industries.

Agricultural exports were to earn the foreign exchange needed to service loans and purchase necessary imports. Developing-country governments had a special role because of the drastic shortage of resources; identifying investment needs and directing resources to priority areas was required. In this view, largely shared by NGOs until the late 1980s, the domestic policy failures which existed were of minimal importance set against the dramatic changes for the worse in the international economy. Widening budget and trade deficits originated in worsening terms of trade shown by real commodity price declines, rising import bills for energy and manufactured goods, and substantial increases in real interest rates. Fewer resources were available for productive investment, and this undermined the possibility of developing the economy successfully.

Developing countries' experience of the 1970s and early 1980s reinforced their reluctance to implement politically difficult, and inevitably unpopular, economic reform measures. Cheryl Payer reviewed the experience of seven countries which requested IMF assistance up to 1970; all were negative experiences, at least for some sections of the community.[14] Similar conclusions were reached by other commentators. Around the world, IMF-World Bank-approved programmes, agreed between the 1970s and the mid-1980s, have been found to have had serious social ill-effects for large sections of the population in Argentina, Brazil, Chile, Costa Rica, Ethiopia, Ghana, South Korea, Jamaica, Mexico, Peru, the Philippines, Sudan, Tanzania, Zambia and Zimbabwe.[15] Indeed there is evidence of substantial social costs in all the seventy countries worldwide that have implemented structural adjustment programmes. Recent research suggests that the structural adjustment programmes could have been greatly improved through better design.[16]

For governments concerned about their own survival, these experiences were particularly threatening: IMF riots, the removal of subsidies favouring urban populations, large increases in under- and unemployment, and the rapid cost-of-living increases directly challenged their *raison d'être* and undermined any popular legitimacy which survived the growing national economic collapse. Governments turned to the Bretton Woods institutions and asked their help to find a way out of the critical economic situation. This delay meant that the extent of adjustment required was far greater than would otherwise have been the case. It also added considerably to the human cost of the programmes eventually agreed.

NGOs insisted that the conventional adjustment model was not necessarily the most appropriate to all conditions. The majority of NGO critics of the structural adjustment programmes have addressed the 'typicality' of all programmes and have identified six objectives for every adjustment programme: reduction of public expenditure; increase in domestic savings; reduction of the state's economic role; liberalisation of the economy; promotion of exports; and promotion of foreign private investment.[17] These objectives have two broad goals: to reduce or remove direct state intervention in the productive and distributive sectors of the economy, and to restrict the state's role to the creation, mainly by manipulating fiscal and monetary instruments, of an institutional and policy framework conducive to the mobilisation of private enterprise and initiative. At their root, NGOs argued, was an almost mystical faith in the private sector which, operating under freer domestic and external market conditions, will provide the motive power for a resumption of economic growth and development. There is a serious misunderstanding in the debate on structural adjustment. For many, the term has become synonymous with the programmes recommended by multi-and bilateral aid donors, but it means no more than to take account of altered economic circumstances and market conditions. 'Instead of focusing on the economic model which the multilateral institutions were created to defend and propagate, they [critics of adjustment] attack the institutions; and instead of focusing on the role of domestic Governments, they choose instead to target a perceived imperialist role'.[18]

Until the late 1980s, NGOs demonstrated little understanding of the importance of economic policy in maintaining a healthy macroeconomic environment. For its part, the Bank failed to accord adequate value to poverty alleviation, environmental protection and human-resource development through much of the 1980s. Similar and more radical analyses were debated at repeated international NGO meetings in the run-up to the 1988 Berlin annual meetings of the Bretton Woods institutions (e.g. the International Coalition for Development Action annual general meetings in 1986 and 1987, and through the Netherlands-based Forum on Debt and Development. Such debates brought to the fore demands to hold the Bretton Woods institutions accountable for the impact of their policies and programmes, in particular the human effects of structural adjustment programmes.

Responding to this call, European NGOs, including some members of the Bank-NGO Committee, helped to organise meetings in Berlin at the same time as the annual meetings of the International Monetary Fund and World Bank. As part of this process, an International Tribunal was held. In the course of this 'popular trial' of the Bretton Woods institutions, testimonies of the hardships suffered by poor and marginalised people around the developing

world was presented by a variety of NGOs, popular organisations
and indigenous peoples. This evidence was heard by a panel of
jurists who delivered the expected guilty verdict. Neither Bank nor
Fund staff (or governors) participated in the tribunal although they
maintained a watching brief over developments. Despite being
marred by violence, the Berlin shadow meeting proved a model
for future NGO events which every year since have shadowed the
Bank/Fund annual meetings.

Criticising the Bank

In response to the Berlin dynamic, the NGO Working Group produced a Position Paper in 1989.[19] This analysed the World Bank's
policies and the relationship between NGOs and the Bank, and
made proposals for reform and policy changes. It asserted the need
for a fundamental rethinking of the development model promoted
by the Bank. This would require the Bank to move from structural
adjustment to structural transformation with priority given to
'the internal needs of developing countries' environmental and
economic sustainability, and the well-being of the poor'. Emphasis
should be placed on the active participation of local people in all
stages of project planning and implementation. Food self-sufficiency
was seen as an important goal, as was the need for the Bank to
endorse land reform. The productive role of women was stressed.
There was a call for the promotion of rural-based and agricultural-
related industries, moving away from export-oriented industrialisation which did not have strong local economic linkages. There
should be a greater role for local government in the development
process and a 'social budget report' should be drawn up for all projects and policies at the design stage. NGOs and popular organisations were seen as 'essential independent channels of local
knowledge' and their expertise should be drawn on more heavily.
Finally, the Paper recommended that local populations and
organisations should be kept informed of the programmatic and
policy initiatives that shape the environment in which they
live and work so that they might participate effectively. The NGO
Working Group's Steering Committee stressed that the Position
Paper and other NGO Working Group documents must be regarded
as 'a constructive effort to bring change to the Bank as an institution, as well as to its policies, through the dialogue and atmosphere
that the World Bank-NGO Committee meetings offered'.

Understandably, the Position Paper met with strong reaction
among Bank staff, who proposed that the NGO Working Group
should amend the Paper. The Working Group decided that it was

inappropriate to change the Paper but agreed to await the Bank's
response before distributing it more widely. In early 1990, the Bank
issued its response which had been prepared by the Bank's Strategic
Planning and Review Department.[20] The Bank asserted that countries with more outward-oriented policies had generally done better
in weathering and overcoming the debt crisis and that the main problem with adjustment lending was that some countries had not sustained their adjustment efforts. Policy reforms aimed at growth
also tended to attack structural inequities, and Bank-supported
adjustment programmes often protected health and education
expenditures of importance to the poor. The Bank attacked the
NGO Position Paper's discussion of structural transformation, saying it was deficient in 'clarity about how countries should deal with
resource constraints'. The section in the Position Paper urging the
Bank to involve NGOs in shaping policies and plans, not just in
implementing Bank-financed programmes, was seen as failing to
reflect the changed thrust in Bank policy in this direction which had
resulted from many years of listening to the Working Group
members. The Position Paper 'has almost nothing positive to say
about national governments or about markets and commercial
enterprise. . .[It] would be stronger if it would devote more space
to assessing NGO performance . . . [and] how NGOs themselves
need to change [which] might suggest ways that NGOs and other
types of institutions (including the Bank) might complement one
another'. The Bank condemned the Paper for showing 'little tolerance for the frailties and complexities that characterise even the
most well-intentioned human efforts. The Position Paper echoes
old debates and stereotypes at a moment when many nations and
institutions are breaking from the patterns of the past and forging
new possibilities'.

Despite the profound differences which the respective papers
demonstrated, two aspects of the process are of particular relevance. First, it marked the beginning of a real, in-depth discussion
within the World Bank-NGO Committee on development policy
and concepts. As importantly, it consolidated the NGO Working
Group's profile as an autonomous entity which interacts and maintains a relationship with the World Bank, while maintaining its own
views, priorities and work programme. For the many NGO critics
of the Committee, this experience was a poignant commentary on
the Committee's ineffectiveness.

Increasing NGO accountabilty

The 1990 Washington Committee meeting brought about further
changes, in response to deepening NGO criticism of NGO member-

ship and representativeness. NGO members were now elected to represent a region. Implicit within this was the requirement that they consult with other NGOs in their region (as is the case with AVARD) and make use of such consultation to represent their region's views in Working Group and Committee discussions. In an effort to renew the Committee's membership, the terms which NGO members could serve were altered so that members who served a full five-year term could not be re-elected for a period of two years. It was recognised that the Committee's output could be substantially improved were NGO members to show greater responsibility and follow up decisions made. To this end, responsibility for particular areas of work were allocated to individual members who would have to report on progress made to the following meeting. Finally, all members were required to report annually on their activities.

Implementing the new approach

The post-1990 Working Group's new assertiveness was given direct expression in the 1991 *Saly Declaration*,[21] adopted by the NGO Working Group in Saly, Senegal. This constituted the first autonomous statement of purpose and work programme by the NGO Working Group. The Declaration acknowledged that the NGO Working Group was 'in a [process of] transition and renewal towards a new pro-active advocacy agenda'. This was based on the positions expressed in the Position Paper and on the Working Group's accumulated experience. The Declaration defined three key roles for the NGO Working Group. First, it should act as a *pipeline*, transmitting information and analysis and offering access to information on the World Bank. Secondly, it should act as *advocate* on behalf of constituencies at national and international levels with the World Bank and governments, parliaments etc. Finally, it should act as a *guarantor* that every effort would be made to feed grassroots experience and information effectively into the World Bank and Bank processes. The fulfilment of these roles provided a clear autonomous agenda for the Working Group's members as well as giving concrete substance to their participation in the World Bank-NGO Committee. The Declaration further insisted on the need for members of the NGO Working Group to act as representatives of a constituency rather than as individuals. This representative relationship would emerge out of an action agenda and would generate accountability and legitimacy with the wider NGO community and the World Bank.

The Working Group then defined the strategy it would follow to achieve this goal. The analysis of the Bank's role in the global financial and economic system would be sharpened. The Group would work at the national, regional and international level, both in the South and in the North. It would make its agenda public and link up with other NGO networks, initiatives and allies. The micro-reality and experience at the grassroots level would be linked to the macro-analysis and the macro-dimension of reality, and there would be an increasing commitment and involvement of the NGO Working Group members in work with their domestic and regional constituencies and in work with the sub-groups.

The Saly meeting also established two sub-groups to focus upon the Working Group's two priority topics, structural adjustment and popular participation, to enable policy discussions with the Bank to be pursued in a more focused fashion. The structural adjustment sub-group decided to concentrate on the production of case studies which would gather empirical evidence of the economic, environmental and social impact of conventional structural adjustment programmes. These should serve as the foundation for a critical evaluation of structural adjustment and a discussion of the alternatives. The Working Group invited the Bank to conduct joint case studies as a means of bridging differences through grassroots analysis in the field. The Bank, however, declined to participate and argued that effects on the poor should be compared with similar countries not undergoing adjustment programmes. With the financial support of the NGO community, the Working Group launched its own studies.

NGO understanding of the stages of adjustment and the opportunities for influencing the process was outlined in 1992. Six stages were identified. The first is the recognition that an economic crisis exists, indications of which will be both external and internal. The second stage is the formal request for IMF and World Bank assistance, which usually comes when all other options have been exhausted. Discussion of the adjustment programme, the third stage, is very wide-ranging with all relevant government ministries being involved. After these discussions, the IMF-World Bank team draws up a policy framework paper which forms the basis of negotiations. The fourth stage is the outcome of the negotiations on the policy framework paper. Once agreement has been reached, the programme is presented for approval by the institutions' executive authorities. When the loan agreement has been signed, the World Bank convenes a meeting of all potential donors at which financial and technical support is pledged. Implementation of the agreement constitutes the fifth stage. This is primarily the government's responsibility although individual donors, e.g. the UN Development Programme and the UN Food and Agricultural

Organisation, may have responsibility for particular aspects. Neither the IMF nor the World Bank are involved in implementation, but they monitor the programme annually. Finally, the effects of the programme can be analysed by comparing the official aims of structural adjustment programmes with the actual experience of the policies.[22]

In order for NGOs to influence the process, it is important that they should have discussions with relevant government ministers and civil servants and with the World Bank Resident Representative at all stages. Copies of the policy framework paper should be obtained and studied and alternative proposals prepared for discussion with the government and World Bank representatives. Lobbies in support of identified improvements should be pursued together with developed-country public-sector unions, targeting both donor and recipient countries' Executive Directors. Meetings should be sought with annual monitoring missions when they are in the country. Problems should be discussed in detail and recommendations for improvements made.

The popular participation sub-group decided to systemise NGO approaches to popular participation and review the twenty projects selected by the Bank as the basis of its internal learning process on popular participation. It also intended to pursue further discussion and elaborate concrete proposals on how to conduct a social audit of projects and programmes. Despite repeated expressions of interest in the subject from the Bank, the sub-group experienced difficulties in proceeding beyond broad statements on the topic elaborated by former Oxfam-UK director, Frank Judd, at the Washington World Bank-NGO Committee meeting in 1989. This led to the sub group's decision to abandon the topic as a focus for continuing work.

The Suraj Kund, India (1991) and Washington (1992) Committee meetings received reports of steady, albeit slow, progress in the work of the two sub-groups. The Suraj Kund meeting was informed that the first phase of the case studies of structural adjustment experience in Mexico, Senegal and Sri Lanka had been fully funded by the NGO community, European NGOs having provided most of the financial support. Difficulties experienced in identifying consultants to carry out the research, however, resulted in the case studies not being available in time for the Washington Committee meeting. The three case studies[23] were finally discussed at the 1993 World Bank-NGO Committee meeting in Washington. A common thread running through all three case studies was that adjustment had failed to achieve all the programme's agreed macro-economic goals. More importantly, from the NGO point of view, the case studies clearly demonstrated severe social costs which accompanied the programmes. For their part, Bank participants argued that some aspects of the case studies' analysis were based on inaccurate information. While they acknowledged that some programme goals had not been achieved within the agreed time period, this was attributed to failures of implementation by governments.[24] Bank staff also acknowledged that severe social costs had accompanied adjustment, although they again insisted that these social costs would have been far greater in the absence of adjustment. Both NGO and Bank participants agreed that far more needed to be done. In pursuit of continuing efforts to refine and improve the efficacy of the programme and project cycle, the Bank undertook to pursue greater transparency in its operations. In order to achieve this, the Bank would seek country-level dialogue with all representatives of civil society and encourage governments to be less secretive.

Sharper intra-NGO disputes

In the aftermath of the Berlin meetings, members of the wider NGO community became more critical of Committee members. Largely for geographic reasons, this criticism was led by US NGOs[25] which organised the NGO meetings shadowing the annual IMF/Bank meetings which were held in Washington for the following two years. European NGOs were particular subjects of this criticism. They were portrayed as virtual 'collaborators' with the Bank because they argued in favour of adopting a reformist approach to the problems arising from IMF-World Bank structural adjustment programmes. They were also accused of following this approach with other problems, such as environmental damage or resettlement of people displaced by projects. By contrast, many US NGOs argued that the Bank was incapable of reform. What was required was root and branch change to the international economy, and particularly to international trade relationships and the development model. Very different reasons lay behind African voluntary development organisations' criticism of their European counterparts. This rested on perceptions of European NGOs' efforts to maintain an 'imperialist' relationship with their African counterparts and underlay the definition of an African voluntary development organisation at the founding conference of the Forum of African Voluntary Development Organisations.

In 1990 John Clark, a former development policy adviser at Oxfam-UK and alternate World Bank-NGO Committee member, commented on the tensions between European and US groups attending the 1990 shadow annual meetings in discussion with representatives of other UK NGOs.[26] On leaving Oxfam-UK to join the staff of the World Bank in 1991, Clark was on the receiving end of personal criticism in the first issue of the US NGO publication *BankCheck*. The article asserted that Clark had been an effective 'fifth columnist' in NGO ranks and 'with friends like these, who needed enemies?'[27]

Personality issues aside, much of the dispute between US and European NGOs probably stemmed from their differing political strategies. The clear divisions between the executive, judicial and legislative branches in the United States has provided opportunities for US NGOs to achieve considerable influence on US policy.[28] Working closely with members of the Congress over a number of years, groups such as the Sierra Club and the Environmental Defence Fund have achieved the introduction of legislation which has affected US World Bank policy in two key ways. Their first major success was to gain access to generally unobtainable World Bank material by requiring the US Executive Director to lodge all World Bank documents in the Library of Congress. Other US NGO-sponsored legislation targeting the Bank's activities was arguably far less positive in its implications. This legislation established the criteria for the US Executive Director's vote on World Bank-financed programmes and projects. In the event of the proposed programme or project falling short of any of a number of environmental and other measurements, the US Executive Director is required to oppose funding. The effect, according to other Executive Directors, has been to isolate the United States within the Executive Board while also disrupting the consensual approach to decision-making. Furthermore, while the legislation has seen an unquestioned increase in the influence of US NGOs, that of other NGOs seeking to influence World Bank policy, programmes and projects has arguably been weakened. Unable to trade improvements to programme and project design for support from the United States, Bank staff and other Executive Directors have less incentive to respond to NGO lobbying positively; and there is one less Executive Director who can respond to NGO lobbying.

The tenth IDA replenishment sharpened the intra-NGO dispute which came to a head at the 1992 Committee meeting. Efforts to gain a substantial additional level of IDA resources had already run into difficulties. Economic recession in the industrialised world meant that by mid-1992, Bank staff believed that the best possible outcome of the replenishment round would be the maintenance of existing resource levels in real terms. This would represent a real cut in available resources because of significant numbers of new IDA members. Earlier in 1992, US environmental NGOs, prominent amongst them the Environmental Defence Fund, Friends of the Earth, Greenpeace and the Sierra Club, had led a lobby of the Congress to block the IDA's replenishment.[29] They insisted that this was necessary because IDA projects and programmes caused environmental destruction and supported structural adjustment programmes. Furthermore, they argued, there was little, if any, alleviation of the lot of poor people from IDA projects and programmes. At the request of the Bank's Executive Directors, Bank staff organised a meeting with developing-country NGO Committee members. The Dutch Executive Director, Evelyn Herfkins, argued strongly to the NGOs that lobbying should be focused on developing-country governments as much as on those of the G7 countries.[30]

In September 1992 a representative group of NGO Committee members met with donor-country Executive Directors. The NGO representatives were from the Senegalese Fédération des associations du fouta pour le développement, the Senegalese Réseau Africain pour le développement intégré, and the Malaysian Third World Network/Consumers Association of Penang. They noted that the IDA had serious shortcomings: it had not secured its poverty alleviation goals; a substantial proportion of IDA lending (around 30 per cent) had supported structural and sectoral adjustment; and, as in other areas of Bank lending, inappropriate projects had brought environmental degradation in their wake. Nonetheless, they emphasised their belief in the urgent need for a successful replenishment of IDA 'which would result in substantial increase in the level of resources available to the IDA'.[31]

The subject of IDA's tenth replenishment and US-led opposition to it was raised in the October NGO Working Group's meeting which followed the full Committee meeting. Working Group members from around the world expressed disquiet at the US NGOs' position and emphasised the importance of an early and successful conclusion to the replenishment negotiations. Agreeing that there were grounds for concern over the use of IDA funds, they nonetheless emphasised that any failure to agree the replenishment would result in a far worse situation for many of the world's countries, especially those in sub-Saharan Africa. As a result, the Working Group instructed Chairperson Mazid N'Diaye to write to the Bank President emphasising the Working Group's support for the replenishment, while expressing concern at the poor environmental and poverty alleviation record of IDA projects.

Difficulties also confronted the work of the popular participation sub-group which struggled to do more than follow the Bank's internal learning process. Sub-group members participated in the

Bank's workshop on popular participation in February 1992 and, at the request of the core group staff, commented on their various reports and proposals. The Washington Committee meeting coincided with the mid-term review of the Bank's internal learning process and the core group's report to the Bank's senior management. The sub-group's difficulties in finding an appropriate working methodology meant that input in this area was probably less valuable than might otherwise have been the case. The sub-group largely acted as a sounding board for the Bank's internal learning group who sought comment on and reaction to continuing internal developments, including the establishment of a $300,000 fund and the elaboration of a participation handbook.

The Washington Committee meeting gave the Bank's President, Lewis Preston, the opportunity to re-emphasise the Bank's priorities – poverty reduction and sustainable development – and stress the institution's need to improve its success rate. The Wapenhans Report, discussed by the Board in 1992, had concluded that the unacceptable rate of project failures was due to a lack of attention to implementation. Mr Preston, stressing his personal commitment to make the practice of popular participation an issue in which the whole Bank structure would be involved, questioned the internal incentive structure. This emphasised the quantity rather than the quality of lending: 'that's no way to run a railroad', he mused. Changes to the incentive structure would be introduced in order to encourage staff to devote greater attention to implementation, rather than emphasising new loans.

Measures were also taken to increase the institution's transparency and accountability. Project Information Documents were introduced. These will be released following approval of the loan by the Board, and are intended to provide information on the Bank's activities in the borrowing country, a core NGO demand throughout the 1980s. The Bank's growing commitment to increasing transparency was reinforced with the announcement of the opening of a Public Information Centre in January 1994. Located at the Bank's Washington headquarters, it is expected to be 'a valuable resource for [those] interested in opportunities to work on Bank-financed projects as well as those seeking country-specific reports'. The Centre will provide Project Information Documents, project appraisal reports, environmental impact assessments, project completion reports and country reports. In the autumn of 1993, the Bank's Board agreed measures to increase the Bank's accountability and established an Independent Inspection Panel. The panel may review Bank project practice to determine whether it has adhered to the institution's procedures, provided

complaints have first been addressed to responsible Bank staff and
not satisfactorily answered. Complaints are only acceptable from
those affected by the project or programme.

Assessing the relationship: beneficial to both?

A number of themes emerge from the foregoing review of the
NGO-World Bank relationship. All provide clear lessons for the
future development of the relationship to the benefit of both.
Before expanding on these, it is important to note that the Bank
has taken on board many NGO criticisms. Among these were the
need for the greater involvement of civil society in all stages of
the project cycle, the need for changes to the design of adjustment
programmes and the importance of taking additional measures to
protect the environment.

Bank staff now frequently consult far more widely, seeking to
draw inputs from a variety of interested parties into project development. The content of adjustment programmes has also changed
significantly; social safety nets, for example, are now routinely
included in the structural adjustment programme design. Country
poverty assessments and environmental impact assessments, as
often as not, involve the participation of representative groups in
civil society in their preparation. But while considerable progress has
been made, NGOs insist that the Bank remains at the very beginning
of a long road of reform needed to improve its performance and
the beneficial impact of its lending on people's development.

NGOs have also been affected by the past 10–15 years. Increasing contact with the Bank has seen an increase in NGO professionalism and competence in previously unfamiliar areas. This is
perhaps most clearly demonstrated in the decade-long debate over
structural and sectoral adjustment; the Bank clearly recognises
that the sophistication of NGO analysis has increased significantly
since the early 1980s. Accompanying their increasing confidence
at the policy level, NGOs have also demonstrated their interest
in increased involvement in all stages of the Bank's project cycle.
This is underlined by the rapid growth of NGO involvement in
Bank projects, to over 240 projects in fiscal year 1993, 30 per cent
of all Bank-supported projects in that year.

A house divided

There is now a general consensus among development and environmental NGOs that the Bank and IMF structural adjustment
programmes are highly damaging to the people and the environ-

ment in developing countries. However the NGOs are clearly divided on what should be the political response. On the one hand, an identifiable group of NGOs perceive the continuing value of dialogue with the Bank. Others wish to alter the Bretton Woods institutions so as to make them unrecognisable, while some want to bring their activities to an end. As the fiftieth anniversary of the Bretton Woods conference was approaching, a significant debate took place.

The reformist position is illustrated by the arguments of Covey and Nelson, two US NGO members of the World Bank-NGO Committee, writing in the journal of InterAction, the umbrella organisation of US NGOs concerned with development. They emphasised their belief that recent developments provided significant opportunities for NGOs seeking constructive dialogue with the World Bank. The key elements were Lewis Preston's emphasis on poverty reduction and four policy changes in the previous six months: a new information disclosure policy, an independent inspections panel, a system of country assistance strategies and a new concern for implementation and follow-through. They also warned that the 'impact of the promised Bank reforms will depend in good part on increased pressure by NGOs and governments'.[32]

As a result of these incremental developments, Covey and Nelson urged four courses of action on NGOs 'concerned about poverty reduction and World Bank policy' that 'want to engage the Bank, whether by monitoring or by collaborating to shape and implement Bank-funded projects'. NGOs need to disseminate information about the Bank's new information policy and the opportunity to appeal through the new Independent Inspection Panel. They should monitor the impact of IDA-financed projects. Good contacts with resident World Bank staff need to be established to raise concerns or make inquiries about the implementation of IDA's anti-poverty mission and, finally, NGOs should communicate to the Bank their own experience with popular participation in sectors or countries where the Bank is at work.[33]

The more radical position was argued by Bruce Rich, the international director of the Environment Defence Fund. He reviewed the Bank's fifty years of activities in an article in the journal *BankCheck* and concluded:

> The World Bank is an institution out of time and place. Fifty years of the Bank as we know it is enough. If, indeed, the role of multilateral institutions is an important one, the World Bank must literally remake itself, open its files, end its secret ways and documents, and learn from its mistakes – not merely on

projects, but in the foundations of its policy prescriptions. It needs to trade-in policies developed by old cold war warriors, and grasp the essential meaning of its favourite new phrase: sustainable development. The World (which after all, provided the Bank with a name) has had enough lies and enough secrecy.[34]

Rich is demanding a very different Bank from the present one. Since he recognises implicitly that there is little possibility of this occurring, he (and others) are demanding the closure of the Bretton Woods institutions.

In 1992 a US NGO, the Development Group for Alternative Policies, hosted a meeting including representatives from Friends of the Earth, the Third World Network based in Malaysia and the European Network on Debt and Development based in Belgium, to plan strategy for the Bretton Woods anniversary in 1994. Their work led to the public launch in May 1994 of the 'Fifty Years is Enough' campaign by some twenty-five US NGOs, with the support of forty-five other NGOs from around the world, endorsing a joint platform. The main demands were summarised as follows:

(1) institutional reform to make openness, full public accountability and the participation of affected populations in decision-making standard procedure at the World Bank and the IMF;
(2) a shift in the nature of economic-policy reform programmes and policies to support equitable, sustainable and participatory development;
(3) an end to all environmentally destructive lending and support for more self-reliant, resource-conserving development that preserves biodiversity;
(4) the scaling back of the financing, operations, role and, hence, power of the World Bank and the IMF and the rechannelling of financial resources thereby made available into a variety of development assistance alternatives; and
(5) a reduction in multilateral debt to free up additional capital for sustainable development.[35]

In general more US NGOs hold radical positions than is the case in Europe, so the campaign took the form of joint action by US NGOs, with external support, rather than the creation of a global coalition. Six months after its launch, the number of endorsements for the platform had grown to 120 US NGOs and 135 'international partners and supporters'. In Europe reformist views were sufficiently strong that the European Network on Debt and Development, the main network for development NGOs, felt unable to put their name to the US platform. The main point of disagreement was that many European NGOs cannot support the call for the financial resources of both the Bank and the Fund to be reduced. British NGOs gave a diverse range of responses: Friends of the Earth, *The Ecologist* magazine and Third World First endorsed the platform and produced their own materials under the 'Fifty Years is Enough' slogan; Christian Aid did not endorse the platform but ran a campaign under their own slogan 'Who runs the World?'; Christian Aid put out materials jointly with the World Wide Fund for Nature, under the reformist title 'Facing the Next Fifty Years'; Oxfam-UK and Ireland refused to associate themselves in any way with the general campaign, but produced, in measured language, their own devastating critique of structural adjustment.[36] Pierre Garland of Oxfam Belgique felt compelled to resign from the World Bank-NGO Committee in order to be free to pursue the campaign vigorously.

The 'Fifty Years is Enough' campaign reached a climax with a very wide range of NGOs, including both those who endorsed the platform and many who did not, descending on Madrid for the Bretton Woods fiftieth anniversary celebrations and the 1994 annual meetings of the Bank and the Fund's Boards of Governors. Again the divisions in the NGO community were evident. Some staged a sit-in at an official press conference, while others strongly disapproved of such tactics. Some concentrated on lobbying the Governors; while others attended both the official and the unofficial events. An unusually high level of conflict occurred in the official proceedings, where there was general agreement that the IMF should issue a new allocation of its Special Drawing Rights, but deadlock on how the allocation should be divided between Eastern Europe and the former Soviet Union, the developing countries and the general membership. For the first time the developing-country governments used their collective veto to prevent a Group of Seven proposal going through. The combination of all these events meant that the Madrid meeting, instead of being an occasion for congratulations and celebrations, saw the Bank and the Fund facing the worst loss of reputation in their history.

While NGOs differ significantly in their rhetoric and their strategies, they would all in practice welcome change towards more open decision-making, effective poverty-alleviation, environmental conservation and debt reduction. The IMF has not begun to move noticeably in this direction, but the Bank is changing. Indeed, there are few senior Bank staff who would dispute the need for the Bank to become more accountable to its members and, increasingly, to the membership's citizens. Clear evidence of this can be seen both in the establishment of the Independent Inspection Panel and in the Bank's disclosure policy. Other supporting evidence includes the emphasis on poverty reduction, the increasing involvement of NGOs in Bank projects, and the growing tendency to exchange personnel with NGOs.[37] The Bank is also making increasing use of NGO personnel on country missions; the Bank team preparing the Zimbabwe poverty report during 1993 and 1994 included Oxfam-UK's policy adviser, Kevin Watkins. Other such missions have included both international and national NGO staff.

Diverse community, diverse responses

Some NGOs, including The Save the Children Fund and Oxfam-UK and Catholic Relief Services in the US, have been helping communities in developing countries improve the quality of their members' lives since before the founding of the Bretton Woods institutions. Others were founded during the 1960s, well after the establishment of the IMF and World Bank. As has been shown, their focus of attention is diverse: in broad terms, NGOs which relate to the World Bank can be grouped into those addressing development or environment issues. But even NGOs which nominally focus on 'development', may target specific social groups – children, the elderly, women, trades union members etc – and similar differentiation can be made in respect to environmental groups.

Inevitably, this diversity has required equally diverse responses on the part of both NGOs presenting their concerns and Bank staff and governors responding to such representations. In the main, NGOs have adopted a threefold approach in dealing with the World Bank. Increasing numbers of NGOs, having strengthened their experienced-based policy capacity, now lobby Bank staff both on specific projects[38] and national economic programmes, particularly structural adjustment.[39] Such lobbying is reinforced by public campaigns which have sought to deny resources to the World Bank; the US-led campaign to reduce the IDA's replenishment is a good example here. The most effective public campaigns have often run parallel to the less public lobbying described above. Sometimes these different roles have been negotiated between NGOs in advance; on other occasions, individual NGOs have pursued both strategies simultaneously. Increasing numbers of NGOs, particularly in developing countries, now actively cooperate with the World Bank, particularly in project implementation but also during other stages of the project cycle, identification, monitoring and evaluation.

The Bank has responded to the NGO community's increased interest in its activities in a number of ways. As a general rule, this response has seen an increase in opportunities for the NGOs to establish a dialogue with Bank staff on topics of mutual interest. Since the establishment of the World Bank-NGO Committee, for example, opportunities for NGOs to participate in World Bank-financed projects have increased, there are regular opportunities for dialogue with senior Bank managers, including the President, and discussions with task managers are increasingly common. Bank-NGO meetings have taken place at a regional level. Furthermore, increasing numbers of the Bank's Resident Representatives in member countries meet regularly with local NGOs, in the course of which concerns over, and experience of, projects and programmes are discussed. The relative benefit of such discussions has varied from country to country, but both Resident Representatives and NGOs which have participated in them emphasise their commitment to continuing and deepening these discussions.

A future for the Committee

After more than a decade, the role of the World Bank-NGO Committee is being jointly reviewed. Past and present NGO Working Group members have on the whole responded positively to questions about the Committee's usefulness. While there was criticism of frequent failures by NGOs to follow through on commitments in the past, recent meetings have seen a new realism permeating decision-making, with NGOs linking undertakings more closely to existing areas of work. This is reflected in the focus agreed by the Working Group – popular participation, structural adjustment, and development funding sources and their monitoring – and in the increased distribution of NGO experience-based analyses as core contributions to the Working Group's and the Committee's activities. The Bank broadly appears to endorse this perception of the Committee's value. However, for both the Bank and the majority of NGOs, the Committee remains just one forum for Bank-NGO dialogue and cooperation. A recent Bank strategy paper emphasised the need to strengthen and focus the Bank-NGO Committee.[40] It also called for increased staff resources to liaise with NGOs; stronger Bank-NGO operational collaboration; the establishment of a funding window for NGO operations; the improvement of government-NGO relations by advising governments of the contribution NGOs can and do make to development; the establishment of sector committees covering key issues of NGO concern; interdepartmental decision-making to ensure that the Bank's response to public criticism is 'owned' by the relevant Bank departments; and a strengthening of the existing NGO Unit.

In effect, the Bank paper endorses the Committee's worth. At the same time, the Bank's contacts with NGOs over the years have contributed to the realisation that the Committee was only one of a number of effective channels of communication with the NGO community. As these other, more specialised, channels have become more effective, Bank staff have come increasingly to value the contribution of NGOs to development, as is shown by proposals for *inter alia* an NGO financing window, action by the Bank to improve government-NGO relations and stronger collaboration with NGOs at early stages in the project cycle.

Building on limited success

Through their continuing dialogue and campaigns, NGOs have had an unquestionable impact on the Bank. This impact is underlined as much by the incorporation into everyday use by Bank staff of key NGO concepts such as 'sustainable development', 'popular participation', or 'people's ownership', as by the preparation of two recent Bank documents, *viz* the Handbook on NGOs and the strategy paper for improving Bank-NGO relations.[41] The draft strategy paper devotes an entire section to explaining to Bank staff '. . . reasons which make the NGO phenomenon so important to the Bank'. These include the expertise of NGOs as evidenced by their experience, skills and local contacts; the scale of NGO operations in both economic and human resource terms; the increasing proportion of bilateral aid being channelled through NGOs; the fact that one-third of Bank-financed projects now involve NGOs; the powerful influence of NGOs with the public, media and donor-country politicians and officials; and increasing NGO emphasis on advocacy – especially regarding the Bank.

However, 'though public understanding of the Bank is important and the political influence of NGOs is a concern, the critical issue is one of its development effectiveness'. The paper further expresses the view that for the Bank to achieve its key priority – poverty reduction – and actually reach the poor, ' . . . requires new partnership and new sources of information and guidance. In seeking sustainable poverty reduction through participatory development the Bank and leading operational NGOs are discovering significant complementarity, underlining the need to forge closer working relations'.

By contrast, community-based organisations which 'have the most intimate knowledge of poverty from which the Bank can learn, . . . in practice have less contact with the Bank'. This represents one of the least successful areas of NGO influence on the Bank from whatever perspective it is viewed. Despite this, Bank staff view the policy dialogue as effective, although it is conducted in the main by advocacy groups which 'often have limited first hand experience of development on which to base their judgement'. NGO criticisms have often been well placed and encouraged major policy shifts and important changes on the ground. Over a number of years, policy and evaluation staff from operational NGOs have sought to base their lobbying on a combination of community-based project experience and better understanding of the country's macroeconomic environment. They believe that the most effective criticism of aspects of the policy advice provided by the Bank to member governments originates in analyses of the impact of policies at the grassroots. What is evident is the need, recognised both by NGOs and the Bank, for greater efforts to improve communication between the grassroots, NGOs and Bank staff so that all projects and programmes can meet the needs of communities better. In recent years, industrial-country NGOs have been heavily criticised by many of their developing-country counterparts, including grassroots organisations. These latter groups have argued that lobbying by industrial-country NGOs is exploitative; this view perceives information being extracted from local communities and concentrated in industrial countries in order to advance the power and influence of industrial-country NGOs who act as interlocutors with their governments and the Bretton Woods institutions.

A growing number of industrial country NGOs have responded to such criticism and sought to assist developing-country partners strengthen their capacity to lobby the aid organisations and development finance institutions. Committee member Coopération internationale pour le développement et la solidarité (Cidse), for example, has offered to finance seminars in developing countries in the course of which partners would be able to further their understanding of the World Bank and how it works. Caritas Internationalis has organised regional seminars intended to increase prospects for national and local cooperation between national Caritas members, their governments and the World Bank. Among other initiatives intended to empower local communities has been that of Oxfam-UK, which encouraged African individuals and groups to write explaining the impact of IMF and World Bank-supported structural adjustment programmes on their own and their communities' lives.

Like other official aid donors, the World Bank is showing increasing interest in bypassing industrial-country NGO intermediaries and relating directly to developing-country NGOs and grassroots organisations. In the light of the Bank's extensive representation at national level, this is understandable. If successfully and

sympathetically implemented, direct links allow developing-country
NGOs and grassroots organisations to communicate their concerns
and experience directly and, inevitably, much more quickly than
in the past when such communication was most often through
third parties. Among the more radical suggestions put forward at
Caritas Internationalis' Latin America regional seminar by Eugene
McCarthy, a Resident Representative of the Bank, was for NGOs
and Bank staff to study each others' projects aiming to reduce
poverty in Mexico's three poorest states, in order to learn from each
others' experience. Equally challenging was McCarthy's suggestion
that NGOs should assist in designing programmes intended to
help Bank staff deepen their understanding of the situation that
poor communities confront.

   Those developing-country NGOs which have pioneered relationships with the Bank's Resident Representatives over recent years
report positive outcomes. However, they emphasise that contact and
exchanges should extend beyond the Resident Representative's
office. Visiting Bank missions, including technical missions, should
meet with relevant members of the NGO community as a matter of
course. They urge that Bank missions should visit grassroots NGO
projects whenever possible to enhance their understanding of the
day-to-day development challenges which local communities face.

Conclusions

NGOs have successfully influenced the World Bank since the beginning of the 1980s. They are increasingly closely involved in the project cycle and in sector work on which Bank policy-making is
based. The influence of NGOs can be expected to increase in the
short- and medium-term future. But one should not overestimate
the extent of this influence. Much of it has arisen from a combination of effective political lobbying of donor-country Governors,
especially those who are Executive Directors, by industrial-country
NGOs, and rising numbers of Bank staff who believe in the effectiveness of NGOs. This has seen NGO issues, such as popular
participation, community ownership of projects etc., enter into
mainstream Bank parlance. If such issues are to become mainstream Bank practice, the value of community ownership of the
project cycle and popular participation at all stages has to be
acknowledged widely within the Bank. In addition, NGOs need to
prioritise their achievement. For this to happen, such development
methodology will have to be endorsed by practical experience. One
way in which this could be hastened would be for the highly

regarded Operations Evaluation Department to compare the economic rate of return of similar projects, some of which would be
participatory while others were not. Bank staff who argue for the
Bank to adopt more participatory methods of development emphasise the importance of such independent endorsement of the benefits of participation. They also emphasise the importance of NGO
support for such studies. Other required changes which NGOs
might usefully support include measures to address the Bank's
culture, not least the need to change the reward system, so as to
encourage task managers to pursue participatory approaches at all
stages of the project cycle.

Some changes of this nature are in the pipeline but others are
still necessary if heavily burdened task managers are to take the
extra time needed for more participatory approaches. Bank staff
also need to be reassured that they will not be penalised in salary
and promotion terms because more participatory approaches slow
down lending. Without such assurances, there is no reason for the
Bank's highly professional staff to seek to adopt participatory
approaches, particularly if they fear that by making fewer loans
their career prospects will suffer. Such campaigning is not particularly eye-catching but NGOs could strengthen existing tenden-
cies within the Bank, which are central to NGO concerns, were they
to pursue these areas. Bank staff have accepted NGO challenges
to increase the institution's transparency and accountability, and
many are attempting to encourage participatory means of working
for development. The challenge confronting NGOs is to build on
their modest gains since the beginning of the 1980s and cooperate
with the World Bank to improve the quality of lives of poor communities in developing countries, while maintaining pressure to
ensure that the Bank's practices continue to improve.

NOTES

1. World Bank, *World Development Report 1987* (Oxford University Press, 1987),
   p. 34.
2. The distribution of the votes in June 1993 in the IBRD and the IDA is taken
   from *The World Bank Annual Report 1993* (Washington, DC: World Bank,
   1993), pp. 199–202 and pp. 217–20 respectively. The votes in April 1993 in the
   IMF are taken from the *International Monetary Fund Annual Report 1993*
   (Washington, DC: IMF, 1993), pp. 166–9.
3. World Bank, *Sub-Saharan Africa, from Crisis to Sustainable Growth: A Long-
   Term Perspective Study* (Washington, DC: World Bank, 1989).
4. World Bank, *World Development Report 1991. The Challenge of Development*
   (Oxford: Oxford University Press, 1991), p. iii.

5. OECD Cooperation Directorate: *Voluntary Aid for Development: The Role of Non-Governmental Organisations* (Paris: OECD, 1988), p. 15.
6. *Ibid.*, foreword by J. C. Wheeler, p. 5.
7. The World Bank *Annual Report 1993, op. cit.*, p. 95.
8. *Ibid.*
9. *Ibid.*, p. 96.
10. Marcos Arruda, *Brief History of the NGO Working Group on the World Bank* (Geneva: NGO Working Group on the World Bank, c/o ICVA, mimeo, 1993).
11. Notable by their absence from this clash were developing country NGOs whose attitude was straightforward. Where the Bank was seen to be deserving of criticism, it was criticised unmercifully, but where it could be used to an NGO's advantage, it was exploited mercilessly.
12. For example ICVA has a programme on Management for Development and has produced major policy documents such as *Guidelines for Improving the Quality of Projects in the Third World Funded by NGOs* (October 1984) and *Suggested Guidelines on the Acceptance of Government Funds for NGO Programmes* (March 1985).
13. *Consensus Conclusions of the WB/NGO Committee Meeting, Santo Domingo* (Geneva: NGO Working Group on the World Bank, c/o ICVA, November 1987).
14. Cheryl Payer, *The Debt Trap: The International Monetary Fund and the Third World* (New York: Monthly Review Press, 1974).
15. Latin America Bureau, *The Poverty Brokers: The IMF and Latin America* (London: Latin America Bureau, 1983); Sue Brandford and Bernado Kucinski, *The Debt Squads: the US, the Banks, and Latin America* (London: Zed Books, 1988); Jackie Roddick *et al., The Dance of the Millions: Latin America and the Debt Crisis* (London: Latin America Bureau, 1988); Giovanni Andrea Cornia *et al.* (eds), *Adjustment with a Human Face*, vol. 2: *Ten Country Case Studies. A Study by UNICEF* (Oxford: Clarendon Press, 1988); Edberto M. Villegas, *Studies in Philippine Political Economy* (Manila: Silangan Publishers, 1984); Fantu Cheru, *The Silent Revolution in Africa: Debt, Development and Democracy* (London: Zed Books, 1989).
16. Ian Goldin and L. Alan Winters (eds), *Open Economies: Structural Adjustment and Agriculture* (London: Centre for Economic Policy Research/OECD, 1992).
17. Akilagpa Sawyerr, *The Politics of Adjustment*, UN Economic Commission for Africa, document number ECA/ICHD/88/29, Addis Ababa.
18. Seamus Cleary, 'Structural Adjustment in Africa' in *Development Review 1989* (Dublin: Trocaire).
19. *Position Paper of the NGO Working Group on the World Bank* (Geneva: NGO Working Group on the World Bank, c/o ICVA, mimeo, December 1989), reprinted in *Development Review 1990* (Dublin: Trocaire, 1990).
20. *A World Bank response to the NGO Position Paper on the World Bank* (Geneva: NGO Working Group on the World Bank, c/o ICVA, March 1990), reprinted in *Development Review 1990* (Dublin: Trocaire, 1990).
21. *NGO Working Group on the World Bank Programme, Saly, Senegal, March 1991* (Geneva: NGO Working Group on the World Bank, c/o ICVA, mimeo, 1991).
22. Seamus Cleary, *International Financial Institutions* (Ferney-Voltaire: Public Services International, 1992).
23. Charles Abeysekera *et al., Structural Adjustment in Sri Lanka: A grassroots perspective*; Alioune Tamchir Thiam, *Structural Adjustment in Senegal: a grassroots perspective*; Equipo Pueblo (coordinator Carlos Heredia), *Structural*

Adjustment in Mexico: a grassroots perspective (Geneva: NGO Working Group on the World Bank, c/o ICVA, all three in mimeo, 1993).

24. NGOs acknowledged that this was accurate in Senegal's case at least. Sri Lanka government representatives who participated in the discussion also insisted that failures to achieve performance targets arose from implementation failures and delays.
25. Including NGOs such as The Development Gap, the Environment Defence Fund, and the Sierra Club.
26. Including ActionAid, the Catholic Fund for Overseas Development, Christian Aid, and the Save the Children Fund at a meeting of the UK Debt Crisis Network.
27. Some of this criticism was clearly a matter of personality. No such criticism was levelled at John Mitchell, formerly World Development Movement Director, when he joined the staff of the World Bank later that year.
28. P. Le Prestre, *The World Bank and the Environmental Challenge* (London: Associated University Presses, 1989).
29. 'Critics Get Tough: Target Bank's Money' in *BankCheck Quarterly*, November 1992, International Rivers Network, Berkeley, California.
30. Address to NGO-World Bank Committee, Washington DC, October, 1992.
31. Mazid N'Diaye, Co-Chair, World Bank-NGO Committee and Chair, NGO Working Group in a letter (dated October 1992) on behalf of the Working Group to the President of the World Bank, Lewis Preston.
32. Jane Covey and Paul Nelson, 'Making the World Bank Responsive to NGO Concerns' in *Monday Developments*, 8 November 1993, p. 11, InterAction, New York.
33. *Ibid.*
34. *BankCheck Quarterly*, September 1993, International Rivers Network, Berkeley, California, USA. Another campaign supporter, The Development Gap, co-sponsors *BankCheck* with the publisher.
35. The material quoted consists of the main heading for each of the five sections of the platform, *World Bank/IMF: 50 Years is Enough US Campaign* (no publishing details given on the document).
36. Oxfam UK and Ireland, Policy Department, *Structural Adjustment and Inequality in Latin America: How IMF and World Bank Policies have failed the Poor* (Oxford: Oxfam, September 1994).
37. The UK-based Save the Children Fund was one of the first NGOs to participate in such an exchange. According to the participants, the positive experience led to an increased understanding of each institutions differing perspective.
38. For example, Indian NGOs, environmental groups and some development NGOs lobbied extensively on the Sardar Sarovar dam; there has also been considerable lobbying of World Bank staff and governors around resettlement concerns arising from the Ruwizi dam in Zaire.
39. Oxfam-UK's 'Africa: Make or Break' campaign is a clear example.
40. World Bank, *Strategies for improving Bank-NGO Relations*, Draft 9.
41. Respectively, Catharine Stevulak and Ann Thomson, *Approaches to Bank/NGO Collaboration* (draft working paper presented at the seminar, World Bank and NGOs: operational policy approaches for collaboration, Washington, 29–30 June 1993) and *op. cit.*, Draft 9.

4

UNESCO AND NGOs: A MEMOIR

Richard Hoggart

UNESCO is in many important and interesting ways so unique an element in the UN system that its differences from the rest need indicating at the start. The main UN bodies provide arenas where matters of high governmental policy can be addressed: matters of war and peace, of security, of economic survival, those issues which need the full diplomatic attention of each government. This is not to say, incidentally, that UNESCO does not concern itself with such things; but it does so as matters to be discussed intellectually and hence, it is hoped, to be better understood. So UNESCO has programmes on peace and peacemaking, and on the causes of war; it is concerned with intellectual strategy, not tactical in-fighting. UNESCO's real difference lies elsewhere. Its central preoccupations are those matters with which, in free societies, individual citizens are or should be directly concerned and governments less directly concerned, or concerned only under the watchful eyes of their individual citizens: education (as compared with government propaganda), individual human rights (which many governments still flout), free communications, and the disinterested pursuit of knowledge of all kinds, from the scientific to the philosophical.

Many societies, particularly in the first decades of UNESCO's life, did not have open democracies, where individuals were free in the above senses. Hence one of the more glaring of UNESCO's continuing difficulties: its Constitution assumes virtues which many governments do not have. Some are worse than others in this respect, of course; but UNESCO's governing bodies and its Secretariat also stub their toes on the unwillingness of some highly-developed and sophisticated parliamentary democracies to live up to the spirit of the Constitution to which they have pledged concurrence. All participants in UNESCO, the NGOs no less than the formally constituent elements, feel this paradox. The best among those involved with UNESCO do not regret this; it arises from the nature of nation states and the frailty of humanity.

Thus, from its inception UNESCO has had an Executive Board

that has been responsible for the execution of UNESCO's programmes. Initially the Constitution specified in Article V that the
Board's members should be 'persons competent in the arts, the
humanities, the sciences, education and the diffusion of ideas, and
qualified by their experience and capacity': they should exercise
their powers on behalf of UNESCO as a whole 'and not as representatives of their respective governments'. The early Boards had
a good proportion of scholars, thinkers, great statesmen from all
over the globe; they were the conscience of the organisation. The
governments subsequently decided they could not all accept independent thinkers being in control of the main decision-making
body. In 1954 the Constitution had been amended, explicitly con-
verting the members of the Board into government representatives.
Even so, when the present writer joined the Secretariat in 1970,
something of the original spirit remained. For example, the member from (not 'of' or 'for') Switzerland was a hugely impressive
Professor of Philosophy. To hear her berate the Board on human
rights or freedom of communication was a joy to those who
worked daily to fulfil UNESCO's purposes, and an embarrassment
to those who did no more than follow instructions.

From a small group of eighteen people, UNESCO's Board has
steadily grown to the current size of fifty-one representatives, as
more continents, regions and states have demanded places; its
debates are therefore inherently more difficult and drawn-out. More
important, when the Board's members formally became nominees
of their governments, continents and regions, a very important
distinction was erased. Conscientious Secretariat members regret
this, but most of them accept it and make more and more tactical
adjustments rather than following the institution's strategic lights.
In November 1993 the General Conference finally eliminated the
last vestiges of the idea of the Executive Board being composed
of independent individuals. The Constitution had been amended
again to specify that the members of the Executive are not the
people who sit as representatives on the Board, but the *states*
who appoint them. All that remains of the original ideals is an
obligation upon the states standing for election to submit the
name and curriculum vitae of the person they intend to designate
as their representative.

Something similar has happened to another of UNESCO's special inventions: the National Commissions. These were intended to
be the crown, the living expression in each country, of UNESCO's
commitment to free intellectual life. They were meant to be composed of highly-qualified and independent individuals, who between
them would cover the whole spread of its interests. They would be

able to advise their own governments and UNESCO itself. It is obvious from the start that such independence would in some states be a myth: the National Commissions in such countries were minor governmental units. In some other states they did have real freedom and their members (whether of the National Commission itself or of its sub-committees on culture, science, communications, education) really were among the best of their kind. They spoke their minds when advising governments and expected the civil servants who attended their meetings to service their work or to act as observers only.

That too has changed over the years and in much the same way as the Executive Board. A minister of government would replace a Commission chairman from outside government – a university vice-chancellor, perhaps. The argument for this and for a selection of Commission members less representative of the intellectual community was always predictable and always the same: if you want to have any clout you must be run by someone who can speak to and for the government of the day. But who then speaks freely for the Constitution? Once again, the NGOs, which had been accustomed to looking for help from intellectually well-informed members of National Commissions, found that advice and support less forthcoming.

All such changes bore heavily also on responsible members of the Secretariat. Except for time-servers or those from states which simply do not recognise the independence of the Secretariat, life for members of the Secretariat became all the harder. The 'independence' of staff can be defended from one secure base: Article VI of UNESCO's Constitution affirms:

> The responsibilities of the Director-General and of the staff shall be exclusively international in character. In the discharge of their duties they shall not seek or receive instructions from any government . . .

Each state member of the organisation also undertakes not to seek to influence the staff. On joining the organisation all officials swear to uphold its basic principles, to become international civil servants rather than agents of their home governments. This allowed the courageous to point out to an erring committee that they were acting against the Constitution, or to refuse an irregular request from the ambassador of a member state, or to point out to colleagues that special favours for their own countries were against the rules; or to support an NGO by invoking the rules on its behalf against undue pressure from a particular member state.

This preamble has been introduced so as to highlight the special nature of UNESCO, its general problems and those of its affiliated NGOs. Instances of the areas in which, even though pressures on all sides have increased, the organisation and its relations with the NGOs are still in good working order, are given in the following pages, as are examples of where the pressures have become regrettable.

Given the peculiar nature of UNESCO it is not surprising that the relationship with its NGOs is also especially strong. As early as the initial Constitution itself, of 16 November 1945, Article XI, section 4, ruled:

> [UNESCO] may make suitable arrangements for consultation and cooperation with non-governmental international organisations concerned with matters within its competence, and may invite them to undertake specific tasks. Such cooperation may also include appropriate participation by representatives of such organisations on advisory committees set up by the General Conference.

In the early years, very close relationships developed on an *ad hoc* basis with a relatively small number of international NGOs. When the number increased significantly in the late 1950s, it became necessary to establish criteria specifying which NGOs were eligible to work with UNESCO and what their role should be. In 1960 the Eleventh Session of the General Conference passed a lengthy resolution formalising the whole system. The resulting *Directives concerning UNESCO's Relations with International Non-Governmental Organisations*, as amended in 1966, are given in the manual of the General Conference, the 'Green Book' of UNESCO's basic working rules.

The 1960 Directives are detailed, helpful and precise as to the rights and duties of NGOs; indeed they are wide, liberal and enabling. An NGO must not have been established by intergovernmental agreement; its purposes and functions must be non-governmental; there must be a wide geographic spread in the NGO's membership; and the NGO must have good communications with its members. 'Consultation and cooperation' are key words. Those duties include providing advice, offering technical cooperation to UNESCO, expressing the views of important sections of public opinion and helping to prepare and execute UNESCO's programme of activities. These are still the main foundations of UNESCO's stated relations with NGOs; but the years since have seen successive attempts to shift or weaken some of the pillars, usually under more illiberal impulses. They have stood the test of time well and are still in force, although the relentless increase in numbers, with a trebling in the total having official relations with UNESCO, from 187 in 1961 to 585 in 1991, has put the system under stress.

In UNESCO, relations with NGOs are based on the degree of cooperation offered by the NGO, unlike the United Nations, where they are based on the range of an NGO's activities. The three categories of relationship all impose significant obligations on NGOs with regard to liaison and the exchange of information. NGOs which make 'regular major contributions to UNESCO's work' and are able to advise 'on the preparation and execution of UNESCO's programme' obtain the highest status, Category A, Consultative and Associate Relations. Category A NGOs are expected to expand those of their activities that are of special interest to UNESCO and promote coordination among NGOs in their field. All the NGOs may receive documents, attend meetings and make statements in all subsidiary bodies of the General Conference. This is similar to practice in the United Nations.

UNESCO offers privileges that would be unthinkable at the UN. The Directives specify that UNESCO should 'strive as far as possible to provide office accommodation' for organisations in Category A. Originally this arose as part of UNESCO's efforts in the 1940s and 1950s to encourage the formation of new international NGOs covering its main activities. Given the shortage of office space, there is no way that UNESCO could offer accommodation to more than fifty NGOs now in Category A; currently just eight of the older NGOs remain with their own offices in the UNESCO building in rue Miollis. Services are also provided to Category A and B NGOs for their biennial conferences with UNESCO on the draft programme and budget. These conferences elect an eighteen-member Standing Committee to cooperate with the Secretariat for the following two years. It too is provided with premises and secretarial facilities.

UNESCO is also exceptional within the UN system in providing Category A and B NGOs with subventions to cover costs of travel, organising meetings, operating research centres, publishing, establishing new national sections and meeting central administrative expenses. At their peak in 1985, the total amount of subventions paid to NGOs was $2.6 million and contracts awarded to implement UNESCO projects totalled $2.3 million. As a result of the budgetary cutbacks following the withdrawal from UNESCO in January 1986 of the United States and the United Kingdom, the subventions had fallen to $1.7 million and contracts to $2 million per annum for the 1990–1991 biennium.

There was, however, growing controversy in the 1980s over the allocation of subventions. The distinction between subventions and contracts had become blurred and some NGOs were failing to meet their obligation to account for the use of money they had received within a reasonable time-period. The first major change was in 1991 when the terms of reference of the Executive Board's Committee on International NGOs were changed to include examination of the Director-General's proposals to grant subventions. Thus the financial decisions ceased to be determined predominantly by the Secretariat's views of the usefulness of NGO activities; political hands made a grab at the purse strings. The final result of a long political process was that from January 1996 subventions will be granted solely to new NGOs or to NGOs from developing countries starting to cooperate with UNESCO. The new subventions will be granted for a maximum of four years. Well-established NGOs will continue to be eligible to receive contracts under UNESCO's own programme. The possibility of more secure financial support, a limited version of the old subventions, remains open with a new provision for medium-term 'framework agreements' for NGOs to work with UNESCO. In principle, it will still be possible for NGOs to maintain their independence, but they will be under direct scrutiny by governments and will be aware that from now onwards the price of taking a decision that is unwelcome to key governments could be the loss of financial support from UNESCO.

The third exceptional feature of UNESCO-NGO relations is the degree to which it is formally specified that NGOs may be involved in policy-making. At the United Nations, the relationship with NGOs never officially goes beyond 'consultation'. At UNESCO, Category A NGOs can expect, in principle, to 'be associated as closely and as regularly as possible with the various stages of planning and execution of UNESCO's activities coming within their particular field'. In practice, the distinctions between the UN and UNESCO are not as sharp as these formal statements suggest. Some prestigious NGOs at the UN do have close working relations with the Secretariat, while some of the smaller NGOs at UNESCO do not have any permanent full-time staff in Paris. Nonetheless the idea that an NGO has a formal right to take part in policy-making makes UNESCO unique.

So, formally, there has been a generous set of guidelines. What did the reality seem like from the perspective of an Assistant Director-General? It is at this point necessary to go back a few decades. From their beginnings, international non-governmental organisations have been regarded with suspicion by some governments, some intergovernmental organisations and some individuals whose work involved contact with NGOs. The League of Nations had seen some NGOs and some bodies similar to them emerge, notably (for a student of UNESCO) the International Institute of Intellectual Cooperation, founded in Paris in 1926. In its intellectual and cultural interests, the Institute had qualities similar to some of what became UNESCO's main NGOs and it did much to nourish fledgling NGOs. However, the Institute was not in itself an NGO: it was an intergovernmental organisation and could almost be described as the mother of UNESCO itself. Ironically, although it was intergovernmental, the criticisms of it from some quarters were similar to those later directed at the NGOs.

Some politicians and diplomats claimed the Institute was 'mandarin', too much associated with universities or at least 'vaguely academic', and so to be treated rather contemptuously by statesmen and others who live in the 'real' world. Hence from the 1920s onwards, and even more sharply in the 1940s – the period of CAME (the Conference of Allied Ministers of Education: the 'father' of UNESCO) – there was a split: between those who wanted individuals and non-governmental bodies to have a part, a working part, in the intergovernmental bodies, and those who would have none of that. Such different views still exist, whether of those radical enough to question the rights of international NGOs to be recognised at all, or more specific differences among those who believed that NGOs could be valuable but who defined and ranked them strictly according to personal professional interests. The years have brought little agreement. The field is large and exceptionally diverse. Meetings of representatives of NGOs are nearer to Noah's Ark than, say, those of a university Senate. Academics can be quarrelsome and divided but they have at least a common tap-root, the pursuit of knowledge for, in the first place, its own sake.

As an Assistant Director-General, I had an unusually wide and varied experience of NGOs. UNESCO's work is, for the purposes of management, functionally divided into huge groups of subjects rather than by the geographical area in which projects are located. In my day, the first half of the 1970s, four ADGs shared the work between them. The other three had relatively simple and coherent briefs: Education, Science, Communications. I had Culture (both in the anthropological and the Matthew Arnoldian sense) including the physical heritage – monuments and sites across the world, the social sciences, the humanities and virtually anything else there was difficulty finding a home for, such as human rights, racism, population, drugs and the environment. It was a great ungainly shopping bag. As a result I had responsibility for UNESCO's relationships with several dozen NGOs in the two major categories, A and B, along with many more in Category C.

One evening the ADG for Science was sitting in my office waiting for me to give him a lift to a reception. He had to wait longer than expected because during a single half-hour calls came in: about an earthquake in Latin America and damage to important religious monuments; about problems at a tricky social scientific conference somewhere in Eastern Europe; about the latest eruption in the Arab-Israeli dispute to do with the care, or the alleged neglect, of each other's holy places; about whether a certain NGO was to be asked to give consultancy services somewhere in Asia; – and a routine call from the DG's office just checking that a paper he was to deliver at a meeting on environmental problems would be ready for him on time. The ADG for Science said he would not receive five such different calls in a couple of days let alone in one half-hour after the official end of the working day.

Yet my account of life with the NGOs, an impressionistic account inevitably but based on much direct experience, will seem limited to some readers simply because its axis was artistic/intellectual/cultural. To me it seemed extensive enough, but, from one angle it can seem circumscribed, only part of a much larger whole. NGOs can be political and ideological (to do with opposing racism, enhancing human rights, defending the environment); they can embrace academics and artists of all kinds together with those professionals who are not strictly academics or artists but whose 'mystery' has social value and quality such as architects and town-planners. NGOs can be polemical or devoted to lobbying or engrossed in their own closed world – or something of all these. So the style, the manner, the thrust will differ from type to type; so will the sense of rectitude and urgency, and the case or difficulty of their intimacies with governments or with their host intergovernmental agency. One thing we can be sure of: they will all believe in the merit and the priority of their cause.

For UNESCO's relationships with its NGOs the key figure, the towering figure, was its first Director-General, Julian Huxley. There had been, of course, a fight at the founding meeting in Church House, Westminster, over where UNESCO's headquarters should be located and which country should supply the first DG. For supporters of the NGO idea, such as the present writer, it is a source of pleasure that the French (as they thought was only right) got the site but the British the DG. Huxley was a splendid example of a very special English type, a product of the intellectual and scientific upper-middle class; a free spirit, eccentric, entirely unbureaucratic (he was reputed to disappear between meetings to sketch the flora and fauna of the Bois de Boulogne and to pass duller parts of official meetings drawing the birds and plants he had seen). He was exceptionally inventive and delighted in mixed bodies where independent thinkers of all kinds were engaged with straight governmental representatives. He was also inspired by that post-war sense of hope for a more decent and intelligent future, which lasted nearly a decade, until the hard-headed pragmatists and the Cold War warriors began to impose their dire spirit, even on UNESCO. Huxley loved to tweak the noses of *apparatchiks* from East or West; most governmental spokesmen bored him but he loved talking to individuals and to groups with intellectual or artistic passions. I treasure the memory of driving him round Paris during UNESCO's celebration of its twenty-first anniversary, in 1971. The old quirky spirit was in full form. He died in 1975.

So Huxley loved NGOs but was rather cavalier towards the proto-col demanded by so many member states. If he met a strong-minded person with bright ideas he co-opted him or her without much, if any, consultation with his Executive Board. He not only encouraged NGOs; he created them when he thought a particular kind of body was needed to promote UNESCO's broad principles and basic pur-poses. He encouraged them because he believed, rightly, that they could and should be more flexible than intergovernmental bodies. Huxley's own account gives an illustration of his approach:

> In the hot summer of 1947, we also set up an International Theatre Institute (for drama, opera, films and ballet) . . . The committee responsible for this comprised many well-known names in dramatic circles, such as the French producer and actor Jean-Louis Barrault, Sir Tyrone Guthrie from England, and Lillian Hellman from the USA. She was a strong liberal, but official US bodies chose to consider her a communist, and pro-tested. However, we stood firm and succeeded in getting the Institute approved as another of UNESCO's international non-governmental bodies. (*Memories II*, Penguin, 1978, p. 18)

In all this Huxley was ably supported by his Deputy Director-General, Jean Thomas, a Frenchman. That pairing of nationali-ties was also apt since Thomas's personality well complemented Huxley's; Thomas was typical of the best type of French intellec-tual, precise, penetrating and, like many from the Grandes Écoles, excellent at linking management skills with the principles they are meant to serve. The debates about the NGOs were, he said, some of the worst in UNESCO. But Thomas, too, gave powerful initial pushes to some NGOs which were later to become major constituent-clients of my Sector – such as the International Council of Museums (ICOM), the International Music Council and the International Theatre Institute – as Huxley had done, especially, to some of the scientific and environmental NGOs.

Huxley and Thomas were also responsible for establishing the principle of giving a basic, operating subvention to NGOs. This principle became a subordinate battleground in the initial dispute on whether NGOs should be welcomed at all. Let them be recognised, then, the argument ran at this point, but let us keep close tabs on them by only giving them funds for contracts, for precise work done according to our briefs. The debate over the proper balance between subventions and contracts continued over the decades. Gradually the noose has tightened to the point that permanent subventions for well-established NGOs are now being phased out.

Huxley and Thomas would have opposed that. They believed that if the aims, the natures themselves, of NGOs were worthwhile such NGOs deserved, from the UN's one specifically intellectual body, basic funding to keep them going, no matter how few or how many contracts they attracted. They believed that strong professional non-governmental international organisations were among the bastions of free speech, whereas UNESCO, whatever its Constitution might say, had constantly to resist encroachments on free speech from its member states. NGOs should not be led to conceive of themselves as lapdogs; they must be free to bite the hand that feeds them. In democracies, this is or should be an accepted, cardinal attitude, held by those who receive their subventions, towards all those bodies which themselves receive their funds from government. Anyone in Britain who has much to do with, for instance, the Arts Council, the British Council or the BBC knows both that the clients of such bodies, being free-born Britons, do not hesitate to bite the hands that feed them and that many people (especially some politicians and civil servants) find the principle hard to take. In authoritarian regimes the rule is, of course, incomprehensible.

It will be plain that I am very much a Huxley/Thomas man. Disinterestedness, like democracy itself, is very hard and perhaps impossible to attain; but it is the right ideal, the right condition to aim for, everywhere. It is easy to assert that free speech and freedom of enquiry must be fought for in authoritarian regimes; open capitalist democracies have their less evident, less unmistakably punitive, ways of calling free speech and free enquiry into question. The arguments drone on: the time is not ripe; the losses will be greater than the gains; we will be misunderstood, thought to be unsure of our own purposes, by other societies towards which we are on ambiguous terms; surely there must be a limit, the point beyond which liberty becomes licence; and so, drearily, on. It is therefore not surprising that Huxley was greatly criticised for his open attitude towards NGOs.

Sewell is more qualified than I am to comment on Huxley's contribution to the history of NGOs:

> Unfortunately for the course of UNESCO's development, Huxley's perception of human affairs did not prompt him to draw his non-governmental framework into a living relationship with his own organisation. He practised engagement only upon an interpersonal scale. His approach to the problem of a surrogate framework consisted of an insufficient number of steps: discover a needy area within one's map of the whole; stimulate someone to set up a corresponding NGO; move on to the next needy area'. (*UNESCO and World Politics*, James F. Sewell, pp. 109–10)

If I read that aright, Sewell is saying that Huxley had not the patience to follow through organisationally, properly to tie the NGOs into UNESCO's activities; that he worked through individuals rather than committees or constitutional plans and so did not cause NGOs to be properly bound into UNESCO. One wonders why, if this was so, Jean Thomas did not put right the deficiency. The argument also sits rather uneasily with the paragraphs on NGOs in UNESCO's key documents from Huxley's time onwards. Certainly, in 1960 the General Conference resolution specifying the Directives on relations with NGOs would seem to have remedied the omission Sewell describes. Certainly, too, the growth in the numbers of NGOs went on rapidly in the early years. In 1948, the year Huxley ended his two-year spell, there were eighty; there was a particularly strong spurt in 1961, when the system was first made more formal, and by 1971 there were almost 300. By 1991 there were 585 but of those only fifty-two, less than one in eleven, were in Category A.

As I have indicated, the heart of the interests of my NGOs was artistic/intellectual. It followed that most were not political or aggressive in polemical ways; but they could be a tricky lot. They ranged from quite formalistic social scientists to the most airily artistic, from pure and disinterested scholars to forceful professional chauvinists; chauvinists for their profession, that is.

Typical of the more effective bodies were the International Council of Museums (ICOM) and its half-brother ICOMOS (Monuments and Sites); International PEN; the International Music Council (very active, with Yehudi Menuhin as its President);

the International Council for Philosophy and Humanistic Studies and the International Association of Art. Then there were the NGOs concerned with various forms of human rights. Oddly, I heard less about them than about the artistic NGOs but am not sure why. Perhaps before they reached me the Social Science Department fielded more of the problems of the NGOs allotted to their bailiwick than the two Culture Departments managed to do. Perhaps artistic NGOs are more likely to be contentious and out to hold their corners at all costs.

The fact is that all Secretaries-General of NGOs must, to repeat, believe there is nothing quite as important as their own NGO's work. That comes with the job; so does, inevitably, a tendency to over-state their case. More simply put, most NGOs, whatever the Constitution or the Manual may say, feel like supplicants. So they woo the members of the Secretariat (whilst sometimes resenting their powers and their higher salaries); or they woo delegates to UNESCO of their key member states or region or faith. Some members of the Secretariat cherish those attentions; they make them feel powerful, generous, bureaucratic patrons. Some Secretariat members are not only emotionally susceptible but politically vulnerable. Article VI of the Constitution may assert the independence of UNESCO's staff, but if the UNESCO delegates from the home countries of Secretariat members lean on them, some may well bend, out of fear or the wish to be liked – or the inevitable mixture of both – if their countries flout that Article and insist on thinking of Secretariat members from their countries as their agents within the organisation.

So I, and the Directors who reported to me, had to watch all such movements as closely as the complex spider's web of communications allowed. It is plain that not all Directors were free men and women. I was, and for a reason not to do with any virtue of mine. I came from a reasonably open democracy; the British delegation did not once in five and a half years attempt to put pressure on me or try to persuade me with compliments. I knew I could easily return to England and a decently paid academic job. Moral courage is well buttressed by such lucky considerations. For someone like me, stubbornness in the face of would-be pressures, rather than moral courage, did service. This was not so for the Secretariat member who would soon be told by the national delegation to go back home if he or she stood out for the principles of international service; consigned perhaps to oblivion, certainly to a job, if job there was, at a tenth of the UNESCO salary, and no perks. Most yielded and stayed in Paris. I know of only one who defected rather than return home, but there may well have been others.

There would be continuous lobbying from the NGOs for higher basic subventions and more contracts, especially from those Category A NGOs with offices provided by and near UNESCO. From the mid-1970s most of those were placed in the new Miollis building only a quarter of a mile from the central, Y-shaped building in Place de Fontenoy. After the building was opened, a minibus trundled all day between the Miollis and the main buildings. NGO staff were still able, as before, to mingle with Secretariat members and with members of national delegations in the restaurants, the bars, the library and the rest areas. So strong was the public image of the more powerful NGOs that many people outside thought they were a full part of UNESCO as an organisation, fully within the Secretariat, fully an organ of the institution. This was not true nor what their best supporter, Huxley, intended; but most of the relevant secretaries-general were naturally not disposed to dispel that confusion. Some were too blinkered to see that in the long term, and with a wider perspective, it would be against their own best interests if they really were organically part of UNESCO. So the tendency to look too much towards the developed world, of which Paris was so exciting a part, and to neglect the needs of the developing world, grew all the stronger. That was one matter for rebuke by the General Conference.

Sometimes NGOs closely related to each other (say, because they each represented one of the major art forms) ganged up so as to try to influence the Secretariat, even though for most of the time they would watch each other warily. Some could use the arcane channels of communication better than others. And sometimes, however much I tried to understand and sympathise with the pressures under which they worked, I became fed up with the routine procession of this kind of *apparatchik*. They all claimed to be free spirits, thinking only of the art or intellectual endeavour they spoke for, but not all of them were.

Such behaviour was not improved by the ambiguous attitudes or root and branch opposition of some member states towards the NGOs. We know those attitudes emerged when NGOs began. In totalitarian states across the globe the idea that encouragement should be given to intellectually free bodies, free above all to criticise them, seemed absurd. Why should such bodies be let loose, they asked? Nor were the democracies altogether free from similar attitudes, but they put their case in more empirical, non-ideological terms. Sewell notes that the Englishman, Lord (Arthur) Salter, made a classic statement stressing 'the necessity of responsible *governmental* participation in order to achieve effective organised international action'. In other words, he was putting the NGOs to one side.

The argument goes on as it has from the beginning, not only about NGOs but about any body within or outside UNESCO that might claim powers other than those directly given by governments. The original National Cooperating Bodies within member states gave way to the UNESCO National Commissions. In some countries these became progressively less free than their predecessors; in others they began unfree. The similarities with the NGOs are obvious. There are also similarities with the changes over the years in attitudes towards UNESCO's Executive Board. As early as the mid-1950s it was noted that, in spite of the Constitution, Board members did not serve 'on behalf of the Conference as a whole [rather than] as representatives of their respective governments; they were speaking precisely for those governments'. Such spokesmen were accorded a closer hearing than those who were not spokesmen but free speakers. That process goes on. We have seen that, progressively, the Board has grown larger and more and more the members have become the voices of their governments.

In all these movements Britain did not, after a few years, behave imaginatively; it was not Huxleyan. It was instead, and at best, vague, and gave an impression of little interest. In the time I knew it, the delegation at UNESCO did include some very effective and decent people; but they were too few and underrated. There was no British ambassador but a very hard-working Principal (a quite low level of the Administrative Class in the Civil Service) with a vestigial staff. This suggested to UNESCO that the United Kingsom thought little of it. To the newer and smaller nations the international platform provided by UNESCO was vastly more important than it was to successive British governments. There was no need for Britain to imitate some of the nations just establishing modern education systems (and those anxious for aid) and attach to UNESCO a full blown ambassador with full staff and panoply; but the gap was altogether too great.

Two instances stick in the memory. In my early days a Convention was drafted, with of course much professional help from NGOs, to discourage the illicit purchase and transfer of cultural property (many poor countries were having their national treasures secretly depleted by the financial lures of the Western world). Most European powers, especially West Germany, sent to the working party experts who were well briefed and cogent. The United Kingdom sent a lawyer who was neither expert nor well-briefed and who, according to orders, opposed the Convention – in a fluting, superior voice which made me blush. Three years or so later came a related but significantly different Convention (also prepared with good professional help from NGOs), that on The

Restitution of Cultural Property (for example, if country X, being wealthy, has three examples of country Y's historic war-canoes, leaving Y itself with none, then an exchange will be agreed). Again, the British representative had instructions to oppose (shadows of the Elgin Marbles). I learned this at a reception the evening before the Convention's working-party began and so fiercely exploded before Britain's Board member that he telephoned London to suggest revised instructions.

The pity is that by the 1970s Britain showed little sign of an active enthusiasm for UNESCO and could almost always be guaranteed to take the *status quo*, unimaginative line. Other countries could be more liberated. At a huge conference in Asia, the Eastern Bloc tried to put through a resolution which would have restricted the intellectual freedom of the Secretariat when preparing, with NGO help, documents on the rights of artists (weasel phrasings such as 'The Secretariat will in all such issues in the first place take into account governmental views ...' disguising the true meaning, which was 'will reflect' or 'will yield to'). Again, most major developed powers, older than the rock on which they sat, were not disposed to argue the case. The NGOs most concerned were naturally alarmed. The New Zealand delegation, prompted by an academic member of the British delegation and me, proposed a revised version. Since the East European delegations had no fall-back position, and probably did not realise the semantic shift in the revised version, it went through. But that was a case of a Secretariat intervention of substance and not to be practised too often. What, I might have asked with the rock-like confidence of my own disinterestedness, if other less disinterested members of staff did that kind of thing!

In the light of the above, a statement in the government's booklet *Britain and UNESCO* of 1966 rings somewhat hollowly: 'One of UNESCO's most frequent activities is to name a problem, call a conference of the people anywhere in the world with the knowledge and experience most likely to provide a solution [which must mean above all the NGOs] and then use their recommendations as a guide to its own action'.

The UK's near indifference was at least less damaging than the active political interventions of some governments. There have been fairly frequent efforts to make NGOs know that they might lose their subventions and contracts if they did not toe a particular line pushed through the General Conference; about links with South Africa, for instance, or much worse, because they were about one government's demands rather than the principle of countering racism, were the regular resolutions against NGO links with 'the Chiang Kai-shek clique' in Taiwan. Even an NGO sympathetic to the battle against apartheid might resent not being able to make up its own mind and being threatened through the power to withhold funds; but such considerations seem entirely beside the point to the representatives of some member states. In 1972, during my last year at UNESCO, PEN, a valuable air-hole to writers suffering censorship in many countries, was violently attacked by Czechoslovakia because it had run an outspoken conference on current limitations on artistic freedom. We in the Secretariat resisted the attack strongly and enlisted support. The Czechoslovaks unwisely insisted on a vote in Conference, and lost it.

The most striking instance of such direct intervention in my experience came in 1973 when Amnesty International, an NGO in Category B and admirably affective, arranged a conference at UNESCO Headquarters on the practice of torture throughout the world. Almost immediately before the meeting was to open, objections were made, by those who knew the finger would be pointed at them, against the use of UNESCO's premises and facilities. UNESCO gave in and Amnesty moved to another venue in Paris.

But NGOs can have more helpful relationships. The Participation Programme used money set aside from the funds allotted to the Core Programme by the General Conference. The PP office, as it was known, could be approached by a National Commission with what was thought to be a good initiative, germane to UNESCO's purposes. It might be a conference or a publication or a modest research project carried out in the applicant member state but it usually involved more than the nationals of that state. Inevitably, such proposals involved relevant NGOs. Once they were approved UNESCO would match dollar for dollar towards the cost.

PP plus NGOs could provide an occasional escape-hole for the more adventurous Secretaries-General of National Commissions in, for example, Eastern Europe, if they wanted to launch an initiative of a sort which would be suspected and endlessly chewed over before, probably, being nervously rejected if it went through their usual channels. My own favourite among such Secretaries-General would, having got the NGOs on his side, earnestly apply for PP funds. By this means he carried out several projects of high intellectual calibre and with the minimum of state interference.

So, at best, a good NGO could have a kind of balancing role between the Secretariat, often under pressure to give way to expediency, and governments who were putting on that pressure. Such NGOs, if properly employed by the Secretariat, could define and refine policy often better than UNESCO itself could. Secretariat members may have been at the frontiers of their disciplines when they began to work for UNESCO: inevitably, the frontiers moved ahead of them as the years passed. NGOs are essential to UNESCO if it is to keep up-to-date and retain the respect of the scholarly, scientific and intellectual communities. Much the same applies to conferences, conventions and the like; NGOs could best sustain the international intellectual dialogue. I had to keep an eye on nine major standard-setting Conventions. The Convention for the Protection of the World Cultural and Natural Heritage, finalised at UNESCO in 1972, was an example of such an instrument. Working parties of experts, mostly proposed by NGOs, were crucial to negotiating an effective Convention. The IUCN has been active in identifying World Heritage Sites that should be nominated for protection, and the Rome Centre for Cultural Property, ICOMOS and IUCN are all specified in the Convention as advisers to the World Heritage Committee.

That ideal has not always been lived up to. Again, Sewell has his doubts: 'UNESCO leaders, particularly Huxley, stand as creators of new NGO units almost more than as makers of roles for joint UNESCO-NGO operation. It has remained for Huxley's successors to try constructing devices for collaboration which are conducive to greater mutual effectiveness. In this they have met with very limited success'. My experience makes it difficult to quarrel with this assessment. Some individual members of the Secretariat work hand-in-glove with their NGOs though for differing reasons, not all of them sound or creditable. But generally the organisation has been too preoccupied with itself, with its day-to-day relations with the Board and the member states, to pay much attention to what might be the ideal relationship with NGOs.

Looking over old notes, I was delighted to rediscover that early in 1970, only a month or so after arriving in UNESCO, I drafted three criteria for our obligatory regular examination of an NGO. Is it at the forefront of its discipline? Is it making reasonable efforts to spread itself, especially in developing countries? Is its proposed programme *complementary* to that of UNESCO? The order and the phrasing were both deliberate, an attempt to recognise all at once the authority of intellectual life, the autonomy of the NGOs and the constitutional duties of UNESCO. Above all, the word 'complementary' recognised that the NGOs have a role beyond that of helping to fulfil UNESCO's programme, that the last word does not come out of an intergovernmental agency. These criteria were adopted and went on the books. I would not alter them if I went back to the Secretariat now, almost a quarter of a century later.

It will be plain that I favour the ideal, though it may be difficult or even impossible to achieve. The idea of NGOs was, and still is, a fine one, a product of the Western democratic belief in freedom of enquiry and free circulation of the findings of such enquiries. The best officers of the NGOs are the blood brothers of the most devoted among the international Secretariat. In saying this one remembers yet again the high optimistic spirit of the immediate post-war years which gave birth to the United Nations itself and its independent agencies. The progressively more-governmentally-controlled idea of UNESCO and, by extension, the risk of narrowing the definition of its relationships with NGOs, had best be regarded as an error; an error to which governments are prone but one which should, progressively, be put right.

But all is certainly not lost. There is a clear disparity between the attitudes of some member states as they are revealed in restrictive acts such as those described above and most of the resolutions about NGOs passed by the General Conference in the last few years. To an eye used to UNESCO's codes, a late resolution against links with South Africa shows the modifying effect of more reasonable member states and, I suspect, of Secretariat drafters (this is not true of the anti-Taiwan resolutions). Earlier anti-apartheid resolutions addressed to NGOs were more restrictive and arm-twisting. The six-yearly report (1983–8) on NGOs in Categories A and B quite rightly urged more widening into the developing world and more cooperation with National Commissions; but this was within a general context of encouragement. The granting of subventions has not been stopped, but redirected to serve a different purpose. The practice of awarding contracts to NGOs has survived a period of financial stringency for UNESCO. This is all indicative of the tensions between member states, and the Executive Board, the National Commissions and the NGOs; or, more precisely, between the liberal intellectual spirits and the formalistic routine minds that will continue to exist *within* each of those elements in and around UNESCO.

5

NGOs AND THE ENVIRONMENT

Sally Morphet*

This chapter considers the role that non-governmental organisations concerned with the environment[1] have played during the twentieth century and the effect they have had on states which were members of the post-Second World War UN system. As a particular group, and through their exposure at the 1992 UN Rio Summit, these international NGOs are generally thought to have had a strong effect both on the UN system and also on certain regions and countries, despite the fact that their aims are often fairly divergent. One measure of the degree to which the UN has changed is that the UN Charter contains no mention of the environment or the conservation of nature, whereas the UN Environment Programme and the Commission on Sustainable Development are now organs of major importance. The international NGOs were primarily, but not solely, responsible for this change.

In order to put their current activities into perspective, the chapter also looks at the way international NGOs have, in the past, attempted to influence international environmental politics at a global level, and to see whether it is now easier or harder for them to influence the system. It therefore discusses how the development of an international knowledge base on environmental issues between the two world wars was harnessed by certain UN specialised agencies and the main body of the UN after 1945: it assesses NGO influence before, at and after the 1972 UN Conference on the Human Environment in Stockholm and the 1992 UN Conference on Environment and Development in Rio.

Harnessing a knowledge base

Even before the end of the First World War, the scientific community, acting through academics and research councils, had started

---

* The opinions expressed are the author's own and should not be taken as an expression of official government policy.

discussions on future cooperation. Subsequently, a meeting held at the Royal Society in London led to the setting up of the International Research Council with four unions in 1919 'for the purpose of facilitating international cooperation in scientific work and promoting the formation of international unions in different branches of science'.[2] The Council was reconstituted in 1931, with the addition of Germany, as the International Council of Scientific Unions (ICSU). 'The ICSU in its rejection of political discrimination as an unacceptable impediment to the free communication of scientists thus maintained, both in character and intent, a strictly non-governmental status'.[3]

The opportunity to use this knowledge base more constructively came with the formation of the United Nations after the Second World War. ICSU was concerned to ensure cooperation with the new UN specialised agencies dealing with scientific questions. It was, not surprisingly, particularly concerned to link up with the United Nations Educational, Scientific and Cultural Organisation (UNESCO), which had been set up in 1946 to promote and develop international and national efforts in the fields of education, natural sciences and social sciences, and to these ends foster international cooperation between specialists and NGOs.

What was needed, as a former President of ICSU pointed out in 1972, was first, a review and evaluation of the present state of knowledge; secondly, identification of areas in which further research was needed and the means by which it could be promoted; thirdly, the promotion of research needed for the advancement of knowledge and the formulation of principles of environmental management; and finally, 'its consummation in *internationally agreed actions* or measures designed to check and control the circumstances of environmental change of proven or potential hazard to man ...'[4] This last point shows clearly that NGOs need ultimately *inter alia* to work with and influence governments, whether through education, networking, the provision of knowledge or as a political pressure group.

Thus at the conference which drafted the UNESCO constitution in 1945, a resolution was passed instructing the Executive Board to consult with ICSU 'on methods of collaboration'. By the terms of the agreement subsequently approved by both bodies, UNESCO undertook to provide financial and secretarial assistance to ICSU. As Julian Huxley, the first Director-General of UNESCO, noted:

It was on Needham's advice that ICSU ... became the first of such bodies to be attached to UNESCO. We provided it with rooms in UNESCO's headquarters in Paris, and salaries for

its staff: previously the Cambridge professor who was its
secretary – and sole executive – had to dictate all its correspondence in his College rooms![5]

This period also saw the founding of what was to become *the* influential body on nature conservation. Huxley notes in his memoirs:

We got back to Paris [in 1948] just in time for a Conference on
Nature Conservation at Fontainebleau, which followed up the
decision of principle, that UNESCO should concern itself with
nature conservation policy, by establishing the IUCN, the International Union for the Conservation of Nature, as an agency
affiliated to the organisation.[6]

The impetus behind this had come from a conference at Brunnen
in Switzerland in July 1947 sponsored by the Swiss League for the
Protection of Nature.[7] Even at that early stage the conference was
attended by delegates from twenty-four countries as well as nine
international organisations. It adopted a draft constitution establishing a provisional International Union for the Protection of
Nature.[8] In 1956 the name was changed to the International Union
for the Conservation of Nature and Natural Resources, abbreviated
to the IUCN, and then in 1990, for publicity purposes, a short
descriptive title, the World Conservation Union, was adopted, with
the full official title being retained for legal purposes.[9]

The IUCN (like ICSU) was a hybrid NGO in that it comprised
governments, government agencies, intergovernmental organisations and NGOs. There was some debate in the mid 1940s as to
whether the proposed new organisation should be incorporated
within the framework of ICSU. It was decided that it should not,
as nature protection 'involved so many matters beyond the bounds
of pure science ... '.[10]

Both ICSU and the IUCN have continued to play a major role
in developing ideas on environmental questions. As Huxley stated,

[The] IUCN has since done a great deal for nature conservation
in many parts of the world – setting up new national parks in
Latin America, aiding those in Africa and helping ecological
research on wild life, as well as cooperating with conservation
bodies in the USA, Germany and elsewhere.

And ICSU

... gave UNESCO much valuable advice – on the peaceful uses
of atomic energy, on regional centres for scientific co-operation
and exchange of knowledge, on the calling of international
scientific congresses, and on liaison with other International

Agencies concerned with science, such as FAO for agricultural science and applied ecology, and WHO for medicine, physiology and social well-being.[11]

The interaction between NGOs and certain specialised agencies

The dynamic interaction between these hybrid NGOs and certain of the main UN specialised agencies proved fruitful. In the 1950s UNESCO provided the IUCN with funds for conservation education, while the UN Food and Agriculture Organisation (FAO) collaborated with it on African conservation problems in the early 1960s.[12] ICSU meanwhile developed a system of planning and research operations through scientific committees as early as 1952 when it formed the Special Committee for the International Geophysical Year (IGY). The successful IGY project was followed by the setting up of nine similar scientific committees within ICSU. These included the Scientific Committee on Oceanic Research in 1957; the Committee on Space Research and the Scientific Committee on Antarctic Research in 1958; and in 1964 the Scientific Committee on Water Research.[13]

The interaction between NGOs and the main United Nations system

The pressure to harness the knowledge available in NGOs to the activities of certain specialised agencies was paralleled (though less adequately) by initiatives in the main UN system through the Economic and Social Council (ECOSOC) and the General Assembly. One of the first manifestations of this was the holding of the UN Scientific Conference on the Conservation and Utilisation of Resources in 1949. The issues it dealt with had not yet attracted great political interest. It is not therefore surprising that many commentators consider that the parallel International Technical Conference on the Protection of Nature, which shadowed the main conference, was ultimately more influential. It was sponsored jointly by the IUCN and UNESCO and met at Lake Success in August/September 1949 and 'may be seen in retrospect as a forerunner of the UNESCO-sponsored Biosphere Conference two decades later'[14] and as laying 'the foundation for international conservation work for much of the 1950s'.[15]

As more developing countries joined the United Nations during the 1950s and, particularly, the early 1960s, these areas of interest became more important and part of the mainstream. This was exemplified by resolutions passed by both UNESCO and the General Assembly in 1962 on the relationship between conservation and development. The latter mentioned the work of the IUCN, and noted the need for the provision of technical assistance to developing countries for the conservation and restoration of their natural resources and their flora and fauna.[16] A UN Conference was subsequently held, in 1963, on the Application of Science and Technology for the Benefit of the Less-Developed Areas. On the whole, however, developing countries were not then convinced that they could be helped by the community of environmental NGOs.

The World Wide Fund for Nature (WWF)

One pointer to the future was the establishment of the World Wildlife Fund (WWF – later the World Wide Fund for Nature) in London in 1961 by the IUCN Board. This, once again, owed much to the endeavours of Julian Huxley who wrote a series of articles on threats to East African wild life in the *Observer* newspaper.[17] WWF objectives included the collection, management and disbursement of funds 'through suitable international or national bodies or individuals for the conservation of world fauna, flora, forests, landscapes, water, soils, and other natural resources'.[18] The WWF, with its well known giant panda symbol, has been extremely successful. It became an actor on the conservation stage in its own right though maintaining a close relationship with the IUCN. It was the forerunner of many NGOs which have tried to bring conservation issues to public attention.

NGOs and Stockholm, 1972

A number of these strands came together in the late 1960s following the unanimous General Assembly resolution (mentioning the important work of both ICSU and the IUCN), at Swedish instigation, calling for a conference on the human environment.[19]

The Paris Biosphere Conference, 1968

The key conference held before Stockholm was the 1968 Intergovernmental Conference of Experts on a Scientific Basis for a Rational Use and Conservation of the Resources of the Biosphere (the Paris Biosphere Conference). This again sprang from a UNESCO initiative, which in its turn was influenced by both ICSU and the IUCN. In the case of ICSU, this influence went back to the setting up of their Special Committee for the International

Biological Programme in 1963 'charged with planning and ensuring the execution of a program on the biological basis of productivity and human welfare'.[20] These proposals had been formulated by one of ICSU's own unions after discussion with IUCN representatives. They became in effect 'an amalgam of the distinctive approaches of the two organisations' and set the pattern of 'IUCN participation in and pressure for greater emphasis to be given to the conservation aspects of international scientific endeavours'.[21]

The main achievement of the Biosphere Conference, apart from adding pressure to the call for a conference on the environment, was the setting up (by 1971) of UNESCO's influential MAB (Man and the Biosphere) interdisciplinary research programme which provided 'within the natural and social sciences a basis for the rational use and conservation of the resources of the biosphere and for the improvement of the relationship between man and the environment'.[22] Its detailed planning was done mainly through almost a hundred national committees under an International Coordinating Council. It provided a rare commodity, 'integrated policy-adaptable information'.[23]

The Scientific Committee on the Problems of the Environment (SCOPE)

In addition to being instrumental in setting up the Biosphere Conference, ICSU subsequently set up a further important committee, the Scientific Committee on Problems of the Environment (SCOPE). Its remit was to report on environmental characteristics which mankind was altering and to emphasise problems of international concern whose solution the scientific competence of the ICSU could further and to provide 'scientific advice to the ICSU and *(when requested) to UN agencies'*.[24]

The fact that SCOPE was, from the beginning, concerned both with the generation of knowledge and with increasing public awareness of environmental problems was particularly significant. It was an indication that NGOs were discovering, as the IUCN and WWF had already done, that by the late 1960s governments needed to be influenced, not only by the methods developed in the 1950s, but also by communication with the increasing number of influential and educated people who were concerned about environmental issues.

After its first meeting in Madrid in September 1970, SCOPE set up working groups on materials which might significantly alter the biosphere: man-made lakes; the feasibility of an international registry of chemical compounds; a planned system of global environmental monitoring (later known as Earthwatch); and environmental problems in developing countries. Four of these projects were supported by the Ford Foundation. The results of the three projects completed at the time were made available to the Stockholm Conference.[25]

The main road to Stockholm

The UN General Assembly resolution calling for a Conference on the Human Environment also asked the Secretary-General to consult appropriate NGOs and in his 1969 report to the General Assembly he made a number of suggestions about the representation of NGOs at the forthcoming preparatory meetings.[26] These and others were unanimously endorsed by the 1969 General Assembly which established the Stockholm Conference's Preparatory Committee.[27] This met for four sessions between 1970 and 1972 and was attended by a number of NGOs as Observers. Representatives of the IUCN and the International Society of Soil Science also participated in the intergovernmental Working Groups created to draft recommendations for presentation to the Conference.[28]

ICSU was also involved. In December 1970 the Secretary-General of the Conference, the Canadian Maurice Strong, asked SCOPE to prepare 'a report recommending the design, parameters, and technical organisation needed for a coherent global environmental monitoring system'.[29] ICSU was also involved through its Committee on Science and Technology in Developing Countries, which was concerned with the environmental impact of technology on developing countries. This had played a complementary role to ECOSOC's Advisory Committee on the Application of Science and Technology to Development. Such developments were helpful in persuading certain developing countries to take a more positive attitude to NGOs. They were also a sign of the growing preoccupation of the main (more political) UN system with problems of development/environment.

NGOs also played a role in rethinking North/South concerns in the context of environmental issues. The differing approaches of developed and developing countries at Stockholm had been reflected in the original commissioning resolution, which had expressed the hope that developing countries would 'derive particular benefit from the mobilisation of knowledge and experience about the problems of the human environment'.[30] This reflects the view at that time that environmental problems were predominantly the result of industrialisation and were not yet the concern of developing countries. Some of the possible clashes were ironed out through a conference at Founex in June 1971, when twenty-seven experts 'expanded the environmental agenda by forging a link between development and environment'.[31] In effect they argued that environmental problems had their origin in both poverty and industrialisation.

A further, major innovation for NGOs was the fact that Maurice Strong commissioned Dr Dubos in May 1971 to act as Chairman of a distinguished group of experts who would serve as advisers in preparing a report which was to

> ... reach out for the best advice available from the world's intellectual leaders in providing a conceptual framework for participants in the United Nations Conference and the general public as well. . . The only restraint on those who prepared the report was a request that they should not prejudge the work of governments at the United Nations Conference by proposing specific international agreements or actions – its main purpose being to provide background information relevant to official policy decisions.[32]

The restraint is worth noting since it illustrates a specific difference between what happened at Stockholm and what was to happen at Rio, where this restraint did *not* apply.

The final report incorporated the views of over seventy contributions made by this large committee of scientific and intellectual leaders from fifty-eight countries. The experts 'provided a great deal of invaluable guidance in the formulation of scientific issues, in suggesting rearrangement of material and in verifying or correcting factual points'.[33] The cost was met by the Albert Schweitzer Chair at Columbia University, the World Bank and the Ford Foundation.

At first glance this 'unique experiment', as Strong describes it, looks as though it had nothing to do with NGOs. But there were a number of interrelationships. First, an NGO, the International Institute for Environmental Affairs (founded in London and Washington in 1971 and renamed the International Institute for Environment and Development [IIED] in 1973), provided overall management of the process. Secondly, a number of the 152 experts consulted had connections with NGOs including ICSU, IUCN, the International Social Science Council (ISSC – set up, like ICSU and the IUCN, with the assistance of UNESCO in 1952), SCOPE, the International Bar Association, the International Union of Architects, the World Association of World Federalists, the World Congress of University Presidents, the World Federation of United Nations Associations and the Society for International Development (founded in Washington in 1957: it now has its headquarters in Rome).

NGOs at Stockholm

The Stockholm Conference was held on 5–16 June 1972. Representatives of 113 states (the Soviet Union and the East Europeans were not represented) attended the conference, as well as members of the UN Secretariat and other intergovernmental organisations, along with

> . . . 255 international and national non-governmental associations. . . . In addition to the NGOs, which were accorded official observer status to attend plenary or committee sessions of the Conference, several hundred other private groups – mostly local or national organisations concerned with ecology or with some aspect of the Conference agenda – participated in the Environment Forum, the Life Forum, or other non-official activities which went on at Stockholm during the period of the official intergovernmental meetings.[34]

The rules of procedure allowed NGOs to observe and speak at open plenary or committee sessions. Invitations to attend were sent both to the recognised NGOs and to NGOs that did not have consultative status with the United Nations through ECOSOC, setting a precedent for the 1992 Rio Summit. These were NGOs of a 'genuinely international character' which, in the judgement of the Secretary-General, were 'directly concerned with the subject matter of the Conference and could contribute to its objectives'.[35] Overall NGOs had more contact with the conference secretariat. Moreover, many of the consultant experts were members of NGOs such as ICSU, SCOPE, and the IUCN.

The alternative proceedings, arranged by the Swedish United Nations Association and the National Council of Swedish Youth and consisting of over 200 groups including the Environment Forum, provided another potential route by which NGOs could influence the conference. There were other counter-conferences, such as the Hog Farm Commune's night rally, attended by Maurice Strong, drawing attention to the need for a commercial whaling moratorium. A further influential experiment was the eight-page newspaper produced by the Friends of the Earth and the *Ecologist* which was delivered daily to conference and NGO delegates.[36]

One new NGO, the Friends of the Earth, came to the fore at Stockholm. This was one of the new more politically-oriented ecology action groups. It was founded in 1969 in the United States[37] by the former Executive Director of the well-established Sierra Club. Through his policy of taking legal action to challenge specific projects as harmful to the environment, he had led the US Internal Revenue Service to revoke the Sierra Club's tax-deductible status as a charity. Under US law, organisations which receive such status can only devote a limited part of their time and resources to influencing public policy. He therefore decided to form an established body 'to have as its specific purpose the task of waging political battles to protect the environment'. This organisation reflected the public mood and the 'environment joined peace and civil rights as one of a trilogy of issues that encompassed the fears and hopes of an emerging generation'.[38] By January 1971 Friends of the Earth had itself become internationalised through the participation in its proceedings of delegates from a number of major European countries. Its aims were 'to promote ... the conservation, restoration and rational use of the natural resources and beauty of the Earth'.[39] This internationalisation enabled it to be accepted onto the Roster of NGOs recognised by ECOSOC.

Not surprisingly a major dispute emerged at Stockholm over leadership between the influential old hybrid NGOs, like ICSU and the IUCN, and the new, more politicised NGOs such as Friends of the Earth. From this, as Feraru puts it, 'emerged the remarkable team of Barbara Ward (Lady Jackson) and Margaret Mead – who kept the "old" and "new" factions from a breach, and who also served as a bridge between the NGOs on the one hand, and government delegates and secretariat officials at Stockholm on the other'.[40]

The end result of Stockholm was a Declaration of Principles concerning the global environment, an Action Plan with 109 recommendations for governments and international bodies (significantly, *not* NGOs) and a resolution to the General Assembly asking for the establishment of a UN Environment Programme, with a Governing Council, a small secretariat and an environment fund financed by voluntary contributions. It also called for NGO collaboration with the United Nations. These proposals were subsequently discussed at ECOSOC and then approved by the General Assembly in December 1972 by 116 votes in favour and ten abstentions.[41] Maurice Strong was elected Executive Director of the UN Environment Programme (UNEP) by the General Assembly on the recommendation of the UN Secretary-General, and Nairobi was selected as the headquarters for the UNEP Secretariat, becoming the first Third World capital to host a major UN body.

An assessment

The NGOs involved in Stockholm, and certain of its preceding conferences, represented a variety of interests – religious, humanitarian, occupational and scientific. Ann Feraru attempted to measure the involvement of these in the context of participation, activity and peer rating.

> By all three measures, the International Union for the Conservation of Nature and Natural Resources (IUCN), the International Council of Scientific Unions (ICSU), and the Friends of the Earth were the most involved of the INGOs in UN environmental activities.[42]

She noted that the NGOs defined their role in terms of one or more of the following objectives – getting information, giving expert assistance, and lobbying and representation – and that these appraisals were accepted by high UN Secretariat officials. Observers from fifty-two international NGOs attended one or more of the four Preparatory Committee sessions. Some held unofficial meetings with delegates which enhanced their influence, and two, the IUCN and the International Society of Soil Science, had representatives on the Preparatory Committee's intergovernmental working groups on soil and conservation.

She suggested, however, that NGOs could have been more influential at Stockholm if NGO access to governments had not varied as widely as it did from country to country. A number of the main international associations noted that the job of lobbying governments was the responsibility of the national member organisations. This process does not seem to have been done with the coherence, appropriateness and persistence that was to be the case in Rio in 1992. Feraru just notes, with respect to the National Reports that each government was expected to submit, 'it is probable that some governments consulted or otherwise involved non-governmental associations – national and international – in the preparation of these reports'.[43]

The presence of the many members of the non-governmental community may, however, have been even more important for its subsequent 'information feedback to their home populations, their governments and their news media. This broadened participation affected not only the substance of conference rhetoric, but influenced public perceptions of the conference'.[44] Feraru's conclusion was that

> ... the INGOs that are likely to be listened to by the international secretariat are those that can help UNEP most – the

scientific experts and the opinion molders. The advice of the former groups, on what UNEP should do for scientific reasons, and of the others on what UNEP should do to get its constituencies' support is most likely to be accepted by the secretariat and transmitted through it to the formal UN decision-making organs, including the new Governing Council for Environmental Programs.[45]

These links have continued. What has changed is the increased influence of political pressure groups such as Friends of the Earth.

NGOs after Stockholm

After Stockholm, concerned NGOs held conferences in New York (while ECOSOC was meeting to discuss the Stockholm recommendations) and later at Geneva (at the time of the first meeting of UNEP) to discuss their own interrelationships and their future relationship with the new environmental secretariat. They set up the Environment Liaison Centre (ELC) in Nairobi in 1974 as a communication link with UNEP. The ELC also became a focus for NGO relations with the UN Centre for Human Settlements (HABITAT) set up in 1978 alongside UNEP in Nairobi. The ELC was supported by a number of major NGOs including the International Institute for Environment and Development, the International Council of Voluntary Agencies, the International Union of Architects, Friends of the Earth International and the International Union of Local Authorities. By 1981 it had almost two hundred member organisations and had gained Category II consultative status with ECOSOC. It published a quarterly bulletin which was distributed to 4,000 NGOs, the majority in developing countries.[46]

The early 1970s does seem to have been a turning point for NGOs dealing with the environment. As Burke has put it in a somewhat oversimplified way: 'In 1970 the environment as an issue was the preserve of scientists, government specialists and private enthusiasts. By 1980 it was an issue high on the political agenda of most nations.'[47] One reason was the activities of Greenpeace which was founded in 1971 'to redress the assault on the natural world by using peaceful direct action', in the first instance by sailing into a nuclear test zone. A further reason may well have been the greater visual impact of events caused by changing global communications patterns including the beginning of 'the switch in dominance from newspapers to television' which is thought to have taken place in the United Kingdom around the early to the mid-1970s.[48] However the change was not as strong as Burke suggested, since the WWF has been a successful advocate of conservation issues to the general public and an excellent fund raiser in the West from the early 1960s. The publication of Rachel Carson's *The Silent Spring* in 1963 and the Torrey Canyon disaster in 1967 were also seminal events.

The sort of change described can be illustrated by the moves made by Friends of the Earth in its post-Stockholm phase when it began to try to operate internationally at five levels, by creating a national constituency for international issues, working bilaterally with non-governmental (and, rarely, governmental) organisations, through the Environment Liaison Centre (ELC) in Nairobi on global environmental issues, through the European Environment Bureau on EEC issues and via the Friends of the Earth International network.[49]

Meanwhile the IUCN was continuing to adapt, not only because its Third World membership was increasing, but also because it needed to deal with the more development-oriented UNEP which, like UNESCO, would be willing to fund some of the IUCN's activities (others were funded by the WWF). It therefore began to issue a series of guidelines for development planning on particular topics, besides pressing UN bodies to become more aware of the ecological dimension of their activities. By 1977 it had revised its structure, recruited Maurice Strong to become Chairman and accepted UNEP funds to prepare a World Conservation Strategy.[50]

The influence of hybrid NGOs, in the context of UNEP, can be seen in the fact that by 1980 both the World Bank (a specialised agency) and the UN Development Programme (a UN special body) had agreed to the Declaration of Environmental Policies and Procedures Related to Economic Development (signed by eight multilateral development funding agencies). With this Declaration these institutions committed themselves to ensuring all their programmes and projects complied with the principles agreed at Stockholm. A new inter-agency mechanism, the Committee of International Development Institutions on the Environment, was created to assure its implementation.[51]

NGOs and Rio, 1992

In 1982, the tenth anniversary of the Stockholm Conference, the ELC counted 2,230 environmental NGOs in developing countries (60 per cent formed after 1972), and 13,000 in developed countries (30 per cent formed after 1972).[52] There was also, as a result of world-wide economic difficulties, a relative decline in government support for international environmental cooperation.[53]

In the early 1980s when North/South relations were in the doldrums, UNEP was one of the few forums that successfully maintained North/South cooperation. Using the scientific expertise of ICSU, the IUCN and WWF, a long-standing tradition started by UNESCO, UNEP launched the World Conservation Strategy in March 1980, which was subsequently welcomed by the General Assembly. The consensus resolution urged all governments and other bodies to take it into account.[54] One commentator notes that 'This high-level policy statement was one of the first to stress sustainability, especially of natural life-support systems in the context of supporting human needs'.[55] This was seen as an endorsement of a new approach which focused not only on the problem of sustainability in developing countries but also that of over-consumption in others. Environmental NGOs were now as closely involved with the main UN system as they were with certain specialised agencies.

The new Southern interest in conservation issues was manifested by the adoption of the World Charter for Nature, an initiative by Zaïre, aimed at protecting animals and plants and their environment through proclaiming principles of conservation.[56] The increased mainstream political concern over environmental problems was illustrated again in 1984 when General Assembly members decided to issue an annual list of banned hazardous chemicals and unsafe pharmaceutical products. The resolution, which specifically made known its appreciation of NGO activity in obtaining appropriate information, was adopted by 147-1 (United States).[57]

The Brundtland Report, 1987

Thinking about North/South issues (and the fact that they were dynamically interlinked) had already been highlighted by the 1980 Brandt Report on international development.[58] This was followed by the formation of the World Commission on Environment and Development which was welcomed by the General Assembly at the end of 1983.[59] Mrs Brundtland had been asked by the Secretary-General to chair the Commission and to prepare a report which was to formulate a global agenda for change.

While the report was being compiled, an overview of the role and contribution of NGOs to environment and development action at the national and international level was given in a report to the Commission by the Environment Liaison Centre. Brundtland subsequently noted that NGOs had played an indispensable role since Stockholm in

... identifying risks, in assessing environmental impacts and designing and implementing measures to deal with them, and in maintaining the high degree of public and political interest required as a basis for action. Several international NGOs have produced significant reports on the status of and prospects for the global environment and natural resource base.[60]

The Brundtland Report, *Our Common Future*, went on to point out that many coalitions of NGOs were now active. These included regional groups providing networks linking environment and development NGOs, and also a number of regional and global coalitions on critical issues such as pesticides, toxic chemicals, acid rain, seeds, genetic resources and development assistance. A global network for information exchange provided through the ELC now had 230 NGO member groups, the majority being from developing countries. Only a few, however, dealt on a broad basis with both environment and development issues. One was the International Institute for Environment and Development which had been a pioneer of the conceptual basis for the environment/development linkage. The Brundtland Report recommended that NGOs should give a high priority to networking on development cooperation projects. It also stated that NGOs and private and community groups could often provide an efficient and effective alternative to public agencies in delivering programmes and projects. The Commission ended by suggesting that international NGOs needed substantially increased financial support.

As a result of the balance between its contributors, the Brundtland Report managed to cross the North/South gap more effectively than had *Only One Earth* in 1971, though this certainly did not mean that a balance had been achieved in terms of the influence of NGOs from the North and South. It was also clear that Brundtland considered NGOs to be extremely important, and that their influence should be furthered at country and global levels. It is worth noting that the attitudes to NGOs outlined in the report have not, on the whole, been the subject of critical comment, though the report has been criticised on a number of other grounds, including the fact that some consider that it failed to do justice to the poor and dispossessed.[61]

The increasing influence of NGOs in the 1980s

ICSU and the IUCN continued to maintain their strong influence on UN bodies in the period after Brundtland. As has already been noted, both the IUCN and the WWF (which achieved 3 million members during the 1980s) helped UNEP prepare the World Conservation Strategy. The IUCN was also asked by Maurice Strong to develop international conservation law.[62] Meanwhile ICSU played a major role as the adviser to another UN specialised agency, the World Meterological Organisation (WMO), and UNEP in setting up the Intergovernmental Panel on Climate Change in 1988 charged with assessing the magnitude of the climate change problem and recommending appropriate responses. They also began to collaborate with the World Resources Institute (WRI), a new policy and research organisation which had been founded in 1982. Strategically placed in Washington DC, WRI absorbed the Washington office of the IIED in 1988.

ICSU, the IUCN and the WWF were, increasingly, joined by other NGOs who took on some or many of a similar range of tasks, including attempts to change political attitudes (at domestic and/or regional and/or international levels) and disseminating research findings. The newer tasks of shifting public attitudes and 'orchestrating pressure' on states, companies and public opinion, often, in the first place, through increasing the membership and finances of individual organisations, were also much in evidence.[63] In the United States long-standing domestically-oriented environmental pressure groups such as the Sierra Club, the National Audubon Society, the Wilderness Society and the National Wildlife Federation increased their membership from 4 million in 1981 to 11 million in 1990. Their combined revenues came to over $300 million.[64] Further organisations with scientific legal expertise set up in the 1960s and 1970s were the Environmental Defense Fund (1967) and the National Resources Defense Council (1970). In the 1980s, however, the fastest growing affiliate of an international NGO in the United States was a relatively new organisation – Greenpeace USA.

A number of these United States NGOs were able to exercise pressure on World Bank environmental policies during the 1980s. They were in a position to be particularly effective, both because the United States was the largest shareholder of the Bank and because they knew how to lobby Congress. Their campaign, which began in 1983, was led by the National Wildlife Federation and the National Resources Defence Council. By 1985 both were cooperating across the North/South divide with Brazilian NGOs, and using the national media to their advantage. A turning point was reached in 1987, when the President of the World Bank announced major changes in World Bank environmental policy.[65]

The value of coordination was apparent even on a national level. A formal committee of the heads of twenty major US NGOs was set up as early as 1983. This agreed to a joint media campaign on six major environmental issues at the G7 Summit at Houston in 1990. They were joined by more than thirty NGO leaders representing 150 groups in fourteen countries who helped make sure the case was heard. 'Press accounts credit the NGOs with keeping the environment on the agenda of the Summit, for the second year running, against the express wishes of the United States Government'.[66]

This domestic expansion and linkage with other national groups, was also reflected on an international level. 'From five international affiliates in the late 1970s, Greenpeace International' had 'become a federation of twenty national organisations, all committed to an overarching international programme with more than 3.3 million members'.[67] By the end of the 1980s Greenpeace (dealing with maritime issues) had become as influential as the organisation founded two years before them, in 1969, the Friends of the Earth. In their interesting study of the influence of Greenpeace on the workings of the London Dumping Convention, Stairs and Taylor note that:

> By the close of the '80s environmental groups such as Greenpeace and their land oriented equivalents (such as FOE, World Wildlife Fund, The Sierra Club etc) had grown into million-dollar, sophisticated multinational operations capable of research, political lobbying, effective media communication and in the case of Greenpeace, active policing on behalf of the environment.[68]

They suggest that Greenpeace, which had had observer status at meetings of the parties to the Convention since the early 1980s, was able to participate and contribute in five ways – through a detailed critical review of scientific justifications for dumping; linguistic aid to non-English speakers within the debating process; scientific and technical advice to 'friendly states' willing to take the floor on key issues, including the drafting of resolutions; willingness to publicise incidents where regulations had been broken; and carrying out primary scientific work.

The independent author of this piece (Taylor) makes a telling point on the way influence can be lost.

> NGOs need to take great care over their own internal dynamic with regard to motivation and policy. As NGOs grow to multinational million-dollar operations and are dependent upon public funding and media coverage of issues, certain inflexibilities and 'hidden agendas' can develop. For example, Greenpeace evolved a policy of world-wide prohibition of sewage

dumping very largely based on the agenda of North Sea campaigners. The transference of this policy to, for example, coastal Malaysia via the LDC [London Dumping Convention], without adequate research, could lead to environmental losses rather than gains – there, sewage is largely uncontaminated by industry, and coastal discharges threaten human health and wildlife: sea dumping could be justified if the costs of land treatment were unrealistic. On this issue, ethnocentrism, and campaign simplicity, led to an uncompromising stand.[69]

The writers go on to argue that legitimacy of governmental decision-making and the quality of decisions are enhanced by NGO participation. It also fosters public education and can increase popular support. 'The influence of NGOs lies in their ability to mobilize popular opinion and persuade decision-makers. If they lose touch with the public, or with the facts, they soon fail'.[70] There is also the important question of who they represent and how to determine public interest. Some have active memberships who participate in policy making, others are run by their staff.

As the environmental movement developed internationally, Northern NGOs began to form alliances across national boundaries involving Third World colleagues. If the Environment Liaison Centre is to be believed, there were about 900 Southern environmental NGOs before 1972; these had increased to 2,230 by 1982.[71] It has been suggested that environmental advocacy groups, women's rights activists and community development groups all emerged in Asia in the late 1970s and early 1980s, following in the footsteps of first generation civil liberties organisations which emerged in the early 1970s.[72] Relevant environmental bodies include the Pesticide Action Network and the Third World Network, both now with worldwide connections and both founded in Malaysia, in, respectively, 1982 and 1984. As Bramble and Porter have noted:

These have greatly broadened the range of subjects on the international environmental agenda – from wildlife conservation and endangered species to rural development and community decision-making; free trade and patenting of biological materials; technology transformation and curbs on multinational corporations; external debt and terms of trade; structural adjustment and 'conditionality'. ... NGOs do not always agree on these tough issues that are central to North-South cooperation. But the dialogue and negotiations among NGOs themselves offer a path for international problem solving that may be a good alternative to the often-paralysed intergovernmental forums.[73]

The main road to Rio

In December 1989, the General Assembly unanimously decided to convene a UN Conference on Environment and Development (UNCED) and to establish a Preparatory Committee.[74] Once again the UN Secretary-General designated Maurice Strong to head an *ad hoc* secretariat to support the Preparatory Committee. ICSU and the IUCN were not specifically mentioned, as they had been in the resolution deciding to convene the Stockholm Conference, but concerned NGOs were called upon to help in the preparatory process. Not surprisingly, many of Maurice Strong's actions were based on his experience in the run-up to Stockholm.

The IUCN's involvement in the immediate preparations for Rio began in a major way in 1990 when Ambassador Tommy Koh, Chairman of the Preparatory Committee for Rio, addressed the 18th session of the IUCN General Assembly and asked for the Union's input and assistance. Subsequently IUCN staff worked with Maurice Strong and his team in drafting the final conference document, Agenda 21. They contributed, in particular, to the sections on biodiversity,[75] forests, oceans and seas, population and resources, environmental education and environmental law.

The following session of UNEP in May 1991 was attended by eleven international NGOs as observers. It decided *inter alia* to hold a special session of the Governing Council in February 1992. At this (attended by fourteen international NGOs as observers), Maurice Strong noted that the core documentation for UNCED consisted of proposals for Agenda 21 which addressed 100 or so programmes that were neither purely environmental nor developmental. Issues of finance also loomed large. The Conference had to be seen as 'the beginning of a global partnership and a new phase of development and environment cooperation'.[76] Those at the session noted the second edition of the World Conservation Strategy, recently published by IUCN/UNEP/WWF: *Caring for the Earth: A Strategy for Sustainable Living* (it was hoped that the Executive Director would bring the Strategy to the attention of delegations at UNCED). In February 1992 at the Fourth World Congress on Parks and Protected Areas in Venezuela, a related document, *The Global Biodiversity Strategy*, prepared by the IUCN in collaboration with UNEP and the WRI, was finally released.

Meanwhile the official Preparatory Committees were continuing. The First and Second proved important in the context of the representation and participation of NGOs at the Summit. As we see in Chapter 2, at the first session Decision 1/1 was taken which, as at Stockholm, allowed concerned NGOs to attend as long as they were directly interested in the matters discussed at the Conference, even if they were not in consultative status with ECOSOC. The Decision also highlighted the need to ensure equitable representation in the preparatory process of NGOs from developed and developing countries, and from all regions, as well as to ensure a fair balance between NGOs with an environmental focus and those with a developmental focus, and to encourage the participation of scientific organisations. This was followed by Decision 2/1 which requested the Secretary-General to invite a number of groups to the forthcoming conference including

> ... all non-governmental organisations accredited to participate in the work of the Preparatory Committee by the conclusion of its fourth session; those organisations should receive invitations to participate as observers at the Conference.[77]

The NGOs with official consultative status at the Preparatory Committees for UNCED were overwhelmingly Northern. As Craig Murphy points out,

> ... while a diverse and multi-vocal chorus of NGOs could be heard alongside all the UNCED preparations, those NGOs with official consultative status at the initial meetings [the Preparatory Committees] included only Northern environmental groups and lobbyists for the older industries who were initially the most resistant to the industrial policies needed for a new world order in which the leading sectors would be less destructive to the environment, and were likely to be the industries producing environmentally improved products.[78]

Interestingly the Southern position on this question leaned towards the positive. The South Centre (the follow-up office of the South Commission) noted in its strategy document for UNCED that 'the countries of the South should strengthen their links with NGOs from the South'.[79]

In a different area, the Fourth Preparatory Committee seems to have been particularly important in the context of women's issues. Non-governmental women's organisations used the lobbying opportunities available there and, in so doing, transformed

> Agenda 21 from a neutral document with little sense of women's distinctive problems to one which is by and large women-friendly, with many injunctions to governments to support local women's groups involvement in managing environment and development, all in the course of four weeks of negotiations at PrepCom IV.[80]

A number of independent, related conferences were also held. On the main non-governmental side, these included an ICSU meeting and a women's meeting in Vienna in November 1991 as well as a major conference in Paris in December 1991 with 'particular efforts being made to secure representation of groups from the South and, within the South, of those from subnational and regional organisations who were closer to the "grassroots"'.[81]

A whole range of other organisations (not necessarily to be classed as NGOs) also met representing *inter alia* the business community, including the influential Business Council for Sustainable Development (a group of forty-eight top executives of multinational companies founded in 1991) and what have been called pseudo-NGOs, such as the Asbestos Institute of Canada, besides representatives of youth and trade unions.[82] Some coordination was provided by the Centre for Our Common Future, a voluntary agency created to follow up Brundtland through its reports of activities and its system of 'working partners', which by 1992 included 198 institutes and coordinating groups of NGOs.[83]

NGOs at Rio

The Rio conference held from 3–14 June 1992 was attended by 178 countries as well as representatives of over 650 NGOs. In his opening speech, the UN Secretary-General, Boutros Boutros-Ghali, paid special tribute to the non-governmental community, arguing that they should have a critical role in the follow-up activities. Maurice Strong noted that no international conference of governments had enjoyed a broader range of participation and greater contributions from NGOs than this one 'and I salute them for this'.[84] It should be noted that the President of the IUCN, Martin Holdgate, also addressed the plenary session of governments. He stressed the need for new partnerships in the pursuit of sustainable development besides emphasising the IUCN's unique potential to contribute in this area.[85]

The Conference produced the Rio Declaration of Principles, the Convention on Climate Change, the Convention on Biological Diversity, a set of forest principles and Agenda 21. The Agenda 'was intended to serve as a kind of road map pointing the direction toward sustainable development'.

It represents an ambitious effort to provide recommendations across the entire spectrum of environment, development, and social issues confronting mankind today. In terms of social and economic issues, it addresses poverty, overconsumption and production, population and human development problems.[86]

There were also repeated calls for the overhaul of the main financial institutions particularly on behalf of Third World NGOs. Northern and Southern states, like many NGOs, were both divided and aware that they had many common tasks on which they might become partners.[87]

Although NGOs were mentioned in other parts of Agenda 21, it was in Chapter 27, on 'Strengthening the Role of Non-Governmental Organisations: Partners for Sustainable Development', that they received most attention. This noted the vital role of NGOs in participatory democracy and the fact that their credibility lay in the responsible and constructive role they played in society. The community of NGOs offered a global network that should be tapped. The objectives set out included the following:

– mechanisms should be developed by society, governments and international bodies to allow NGOs to play a responsible and effective partnership role;
– the United Nations and governments should review formal procedures and mechanisms for involving NGOs at all levels from policy making and decision-making to implementation;
– a mutually productive dialogue should take place at the national level between all governments and NGOs; and,
– governments and official bodies should promote NGO participation in the conception, establishment and evaluation of official mechanisms and formal procedures for the review of the implementation of Agenda 21 at all levels.[88]

In his final speech to the Conference, Maurice Strong noted that intergovernmental and non-governmental organisations 'had contributed so much to our work, the Global Forum [to which the IUCN also contributed] especially'. He added:

We must also expand the participatory process that has meant so much to us here – participation of people through non-governmental organisations in the implementation of Agenda 21, and indeed in the United Nations itself. I believe we need to review entirely the system of arrangements within the United Nations for greater participation of these organisations.[89]

This was followed up, in part, in the proposed revisions to the UN medium-term plan for 1992–7, which suggested that the objectives of Agenda 21 remained the basis of the work of the secretariat in its effort to assist governments, in concert with UN agencies, NGOs and others, in realising the benefits of the Rio outcome. In addition, UNEP was mandated to empower major groups including women and NGOs for environmental action. This was to be done by strengthening the role of formal NGOs and specialised professional groups; establishing procedures and mechanisms for consultation, review and cooperation of NGOs in the implementation of Agenda 21; forging partnerships with entrepreneurs in the business community to embrace the concept of stewardship; and establishing links and effective partnerships with the scientific and technological community.[90]

An assessment

The influence of NGOs at Rio was similar to, but overall much more extensive than seems to have been the case at Stockholm. The influence of the knowledge-based, mainstream, heavyweight organisations such as the IUCN and ICSU was maintained. Once again, they were able to shape both Agenda 21 and also the two Conventions on climate change and biodiversity. As with Stockholm, they were involved in the planning process from the beginning. Newcomers of their ilk, such as the WRI, were also influential. Networking remained one key to influence: it is relevant that the WRI, as has already been noted, worked with the IUCN and UNEP to produce the Global Biodiversity Strategy.

It is more difficult to assess the overall influence of the wide variety of NGOs who turned up for the conference. One assessment states:

> Other important actors in the UNCED process were the non-governmental organisations ... However, it is still unknown how effective they proved in the UNCED process. In the view of two knowledgeable observers of the UNCED process, the NGOs spent more time networking with one another than specifically influencing the negotiations and the wording of specific texts. This was particularly so in the Rio Earth Summit itself, where many NGOs largely participated in a companion event to the Earth Summit, the Global Forum, the site of more than 600 exhibition booths where NGOs, International Organisations, and others exchanged views and in some cases drafted 'alternative treaties' in a process quite separate from the UNCED negotiations. Yet it must be said that the international NGO networking that took place during much of the UNCED process may well prove to be a key ingredient in ensuring successful implementation, at the national level, of the far-reaching measures adopted in Rio.[91]

The conventional view concerning the input of NGOs at the conference was put by James Speth, then Director of the WRI:

... Rio, signaled the rise of an increasingly powerful group in international diplomacy: non-governmental organisations (NGOs). The Earth Summit brought together an international community of scientists, policy experts, business groups, and activists representing a wide array of interests. Although far from cohesive themselves, NGOs worked together surprisingly well throughout the summit process, lobbying and educating delegates, helping draft agreements, and communicating with the 9,000 journalists who covered Rio.[92]

The pointer to future influence, which links with the change in Agenda 21 achieved by women's groups at the Fourth Preparatory Committee, may have been provided by Thomas Harding, director of a small non-profit media organisation. He wrote in September 1993:

One of the few generally agreed-upon positive outcomes from the Earth Summit in Rio was that environmental groups became more sensitive to integrating social awareness into their ecological thinking. This occurred mainly as a result of pressure from third world groups concerned that northern environmentalists were setting the environment before development issues, as well as from women's groups angry that reproductive rights were being placed below consumption issues in the debate over population.[93]

He also pointed to the rise of the environmental justice movement in the United States in the early 1980s, as communities realised that they were the target of toxic dumping and the placement of hazardous industries. The concerns of resource users (miners, fishermen, loggers etc.) and those concerned with environmental justice had to be taken into account if environmental groups were to avoid attack.

This thinking on one radical edge chimed in with the new emphasis being placed on those representing 'civil society' within the United Nations. Rowlands, for instance, notes that,

the importance of 'civil society' was demonstrated at UNCED ... Rio will be remembered for showing that governments alone cannot address the environmental crisis. Politicians are beginning to accept they cannot have a decision-making monopoly on these issues.[94]

The final assessment of the influence of NGOs at Rio is likely to be complex: it is too early to take more than a preliminary view. There is however, no doubt that any overall assessment would, as at Stockholm, have to give pride of place, once again to ICSU and the IUCN. A further candidate could be the WRI.

NGOs after Rio

The continuing involvement of the IUCN and ICSU remained noticeable after Rio. The IUCN contributed to UNEP task forces on technical aspects of the Biodiversity Convention, and on how countries could prepare national biodiversity plans. As its 1992 Annual Report pointed out, 'As the Convention enters into force, the IUCN is uniquely placed to provide professional support to the Parties to the Convention and their Secretariat'.[95] UNEP continued to rely heavily on both. In its June 1993 report to the new Commission on Sustainable Development, UNEP noted that it was cooperating with UNESCO and ICSU in the development of the Global Climate Observing System. It was also exploring the development of a Global Terrestrial Observing System to help determine the effects of climate change on terrestrial ecosystems in cooperation with the FAO, WMO, UNESCO and the IUCN. It also drew attention to the World Conservation Monitoring Centre, a collaborative organisation among UNEP, WWF, the IUCN and the WRI which would continue to provide assessments of the distribution and abundance of the world's species.[96]

In December 1992, the UN General Assembly requested ECOSOC to set up a high-level Commission on Sustainable Development (CSD), as a functional commission of ECOSOC, in order to ensure the effective follow-up of UNCED. The resolution stated that the new Commission's rules of procedure 'should allow its members to benefit from the expertise and competence of relevant intergovernmental and non-governmental organisations'.[97] The following month the UN Secretary-General put out a report on the proposed rules of procedure for the CSD.[98] He noted that UNCED had been characterised by 'unprecedented involvement' of NGOs. He recommended that the CSD encourage participation of NGOs including those dealing with industry and business and the scientific communities. He also recommended that procedures should be established for an expanded role for NGOs, including those related to major groups, with accreditation based on the procedures used for the conference.[99] Subsequently the CSD decided at its first organisational session in February 1993 that it would determine ways to consider reports and contributions from entities outside the UN system, including non-governmental organisations.[100]

In February 1993 ECOSOC decided that NGOs in consultative status with ECOSOC, any NGO accredited to participate in UNCED and others considering themselves relevant and competent in areas pertaining to the work of the Commission who had gained ECOSOC approval could be accredited to the first session of CSD in June 1993.[101] Ultimately some 350 NGOs participated. Their impact continues to be based, as so often before, on the expertise they can contribute. The UN Secretary-General noted in February 1994,[102] in the context of an Open-Ended Working Group of the CSD, that most of the work on national environmental funds had been done by NGOs such as the WWF, Nature Conservancy and Conservation International. Other contributions had come from bilateral technical programmes and the Global Environment Facility.[103] NGOs are now in the process of trying to ensure that they maintain appropriate relations with this Facility (as well as the CSD) which held its first Council meeting in July 1994.

Conclusions

This chapter has concentrated on four particular types of NGOs: the well-established scientific, hybrid NGOs, ICSU and the IUCN plus the latter's fundraiser and populariser the WWF; secondly, the two other, high-status, high-expertise NGOs, the IIED and the WRI; thirdly, the major international 'political' NGOs such as Friends of the Earth and Greenpeace; and lastly, some influential national NGOs such as the United States Sierra Club. It has tried to see how and why they came into being and in what ways they have managed to influence global environmental politics. Their interrelationships and capacity for networking are both close and complex, as can be illustrated by the fact that Friends of the Earth, Greenpeace and the IIED are all NGO members of the IUCN.

The major NGOs appear to have influenced global environmental politics in two important ways. The first relates to their contribution to the building up of an accessible, international knowledge base which, as the President of ICSU pointed out in 1972, is a prerequisite for taking appropriate internationally agreed action.[104] The second relates to their abilities to influence major UN bodies (all run by governments) or governments separately to take the appropriate actions. The tactics involved in promoting the second often vary from institution to institution, from government to government and from decade to decade.

The first crucial step after the Second World War was taken by Julian Huxley who realised that governments and the international community, represented by UNESCO, needed to involve the world scientific community, represented by hybrid NGOs with an inheritance from the system of scientific unions, in the new UN institutions. ICSU and the IUCN dominated the discussion of environmental issues in the UN system, especially the specialised agencies, from the late 1940s to the late 1960s. The IUCN also, through its initiative in setting up the WWF in 1961 to popularise and to raise funds for environmental work (which had previously been, in part, provided by UNESCO), showed the way to the more political groups such as the Friends of the Earth and Greenpeace which were set up in the context of the first major UN environmental conference at Stockholm in 1972.

The burgeoning interest in environmental issues from the 1970s onwards owed much to changes in world-wide communication patterns, rethinking by governments (helped by ICSU and the IUCN) and the increasing numbers of educated and influential people interested in these subjects. There was, moreover, growing pressure from the increasingly powerful Northern NGOs as well as the slow but persistent development of Southern NGOs (more than 2,200 in 1982). Nonetheless, certain Northern NGOs began to lose support in the mid-1990s. Greenpeace, for instance, decided to cut its international staff by one-tenth at the end of 1994. This may presage a decline in the resources available to some of the major NGOs.

These processes were accelerated in the context of the scientific and political preparations for the 1992 Rio Summit. ICSU and the IUCN, joined by the IIED and WRI, continued to ensure that the interface between scientific knowledge and its development was transmitted into the main UN system while major, more political, NGOs (including some from the South) exerted pressure on governments either directly or indirectly. Interestingly this included pressure to reform/change UN institutions, most notably the World Bank.

The current situation was succinctly described by the UN Under-Secretary-General for Policy Coordination and Sustainable Development, Nitin Desai.[105] He stated:

> NGOs and, more generally, organisations of the civil society no longer simply have a 'consumer relationship' with the United Nations. They have increasingly assumed the role of promoters of new ideas, they have alerted the international community to emerging issues, and they have developed expertise and talent, which, in an increasing number of areas, have become vital to the work of the United Nations both at the policy and operational levels. If we recall the process of the preparations for the Earth Summit, we can see very clearly that their contributions were essential to the shaping of the agenda, to the process of public mobilisation around the concept of sustainable development, and to the building of the political commitments which made the adoption of the Rio Declaration and Agenda 21 possible.

The newer NGOs are, in fact, now doing what ICSU and the IUCN have been doing since they joined forces with UNESCO in the late 1940s.

NOTES

1. This means both NGOs exclusively concerned with the environment, and others concerned with questions (e.g. human rights) with an environmental dimension.
2. J. Eric Smith, 'The Role of Special Purpose and Nongovernmental Organizations in the Environmental Crisis', *International Organization*, vol. 26 no. 2, spring 1972, p. 306.
3. *Ibid.*, p. 306.
4. *Ibid.*, emphasis added.
5. Julian Huxley, *Memories II* (London: Penguin Books, 1978), p. 17. Professor Needham was a leading British biologist.
6. *Ibid.*, p. 56.
7. A detailed history of the origins and evolution of the IUCN is given in Chapter 3 of Robert Boardman, *International Organisation and the Conservation of Nature* (London: Macmillan, 1981), pp. 25–40.
8. Lynton Keith Caldwell, *International Environmental Policy Emergence and Dimensions* (Durham, NC: Duke University Press, 1984), pp. 36–7.
9. Resolution 18.1 of the 18th session of the General Assembly of the IUCN, Perth, 28 November–5 December 1990.
10. See Boardman, *op. cit.*, p. 40.
11. See Huxley, *op. cit.*, pp. 18 and 56.
12. See Boardman, *op. cit.*, p. 45.
13. See Smith, *op. cit.*, pp. 309–13.
14. See Caldwell, *op. cit.*, p. 39.
15. See Boardman, *op. cit.*, p. 43 and, for more detail, pp. 51–2.
16. UN General Assembly Resolution 1831(XVII) of 18 December 1962.
17. Boardman, *op. cit.*, pp. 54 and 100.
18. *Ibid.*, pp. 108–9.
19. UN General Assembly Resolution 2398(XXIII) of 3 December 1968.
20. See Smith, *op. cit.*, p. 314. For more details on the Swedish initiative, see pp. 154–5 of Olle Dahlen, 'A Governmental Response to Pressure Groups - The Case of Sweden' in Peter Willetts (ed.), *Pressure Groups in the Global System* (London: Pinter, 1982).
21. See Boardman, *op. cit.*, p. 64–5.
22. *Ibid.*, p. 65.
23. See Caldwell, *op. cit.*, p. 268.
24. See Smith, *op. cit.*, pp. 316–17, brackets in the original but emphasis added. SCOPE was originally the 'Special Committee . . .' and later became the 'Scientific Committee . . .'
25. *Ibid.*, p. 318.
26. *Problems of the Human Environment. Report of the Secretary-General*, UN doc. E/4667 of 26 May 1969.
27. UN General Assembly Resolution 2581(XXIV) of 15 December 1969.
28. Anne Thompson Feraru, 'Transnational Political Interests and the Global Environment', *International Organization*, vol. 28, no. 1, winter 1974, pp. 34 and 43.
29. See Smith, *op. cit.*, p. 318.

30. Resolution 2398(XXIII), *op. cit.* Almost the same wording appears in E/4667, *op. cit.*, p. 25, para. 88(d).
31. Marc Williams, 'Rearticulating the Third World Coalition: the role of the environmental agenda', *Third World Quarterly*, vol. 14, no. 1, 1993, p. 17.
32. Barbara Ward and René Dubos, *Only One Earth: The Care and Maintenance of a Small Planet* (London: Penguin Books, 1972), pp. 9–10.
33. *Ibid.*, p. 11.
34. See Feraru, *op. cit.*, p. 35. There does not seem to be general agreement on the number of NGO observers at the Stockholm Conference. While Feraru gives a figure of 255, Willetts gives 298. See Peter Willetts, 'The Pattern of Conferences', in Paul Taylor and A. J. R. Groom (eds), *Global Issues in the United Nations Framework* (London: Macmillan, 1989), p. 52.
35. UN doc. A/CONF.48/PC.11 of 30 July, 1971, p. 65, which was finally endorsed by General Assembly Resolution 2850(XXVI) of 20 Dec 1971.
36. See pp. 116–17 of Tom Burke, 'Friends of the Earth and the Conservation of Resources' in Peter Willetts (ed.), *Pressure Groups. . .*
37. This account is taken from Tom Burke, *op. cit.*, pp. 105–24.
38. *Ibid.*, See p. 106.
39. *Ibid.*, p. 107.
40. Feraru, *op. cit.*, p. 49.
41. UN General Assembly Resolution 2997(XXVII) of 15 December 1972.
42. Feraru, *op. cit.*, p. 37.
43. *Ibid.*, p. 47.
44. Caldwell, *op. cit.*, p. 57.
45. Feraru, *op. cit.*, pp. 53–4.
46. See Willetts (ed.), *Pressure Groups . . .*, p. 117.
47. *Ibid.*, p. 110.
48. Jonathan Benthall, *Disasters, relief and the media* (London: I. B. Tauris, 1993), p. 201.
49. See Willetts (ed.), *Pressure groups . . .*, p. 114.
50. See Boardman, *op. cit.*, pp. 114 and 123.
51. Peter S. Thacher, 'The Role of the United Nations' in Andrew Hurrell and Benedict Kingsbury (eds), *The International Politics of the Environment* (Oxford: Clarendon Press, 1992), pp. 190–2.
52. See Caldwell, *op. cit.*, p. 265.
53. *Ibid.*, p. 278.
54. UN General Assembly Resolution 35/74 of 5 December 1980, paragraph 9.
55. See Thacher, *op. cit.*, p. 189.
56. UN General Assembly Resolution 37/7 of 28 October 1982, passed by a vote of 111 in favour to 1 against (USA) with 18 abstentions.
57. UN General Assembly Resolution 39/229, 'Protection against products harmful to health and the environment', of 18 December 1984, passed by a vote of 147 in favour to 1 against (USA).
58. *North-South: A programme for survival. Report of the Independent Commission on International Development Issues* (London and Sydney: Pan Books and Cambridge, MA: MIT Press, 1980).
59. UN General Assembly Resolution 38/161 of 19 December 1983 welcomed the establishment of the Brundtland Commission and Resolution 42/197 of 11 December 1987 welcomed the report and decided to transmit it to all governments.
60. World Commission on Environment and Development (WCED), *Our Common Future* (Oxford University Press, 1987), pp. 326–7.
61. Peter Doran, 'The Earth Summit (UNCED)', *Paradigms*, vol. 7, no. 1, Summer 1993, p. 58. For a critique of ideas on sustainable development see also

Craig N. Murphy, 'The State of the United Nations: 1992', *ACUNS Reports and Papers 1992*, no. 3, pp. 52–7.

62. *Ibid.*, p. 55.
63. See Hurrell and Kingsbury (eds), *op. cit.*, p. 20.
64. Barbara J. Bramble and Gareth Porter, 'NGOs and the Making of US Policy' in Hurrell and Kingsbury (eds), *op. cit.*, p. 317.
65. For a detailed account of the pressures exerted see Bramble and Porter, *Ibid.*, pp. 325–336. See also Seamus Cleary, Chapter 3 of current volume, and Philippe le Prestre, *The World Bank and the Environmental Challenge* (London: Associated University Presses, 1989).
66. *Ibid.*, p. 313.
67. *Ibid.*, p. 317.
68. Kevin Stairs and Peter Taylor, 'Non-Governmental Organizations and the Legal Protection of the Oceans: A Case Study' in Hurrell and Kingsbury (eds), *op. cit.*, p. 113.
69. *Ibid.*, pp. 133–4.
70. *Ibid.*, p. 135.
71. See Caldwell, *op. cit.*, p. 265.
72. Sidney Jones, 'The Organic Growth Asian NGOs have come into their own', *Far Eastern Economic Review*, 17 June 1993, p. 23. See also the Introduction in Thomas Princen and Matthias Finger (eds), *Environmental NGOs in World Politics: Linking the local and the global* (London: Routledge, 1994).
73. See Bramble and Porter, in Hurrell and Kingsbury (eds), *op. cit.*, p. 322.
74. UN General Assembly Resolution 44/228 of 22 December 1989.
75. IUCN was the first body to draft a biodiversity convention in the mid-1980s. These ideas were built on by UNEP after 1987 with the help of both FAO and UNESCO. See *1992 Annual Report IUCN*, Gland, Switzerland, p. 10. See also Shanna L. Halpern, 'The United Nations Conference on Environment and Development: Process and Documentation', *ACUNS Reports and Papers*, no. 2, 1993, p. 26.
76. UNEP Report of the Governing Council on the work of its third special session, 3–5 February 1992, *GAOR 47th session, supplement no. 25*, p. 8.
77. Decision 1/1 adopted on 14 August 1990 is given in *Report of the Preparatory Committee for the United Nations Conference on Environment and Development*, UN doc. A/45/46, pp. 22–3. Decision 2/1 adopted on 18 March 1991 is given in the report on the Preparatory Committee's second session, UN doc. A/46/48, pp. 21–2. See Appendix B.
78. See Murphy, *op. cit.*, pp. 58–9.
79. *Environment and Development Towards a Common Strategy of the South in the UNCED Negotiations and Beyond*, The South Centre, Geneva (1991), p. v.
80. 'UNCED, its "Stakeholders", and the post-UNCED process', unpublished paper, Jacqueline Roddick, Institute of Latin American Studies, University of Glasgow, p. 5.
81. *Ibid.*, p. 4.
82. Ian H. Rowlands, 'Environment and Development: The Post-UNCED Agenda', *Millennium*, vol. 21, no. 2, pp. 217–8.
83. See Roddick, *op. cit.*, p. 4.
84. *Report of the United Nations Conference on Environment and Development*, vol. IV, A/CONF.151/26 (Vol. IV), 28 September 1992, p. 50.
85. *1992 Annual Report IUCN*, *op cit.*, p. 10.
86. Biliana Cicin-Sain and Robert W. Knecht, 'Implications of the Earth Summit for Ocean and Coastal Governance', *Ocean Development and International Law*, vol. 24, 1993, p. 331.
87. See Rowlands, *op. cit.*, pp. 216–7.

88. The wording given is a paraphrase of UN doc. A/CONF.151/26 (vol. III), *op. cit.*, p. 21, paras 27.5–27.8.
89. UN doc. A/CONF.151/26 (vol. IV), *op. cit.*, p. 74.
90. *Proposed Revisions to the Medium-Term Plan for the Period 1992–1997*, UN doc. A/47/6 of 15 September 1992, pp. 5 and 28–9.
91. See Cicin-Sain and Knecht, *op. cit.*, p. 336.
92. James Gustave Speth, 'A Post-Rio Compact', *Foreign Policy*, no. 88, fall 1992, p. 146.
93. Thomas Harding, 'Mocking the Turtle', *New Statesman and Society*, 24 September 1993, pp. 45–6. More about this organisation, Small World, is given in *Development Dialogue*, 1991.
94. Rowlands, *op. cit.*, p. 220. A useful assessment of the overall work of NGOs primarily focused on development NGOs, is given in Inge Kaul *et al., Human Development Report 1993* (Oxford University Press for the UNDP, 1993).
95. 1992 Annual Report IUCN, *op. cit.*, p. 10.
96. Report of the Governing Council of the UN Environment Programme on Plans to Implement Agenda 21, E/CN.17/1993/14, 7 June 1993, pp.6 and 9.
97. UN General Assembly Resolution 47/191 of 22 December 1992, quotation from operative paragraph 8.
98. Institutional arrangements to follow up the UN Conference on Environment and Development, Rules of Procedure of the Commission on Sustainable Development, Report of the Secretary-General, E/1993/12, 29 January 1993.
99. *Ibid.*, pp. 5–6. For more detail on this question see Chapter 2 of this volume.
100. Report of the Commission on Sustainable Development on its organisational session, 24–26 February 1993, E/1993/25, 3 March 1993.
101. ECOSOC Decision 1993/215 of 12 February 1993, in UN Doc. E/1993/93, pp. 97–8. See Appendix B.
102. Financial resources and mechanisms for sustainable development: overview of current issues and developments, Report of the Secretary-General, E/CN.17/ISWG.II/1994/2, 22 February 1994, p. 23.
103. The Global Environment Facility began operations in December 1991 to fund projects with a demonstrated global environmental benefit. It is operated jointly by UNDP, UNEP and the World Bank. Its creation was strongly endorsed by the WWF. See Alexander Wood, 'The Global Environment Facility Pilot Phase', *International Environmental Affairs*, vol. 5, no. 3, summer 1993, p. 219.
104. See Smith, *op. cit.*, p. 306.
105. See Nitin Desai's address to the Organisational Session of the Open-Ended Working Group of ECOSOC on the Review of Arrangements for Consultations with Non-Governmental Organisations on 17 February 1994.

6

NGOs AND THE HUMAN RIGHTS OF WOMEN AT THE UNITED NATIONS.

Jane Connors

Introduction

One of the more striking aspects of the Vienna Declaration and Programme of Action,[1] adopted by the Second World Conference on Human Rights in Vienna on 25 June 1993, is the amount of space devoted to the human rights of women. The balance of the Declaration and Programme of Action recognises no new rights and makes few conceptual advances in the field. Rather, it reaffirms existing rights and their universality, indivisibility, interdependence and interrelationship. The paragraphs concerning women, however, represent unprecedented advances in human rights thinking. Large steps have been taken towards the full acknowledgement of women's rights as human rights, while the human rights agenda of the United Nations has expanded to include areas such as violence against women, both in the public and private sphere, and other gender-specific abuses.

The advances reflected in the Vienna Declaration and Programme of Action are, to a great extent, attributable to the activities of a select group of activists and NGOs who have worked to redefine the meaning of human rights to encompass the specific experiences of women. Their work, which is relatively recent, has gone some way to reclaim human rights for women and to reverse the pattern of neglect of women's human rights by the United Nations and the human rights community, including mainstream non-governmental organisations. Their work has also revealed the potential of the human rights framework for women's organisations and will create an opportunity for creative collaboration between mainstream human rights NGOs and women's NGOs.

What follows is an account of the development of the recognition within the United Nations of human rights for women and the activities and influence of NGOs in that development. It considers two areas: the work of women's NGOs in the development of human rights standards and the implementation of those

147

standards, and the role of human rights NGOs in the development and implementation of standards to promote the human rights of women. Although there are a number of studies which examine the role of NGOs in UN human rights standard-setting and implementation generally,[2] and there is now a growing literature on the subject of women's human rights,[3] there has been little attempt to intersect these two fields of study. Thus, a thorough analysis of the contribution of NGOs specifically to women's human rights has yet to be undertaken. Indeed, the whole subject of the contribution of NGOs to the work of the United Nations relating to women remains undeveloped. Although many commentators refer to this contribution as invaluable,[4] the handful of researchers who have documented it confine their attention to the growth in number, influence and sophistication of women's NGOs during the UN Decade for Women (1975–85), their profile and concerns at the three 'women's conferences' which took place during the Decade and their impact on questions such as development and, more recently, the environment.[5]

Two themes emerge from the account which follows. First, although non-governmental organisations devoted to women's issues have been active in UN affairs since the foundation of the organisation, their concern for human rights standard-setting and implementation has been peripheral. The early examples of these organisations confined their attention to social, humanitarian and peace issues and those established during the International Women's Decade primarily addressed questions related to economic development in the South. Secondly, the issue of the disadvantages and injustices experienced by women because of their gender has been largely neglected. Both the main international organs established for the promotion and protection of human rights within the United Nations and traditional human rights NGOs, such as Amnesty International, the International Commission of Jurists, the International League for Human Rights, the International Human Rights Law Group, Americas Watch and the Lawyer's Committee for Human Rights, have been slow to recognise the issue.

Human rights and women's international non-governmental organisations

The League of Nations to the Commission on the Status of Women (CSW)

Although the concept of legally enshrined human rights is the creature of the United Nations, standard-setting in certain areas predated its establishment. For example, trafficking in women[6], employment[7] and nationality[8] were the object of international standard-setting by diplomatic conferences and by the International Labour Organisation in the early part of this century. Similarly, the Covenant of the League of Nations called for humane conditions for all, irrespective of sex, the suppression of traffic in women and, in Article 7 of the Covenant, specifically provided that employment connected with the League would be 'open equally to men and women'.

Even at this early stage, women's international organisations were active in intergovernmental relations. The formulation of agreements relating to trafficking was largely the result of lobbying by anti-slavery activists and organisations and women's organisations.[9] In her analysis of the relationship of women to the League of Nations, Carol Miller[10] found reference to at least twenty women's international organisations working in Geneva at the time, with dozens more national societies sending deputations and corresponding with the League. The best known of these include the Women's International League for Peace and Freedom, the World Young Women's Christian Association, the International Council of Women, the International Federation of University Women and the International Woman Suffrage Alliance, which was later renamed the International Alliance of Women for Suffrage and Equal Citizenship. Carol Miller's account of the experience of these organisations reveals that the League confined their activities to social and humanitarian issues. The League certainly perceived that women's organisations had an important contribution to make to its work. League Secretariat members attended annual meetings of many of these organisations and solicited their views on aspects of the League's activities.[11] Their contribution, however, was confined to influencing public opinion in favour of the League and its policies and acting as assessors on the Advisory Committee on the Traffic in Women and on the Child Welfare Committee. Carol Miller suggests that, to a large extent, the organisations themselves unconsciously reinforced the narrow perception of their role.

Human rights and the CSW: the early years

For example, the Joint Standing Committee of the Women's International Organisations based in Geneva and the Council for the Representation of Women in the League of Nations in London lobbied national governments and the League to improve the position of women within the League. They argued that their capacity for contribution to its work went beyond social, humanitarian and peace issues.[12] The efforts of women's groups, however, appear to be specifically focused towards those concerns. Correspondence from these organisations with the League predominantly relate to issues concerning refugees, traffic in women and children, health and education, the welfare of children, the nationality of women and other questions concerning the status of women.[13] Similarly, in 1921 the London-based Council for the Representation of Women in the League of Nations protested at the British government's failure to send a woman delegate to a conference on the traffic in women and children, stating that this area was 'a tragedy which is supremely a woman's'. Moreover, among the conclusions of the 1929 Congress of the International Woman Suffrage Alliance is the suggestion that the League should make greater use of the 'special knowledge of women'.[14] There were some women's NGOs with wider concerns. Although described by Carol Miller as having less influence than other bodies,[15] the Women's International League for Peace and Freedom (WILPF), which had been founded in 1915 with the specific aim of total and universal disarmament and the prevention of war,[16] raised economic and international law issues.[17] WILPF established an international headquarters in Geneva in 1920 and its lobbying had influence on various areas of the League's work.[18] Again, a number of British and US women's societies presented proposals for a Women's Bureau within the League; that proposed by the International Alliance of Women recommended the establishment of a permanent international women's office modelled on the ILO, with an annual conference of women.[19]

NGO lobbying resulted in a joint request by ten Latin American delegations to have the status of women and the question of an equal rights treaty placed on the agenda of the Assembly of the League. At the invitation of the Secretary-General, women's NGOs presented statements to the 1935 Assembly during which they expressed concern that governments increasingly ignored prescriptions in constitutions which enshrined the equal rights of women and restricted their employment. Governments and NGOs were canvassed for observations regarding possible action and an expert committee, which met three times until it was brought to an end by the Second World War, was appointed to investigate the legal status of women throughout the world.

When the United Nations was being established, women's organisations were anxious to maintain the gains they had made in the League. At San Francisco in 1945, a number of women's activists and organisations working under the umbrella of the Inter-American Commission on the Status of Women were successful in having equal rights of men and women and non-distinction on the basis of sex included in five Articles of the UN Charter.[20] Once the consultative system for NGOs was working, ten women's NGOs were in the first batch of thirty-two NGOs given Category B status in 1947.

These women lobbied successfully for the Economic and Social Council of the UN (ECOSOC) to establish a Sub-Commission on the Status of Women, the mandate of which was to give the Commission on Human Rights special advice on problems relating to the status of women.[21] Further lobbying, particularly by the Sub-Commission's Chair, Mrs Bodil Begtrup, transformed it in 1946 into a full Commission of the Economic and Social Council.[22] Mrs Begtrup, president of the Danish Council of Women, said at the second session of ECOSOC that women did not want to be dependent on the 'pace of another Commission'.[23] The Commission (CSW) has been described by John Humphrey, the first Director of the UN Division of Human Rights, as a 'kind of lobby for women of the world'.[24] Although composed, like the Commission on Human Rights, of government appointees, the CSW was closely linked with the women's NGO community. Many governments appointed delegates such as Bodil Begtrup or Jessie Street, chairman of the Australian Women's Charter Conference and of the UN Association of Women of New South Wales.

The blurred distinction between Commission 'insiders' and non-governmental 'outsiders' is a recurring theme in the context of the promotion of women's rights, both by the CSW and generally. For example, the Inter-American Commission on the Status of Women was not only one of the groups active at San Francisco but it went on to have some of its members serve as delegates to the early sessions of the Commission on the Status of Women.[25] Another example, although in another context, is Helvi Sipila, Assistant Secretary-General for Social Development and Humanitarian Affairs within the United Nations, who was appointed Secretary-General of the 1975 International Women's Year. She had been president of the Finnish Girl Guides and president of the International Federation of Women Lawyers. As John Humphrey points out, the CSW has evoked more personal commitment from its delegates than any other UN body.[26] This is largely because delegates chosen to represent their countries at the Commission have usually been women, with only a handful of delegates being men. As such, the CSW is an unusual UN body. Furthermore, most appointees have continued to rely for political, intellectual and moral support on the women's national and international NGOs from which they were drawn.

At the time, the establishment of the Commission was a victory for this determined. group of women. Several member states, including the United States and the United Kingdom, opposed its formation on the grounds that women's rights could be catered for within the rubric of human rights.[27] While not underrating the real achievements of the Commission on the Status of Women in addressing women's concerns,[28] its existence has, ironically, contributed to the neglect by both the traditional UN human rights framework and human rights NGOs of issues of concern to women. These bodies point to the Commission as the body responsible for such questions. At the same time, although there were early attempts by some NGOs and Eastern European countries to have the CSW monitor the implementation of the rights of women in individual countries,[29] the Commission itself, and those NGOs who have allied themselves to its work, have been able to avoid human rights concerns by pointing to the traditional human rights framework. The separation of the concerns of the human rights bodies within the United Nations was compounded in 1973 when the CSW Secretariat was removed from the Division of Human Rights within the Department of Political and General Assembly Affairs to the Centre for Social Development and Humanitarian Affairs within the Department of Economic and Social Affairs. From 1979, moreover, the concerns of both drifted even further apart when the CSW and its Secretariat were moved to Vienna.[30]

With the establishment of the Commission on the Status of Women, most international women's NGOs devoted their attention to its activities. Women did, however, participate in the drafting of the Universal Declaration of Human Rights, a process one commentator has described as a 'struggle'.[31] Although the Universal Declaration contains few references to women's rights, it was a progressive document for its time. This was largely as a result of vigilance on the part of female delegates to the Commission on Human Rights and lobbying by the Commission on the Status of Women and non-governmental organisations such as the International Council of Women, the International Union of Catholic Women's Leagues and the Women's International League for Peace and Freedom (WILPF). The three officers of the CSW were entitled to attend and participate without voting when the rights of women were being considered.[32] Although attracting little support from the female chair of the Commission on Human Rights, Eleanor Roosevelt,[33] these efforts managed to ensure that the language of the Declaration, despite the fact that it speaks of a spirit of 'brotherhood', clearly encompassed women as well as men. Moreover, although the document privileges the family as an institution, it does provide for equality of rights within it. The influence of these women and organisations was also responsible for the rights of equal pay and suffrage and the establishment of equal rights with respect to marriage and dissolution of marriage, although there were energetic, but unsuccessful, efforts to ensure that no rights to divorce were enshrined.[34]

Several women's NGOs maintained offices in Geneva so as to contribute to all areas of the work of the nascent United Nations. WILPF, for example, was granted consultative status with ECOSOC in 1948.[35] This was despite an objection by the Women's International Democratic Federation, a communist NGO with similar status, which accused it of being a 'reactionary and pro-fascist organisation'. WILPF was also admitted to consultative status with UNESCO and to specialised consultative status with the Food and Agriculture Organisation. As part of an NGO advisory panel, WILPF recommended that the United Nations establish a permanent agency for child welfare, a step taken with the creation of UNICEF in 1950. It also lobbied for the creation of the office of the UN High Commissioner for Refugees (UNHCR)[36] and participated with other NGOs in the plenipotentiary conference at Geneva at which the Convention on the Status of Refugees was drafted. This occasion was characterised by an exceptional degree of involvement, for that time, of NGOs in drafting a convention and attending its signature by government representatives.[37]

WILPF and other women's NGOs, including the International Federation of University Women, the International Council of Women, the International Federation of Business and Professional Women and the International Union of Catholic Women's Leagues (renamed the World Union of Catholic Women's Organisations in 1952), participated in the drafting of the twin Covenants on human rights by the Commission on Human Rights, a process that began in 1947 and was largely completed by 16 April 1954. WILPF opposed both the division of the rights into two legal instruments[38] and the reiteration, in article 3 of both Covenants, of the non-discrimination guarantee which is to be found in the Universal Declaration. WILPF argued that article 3, which enshrines the right of equal enjoyment by men and women of the rights enumerated in the Covenants, would serve little purpose given the guarantee in the Universal Declaration and it would be better to await the result of the implementation of its terms.[39]

Most women's NGOs, however, focused their attention on the Commission on the Status of Women. The CSW embarked on an ambitious programme of work including studies, seminars, the elaboration of international standards and the review of reports submitted by states. It also stimulated action in favour of women by the United Nations, its specialised agencies and other organs, including the provision of technical assistance to benefit women in developing countries. One commentator has observed that 'in no organ of the United Nations do international non-governmental organisations play a more active and influential role than in the Commission'.[40] Certainly, since its establishment, at least thirty international women's organisations in consultative status, representing a broad spectrum of religious, professional, educational and civil interests, have regularly participated in the sessions of the CSW. Further, many women's groups who cannot participate in CSW sessions because they do not meet the Council requirements for consultative status, attend its meetings.

The early work of the CSW was devoted to the political rights of women and the legal rights of married women. It resulted in the formulation of the Convention on the Political Rights of Women and the Convention on the Nationality of Married Women. The former was an initiative of the Latin American delegates to the Commission,[41] while the latter was influenced by a model convention drafted by the International Alliance of Women at its meeting in 1923. At the same time, the CSW contributed to the activities of other branches of the United Nations. For example, its lobbying resulted in the explicit reference to sex equality in article 3 of the two Covenants on Human Rights, while article 23 of the International Covenant on Civil and Political Rights, guaranteeing equality of rights within the family, is a direct result of a CSW request that article 16 of the Universal Declaration on Human Rights be reflected in its provisions.[42]

Although much of the work of the CSW and, therefore, much of the work of women's NGOs, was related to human rights, the concept of human rights and the activities of the mainstream human rights organs within the United Nations were not priorities for many organisations concerned with women's affairs. Accordingly, women's NGOs paid little attention to the mainstream human rights framework and mechanisms within the United Nations. Although there were exceptions, particularly among the well-established NGOs such as WILPF and the International Alliance of Women, they rarely lobbied the Commission on Human Rights or the Sub-Commission on the Prevention of Discrimination and Protection of Minorities. Similarly, although again there were exceptions – and these tended to be the same as those above – women's NGOs were rarely involved in the ILO or UNESCO.

Within the mainstream human rights system of the United Nations, women's NGOs were most involved with the Working Group on Contemporary Forms of Slavery and the Working Group on Traditional Practices. The former considers, among other issues, traffic in women and children and, since 1992, the question of 'comfort women'.[43] Established primarily through the efforts of an NGO,[44] it has assumed a monitoring role for several major conventions dealing with traffic and prostitution, including the 1949 Convention for the Suppression of the Traffic in Persons and of the Exploitation of the Prostitution of Others.[45] Considerable use is made of the Working Group by NGOs such as the International Abolitionist Federation, the International Council of Women and the Minority Rights Group, who pass on information and register complaints.[46] The Working Group has provided a forum for NGOs, who submit information on specific situations.[47] Indeed, NGO activity in this area has meant that states referred to in NGO submissions frequently attend and respond to allegations of violations.[48]

In the early 1960s, steps were taken within the CSW towards the elaboration of human rights standards specifically for women. In November 1963, twenty-two developing and East European countries introduced a resolution at the 18th session of the General Assembly calling for a declaration on the elimination of discrimination against women. Anticipating some resistance, the sponsors of the resolution tied the aim of the declaration to development, arguing that women's participation in the development of nations was essential and that discrimination impeded development. Debate in the Third Committee centred on whether the Commission should tackle practical, programmatic questions of women's integration into the development process or deal with law and policy reform to eliminate discrimination. Western Europeans argued in favour of the former view, while the newly independent nations urged that a declaration was needed to ensure equality of women and enhance prospects for development. In the event, final votes to begin work on a declaration were unanimous in the Third Committee and the General Assembly, with the resolution inviting governments, UN specialised agencies and NGOs to send comments and proposals to the Secretary-General.[49]

Drafting of the declaration took place from 1965, based on a memorandum by the Commission on the Status of Women compiled from replies from thirty-three governments, fifteen NGOs and four specialised agencies.[50] The memorandum suggested that women's education was a priority and stressed that tradition and culture, especially as exemplified in marriage and family law, were major constraints on women's equality, although there were some respondents who extolled the role of women as mothers and family members.

Eight industrialised countries – Denmark, Finland, France, the

Netherlands, Norway, Sweden, Britain and the United States –
responded to the Secretary-General's request for comments. All
except the United States suggested that the new declaration be
limited to combining the existing conventions concerning the rights
of women or to re-emphasising the importance of education. Only
three of the original developing country sponsors – Afghanistan,
Argentina and Morocco – responded, with Afghanistan stating
that overcoming discrimination required 'combatting of traditions,
customs and usages which thwart the advancement of women . . .
[and] intense educational efforts . . . designed to enlighten public
opinion'. Its response also suggested that 'amends' be made to
women by granting them special privileges. Other respondents
underlined the need for home and child-care services to encourage
women's activities outside the home and the need for public education campaigns advocating equality. China noted that civil laws
often denied married women rights with respect to property, while
Nepal suggested that no marriage should be allowed where the age
difference between the spouses was more than twenty years. The
United Arab Republic argued for equality in nationality and domi-
cile, and for aid to widows and divorcees, and again stressed the
need for educational campaigns.

The seven Eastern European respondents all strongly supported
the proposed declaration, submitting detailed suggestions and
adding criminal law and the problems of unmarried mothers to
the list of issues. With the exception of the YWCA, which suggested that adoption of a declaration might give the impression
that the work of the CSW was finished, NGO respondents were
unanimous that a declaration would be particularly useful in
illustrating world-wide discrimination against women. They suggested that the concerns of the declaration should encompass
family and criminal law, discrimination against single women and
female heads of household, prostitution, employment and education. None of the respondents – governmental, intergovernmental
or non-governmental – mentioned women's health, an issue that
emerged during drafting. The FAO, however, did point out that
discrimination against rural women included lack of recognition
of their work, especially in food production, and their need for
satisfactory housing and education. UNESCO indicated that
although an existing convention on education allowed for equivalent education in separate male and female educational systems,
co-education would be better.

At the CSW, a drafting committee was appointed, composed of
delegates from Austria, Colombia, Guinea, Iran, Mexico, the
Philippines and Poland – the countries that had sponsored the

original resolution – and the Dominican Republic, France, Ghana, the Soviet Union and the United States. Drafting began, with the cooperation of other members of the Commission, representatives of governments that were not members of the Commission, UN specialised agencies and twenty-two NGOs, including the fifteen that had previously submitted responses. The drafting committee selected Poland's draft as its working document. In its preamble, this document linked 'equality, development and peace', a linkage first made in 1926 by the International Alliance of Women[51] and later to become the major theme of the UN Decade for Women. It defined and condemned discrimination and included eleven articles that covered all the issues which had featured in government and NGO responses. The final article called on women's organisations to undertake educational campaigns to inform women and men of the principles of the declaration. It also called on governments, individuals and NGOs 'to do all in their power to promote implementation' of the principles of the declaration and those on women's equality contained in the UN Charter and the Universal Declaration of Human Rights. Although the drafting process was to take a further four years, the General Assembly adopted the Declaration on the Elimination of Discrimination against Women on 7 November 1967.[52]

The CSW was given the task of overseeing the implementation of the Declaration. It received reports, consolidated into a four-year reporting cycle in 1972, from states, specialised agencies and NGOs. Unfortunately, as the Declaration did not constitute a treaty and lacked binding force, few reports were received. In 1974, for example, only thirty-four states and fourteen NGOs submitted reports.[53] To a certain extent, reporting under the Declaration was also affected by the identification of development as a major concern of the United Nations. This was to have significant implications for both the CSW and women's NGOs. Many were beginning to devote their activities to economic and development issues, and a number, particularly those of the South, categorised the struggle for women's rights, manifested in the Declaration, as Western, bourgeois and essentially irrelevant.

The CSW had first actively turned its attention to economic and social development in 1966, when it requested the Secretariat, through the Economic and Social Council to prepare a questionnaire for member states and NGOs on the issue.[54] The response from seventy-seven governments and thirty-six NGOs caused the CSW to reconsider its stress on rights. There were three other seminal influences in this shift of focus: Helvi Sipila, designated as special rapporteur to the CSW on the interrelationship of family planning and the status of women, prepared a study[55] between 1968 and 1974 which sought to integrate an equal rights approach with development concepts; in 1970, as its response to the General Assembly's First Development Decade, the CSW endorsed a Programme of Concerted Action, which set out minimum targets for all member states to achieve in education, training, health, unemployment and maternity protection for women;[56] and Ester Boserup produced her study, *Women's Role in Economic Development*.[57] So different was the new emphasis that Margaret Bruce, Assistant Director of the Division of Human Rights, responsible for the Section on the Status of Women, noted that in 1970 the CSW 'recast its programme of work giving less emphasis to 'rights' and more to the 'roles' of women'.[58] As the focus of the Commission and other parts of the United Nations moved to women's 'roles', particularly in the context of 'development', so too did the focus of women's NGOs.[59] Much of the work of the CSW and women's NGOs became further bound up with International Women's Year, designated by the General Assembly to take place in 1975.[60] This proposal had originated with a group of NGOs and members of the CSW who had become concerned with the slow progress of the Development Decade and it was unanimously endorsed by the Commission at its 24th Session.[61] The focal point of International Women's Year was a World Conference, which was followed by a Women's Decade during which two further world conferences devoted to the concerns of women took place.

The Women's Decade and the Women's Convention

During the Decade, women's NGOs proliferated in number and nature. The traditional, structured organisations had their origins in the suffrage movement, in religious, welfare or propaganda movements, or represented associations of women professionals. The new NGOs included organisations concerned with such diverse areas as peace, domestic violence, breast milk substitutes, female sexual slavery, labour and, most important, economic development. NGOs of various levels of organisation and formality were established in all parts of the world, with a striking number emerging in the South out of grass-roots activity.

The growth of NGO activity in issues relating to women is testified to by the incremental growth in the UN Women's Decade conferences and the NGO forums held in parallel with them. The first was in Mexico in 1975. It was attended by 133 member states, twenty-three UN organisations and 114 international NGOs. It

approved the World Plan of Action[62] and established the UN
Voluntary Fund for Women (UNIFEM).[63] The Mexico Tribune
proved to be the largest of the three parallel non-governmental
meetings organised since the 1972 Stockholm environmental conference. Six thousand people from all over the world registered for
the Tribune, including representatives of 114 NGOs with consultative status. These were diverse and included the International
Planned Parenthood Federation, the International Council of
Women, the World Federation of United Nations Associations,
WILPF, the International Council of Nurses, the International Bar
Association and the International Federation of Business and Professional Women. Organisations without consultative status also
registered; they included the Women's Electoral Penguin Club of
Australia, the Women's Organisation of Iran and the Italian
Feminist Movement. Tribune participants were able to attend 192
informal sessions which concerned topics relating to law and the
status of women, population and planned parenthood. In common
with other NGO forums, a daily newspaper, entitled *Xilenon*, after
the Aztec goddess of tender corn, was produced.

The Mexico Conference stimulated communication between
women and, despite the political differences among them, particularly between First World women and those from the South, women's
consciousness was raised and common problems identified. NGO
networks formed in Mexico City expanded, while many actively
aimed to influence governments to alter discriminatory laws and
practices. For example, the sections in each country of the International Council of Jewish Women, the International Federation of
Business and Professional Women, the International Federation of
University Women, the Soroptimists, the Women's International
Zionist Organisation, the World Union of Catholic Women's Organisations and the Young Women's Christian Association began to
urge governments to support laws granting women equality.[64]

The important contribution of NGOs in promoting the acceptance
of the work of the CSW and the success of the Mexico Conference
led the CSW, at its 1978 session, to support the participation of
local, national and regional NGOs in the regional preparatory
meetings which were held before the 1980 mid-decade conference
in Copenhagen. This time 135 NGOs were represented at the main
intergovernmental conference, twenty-four of which were specifically 'women's NGOs'.[65] There were substantially more participants in the Copenhagen NGO Forum than there had been in
Mexico, with 8,000 registering and at least 1,000 more attending.
The Forum was also more activist in tone than the Mexico meeting,
with the traditional women's groups – those with consultative

status – having moved into more feminist activity and 'women and development' groups having proliferated since Mexico. These two groups were joined by a new variety of women's NGO, involving militant or radical feminists, whose concerns included rape, sexual harassment and domestic violence. While the Mexican Tribune had offered participants 200 meetings over the two-week period, 150 to 175 workshops were held on each day at the Copenhagen Forum. This was largely because, as one commentator has put it, there were 'three Forums within the Forum': [66] Vivencia!, which aimed to be spontaneous, Exchange, which was concerned with creating a network of Third World feminists, and the International Women's Studies Federation, which held a series of scholarly inter-disciplinary seminars.

The momentum created by the two conferences of the UN Women's Decade was in clear evidence at the Nairobi End of Decade Conference in 1985. This was attended by 1,500 official participants and 14,000 women, who took part in the Forum. Again, Forum participants were able to attend hundreds of activities, but this Conference and Forum prompted a deeper understanding of the interdependence of local and global problems.

Although the major concern of the International Decade for Women, and of the majority of those NGOs which emerged during it, was with the issue of women in development, the Decade also saw the translation of the Declaration on the Elimination of Discrimination against Women into treaty form in the Convention on the Elimination of All Forms of Discrimination against Women (the Women's Convention). [67]

Against the background of the Declaration, the CSW proposed the elaboration of a convention, a suggestion which was sanctioned by a resolution of the Mexico Conference. Although the Polish delegate had called for the translation of the Declaration into a convention as early as 1968, the CSW seriously embarked on its drafting at its 1976 session, with a working paper containing four draft conventions. [68] The first was a text based on replies from governments and the report of the original working group which had been established by the CSW. The other drafts came from Benin, Indonesia and the All African Women's Conference, a non-governmental organisation. An additional draft was presented to the Commission by Belgium. [69] Some portions of the Belgian text were taken into account during the discussion of individual articles, but the original Working Group text formed the basis of most discussion, the other texts being disregarded. Drafting of the Convention was, by and large, the work of member states, although established non-governmental organisations dedicated to issues of concern to women contributed. These included the International Council of Social Democrat Women, the International Federation of University Women, the World Young Women's Christian Association, the International Planned Parenthood Federation and the All African Women's Conference.[70] One non-governmental organisation concerned with general issues, the International Confederation of Free Trade Unions, contributed to the drafting of article 11, concerning women and work. It registered opposition to any hasty revision of ILO conventions concerning night work, being apprehensive about enshrining in a UN convention standards of protection for women which were not directly related to their maternal function. Although concerned with the entitlement of women to pensions, retirement and maternity protection and supportive of the idea of shared responsibility in the home, the ILO held that these issues were its province and that it should be responsible for their regulation.[71]

By the end of its 1976 session, the Commission had completed its drafting task. Responsibility then shifted to a 'Working Group of the Whole' of the General Assembly's Third Committee. Although presented with a complete draft, from 1977 to 1979 it worked on draft articles and amendments. It was a difficult process. The fifteen paragraphs of the preamble, which one commentator argues diverge 'further from the central issues . . . than does the preamble to any other human rights treaty',[72] proved particularly problematic. Many delegations considered that some of the issues raised were outside the scope of the Convention and were politically controversial. Preambular paragraphs 10 and 11, concerning equality between men and women in the context of racism and apartheid, international peace and security, general and complete disarmament and the self determination of peoples attracted considerable debate.[73] The sixth preambular paragraph, which states that discrimination against women continues to exist despite the existence of various human rights instruments, provoked the socialist country representatives to disagree with such a 'broad formulation since discrimination against women had been eliminated in their countries'.[74] The Working Group's first meeting only managed to consider the preamble and articles 1–10, while the next session, in March 1979, covered only articles 10–16. The experience of the draft Convention before the full Third Committee did not, however, reflect these difficulties. There, discussion of the draft occupied only two days, after which adoption by the General Assembly was recommended.[75] This 'uncharacteristic speed' has been attributed by one commentator to either 'the comprehensiveness of the preparatory work or . . . the Third Committee's relative lack of interest in the issue, or both'.[76]

The Convention wa$ opened for signature on 1 March 1980 and the first signatories acceded to its terms at the Copenhagen Conference. It was less than two years – by 3 September 1981 – before the minimum number of twenty ratifications required to bring the Women's Convention into force had been achieved.[77] In April 1982, representatives of the states parties met to elect the twenty-three members of the Committee on the Elimination of Discrimination Against Women (CEDAW) as provided for by article 17 of the Convention. In October of that year, the new Committee met at the UN International Centre in Vienna, where the Branch (now Division) for the Advancement of Women, which serves as the secretariat for the Committee was then based. In opening the meeting, the Director of the Branch said that a 'new chapter in the long struggle for equality and the integration of the process of development had begun'.[78]

Although early sessions of the CEDAW were devoted to organisational matters, the substantive work of the Committee had begun by 1983 by when fifty-one states had ratified or acceded to the Convention and thirteen governments had submitted reports on the implementation of its provisions in accordance with its requirements. The Director of the Branch for the Advancement of Women attributed the increasing number of ratifications to the work of national and international non-governmental women's organisations.

NGOs and the Women's Convention

By the time of the 1985 World Conference which marked the end of the International Women's Decade in Nairobi, the CEDAW's work had gained little attention. Women's groups had worked for ratification and were continuing to do so, but they were not yet following the process of reporting and review. They chose to focus on the World Conference and on issues such as economic development, regarding them as more tangible and important than concepts of equality and non-discrimination. The process of drafting and adopting the Convention and the activities aimed at securing ratifications had, nonetheless, suggested that discrimination impeded development and that inequalities between men and women prevented women from achieving full citizenship. Accordingly, focus within the United Nations and among NGO activists began to shift from almost exclusive concentration on issues of women in development to questions of equality and the influence of law and custom on women's status.

During the Nairobi NGO Forum, workshops were held focusing on the Convention, legal literacy, legal services and the power of NGOs to influence public policy. Over 500 women and men from over fifty countries attended a week-long workshop series cosponsored by the Commonwealth Secretariat's Women and Development Programme and two US university-based development programmes, which received the encouragement of a number of CEDAW members. Out of this workshop series, the International Women's Rights Action Watch (IWRAW) global network was formed 'to monitor, analyze and encourage law and policy reform in accordance with the principles of the UN Convention on the Elimination of All Forms of Discrimination Against Women'. At the same time, the 'Forward Looking Strategies for the Advancement of Women', the document adopted by consensus by the official conference, included numerous paragraphs referring to the Convention and the need for legislation, legal reform and policy change to improve the status of women.

While IWRAW grew out of the Nairobi workshop series, the idea for an international network to monitor and support the work of the CEDAW was that of Arvonne Fraser and Rebecca Cook. The former was the Director of the Women, Public Policy and Development Project at the University of Minnesota's Humphrey Institute of Public Affairs, while Rebecca Cook was a lawyer at the Development Law and Policy Program at Columbia University's Center for Population and Family Health. Their view was that without an independent constituency group to maintain and put pressure on the CEDAW and governments, the Women's Convention was likely to be ignored. They also believed that the time had come to establish women's rights as part of international human rights. This would serve to revitalise the traditional women's NGOs and give focus to the field of women in development. It would be backed up by the substantial database relating to women which had been created during the Decade by government agencies, the UN system and independent researchers. IWRAW was officially launched in February 1986 at a seminar preceding the meeting of the CEDAW. Today, IWRAW has a core staff in Minnesota, an advisory board and about 5,000 individuals and organisations around the world connected to the network. A regional IWRAW network has been formed in the Asia Pacific region and one is being formed in Africa to document discrimination against women, bring test cases, provide public education and hold local and regional training sessions.

Central to IWRAW's concerns is the theme that work on international human rights must pay special attention to women's rights.

To this end, IWRAW promotes the idea of women's rights as human rights. Its work is focused directly on the activities of the CEDAW and the elaboration of the provisions of the Convention. IWRAW monitors the Convention and the activities of the Committee, supplying information and parallel reports to CEDAW members and supporting other, particularly national, NGOs which wish to prepare and submit parallel reports. It also provides input into the General Recommendations and suggestions which the CEDAW is entitled to make, based on country reports, by virtue of article 21. IWRAW publishes a quarterly newsletter – *Women's Watch* – and since 1988 has published a report of the proceedings of the annual meeting of the CEDAW.

Although women's NGOs other than IWRAW pay some attention to the work of the CEDAW and there is growing interest in its activities from human rights NGOs, IWRAW has forged a unique link with this UN treaty body. The Women's Convention itself contains no formal machinery by which NGOs can contribute to the implementation of its terms. During the drafting, a group of NGOs had proposed that a system be established which would give NGOs the right to present to the Committee information and recommendations relating to the observance of the provisions of the Convention, but this was not accepted.[79] The Convention on the Rights of the Child is therefore the only human rights treaty which specifically gives NGOs a role in the monitoring process.[80] During the process of examination of country reports, the CEDAW has consistently questioned states parties on the extent of the involvement of NGOs and women's groups in the preparation of state reports. It has not, however, developed any formal procedure by which it receives reports from NGOs either generally or on a country-specific basis.[81] CEDAW members have been prepared to accept information from NGOs informally, the bulk of such information being provided by IWRAW. Each year members of IWRAW have held an informal meeting with members of the CEDAW, generally on the eve of their meeting. This has been greatly helped by the fact that most CEDAW experts are themselves drawn from the women's NGO community, some even being members of the IWRAW network. One such is Norma Monica Forde, the Barbadian expert. She served on the CEDAW for two terms and was active in the Nairobi workshops which served to form the core of the IWRAW network.

The contribution of NGOs has, in general terms, been limited to information to assist the CEDAW in the examination of country reports.[82] Increasingly, however, NGOs have sought to influence the general recommendations formulated by the CEDAW which elaborate its view of the content of the rights guaranteed in the Women's Convention. In its 1989 session, the CEDAW responded with a short general recommendation to NGO concerns about violence against women – a subject which is not explicitly addressed in the Convention.[83] In 1992, the CEDAW went further, issuing an explicit recommendation and series of comments showing exactly how violence was covered by the Convention.[84] This followed further lobbying, and increased attention paid to the issue by the CSW, which had resolved during its 1991 session to formulate a separate international instrument to confront the problem.[85] Formulation of the recommendation was assisted by Andrew Byrnes, a core member of IWRAW, and Donna Sullivan, then staff attorney at the International League for Human Rights. A one-day meeting on the issue of violence against women, jointly organised by IWRAW and the International League for Human Rights and held on the eve of the 1992 CEDAW session, which was attended by at least two-thirds of CEDAW experts, informed much of their work towards the recommendation.

The CEDAW is currently involved in a programme of examining individual articles of the Convention or themes which cut across a number of articles of the Convention. This work forms the basis of further general recommendations which are formulated on the basis of the Committee's examination of states parties' reports and input from the secretariat, specialised agencies and other UN organisations, as well as from interested NGOs. There is a preliminary background paper on the issues chosen by the Committee, which is prepared after consultation with various bodies, including NGOs, and then there is further circulation of the paper to allow for wide comment. This provides important opportunities for NGOs and individuals to become involved in the implementation of the Convention. Themes for consideration have included the family (1993) and equality of political participation and public life (1994). These themes have both been the subject of IWRAW studies and recommendations.

Human rights NGOs and women's human rights

While NGOs that focused on the concerns of women found themselves predominantly bound up with questions such as women and development, rather than issues of human rights, traditional and established non-governmental human rights organisations were slow to recognise the specific claims of women. Like the women's NGOs, they took some time to appreciate the linkages between the work of these two sectors of the NGO community.

Various reasons can be advanced to explain this. First, the concerns of the traditional human rights NGOs reflect the UN human rights framework itself. This framework, having emerged out of a political discourse in which women took little part,[86] establishes human rights standards and implementation mechanisms that relate more closely to issues of central relevance to the lives of men than those of women. Most rights recognised in the framework of international human rights are concerned with the life of an individual in the public sphere and protect the individual from incursions of state authority in that context. Few international instruments encompass violations perpetrated by actors other than the state or those who act pursuant to its authority. For example, the Universal Declaration of Human Rights enshrines rights such as freedom from slavery or servitude, torture, arbitrary arrest and detention, and guarantees rights to nationality, fair and public hearing and freedom of religion and speech.[87] It is clear that women, like men, should be entitled to 'public' rights of this nature, but women are more likely to experience violations in the private sphere, which are perpetrated by private individuals, rather than the state. Despite the fact that these private violations may be the result of the maintenance by states of a cultural, social or legal system which tolerates such abuses or fails to take positive measures to prevent their occurrence, they rarely meet the definition of abuses of internationally-recognised human rights. Examples of violations to which women are commonly subject which are essentially 'private' rather than 'public', and which, therefore, are rarely perceived as meeting the definition of a violation of human rights because they are not attributable to the state, include domestic violence, sexual abuse in the workplace and elsewhere, trafficking and denial of reproductive choice.

Mirroring the concerns of human rights law with state incursions on individual rights, traditional human rights NGOs typically focus on violations of the rights of individuals in the public sphere. The mandate of Amnesty International, for example, is focused directly on violations of human rights in the public sphere by the state and its agents. It confines its work to securing the release of prisoners of conscience, fair and prompt trials for all political prisoners, opposition to the death penalty and torture or other cruel, inhuman or degrading treatment or punishment of all prisoners or other detained or restricted persons. Although, sadly, a growing number of women are subject to violations within its mandate,[88] and in many cases their experience is different in kind or degree because of their gender[89], the victimisation of most women falls outside this clear mandate.

Again, in traditional human rights discourse, although many people subscribe to the concept of the indivisibility of civil, political, economic, social and cultural rights, primary attention is usually given to civil and political rights. The focus of most human rights NGOs has also been on civil and political rights. These rights, although essential for both women and men, are perhaps of less relevance to women in their daily lives than economic, social and cultural rights, which might serve to protect them from the adverse impact of development policies or the effects of environmental degradation. These two factors, essentially reflecting traditional concepts of international human rights law, are central in explaining the neglect of issues of concern to women by traditional human rights NGOs. There are, however, other important if less doctrinal reasons. The NGO human rights establishment is dominated by men and, accordingly, to a great extent concerns itself predominantly with issues of central importance to men. Moreover, the institutional framework has encouraged the separation of the idea of human rights, as reflected in bodies such as the Commission on Human Rights and the Human Rights Committee, from the idea of non-discrimination on the basis of sex, reflected in organisations such as the CSW and the CEDAW with responsibility for the rights of women. Those dedicated to human rights have been able to ignore women's concerns, and those bodies dedicated to women's issues have been able to ignore human rights and concentrate on areas such as women in development. As these bodies have followed their separate concerns, so also have the NGOs which relate to them. Thus, human rights NGOs have paid little attention to the concerns of women and women's NGOs have developed little interest or expertise in human rights. The institutional separation and lack of collaboration between both groups was compounded by the geographical separation between institutions which occurred in 1979 with the removal of the Branch for the Advancement of Women, the CSW and the CEDAW to Vienna. Few traditional human rights NGOs consistently monitored the CSW and the CEDAW after 1979, and only the well-established women's NGOs, such as the International Alliance of Women, the WILPF and the International Federation of Business and Professional Women, who were already based in Geneva, contributed to the work of the Geneva-based human rights organs of the United Nations.

Traditional human rights NGOs began to manifest awareness of the particular concerns of women during the latter half of the 1980s, just as the CEDAW was developing a more structured approach to its work. Perhaps the first traditional NGO to reflect on human rights of women was the International League for Human Rights, whose experience at the 1975 Mexico City Conference apparently led it to change its name from the International League for the Rights of Man.[90] This NGO has produced occasional material on women's human rights, including briefs on UN bodies dedicated to the issue of discrimination on the basis of sex[91] and commentary on a number of states parties' reports for the CEDAW;[92] and, as will be recalled, it collaborated with IWRAW in holding a conference on the eve of the meeting of the CEDAW in 1992.

Amnesty International attended both the official and non-governmental conferences in Nairobi and had, from time to time, made statements to the Commission on the Status of Women[93] where the issues with which the CSW was concerned fell clearly within its mandate. In October 1984, Amnesty International campaigned around the theme of 'Forgotten Women' for its Prisoner of Conscience Week. In 1989, however, Amnesty's rather desultory approach to violations of women's rights was boosted when the International Council Meeting agreed Decision 15. This recognised the importance of human rights violations against women, encouraged efforts to deal with such violations and resolved to give this work a higher profile within its campaigns. It agreed to allocate increased resources to the research and production of materials for this work and to seek safeguards and protection for women subject to gender-specific violations. During the same International Council Meeting, Amnesty also held its first international meeting on women and human rights.

Amnesty's new commitment to the concerns of women was evident when it held its first Intersectional Meeting on Women and Human Rights in Geneva in February 1991 and when it released its first report devoted solely to abuses of women. This report, *Women in the Front Line*, which was published in March 1991, detailed a range of human rights abuses which are primarily suffered by women. Its aim was to mobilise international support for the protection of women and, by extension, the societies in which they live. *Women in the Front Line* has been followed by other reports, including *Rape and Sexual Abuse: Torture and Ill Treatment of Women in Detention*[94] and a country report on Tunisia, detailing the plight of women dissidents and prisoners.[95] Amnesty has organised campaigns related to abuses of women's human rights, produces a human rights bulletin about women prisoners of conscience – *Interact* – encourages the establishment of Women's Action Networks and has appointed women's officers in a number of its country sections.

Amnesty International is not the only traditional human rights NGO which has attempted to integrate into its work the issues relating to women's human rights. In 1990, Human Rights Watch founded its Women's Rights Project, which has now collaborated with the various Watch Committees in the production of over seven influential reports relating to the violation of the rights of women, while the International Human Rights Law Group launched its Women in the Law Project (WILP) in September 1992. Among WILP's reports to date are *No Justice, No Peace: Accountability for Rape and Gender-Based Violence in the Former Yugoslavia* (June 1993) and *Token Gestures: Women's Human Rights and UN Reporting. The United Nations Special Rapporteur on Torture* (June 1993). The latter study concludes that while the former UN Special Rapporteur on Torture, Professor Peter Kooijmans, did much to raise international awareness of torture and the actions needed to combat it, he failed to investigate adequately and condemn many well documented instances of systematic torture or ill-treatment of women. Responsibility, the report argues, must be shared with NGOs who have failed to provide information on specific cases of torture and ill-treatment of women. The International Commission of Jurists has also recognised that women have been largely forgotten by human rights NGOs, and it documents gender-related violations as well as providing training courses in this area.

The Second World Conference on Human Rights

June 1993 saw the Second World Conference on Human Rights and what has been described as the 'extraordinary success of women's rights activists worldwide to end the historic disregard of human rights violations against women'.[96] The Conference marked a new appreciation by human rights activists of gender-specific human rights violations, as well as a new appreciation by women's rights activists of the value of the idea of international human rights. The Conference also revealed, particularly to women's NGOs, the value of cooperation and linkages across interests and across the North/South divide.

Much of the recognition in Vienna of gender-specific abuses as human rights violations was the result of the efforts of a group of women's NGOs which had worked hard to recapture the discourse of human rights for women. Among them was the Centre for Women's Global Leadership at Rutgers University, New Jersey, which in 1990 had decided to focus on redefining human rights from a feminist perspective. This was explored at its initial Leadership Institute in June 1991, which brought together NGO activists from all regions of the world to discuss ways to promote dialogue between women's NGOs and human rights NGOs. Participants at the Rutgers Institute chose to focus on violence against women, an issue so far excluded from the rubric of human rights because of its private, non-state nature. They believed that the subject required analysis within the context of human rights standards and gender discrimination. There would be sixteen days of activism against gender violence and they would organise a global petition for the United Nations to recognise women's human rights at the forthcoming World Conference on Human Rights. The activism would begin on 25 November 1991 – the day on which, in 1960, the three Mirabal sisters, political activists in the Dominican Republic, were murdered. It has been designated a day of international protest against violence against women. Sponsorship for the petition was initially shared by the Centre for Women's Global Leadership with the World YWCA and the International Women's Tribune Centre, which had been established at the time of the Mexico Conference Tribune. NGO activists who attended the second Leadership Institute at Rutgers in 1992 also decided, in local and regional hearings, to gather testimonies on abuses against women. These would be channelled to the Commission on Human Rights so as to testify to the need for effective mechanisms to respond to women's human rights concerns.

Women's NGOs were active at the official regional preparatory meetings of the World Conference on Human Rights, ensuring that the government declarations and resolutions identified women's human rights as concerns to be addressed at the final Conference. NGO activity, which in regions such as Africa involved sub-regional meetings,[97] resulted in the Declarations of all the official preparatory meetings acknowledging the special claims of women to protection from human rights abuses.[98] Their concerted activities, and those of the NGO women's caucus at the final preparatory meeting held in Geneva from 19 April to 7 May 1993, meant that by the time of the Conference in June, many of the gains by women that appear in the Vienna Declaration and Programme of Action had been agreed.[99]

In essence, these gains are in five areas. First, violence against women, sexual harassment, sexual exploitation and trafficking in women are classified by the conference document as human rights abuses, with violence against women in situations of conflict being clearly defined as violations of both human rights and humanitarian law.[100] This was a direct result of NGO activism which had identified the issue as of immense significance to women in all areas of the world. This view was undoubtedly reinforced by evidence of the sexual violence perpetrated against women in the conflict in the former Yugoslavia, which had been the subject of eighteen

NGO submissions to the Human Rights Commission at its 49th session in 1993. Endorsement was given to both the draft Declaration on the Elimination of Violence against Women and the decision of the Commission of Human Rights to appoint a special rapporteur on violence against women at its 1994 session.

Secondly, again as the result of the advocacy of women's rights activists, the reaffirmation of the principle of the universality of human rights incorporates women's human rights as 'an inalienable, integral and indivisible part of universal human rights'.[101] Thirdly, the human rights of women are to be integrated into all UN human rights activities, with recommendations stressing increased cooperation between the Commission on Human Rights, the CSW and the CEDAW and between the Centre for Human Rights and the Division for the Advancement of Women.[102] Fourthly, universal ratification and strengthening of the implementation of the Women's Convention, by both the addition of an optional protocol providing a complaints procedure and a process to address the large number of reservations[103] to its terms, is recommended.[104] Finally, although in no way matching the progress made in relation to the issue of violence against women, the conference document acknowledges some contexts, for example, health, where women suffer disproportionate denial of economic, social and cultural rights.[105]

Advances made by women's NGOs at the Vienna Conference are not, however, limited to the content of the conference document. The World Conference on Human Rights itself marked a turning point in women's participation in the United Nations as an arena in which to advance women's human rights. Women in all regions, particularly Asia, formed an active and effective lobby presence in the preparatory meetings for the Conference, participating directly in defining NGO positions and lobbying on women's issues in the regional preparatory meetings in Tunis, San José and Bangkok. The San José preparatory meeting, which was accompanied by a two-day NGO meeting, was strongly influenced by feminist NGOs and activists. They worked with a sixteen-point statement developed during La Nuestra, a satellite meeting of feminists who had met in San José, Costa Rica in December 1992. Similarly, the NGO Declaration presented at the Regional Meeting for Asia and the Pacific, held in Bangkok in March 1993, cited the invisibility of women's rights as one of the key challenges in human rights and agreed on the urgent need to address women's rights as human rights.

The Vienna Conference was perhaps the first time in the history of the women's movement that women participated fully to ensure that women's rights would be integrated into international and regional human rights policy. The presence of women in Vienna was evident on many levels. During the NGO Forum, 'All Human Rights for All', which ran from 10–12 June 1993 and was open to all NGOs, the Global Campaign for Women's Human Rights occupied key locations in the Forum premises. This included a 'Rights Place for Women' which afforded display areas for materials and office facilities for women organising workshops, with an adjacent women's press room. Although most chose to take part in the Working Group on Women, women's NGOs took part in all working groups at the NGO Forum and the joint NGO statement affirmed women's rights as human rights. Of the scheduled parallel activities, fifty-five related to women and thirty-two women's NGOs were scheduled participants. The concerns of these NGOs were many and diverse, including trafficking, female genital mutilation and women in war, both past and present and including women in the former Yugoslavia. Although they had diverse interests, most of these NGOs stressed the significance of the identification of violence against women as an issue of human rights and the importance and validity of this issue across class, country and culture. Indicative of this was the pivotal event of the non-governmental conference, the Global Tribunal on Women's Human Rights. The Tribunal, which drew more than a thousand people to an auditorium, took the form of testimonies from thirty-three women from twenty-five countries who described the abuses they had suffered or witnessed. In consultation with women legal advisors, a panel of four judges issued a detailed response to the testimonies and urged the establishment of an international criminal court for women. The Tribunal itself was the culmination of the worldwide petition drive, begun at the Centre for Women's Global Leadership at Rutgers in 1992, which called upon the United Nations to address violations of women's human rights. When the petition was presented to the Vienna Conference it had more than 900 sponsoring organisations internationally and 500,000 signatures.

The activities of women's NGOs extended to attempts to influence the official conference. Throughout the Conference, an NGO Women's Caucus met daily to develop strategies to influence the official conference and to continue to press for women's human rights. UNIFEM also hosted a daily caucus in the official conference area which allowed women governmental and non-governmental delegates and those responsible for implementing the UN mandates – the agencies – to come together. Submissions to the official Conference were made by a wide variety of organisations. They included both the traditional, well-established NGOs as well as the more recently formed organisations, and the regions were well represented. There had also been a submission from the Women's Caucus for the final Preparatory Committee for the Conference.[106] The attention of the conference was drawn to the enormous numbers of letters and petitions which had been received relating to violations of women's rights, but their numbers made it impossible to reproduce them in an official document.[107]

Submissions related to women's human rights were also made to the Vienna Conference by NGOs which were not normally primarily concerned with the interests of women. For example, the International Human Rights Law Group contributed a statement related solely to the promotion of the human rights of women. This had been co-sponsored by eighty-two human rights and women's rights NGOs.[108] Amnesty International's comprehensive submission relating to human rights generally devoted some attention to the specific concerns of women.[109] The submission of the Montreal-based International Centre for Human Rights and Democratic Development to both the NGO Forum and the official Conference placed significant emphasis on the rights of women.

Conclusions

It would be safe to claim that apart from the perennial issues of the indivisibility and the universality of human rights, the concerns of women dominated both the World Conference on Human Rights and its attendant NGO Forum. Certainly, women's rights and, within that, their right to be free from violence, was placed squarely on the world agenda. What remains to be seen is whether the substantive gains manifested in the official conference document will be realised and whether those less obvious gains – the increased attention paid by women's NGOs to human rights concerns and the correlated increased attention paid by human rights NGOs to the concerns of women – will be maintained.

In the wake of Vienna, women's NGOs have stressed the need to become more effective actors in the United Nations, its human rights programmes, its development, peacemaking, humanitarian and other activities. But there remains the risk that women's NGOs will fail to maintain the momentum required for a rights-based approach to issues and slip back into the familiar concerns of women and development. There is already some evidence of this in the preparations of the CSW and the final documents of the five regional preparatory commissions for the World Conference on Women which will be held in Beijing in 1995.[110]

At the same time, the new consciousness within the human rights NGO establishment of the importance of the concerns of women is similarly fragile. In this context, it is encouraging to note

Amnesty International's submission to the 50th session of the UN Commission on Human Rights.[111] This supports the activity within the United Nations which addresses violence against women and notes that during the previous six months alone Amnesty had taken action to try and stop human rights violations under all aspects of its mandate against women in 50 countries in all regions of the world. Amnesty has made it clear that it intends to be involved in the 1995 Women's Conference for which it has produced recommendations[112] and it monitored the 1994 sessions of both the CSW and the CEDAW. Amnesty also plans to mount a campaign on women's human rights during 1995. It is also encouraging that the International Human Rights Law Group and Human Rights Watch remain committed to the concept of women's human rights and that these NGOs, as well as the International Centre for Human Rights and Democratic Development, were active during the 50th session of the Commission on Human Rights when the resolution establishing the Special Rapporteur on Violence against Women was being formulated.[113] This apparent commitment of these NGOs to the idea of women's rights as human rights must be matched by a continuing commitment amongst women's NGOs. It is also hoped that the lessons of the Vienna Conference which, in essence, indicate that a linked, cooperative approach by a body of women's NGOs can achieve significant gains, will be replicated in other contexts throughout the work of the United Nations.[114]

NOTES

1. UN doc. A/CONF.157/23, see 32 *International Legal Materials (ILM)* 1161, 1993, p. 3.
2. David Weissbrodt, 'The Contribution of International Nongovernmental Organisations to the Protection of Human Rights' in Theodor Meron (ed.), *Human Rights in International Law: Legal and Policy Issues* (Oxford: Clarendon Press, 1984), p. 403; Harry J. Steiner (ed.), *Diverse Partners: Nongovernmental Organizations in the Human Rights Movement* (Harvard Law School and Human Rights Internet: 1990).
3. Rebecca J. Cook, 'Women's International Human Rights: A Bibliography', *New York University Journal of International Law and Politics*, vol. 24, no. 2, pp. 857–88.
4. Typical, but perhaps more eulogistic than most, is the comment of Margaret K. Bruce, former Assistant Director of the Division of Human Rights in the UN Secretariat: 'A word must be said here about the contribution of the non-governmental organisations without whose active interest and support the efforts of the United Nations would not have had the same impact and value for women everywhere. Among the many activities undertaken by those international non-governmental organisations who enjoy consultative status with

the Economic and Social Council mention may be made of their efforts to make known the norms established by the United Nations and its other work to promote the status of women, and to encourage Governments to observe the standards laid down and to make full use of the various forms of international assistance available'. *Revue des droits de l'homme*, vol. 4, 1971, p. 369.

5. Georgina Ashworth, 'The United Nations "Women's Conference" and International Linkages in the Women's Movement' in Peter Willetts (ed.), *Pressure Groups in the Global System* (London: Pinter, 1982), p. 125; I. Tinker and A. Jacquette, 'UN Decade For Women: Its Impact and its Legacy', *World Development*, vol. 15, no. 3, 1987; Caroline Moser, 'Gender Planning in the Third World: Meeting Practical and Strategic Needs', Kathleen Newland, 'From Transnational Development and the International Decade for Women' and Fred Halliday, 'Hidden from International Relations: Women and the International Arena' in Rebecca Grant and Kathleen Newland (eds), *Gender and International Relations* (Buckingham: Open University Press, 1991).

6. International Agreement for the Suppression of the White Slave Traffic (1904) and International Convention of the same name, League of Nations Treaty Series (LNTS), vol. I, pp. 84–94; International Convention for the Suppression of Traffic in Women and Children, LNTS, vol. ix, pp. 416–33; International Convention for the Suppression of the Traffic of Women of Full Age, LNTS, vol. CL, pp. 431–43.

7. Convention Concerning the Employment of Women Before and After Childbirth, adopted by the ILO, Convention no. 3, 1919; Convention Concerning the Employment of Women during the Night, ILO Convention no. 4, 1919; Convention Concerning the Employment of Women on Underground Work in Mines of All Kinds, ILO Convention no. 45, 1935.

8. Hague Convention on the Conflict of Nationality Laws, 1933; Montevideo Convention on the Nationality of Married Women, 1933.

9. Kathleen Barry, *Female Sexual Slavery* (New York: Avon Books, 1979).

10. Carol Miller, 'Women in International Relations? The Debate in Inter-War Britain' in R. Grant and K. Newland (eds), *op. cit.*, p. 64.

11. *Ibid.*, p. 69.

12. Gertrude Bussey and Margaret Tims, *The Women's International League for Peace and Freedom, 1915–1965* (London: Allen and Unwin, 1965), p. 74.

13. Carol Miller, *op cit.*, p. 69.

14. *Ibid.*, p. 70.

15. *Ibid.*, fn. 29, p. 80.

16. Catherine Foster, *Women for All Seasons: The Story of the Women's International League for Peace and Freedom* (Athens, GA: University of Georgia Press, 1989), Chapter 1.

17. Gertrude Bussey and Margaret Tims, *op. cit.*, Chapters 3 and 7.

18. For example, Gertrude Bussey and Margaret Tims, *op. cit.*, p. 71, quote the following published in the journal of the International Narcotic Education Association of October 1930: 'The decisions taken by the Council [of the League of Nations] were of the utmost importance and it must be noted that they were favourably influenced by the resolutions adopted by the conference of the Women's International League for Peace and Freedom.' Chapters 3 to 15 of Bussey and Tims's monograph details the significant lobbying for peace by WILPF at the League.

19. C. Miller, 'The interaction of national and transnational women's networks with the League of Nations Secretariat', paper presented to the British International Studies Association Conference, December 1991.

20. Statement by the representative of the Inter-American Commission on the Status of Women E/CN.6/SR.29 (1948). The relevant Articles of the UN

Charter are 1, 8, 13, 55 and 76.
21. UN doc. E/38/Rev.1/Add.1.
22. ECOSOC Resolution 1/5 of 16 and 18 February 1946 established the Commission on Human Rights and a Sub-Commission on the Status of Women, with an initial nucleus of seven named women. Resolution 2/11 of 21 June 1946 changed the status of the Sub-Commission to a full Commission of fifteen members. Resolution 48(IV) of 29 March 1947 in its first paragraph defined the functions of the Commission.
23. John P. Humphrey, 'The Memoirs of John P. Humphrey, First Director of the United Nations Division of Human Rights', *Human Rights Quarterly*, vol. 5 (1983), p. 406.
24. John P. Humphrey, *Human Rights and the United Nations: A Great Adventure* (New York: Transnational Publishers, 1984), p. 30.
25. Arvonne S. Fraser, *The UN Decade for Women: Documents and Dialogue*, (Boulder, CO: Westview Press, 1986), p. 6.
26. *Ibid.*
27. Ashworth, *op. cit.*, p. 128.
28. Laura Reanda, 'The Commission on the Status of Women' in P. Alston (ed.), *The United Nations and Human Rights: A Critical Appraisal* (Oxford: Clarendon Press, 1992), p. 265.
29. *Ibid.*, p. 273–4, notes that some NGOs and Eastern European countries sought to raise questions of discrimination in individual countries from the floor in early sessions of the CSW. Cold War tensions effectively terminated this attempt and since that time it has been conventional for NGOs and members to refrain from commenting on individual countries, but to focus on trends.
30. The Commission and its Secretariat shifted to New York in the latter part of 1993.
31. J. Morsink, 'Women's Rights in the Universal Declaration' *Human Rights Quarterly*, vol. 13 (1991), p. 230.
32. Special provision was made for this in an ECOSOC Resolution, largely as a result of lobbying by the CSW. See Resolution 46(IV) of 28 March 1947, under 'Report of the Commission on Human Rights' section A, Paragraph (f). See also Morsink, *op. cit.*, p. 231.
33. Morsink, *op. cit.*, p. 231.
34. *Ibid.*, pp. 241–50. Article 16(1) of the Declaration asserts that men and women are 'entitled to equal rights as to marriage, during marriage and on its dissolution'.
35. Bussey and Tims, *op. cit.*, p. 197.
36. Catherine Foster, *op. cit.*, pp. 25–6.
37. Bussey and Tims, *op. cit.*, p. 201.
38. *Ibid.*, p. 200.
39. E/CN.4/SR.371, p. 17 and see M.J. Bossuyt, *Guide to the Travaux Préparatoires of the International Covenant on Civil and Political Rights* (Dordrecht: Martinus Nijhoff, 1987), p. 76.
40. Elise Boulding, 'Female Alternatives to Hierarchical Systems, Past and Present', *International Associations*, Issue 6–7, 1975.
41. The Organisation of American States had already formulated the Bogota Inter-American Convention on the Granting of Political Rights to Women, in 1948.
42. Bossuyt, *op. cit.*, p. 446 ff. See, further, Laura Reanda, *op. cit.*, at p. 279, where she notes that ECOSOC Resolution 48(IV) 1947 authorised the officers of the CSW to be present when sections relevant to women were being debated during the preparation of the International Bill of Rights. The resolution also requested the Sub-Commission to invite the CSW to send a representative to

its meeting when issues relating to the discrimination on the basis of sex were discussed. The right of the CSW to participate in all relevant meetings of the Commission on Human Rights was extended by ECOSOC Resolution 566 (XIX) in 1955. Similar resolutions of UNESCO and ILO allowed the CSW to have a role in the elaboration of the multilateral treaties of these agencies: see Bruce, *op. cit.*, pp. 378–84.

43. This is the phrase used to describe women who, against their will, were established in brothels to provide 'comfort' for Japanese servicemen during the Second World War.

44. Kathleen Barry, 'International Politics of Female Sexual Slavery' in Kathleen Barry, Charlotte Bunch and Shirley Castley (eds), *International Feminism: Networking Against Female Sexual Slavery* (New York: International Women's Tribune Centre, 1984), pp. 21–31 at p. 23, suggests that the Working Group was established as a result of the efforts of the former secretary of the Anti-Slavery Society, Patrick Montgomery. She indicates on p. 24 that on his retirement the Society had refocused its concern away from trafficking in women of full age.

45. General Assembly Resolution 317(IV) of 2 December 1949.

46. Laura Reanda, 'Prostitution as a Human Rights Question: Problems and Prospects for United Nations Action', *Human Rights Quarterly*, vol. 13 (1991), p. 214.

47. NGO access to this Working Group was extended in 1991 when the Commission on Human Rights adopted Resolution 1991/58 (6 March 1991), which extended access beyond NGOs with consultative status to all interested organisations.

48. Reanda, 'Prostitution as a Human Rights Question', *op. cit.*, p. 214. Reanda notes at p. 211 that the International Abolitionist Federation, an NGO established with the aim of eradicating, rather than regulating, prostitution was instrumental in the 1987 proposal to the Working Group for an implementation protocol to the 1949 Convention. The proposal was endorsed by the Working Group, adopted by the Sub-Commission, but not accepted by the Commission on Human Rights.

49. Arvonne S. Fraser, 'The Convention on the Elimination of Discrimination Against Women', unpublished, pp. 2–10, and UN General Assembly Resolution 1921(XVIII) of 5 December 1963.

50. United Nations, *Draft declaration on the Elimination of Discrimination Against Women: Memorandum by the Secretary-General* E/CN.6/426, 30 October 1964.

51. Fraser, *op. cit.*, p. 6.

52. UN General Assembly Resolution 2263(XXII) of 7 November 1967.

53. Margaret E. Galey, 'Promoting non-discrimination against Women, the UN Commission on the Status of Women', *International Studies Quarterly*, vol. 23, no. 2, June 1979, p. 287.

54. Bruce, *op. cit.*, p. 396 ff.

55. H. Sipila, *Study on the Interrelationship of the Status of Women and Family Planning*, E/CN.6/575/Add.5.

56. Galey, *op. cit.*, p. 278.

57. Ester Boserup, *Women's Role in Economic Development* (London: Allen and Unwin, 1970); also as (London: Earthscan Publications, 1989).

58. Bruce, *op. cit.*, p. 391.

59. Ashworth, *op. cit.*, p. 130.

60. UN General Assembly Resolution 3010(XXVII) of 18 December 1972.

61. Laura Reanda, 'The Commission', *op. cit.*, p. 291.

62. UN doc. E/CONF.66/34.

63. Galey, *op. cit.*, p. 273 at p. 281.
64. *Ibid.*, p. 294.
65. Ashworth, *op. cit.*, p. 135.
66. Ashworth, *op. cit.*, pp. 136–7.
67. UN General Assembly Resolution 34/180 of 18 December 1979.
68. 'Working Paper prepared by the Secretary-General on the Draft Convention on the Elimination of All Forms of Discrimination Against Women', E/CN.6/591 (1976).
69. Addendum to the Working Paper prepared by the Secretary-General on the Draft Convention on the Elimination of All Forms of Discrimination against Women, E/CN.6/591/Add.1 (1976).
70. Lars Adam Rehof, *Guide to the Travaux Préparatoires of the United Nations Convention on the Elimination of All Forms of Discrimination against Women* (Dordrecht: Martinus Nijhoff Publications, 1993). See also UN doc. E/CN.6/591, pp. 7–9, p. 53 and Annex 1, pp. 63–65 and p. 67 and UN doc. E/CN.6/SR.613, pp. 10–11. The ICSDW had access to the UN by virtue of being the women's section of the Socialist International.
71. UN doc. E/CN.6/SR.613 pp. 10–11.
72. N. Burrows, 'The 1979 Convention on the Elimination of All Forms of Discrimination Against Women' *Netherlands International Rev*, vol. 32, p. 423 (1985).
73. Report of the Working Group of the Whole on the Drafting of the Convention on the Elimination of All Forms of Discrimination against Women, A/C.3/32/L.59 (1977) paras.44–9.
74. *Ibid.*, para.34.
75. A/C.3/34/SR.70–3 (1979).
76. Roberta Jacobson, 'The Committee on the Elimination of Discrimination against Women' in P. Alston (ed.), *The United Nations and Human Rights: A Critical Appraisal* (Oxford University Press, 1992), pp. 444–72.
77. Barbados, Byelorussian SSR, Cape Verde, China, Cuba, Dominica, the German Democratic Republic, Guyana, Haiti, Hungary, Mexico, Mongolia, Norway, Poland, Portugal, Rwanda, Saint Vincent and the Grenadines, Sweden, Ukrainian SSR, the Soviet Union.
78. *The Work of CEDAW*, vol. 1, 1982–1985 (ST/CSDHS/5) 1989, p. 3.
79. UN doc. E/CN.6/NGO.272 and Add 1.
80. Convention on the Rights of the Child, UN General Assembly Resolution 44/25 of 20 November 1989, article 45.
81. Andrew Byrnes suggests that there is no reason why the CEDAW should not develop a formal process for the involvement of NGOs in its work. He points out that both the Economic, Social and Cultural Rights Committee and the Committee against Torture have asserted the right to receive information from non-governmental organisations in consultative status with the Economic and Social Council, although no such power has been asserted by the Human Rights Committee, see Andrew Byrnes, 'The "Other" Human Rights Treaty Body: the Work of the Committee on the Elimination of Discrimination against Women', *Yale Journal of International Law*, vol. 14, no. 1, pp. 1–67, esp. p. 36 ff.
82. See, for example, IWRAW, *1992 'A&Q': An Analysis of Country Reports to CEDAW and the Questions they Suggest*, (University of Minnesota, 1992) and *1994 IWRAW to CEDAW Country Reports* (University of Minnesota, December 1993). National NGOs have also provided material. For example, at the time of Japan's first report in 1988, material was supplied to CEDAW by a Japanese women's rights NGO (UN doc. CEDAW/C/SR.108, paras 13, 16 (1988); a Bangladesh NGO provided CEDAW with an alternative report

at the time of the presentation of its second report in 1993; while in 1994, at the time of Japan's second report, a large contingent of Japanese human rights NGOs lobbied CEDAW on the subject of Japanese 'comfort women', see note 43, above.

83. Report of CEDAW on its eighth Session, UN doc. A/43/38, General Recommendation no. 12.
84. Report of CEDAW on its eleventh Session, UN doc. A/47/38, General Recommendation no. 19.
85. The Economic and Social Council adopted a resolution on 'Violence against women in all its forms' in May 1991 (ECOSOC Resolution 1991/18) in response to a recommendation made by the CSW at its 35th session in 1991. The Council resolution recommended that an expert group meeting with the brief to develop a framework for an international instrument on violence against women should be held by the Division for the Advancement of Women. The expert group meeting in November 1991 (UN doc. EGM/VAW/1991/1) and a Working Group of CSW in August 1992 drafted a Declaration that was adopted at the CSW session in March 1993. The CSW text was endorsed in ECOSOC Resolution 1993/10 of 27 July 1993 and adopted by General Assembly Resolution 48/104 of 20 December 1993.
86. Noreen Burrows, 'International Law and Human Rights: The Case of Women's Rights', in Tom Campbell (ed.), *Human Rights: From Rhetoric to Reality* (Oxford: Blackwell, 1986), p. 80.
87. Universal Declaration of Human Rights, UN General Assembly Resolution 217 A(III), 10 December 1948.
88. Amnesty International, *Women in the Front Line* (London: AI Index ACT 77/01, 1991).
89. See, for example, Americas Watch, *Criminal Injustice, Violence Against Women in Brazil* (New York: Human Rights Watch, October 1991).
90. IWRAW, *The Women's Watch*, vol. 2, no. 1, 1988, p. 1.
91. Andrew Byrnes, *Ending Discrimination Against Women* (New York: International League for Human Rights, 'In Brief: Human Rights at the United Nations', pamphlet series no. 2, October 1988).
92. The ILHR produced commentaries on the report of the Czech and Slovak Republics for CEDAW in 1992. Its commentaries for the Human Rights Committee on a number of states parties reports prepared under its terms have also raised issues relating to women.
93. See statement by Amnesty International to the 32nd Session of the Commission on the Status of Women on the Ill Treatment of Women in Custody, SGO/HMC/AR, 22 February 1988.
94. Amnesty International, *Rape and Sexual Abuse: Torture and Ill-Treatment of Women in Detention* (London: AI Index ACT 77/11/91, December 1991).
95. Amnesty International Index MDE 30/02/93.
96. Donna J. Sullivan, 'Women's Human Rights and the 1993 World Conference on Human Rights', *American Journal of International Law*, vol. 88, 1994, p. 152.
97. *WILDAF News*, Issue 5 (Harare: Women in Law and Development in Africa, 1993).
98. Sullivan, *op. cit.*, pp. 152ff.
99. See Report of the Preparatory Committee, UN doc. A/CONF.157/PC/98 at pp. 25-6 and 40-2.
100. UN doc. A/CONF.157/23 at, p. 7, p. 10 and 19.
101. *Ibid.*, p 7. See Sullivan, *op. cit.*, p. 158.
102. *Ibid.*, pp. 18-22.
103. Belinda Clark, 'The Vienna Convention Reservations Regime and the

180 *Jane Connors*

Convention on Discrimination Against Women', *American Journal of International Law*, vol. 85, 1991, p. 281; Rebecca Cook, 'Reservations to the Convention on All Forms of Discrimination against Women', *Virginia Journal of International Law*, vol. 30, 1990, p. 643.

104. UN doc. A/CONF.157/23 at p. 19.
105. *Ibid.*, at pp. 7, 19, 18, and 26.
106. UN doc. A/CONF.157/PC/63/Add.25.
107. *Ibid.*, 3/Add.6.
108. *Ibid.*, 3/Add.22.
109. Amnesty International Index IOR 41/16/92, p. 20.
110. The World Conference on Women planned for 1995 has been authorised to assess women's status in the light of the objectives of the Nairobi Forward Looking Strategies for the Advancement of Women to the Year 2000; mobilise women and men at the policy and grass roots levels to achieve these objectives; adopt a platform of action focusing on fundamental obstacles to the advancement of women; and to determine the priorities to be followed from 1996 to 2001 for the implementation of the strategies within the United Nations.
111. Amnesty International Index IOR 41/38/93.
112. Amnesty International, *Equality by the Year 2000* (London: AI Index IOR 41/06/94) September 1994.
113. Resolution 1994/45: E/CN.4/L.11/Add.5, p. 3.
114. The approach adopted by women's NGOs at the World Conference on Human Rights was replicated during the preparations for the International Conference on Population and Development held in Cairo in September 1994. At its NGO Forum, the Women's Caucus, regularly attended by 400–500 people, proved to be the largest and most influential lobbying group. A similar approach by women's NGOs could be seen in the preparations for the 1995 Summit on Social Development.

7

AMNESTY INTERNATIONAL AT THE UNITED NATIONS

Helena Cook

Introduction

From its inception Amnesty International (hereinafter referred to simply as 'Amnesty') was based squarely within the international legal order framed by the United Nations Charter and the Universal Declaration of Human Rights. It began when Peter Benenson, a London lawyer, launched his 'Appeal for Amnesty' in *the Observer* newspaper in 1961 to campaign for the release of people imprisoned for their opinions. Benenson based his campaign on Articles 18 and 19 of the Universal Declaration of Human Rights and included as one of his four main aims a call for 'effective international machinery to guarantee freedom of opinion'. The Appeal was originally intended to run for only one year. It turned out to be the foundation stone of a world-wide international human rights organisation that has become one of the leading non-governmental players within the human rights movement.

Thirty-three years later, Amnesty's basic objective in its Statute remains to contribute to the observance throughout the world of the Universal Declaration of Human Rights – the fundamental document that underpins the international system of human rights protection. As one of its very early Annual Reports stated, 'Until such time as every government observes every Article of the [Universal] Declaration it will remain a symbol of our potentialities and an indictment of our failures'.[1] Amnesty's work within intergovernmental organisations, such as the United Nations, is a core element of its efforts to secure universal observance of the Declaration and the organisation devotes considerable time, expertise and resources to these activities. This work extends to a wide range of organisations, including the Organisation of American States, the Organisation of African Unity, the Council of Europe, the European Union, the Conference on Security and Cooperation in Europe, the Commonwealth and the League of Arab States. However, its most extensive programme by far at the intergovernmental level is in respect of the United Nations.[2]

This work is based on four fundamental principles that are central to the international human rights system: first, that human rights are universal and indivisible and that the Universal Declaration is indeed a 'common standard of achievement for all peoples and all nations'; second, that respect for human rights is a legitimate concern of the international community and not exclusively an internal matter for individual states; third, that each state can be held to account internationally to ensure that it is fulfilling its responsibility to promote and protect human rights; and fourth, that the international community comprises not only states but also individuals and NGOs that have their own particular role to play in the international promotion and protection of human rights and in the work of intergovernmental bodies such as the United Nations. Through its UN work, Amnesty seeks to encourage the development of international standards, derived from the Universal Declaration, regulating the way in which governments treat their citizens; to see that governments respect these international human rights obligations that they themselves adopt; and to ensure that they are held accountable whenever they fail to do so.

In the wake of the 1961 campaign, the world-wide Amnesty movement grew rapidly. It developed principally through the formation of local groups of Amnesty members, each working on the cases of three 'adopted' prisoners of conscience. In countries with a sufficient network of functioning groups, Amnesty 'Sections' were set up. Initially concentrated in Western Europe, by the early 1970s 2,000 Amnesty groups had been formed and Sections were established in thirty-two countries in all regions of the world. Today the organisation has over one million members and subscribers and the number of groups tops 8,000 in seventy different countries, with Amnesty Sections in forty-eight of those countries.

Amnesty developed from a conviction that public awareness of human rights violations and the pressure of public opinion are powerful and essential weapons against government repression. It focused on the lives of real people rather than on horrific statistics and enabled ordinary citizens all over the world to speak out on behalf of other individuals. One of its special characteristics is the close cooperation between enthusiastic and dedicated volunteer members and full-time professionals and experts. It relies on a combination of both simple techniques, such as letter-writing and urgent appeals to governments, and specialised professional and technical work. The organisation has always placed a high value on the quality and accuracy of its information. It tries to ensure that its recommendations to individual governments and those to intergovernmental organisations are practical, rooted in reality and based on its own experience and knowledge derived from in-depth and extensive research and fact-finding.

Contrary to a wide-spread perception, Amnesty does not work actively and in the same way on the full range of human rights. Although its scope has evolved significantly from its original focus on prisoners of conscience and freedom of opinion and expression, Amnesty still adheres to a precisely defined mandate agreed by the world-wide body of Amnesty members. Its work to *promote* human rights, such as its education programmes and campaigns for ratification of international treaties, extends to all rights – civil and political and economic, social and cultural rights. In the area of human rights *protection*, however, the main focus of its campaigning and other activities is:

– to free all prisoners of conscience; these are people detained anywhere for their beliefs or because of their ethnic origin, sex, colour or language who have not used or advocated violence;
– to ensure fair and prompt trials for all political prisoners;
– to abolish the death penalty, torture and other cruel treatment of prisoners; and
– to end extrajudicial executions and disappearances.

Amnesty also opposes specific abuses by opposition groups: hostage-taking, torture and killings of prisoners and other deliberate and arbitrary killings.[3]

The international human rights system is fundamental to Amnesty's credibility and legitimacy. The human rights treaties and other standards provide it with a consistent and uniform code by which to assess every government and a defence against accusations of bias or the imposition of personal standards or values. This is imperative for an organisation that sets great store by its independence and impartiality. Although in some areas, most notably that of Amnesty's absolute opposition to the death penalty, the organisation's own position may be ahead of the current status in international law and practice, its position still reflects an important body of international opinion and clearly emerging trends.

From its earliest days Amnesty recognised the importance of working directly in and through the UN system, both to expose violations and to advance the frontiers of human rights protection. As an outsider in this governmental club, Amnesty's most potent weapon is awareness-raising – bringing human rights concerns into the public arena and using the momentum created by public opinion as a catalyst for international action. It has been able to use the United Nations to champion the cause of individual victims against the very governments that are the members of that body. It has created pressure on those same governments to broaden and strengthen the UN's system of checks and balances that curtails their authority to abuse the rights of their citizens with impunity. Using the UN's own procedures, it has subjected the actions of governments to the scrutiny of their fellow governments and the rest of the world. When looked at in this light, it is extraordinary that NGOs like Amnesty are respected and taken seriously at the UN and have been able to exert considerable influence there. Yet over the years NGOs have come to be recognised as important participants at the UN in their own right.

It is difficult to quantify precisely what impact Amnesty has within the United Nations. It is impossible to attribute specific results solely to a particular NGO initiative. NGOs can and do set a political process in motion and shape the outcome, but one cannot isolate the impact of NGOs from that of other players or factors. Political developments, public opinion, changes of government and the shifting of international alliances are often critical. Government delegates, UN officials and others may play a key role in achieving a particular result. Amnesty representatives could tell many stories of freak events, chance meetings or casual remarks over lunch that had as much impact as a carefully planned lobbying action. Sometimes a good result is achieved for the wrong reasons and against all odds. To be effective at the UN, NGOs must be opportunists, able to seize on the unexpected and make the best use of an unforeseen event.

This chapter examines the main areas of Amnesty's UN work and describes some of the ways in which Amnesty operates in this intergovernmental forum. It should be borne in mind that Amnesty is never acting alone, but is contributing to a complex process involving many others, including government and UN officials, human rights experts, NGOs, the media and the public.

Amnesty and the UN system

Amnesty began working directly at the United Nations very early in its history. Peter Benenson first secured Category B consultative status for the organisation in 1964. That same year Amnesty convened meetings of interested NGOs to review the further development of the international protection of human rights and promoted resolutions at the UN in favour of a High Commissioner for Human Rights and for a moratorium on the use of the death penalty.

In formal terms consultative status gives the organisation international standing and enables it to attend relevant UN meetings, to submit documents and to make statements. However, the way in which NGO access and participation have developed in practice has given Amnesty much greater scope for formal and informal participation at the UN than is suggested by the wording of ECOSOC Resolution 1296(XLIV) which now governs such status. Consultative status opened the door for Amnesty to undertake a whole range of vigorous political and campaigning initiatives at the UN.

The United Nations also provides a forum for direct access to governments. Amnesty's varied interests at the UN give it a broad platform on which to engage government delegates in debate and to build confidence and respect. Not infrequently, Amnesty's access to a country has been facilitated by the government's diplomatic representatives in New York or Geneva. Even today, in respect of those few governments that persist in refusing access or dialogue, the UN offers a rare, if not the only, opportunity for Amnesty to have direct contact with that government's representatives.

The United Nations is an important meeting place for NGOs from all over the world. From its earliest days Amnesty has been an active member of the Conference of Non-Governmental Organisations in Consultative Status with ECOSOC and was a member of its Bureau for many years. In recent years Amnesty has increasingly participated in joint NGO initiatives at the UN, which can carry great weight. The organisation can also help NGOs without the same level of UN access or expertise by informing them of developments and by alerting them to the significance of tiny changes in wording or emphasis in resolutions that may appear trivial but in fact indicate important political shifts. Contacts with NGOs at the international level also assist in mounting effective broad-based campaigns at the national level by Amnesty's Sections.

Amnesty's early work with the United Nations was directed towards standard-setting and tended to be carried out at the highest levels of the organisation. By the mid-1970s a more extensive UN programme was being developed at the International Secretariat, Amnesty representatives were attending UN meetings regularly and cases and information were routinely submitted to the few international procedures then available. The first Amnesty representational office to the UN was established at this time in New York, although permanent representation to the UN in Geneva was not secured until 1988. It was also recognised early on that there was enormous potential for greater involvement in UN work by Amnesty members. As the membership grew, educational materials and lobbying and campaigning techniques were gradually developed to encourage this. Today, an extensive UN programme is carried out by the joint efforts of professional staff in the Secretariat's Legal and Inter-national Organisations Programme, including its New York and Geneva offices and its volunteer representatives to the UN in Vienna, and by the activities of Sections and members in their own countries. This combination of national action and direct input to UN bodies has greatly enhanced Amnesty's impact at the UN.[4]

Full-time professional staff, including legal experts, enable Amnesty to field well-briefed, experienced representatives at the United Nations. They have the necessary political, technical or country specialisation and can build and maintain contacts with government delegates, UN staff, NGOs and the media. Amnesty can therefore follow UN developments closely at first-hand and it has access to a large volume of documentation and information. Its UN presence also contributes to a better understanding by governments and others of what Amnesty is and does. It provides an important channel for Amnesty's information and a means of conveying its concerns to a wide audience, thereby laying the groundwork for initiatives that Amnesty seeks to pursue at the UN.

Equally essential are the complementary efforts of Amnesty's world-wide membership directed at their own governments. Government positions at the UN are, of course, influenced by domestic fac-tors and national policies, and are often decided well in advance of UN meetings. As many NGOs are frustrated to discover when they first go to the UN, on some questions there may be limited scope for influencing governments at the meeting itself. Amnesty acts while governments are still formulating their positions. Amnesty members around the world inform their governments of Amnesty's current concerns and lobby for UN action. Letters, meetings with govern-ment officials and other direct approaches by members may be sup-plemented by securing parliamentary or public support and media attention as well as working with national NGOs and interest groups. This not only alerts governments to pressing issues or concerns but gives Amnesty some advance indication of the positions which dif-ferent governments will take at the UN. Amnesty members also cam-paign nationally for ratification and implementation of human rights treaties, for effective human rights policies, and for bilateral pressure on other governments which are violating human rights. It should be noted, however, that under Amnesty's working rules members do not work on human rights concerns or cases in their own countries, whether or not these have been the subject of UN action.

Amnesty staff and members regularly attend meetings of rele-vant governmental and expert UN bodies. They monitor closely the formal debates, deliver Amnesty's statements, lobby for resolutions and participate in drafting groups. They also engage in an endless round of informal discussions with government delegates, NGOs and UN staff. At any UN meeting the discussions in the coffee lounges and corridors are as important as, if not more important than, the official speeches. UN work also calls for participation in a host of related international meetings and discussions with government and UN officials, other NGOs and human rights experts. Amnesty makes full use of all the relevant UN human rights mechanisms and procedures and sends huge volumes of information and case material to the UN for action. Hard-pressed government delegates are increasingly seeking out NGO information and proposals at the UN; it is not unknown for Amnesty to be vilified at the UN by a government it has criticised, only to be approached by that same government seeking information it can use against another government.

Much of Amnesty's UN work is directed towards those UN bodies which are explicitly mandated to deal with human rights, principally the Commission on Human Rights and its subsidiary body, the Sub-Commission on Prevention of Discrimination and Protection of Minorities, as well as ECOSOC and the General Assembly. It tends to concentrate its efforts on the issues and mechanisms that deal with the concerns of its mandate.

Amnesty does not, however, confine itself to the human rights bodies, but seeks opportunities through other parts of the UN system to raise human rights issues. The UN programme on crime prevention and criminal justice, for example, has been heavily involved in drafting some of the human rights standards. Amnesty participated actively in this during the 1970s and 1980s, including the five-yearly UN Congresses on the Prevention of Crime and the Treatment of Offenders. Amnesty is now trying to encourage this programme to keep human rights at the forefront of its work, following the establishment in 1992 of a new governmental Commission on Crime Prevention and Criminal Justice that appears reluctant to address human rights issues.

It is, however, an uphill task to break through the compartmentalisation of the UN system. Amnesty has had little success in raising human rights violations specifically affecting women at the Commission on the Status of Women. This Commission has not been willing to take up these issues, arguing that they are within the remit of the human rights programme; it even prohibited Amnesty from naming individual countries in a 1991 statement. The UN Development Programme has also been reticent to tackle human rights issues directly and Amnesty is currently exploring ways to bring its concerns more directly into this programme.

A new direction for Amnesty's work at the UN has been in the area of peace-keeping. As the UN has rapidly expanded these operations in the past six years, human rights have played an increasingly prominent role. Amnesty has made many recommendations to improve the human rights components of peace-keeping operations and post-conflict peace-building. This has also brought Amnesty into much closer contact with the Security Council, with other committees of the General Assembly and with departments in the New York UN Secretariat where Amnesty was previously largely unknown.

Several of the specialised structures attached to the UN also occupy an important place in Amnesty's programme of work at the UN. It works closely with the UN High Commissioner for Refugees on all aspects of its refugee concerns. In 1993, for example, Amnesty significantly stepped up pressure on the governmental Executive Committee of UNHCR to counter moves by several refugee-receiving countries which it warned were systematically undermining the international system of refugee protection.[5] It has also been lobbying actively in the past couple of years to get the Commission on Human Rights to cooperate more closely with UNHCR and to pay more attention to refugee issues as a major human rights concern. Amnesty works with a number of the UN specialised agencies, such as the UN Educational, Scientific and Cultural Organisation (UNESCO – where it was granted consultative status in 1975), the International Labour Organisation (ILO) and the World Health Organisation (WHO). This work may be on a regular basis, such as Amnesty's biannual submission of individual cases to UNESCO's Committee on Conventions and Recommendations and its lobbying of governments, employer organisations and trade unions to raise country concerns at the annual International Labour Conferences.[6] Collaboration with an agency can also be *ad hoc* on specific initiatives or issues related to the agency's mandate, such as with UNESCO on human rights education programmes or with WHO on the role of medical personnel in the treatment and protection of prisoners.

Most of the activities outlined above are the regular 'bread and butter' work for a human rights NGO active at the UN. There are also major international conferences, summits or commemorative events organised under UN auspices at which NGOs can play an important role. Preparation for these may extend over several years and involve regional and inter-regional pre-meetings. It is commonplace for NGOs to hold their own parallel events during such conferences as well as participating in the official governmental meetings. The recent major event of this kind for the human rights community was the turbulent World Conference on Human Rights held in Vienna in June 1993 which took over two years of preparation.[7] Other recent conferences in which Amnesty has played a role include the 1991 World Summit for Children and the 1988 fortieth anniversary of the Universal Declaration of Human Rights. It is currently preparing for the Fourth World Conference on Women and the fiftieth anniversary of the UN, both taking place in 1995.

Contributing to the development of the UN system

Standard-setting

The body of human rights treaties and other standards and guidelines adopted by the United Nations are among Amnesty's primary working tools. No government wants to be accused of openly flouting these international standards of behaviour. Thus Amnesty's criticisms of a particular government's practice and its recommendations for improvements carry far greater weight when they are based on norms set by the UN. Amnesty has, therefore, actively encouraged and participated in the development of new treaties and standards. Most of these standards have been drafted in the context of the UN human rights programme or its programme on criminal justice and now cover, to a greater or lesser extent, all the main areas of Amnesty's mandate.[8]

One of the most compelling examples of Amnesty and other NGOs acting as catalysts in the development of international standards is in respect of the practice of torture.[9] Amnesty's first world-wide Campaign for the Abolition of Torture was launched in December 1972. Aimed at making torture 'as unthinkable as slavery', it sought to generate a world-wide public outcry against torture and to bring pressure to bear on governments to devise effective legal machinery to enforce the international prohibition of torture contained in Article 5 of the Universal Declaration of Human Rights. The campaign included publicising the extensive practice of torture in all regions of the world, diplomatic and political representations to governments and intergovernmental bodies, promotion of a UN resolution for a Convention against Torture and regional conferences on torture by Amnesty's Sections. Amnesty members collected over a million signatures for a petition calling on the UN to condemn torture.

In 1973 several governments at the General Assembly referred to Amnesty's campaign and a resolution was finally adopted condemning torture and other cruel treatment.[10] That same year Amnesty published its *Report on Torture*, a comprehensive world survey of torture, and in December convened an International

Conference for the Abolition of Torture to coincide with the twenty-fifth anniversary of the Universal Declaration. This major event brought together over 300 participants from governments, the United Nations, NGOs and Amnesty's membership and was widely covered in the media. Amnesty decided to turn the one-year campaign into a continuing programme to build on the extraordinary momentum and publicity that had so far been generated. In 1974 Amnesty established its Urgent Action network to draw immediate attention to urgent human rights cases and to enable individual participants around the world to send express letters and cables on behalf of victims at risk. Although not limited to such cases, this network was particularly suited to stimulating action against torture and it served to intensify public awareness of the barbarity of torture in a very direct and personalised way.

The NGO-led mobilisation for international action against torture was brought sharply into focus when the Allende Government was overthrown in Chile in September 1973, unleashing a wave of brutality in the country, and when the 1974 coup in Portugal uncovered shocking evidence of torture under the former regime. These events, against the backdrop of NGO campaigning, set in motion a whole programme of standard-setting relating to torture and the protection of prisoners. In Resolution 3218 (XXIV), the 1974 General Assembly called on the 1975 Fifth UN Congress on the Prevention of Crime and the Treatment of Offenders to consider rules against torture, safeguards against arbitrary detention, a code of ethics for law enforcement officials as well as principles of medical ethics which the WHO was invited to draft. Amnesty spent a year preparing for the Congress – lobbying governments, submitting a 16-page document with a series of recommendations and sponsoring two seminars on torture at the Congress itself. A draft Declaration against Torture was finally approved at the 1975 Crime Congress and adopted by the General Assembly two months later.[11]

Amnesty and other NGOs continued their campaigning against torture which, from the outset, had included a call for a legally-binding treaty. These efforts were again cited by governments at the United Nations in 1977 when, spurred by the political impetus created by the death in custody of Steve Biko, the South African Black Consciousness leader, the General Assembly called on the Commission on Human Rights to draft a Convention against Torture.[12]

The drafting took seven years, but eventually resulted in the adoption of the Convention against Torture and Other Cruel, Inhuman or Degrading Treatment or Punishment in 1984.[13] Amnesty participated actively throughout the preparation of the Convention, both by attending the drafting sessions and by lobbying governments to ensure that a number of key principles were included in the text. The issues on which Amnesty focused were: the obligation on states to extradite or try alleged torturers; universality of jurisdiction in respect of torturers to ensure that they could be tried regardless of their nationality or where the offence was committed; an effective implementation mechanism in the treaty; extending all relevant provisions to ill-treatment as well as torture; rehabilitation of victims; and ensuring that only punishments considered lawful under *international* law would be excluded from the definition of torture. These efforts were not wholly successful but did contribute to strengthening some aspects of the final Convention.

As part of its continuing work against torture, Amnesty has also joined in more recent efforts to revitalise an Optional Protocol to the Convention against Torture. This would establish an international inspection system by independent experts of all places of detention in a state party. The draft Protocol was first introduced more than ten years ago but was stalled in the Commission on Human Rights. Amnesty joined in an NGO initiative, led by the Swiss Committee against Torture,[14] to revise and update the text. Amnesty participated in two expert meetings in 1990 to revise and promote the draft and its members began lobbying governments to urge the Commission on Human Rights to act.

Costa Rica's agreement in 1991 to introduce the NGO text at the Commission was important but there was no agreement to begin work on the text. 1992 was a critical year; if drafting did not get under way, the momentum would be irretrievably lost. Intensive NGO lobbying before and especially at the 48th session of the Commission was stepped up; Amnesty devoted one oral statement entirely to the Optional Protocol, exposing the fallacy of the excuses being used to delay it indefinitely. Finally, thirty-nine states co-sponsored Resolution 1992/43, agreeing by consensus to set up a drafting group, in which Amnesty is currently participating.

Unlike several other NGOs active in standard-setting,[15] Amnesty refrains, as a matter of policy, both from supporting specific draft texts and from putting forward its own drafts. Instead it concentrates on promoting and lobbying for the essential principles and issues that it considers ought to be included in the text. This enables it to maintain a certain distance from the process of government negotiation that is involved in reaching final agreement on a text, a process which often results in weakening compromises.

The participation of NGOs in working groups set up by the Commission or Sub-Commission to draft new human rights texts has long been a recognised practice. In the early days, NGOs had to sit at the back of the room, but today they are more likely to be sitting side by side with official delegates and can intervene relatively freely. One commentator has observed that '[a]t that level of working groups – low in the hierarchy of the UN machinery, but important in terms of legal expertise and technical skills – the NGOs often act as full participants and sometimes as principal actors'.[16] The work is serious, detailed and often painfully slow. One Commission drafting group in which Amnesty is currently participating has been working for more than ten years on a draft Declaration on human rights defenders.[17] In order to make an impact, it is important for an NGO to send delegates with a real grasp of the issues and with expertise in drafting and, as far as possible, to maintain continuity in its delegates, building on their familiarity of the issues, the process and of the other players involved. It has been observed that '[e]xpertise is a key quality, but also important are diplomatic skills, good relationships and contacts and a clear vision about objectives'.[18]

While NGO participation in Sub-Commission and Commission working groups has not been challenged (although it is not formalised in any procedural rules), NGOs have encountered difficulties in higher UN bodies. Despite intensive lobbying and vociferous protests, NGOs were effectively excluded even from silently observing the drafting of the final document of the 1993 World Conference on Human Rights, both in the Preparatory Committee and at the Conference itself. Governments' unease about the exclusion was reflected in the fact that 'formal' sessions of the drafting group were declared open to NGOs, but then neatly circumvented by having all the real work go on in closed informal meetings. At the subsequent session of the General Assembly, which was considering the crucial question of the establishment of a High Commissioner for Human Rights, Amnesty resumed intensive lobbying for NGOs to observe the working group on the issue set up by the Third Committee. Eventually it was left to the discretion of the Chairman to decide on NGO access according to the sensitivity of the debate. NGOs were only allowed into a few sessions, but these did include some highly sensitive discussions on the High Commissioner's mandate.

Sometimes NGOs have been able to seize unexpected opportunities to advance standard-setting. In 1988 a rather uninspiring draft Declaration on Unacknowledged Detention was languishing in the Sub-Commission, having been rejected by the Commission. Its author was reluctant to abandon it and several NGOs, including Amnesty, worked with a number of Sub-Commission experts to turn it into the first draft of a Declaration against 'disappearances'.

Among NGOs, the International Commission of Jurists took the lead on advancing this text through the system, but Amnesty remained closely involved in the drafting and in lobbying until the adoption by the General Assembly in 1992 of the Declaration on the Protection of All Persons From Enforced Disappearance.[19]

As a draft text moves through the UN hierarchy towards final adoption by the General Assembly, NGOs must remain vigilant to ensure that it is not re-opened and weakened in the process. The Body of Principles for the Protection of All Persons under Any Form of Detention or Imprisonment gave Amnesty particular cause for concern. In 1980 the General Assembly referred this to its Sixth Committee (legal matters) which re-opened the entire draft and set about progressively weakening it. Unable to intervene directly in a General Assembly working group, Amnesty embarked on strong lobbying to defend essential elements of the text, encouraging its members to draw on the expertise of Amnesty lawyers. A detailed commentary on the draft text was sent to governments in 1986, in which Amnesty expressed concern about the delay and noted that some delegations seemed to have lost sight of the purpose of the exercise and that the text was even falling below existing standards.[20] The following year, in a last-ditch attempt to save the text, Amnesty appealed to the Sub-Commission, which had originally drafted a strong text of the Principles, in the hope that another UN body might have more impact on the Sixth Committee. The Sub-Commission's concerns, transmitted through the Secretary-General, did appear to have a positive effect. The Body of Principles was eventually adopted by the General Assembly in 1988[21] in a strengthened form that addressed many, although not all, of Amnesty's concerns. Introducing the text, the Chairman of the working group said 'I can also add that the role played by some non-governmental organisations, such as Amnesty International, in stimulating delegations and in keeping public opinion in many countries abreast of the developments in the Working Group has been of the utmost importance'.[22]

Strengthening UN mechanisms and procedures

An extensive body of international norms and standards is, of course, of little or no value unless governments put them into practice. One aim of Amnesty's UN work is to contribute to the gradual development and strengthening of international mechanisms to monitor implementation and to call governments to account.

The UN procedures have developed over the years in a piecemeal and uncoordinated way. The 1993 UN World Conference on Human

Rights, the first high-level conference devoted solely to human rights since the Tehran Conference in 1968, presented a rare opportunity to step back and review the system, with a view to coordinating and consolidating it. Its primary objectives included a thorough review of all the UN's human rights methods and mechanisms and the formulation of concrete recommendations to reform and improve them and to provide them with adequate resources.[23]

The proposed Conference had been conceived in the euphoria surrounding the dramatic political changes in Eastern Europe, but when preparations began in 1991 it quickly became clear that there was little enthusiasm for making major advances in the system of human rights protection. A deep sense of disillusionment and inertia rapidly set in. It seemed impossible for governments to reach agreement on anything. With many others in the human rights community, Amnesty was acutely conscious of the risk that opening up the entire human rights system to scrutiny could result in its being seriously undermined. However, it also believed that the Conference presented a unique opportunity that should achieve more than cosmetic changes.

In 1992 Amnesty initiated a series of discussions on reform of the UN system, first at an expert seminar and then at its major International Conference on 'Disappearances' and Political Killings held in the Netherlands to prepare a forthcoming world-wide campaign. Drawing on the conclusions from these discussions, Amnesty proposed the establishment of a UN High Commissioner for Human Rights as its priority for action by the World Conference. The proposal for a High Commissioner had been on and off the UN agenda for many years. In a substantial paper submitted to the World Conference, Amnesty placed this post in the present-day context of the existing system and its shortcomings.[24] A major campaign was planned to get the post of High Commissioner on the Conference agenda. Amnesty systematically raised the issue in its statements and in discussions at the preparatory governmental, NGO and expert meetings taking place in the run-up to the Conference, as well as building public pressure for action through its membership and via the media.

When Amnesty launched its proposal in October 1992 at the Africa regional meeting it attracted little interest. However, the idea of a High Commissioner gradually gained ground, notably at the regional meeting for Latin America in January 1993 where Costa Rica finally took up the proposal. With some difficulty, the final Declaration of that meeting proposed that '... the World Conference consider the possibility of asking the General Assembly to study the feasibility of establishing a United Nations Permanent

Commissioner for Human Rights'.[25] The establishment of a High Commissioner featured more firmly and positively in the conclusions of a 1993 inter-regional meeting held under the auspices of the Council of Europe. Although the Asian governments ignored it at their regional meeting, Asian NGOs took it up at their parallel meeting, as did several other NGO and expert meetings in the run-up to the Conference. It also featured as one of the main recommendations of the parallel NGO Forum in Vienna, attended by thousands of NGOs. In the matter of a few months, as one Western government noted, the High Commissioner had become one of the leading issues at the Conference and could not be ignored.

Although the proposal was included in the draft final document of the Conference, hammered out in advance in meetings from which NGOs were barred, it was still perhaps the most controversial issue in Vienna. There, Amnesty stepped up its public campaign and, undeterred by the exclusion of NGOs from the final drafting, mounted a constant 'guard' outside the drafting meetings, taking every opportunity to discuss progress with the delegates. Finally, after all-night deliberations, the Conference requested the next session of the General Assembly to take up the question of the High Commissioner as a matter of priority.[26]

This marked the start of another round of intensive lobbying by Amnesty on the issue in preparation for the 48th session of the General Assembly.[27] Other NGOs joined in these efforts but the active NGO community at the General Assembly is much smaller than at the Geneva human rights meetings. When the session got under way Amnesty's representatives worked frenetically, first to ensure that the issue of the High Commissioner would be taken up, later to secure NGO access to the debate and finally to secure the strongest possible mandate for the post. Discussions in New York with government delegates from all regions of the world, including those very much opposed to the post, were supplemented by a series of press releases and urgent calls for lobbying on specific points by Amnesty members in their own countries at critical junctures in the debate. The landmark decision of the General Assembly to establish the post of High Commissioner for Human Rights was the culmination of an extraordinary process and remained highly controversial to the last moment.[28] The price paid for a consensus resolution was that the mandate was much weaker and vaguer than Amnesty had worked for. However, it was left sufficiently open to allow a creative and committed High Commissioner room to manoeuvre in the political minefield in which the post will operate. For Amnesty the challenge is now to mobilise all its techniques to ensure that this does indeed represent a major step forward for human rights protection.

The High Commissioner may be one of the most dramatic recent developments within the UN human rights system, but in many ways the so-called thematic mechanisms were far more ground-breaking in political terms. They represented a major step forward from the comparatively safe waters of standard-setting to the much more turbulent seas where the behaviour of any government could be publicly scrutinised and criticised. From its earliest involvement in UN drafting, Amnesty had consistently called for effective international machinery to be set up to ensure the implementation of these standards. The first such mechanism, the Working Group on Enforced or Involuntary Disappearances, was established in 1980 and opened the way for similar mechanisms to address other categories of grave violations.

The work of Amnesty and other NGOs was again important in this connection, particularly in focusing international attention on the critical issues which needed to be addressed. Torture, the death penalty and other political killings were all priorities on Amnesty's campaigning and action agenda in the 1980s when the Commission set up its theme mechanisms dealing with these categories of violations.

The Special Rapporteur on summary or arbitrary executions came next, in 1982, when the Director of the UN Division of Human Rights opened the Commission with a strong statement addressing the UN's obligation to confront the problem of 'deliberate killings perpetrated by organised power' without any legal basis.[29] The issue was already prominent on the international agenda following resolutions by the Sixth Crime Congress in 1980 and the General Assembly in 1980 and 1981. Amnesty had even made an exceptional call in 1979 for a special session of the Security Council to discuss the rise in political killings and the resulting threat to peace and security. At the 1982 Commission it was the Danish delegation, citing an Amnesty statement, which introduced the resolution to establish the new Special Rapporteur to address both the arbitrary use of the death penalty and extra-legal executions.

Torture was still very much on the UN agenda at this time and the idea of a third thematic mechanism to deal with torture was gaining ground. In early 1984 Amnesty renewed its world-wide campaign against torture, publishing another major survey, *Torture in the Eighties*. Amnesty also stepped up its lobbying for a theme mechanism on torture, a proposal it had raised informally with human rights experts and some key governments in 1983. At the Commission's 1985 session, Argentina – recently emerged from military rule – introduced Resolution 1985/33, establishing the Special Rapporteur on torture.

There still remained, however, no UN mechanism capable of taking up the issue which was at the heart of Amnesty's work – prisoners of conscience. Amnesty was continuing to press for UN action in this area but was initially reticent about seeking a specific UN mechanism lest 'prisoner of conscience' be given a restrictive international definition that could undermine its own work.

The opportunity came in 1991 when the Commission took up a Sub-Commission report on administrative detention. Its various recommendations for action opened up the possibility of creating a new mechanism which could take up cases of prisoners of conscience. Amnesty, still nervous that the initiative might backfire with a very narrow definition, had an unusual opportunity to press for a broader mandate when Amnesty and the International Commission of Jurists were invited to attend the informal government discussions during the Commission. The final decision secured a reasonably flexible mandate which the new Working Group on Arbitrary Detention has interpreted widely to include prisoners of conscience.

Amnesty has also sought to introduce new proposals at the United Nations for the more effective monitoring of the human rights situation in a country. The traditional method of sending a UN expert to the country once or twice a year gives only a summary overview of conditions and has little protective value. However, the use of on-site human rights monitors as part of new-style peace-keeping operations opened up a new range of possibilities for UN action. In the immediate aftermath of the Gulf War in 1991 and the onslaught of human rights violations that followed inside Iraq, Amnesty called on the UN to base monitors in that country with the authority to intervene with the authorities and to take remedial and protective action on behalf of victims of violations.[30] This proposal was later strongly advocated by the UN expert on Iraq and endorsed by the General Assembly, but has not so far been implemented. Although the disastrous experience in 1993/4 of the International Civilian Mission in Haiti represents a set-back to the development of UN monitoring operations,[31] Amnesty has repeated its call for on-site monitoring in other countries. Some UN experts have made similar recommendations and a step in this direction has been taken in the former Yugoslavia. In 1994 a call for monitors in Rwanda was one of the first actions taken by the new High Commissioner for Human Rights. While the UN human rights programme is a long way from becoming really operational in this way, the idea of on-site monitors, unthinkable a few years ago, is now firmly on its agenda as an option to be explored.

Using the UN machinery

There are many ways in which Amnesty can raise its concerns at the United Nations. These include submissions to the formal procedures set up to examine individual cases, particular types of violations or specific country situations. These human rights mechanisms may be established under the terms of an international treaty or they may be set up by the political bodies of the UN, such as the Commission on Human Rights. There are in addition a variety of opportunities for using UN meetings to draw attention to human rights violations and to lobby governments or UN experts even when no formal machinery exists.

Amnesty regularly feeds an enormous volume of information into the UN system through formal mechanisms and other channels. NGOs are by far the main providers of information to the UN human rights system – if it had been dependent on governments, it would have ground to a halt long ago. A member of the Working Group on Enforced or Involuntary Disappearances has described NGOs as 'the fuel and the lubricant which allow the machine to function and speed the working up'.[32]

Amnesty makes the fullest possible use of the UN machinery dealing with the violations within the organisation's mandate. It seeks action to protect individuals and, by publicly exposing violations, maintains pressure on governments to improve their human rights record. Individual cases and country situations are submitted to relevant UN procedures. Amnesty's oral and written statements to UN meetings and conferences will often detail cases and country concerns. Case and country briefings are routinely sent to UN experts and committees, such as the Commission's country rapporteurs and the Human Rights Committee. Amnesty reports are circulated to UN staff and to government missions to the UN, and government delegates often request information on specific countries, cases or issues. Reports and press statements timed to coincide with relevant UN debates serve to highlight particular concerns. In cases of special concern or urgency, Amnesty may appeal for action directly to the UN Secretary-General or to other senior UN officials.

As one of the main suppliers of information to the UN system, Amnesty bears a heavy responsibility. Several UN mechanisms would hardly have anything to work with if it were not for Amnesty's materials. This degree of dependency is undesirable for all concerned and Amnesty consistently attempts to inform other NGOs, particularly those without ready access to the UN, about the mechanisms, how they work and how to submit information to them in an effort to broaden and strengthen this vital information base.[33]

Amnesty's input is not limited to raising case and country issues, however. It also contributes actively to studies and debates on emerging human rights issues at the UN. Much of this work is carried out, or at least begins, in the Sub-Commission on Prevention of Discrimination and Protection of Minorities. Issues under consideration there in respect of which Amnesty has had a significant input include states of emergency, the independence of judges and lawyers, the right to a fair trial, conditions of detention, the use of the death penalty (particularly in respect of minors), freedom of opinion and expression, impunity, the rights of indigenous peoples and freedom of movement.

Raising country situations at the Commission on Human Rights

Two separate procedures have gradually evolved over the years by which the Commission on Human Rights can take up violations in individual countries. The so-called 'public procedure', by which the Commission debates and may take action in respect of a country in open session, is based on ECOSOC Resolution 1235(XLII) adopted in 1967. Three years later ECOSOC adopted Resolution 1503(XLVIII) establishing a parallel confidential procedure, described below, known as the '1503 procedure'.

Seeking the strongest possible action at the Commission on Human Rights in respect of individual country situations is a high priority for Amnesty. Before each annual session of the Commission, Amnesty publishes a document highlighting new country situations which require attention and makes recommendations in respect of those countries which are already on the Commission's agenda. For the 1994 session, Amnesty's document for the Commission covered no less than twenty-nine different countries including Algeria, China, Haiti, Indonesia, Iraq, Peru, Sri Lanka, Sudan, Togo, the former Yugoslavia and Zaïre.[34] The relatively new power of the Commission to convene a special session in response to a human rights emergency, outside its regular annual meetings, has provided Amnesty with an additional means of putting pressure on the Commission to act on appropriate country situations.[35] In May 1994 the organisation made its first direct call for such a session on Rwanda.

The practice in the Commission has changed radically from the days when it was only interested in South Africa and the Israeli-Occupied Territories. However, it is still notoriously selective in the countries that are taken up. Some of the countries with the worst

human rights records have never yet been under investigation and
are often themselves members of the Commission. External political
developments heavily influence which countries are addressed, as
evidenced by the Commission's recent focus on Iraq and the former
Yugoslavia. However, NGOs can still play a particularly influential
role here by focusing public attention on a wide range of country
situations, keeping up the pressure on the UN to act and countering
the political bias inherent in a body composed of governments.

The Commission has no real power of enforcement to compel
a country to stop violating the rights of its citizens. Its strongest
measure of censure under the public procedure is to appoint an
expert to study the situation. Alternatively it may call for a report,
adopt a resolution or agree to a statement on the situation by the
Chair. The political impact of these measures lies largely in the
international public censure when a country is singled out in this
way. The intensive efforts which countries invest in seeking to
avoid these measures is some indication that they do have an effect
and are taken seriously.

A great deal of effort is required to build the momentum and the
support for a country resolution to be adopted. Work must begin
long before the Commission session. NGOs must also be alert to the
political advantage that the target government may derive from a
very weak resolution or one that is voted down. It is essential to provide reliable, balanced, comprehensive and up-to-date information
on the country situation in question. The task is much easier if
governments are already feeling domestic pressure to take action at
the international level. Amnesty members routinely lobby their own
governments to take action on country situations before the Commission. These country situations will also feature in Amnesty's UN
statements and will be raised in discussions with government delegates. NGOs are increasingly coordinating lobbying efforts on
particular countries for the maximum impact. While NGOs may
often struggle to get the Commission to look at new countries,
there are also many occasions when governments themselves are
seeking to take an initiative and turn to NGOs for information.

The political balance in the Sub-Commission is rather different
from that of the main Commission. The Sub-Commission is smaller and officially its members are experts on human rights rather
than government representatives. Sometimes a resolution on a new
country situation adopted by the Sub-Commission may help in
building momentum for action at the Commission but it is not
generally decisive. The Sub-Commission has on occasion been able
to adopt resolutions on country situations that have proved unacceptable at the Commission. Such resolutions do serve to put some

public pressure on a government, although this does not carry nearly the same weight as action at the Commission. Amnesty highlights new country situations of concern in its oral statements to the Sub-Commission, in the provision of country reports to the experts on request, in discussions with individual experts during the sessions and in joint initiatives with other NGOs. However, the Sub-Commission can also be very resistant to taking up new countries. Some of the experts are patently not independent of their governments and will fight as hard as any government to avoid the adoption of damaging country resolutions.

The 1503 procedure

The confidential procedure for dealing with country situations has evolved considerably since it was first established by ECOSOC in 1970. Under the '1503 procedure' complaints about human rights violations submitted by individuals and NGOs are considered first by the Sub-Commission and then by the Commission in a four-stage process behind closed doors. The aim is to identify those situations which appear to reveal 'a consistent pattern of gross and reliably attested violations of human rights'. The Commission may then decide on further steps it will take with the governments concerned to address these situations. This was one of the first international procedures which Amnesty used at the United Nations. Its first submissions concerned Brazil and Indonesia. Since those early days Amnesty has continued annually to prepare comprehensive and detailed reports on carefully selected country situations for submission under this procedure. In 1993 it made nine such submissions on Bahrain, Chad, China, Morocco, Sudan, Syria, Tunisia, Turkey and Uganda.

The 1503 procedure is seemingly both flexible and comprehensive. There are no restrictions as to the countries or the issues which can be submitted for consideration under it. Information can be submitted by any source and in any format. The main problems with this procedure are its excessive secrecy, the length of time the whole process takes and the fact that decisions taken behind closed doors are as highly politicised as those taken by governments under the public procedure described above. The '1503 procedure' starts in the Sub-Commission which decides which submissions merit being forwarded to the next Commission session, six months later. The Commission examines these in closed session, usually with a representative of the government present to respond to questions. It may then decide to drop the country from further consideration, to keep it pending to the next session or to take further action which, among other steps, can include appointing a country rapporteur.

The process is completely confidential. NGOs and other sources are never informed directly at any stage whether their complaints have been taken up, are given no reason for those which fail and never have the chance to update the information first submitted, although one cycle of the process lasts some ten months, during which a situation can change radically. Nor do sources hear the government's response or have an opportunity to comment on it. The only information provided is at the end of the Commission session when the countries considered by the Commission and those it has decided to drop are named. Further action taken by the Commission on countries which remain under the procedure, including the appointment of a rapporteur, is not revealed. Thus NGOs have no formal way of updating information on countries kept pending or of briefing a 1503 rapporteur on the latest developments.

These severe deficiencies have led Amnesty and others to be increasingly critical of the procedure. However, the very secrecy with which it operates makes it very difficult for those NGOs which use it to play an active or effective role in its evaluation or reform. NGOs are, understandably, reluctant to be the architects of the demise of any international procedure which offers a means for grave human rights situations to be addressed, however imperfectly. Although it has been argued that its deficiencies are actually damaging to the protection of human rights and to the credibility of the international system,[36] NGOs are unlikely to attack it head on as long as it presents some means of dealing with situations that are not being more effectively tackled elsewhere.

The thematic mechanisms

The thematic mechanisms are the rapporteurs and working groups set up by the Commission on Human Rights to address particular themes, such as torture or religious intolerance, on a global basis. There are now thematic mechanisms covering all the core human rights violations against which Amnesty campaigns.[37] The ones which Amnesty uses most extensively in the course of its work are those dealing with disappearances, summary or arbitrary executions, torture and arbitrary detention. The observations in this section relate mainly to these. The organisation also periodically submits relevant cases and information to other thematic mechanisms, such as the Special Rapporteur on religious intolerance, and draws on their findings and recommendations where these relate to matters within its mandate. The new rapporteurs dealing with racism, freedom of opinion and expression, violence against women and the independence of the judiciary are also relevant to Amnesty's work, but they have only just begun to function and it remains to be seen how they will develop their mandates and methods of work.

For Amnesty these are flexible, rapid procedures capable of handling a large volume of cases in respect of any country. They are the most direct way to raise individual cases at the United Nations. There is no requirement that a state expressly recognise or accept their competence, unlike the treaty-based individual petition procedures. There are no complicated rules of admissibility or procedure. A number of these mechanisms have developed emergency procedures and can act within hours of receiving a case. Although their response may be limited to sending a fax to the government concerned, the mere fact of putting a government on notice that an individual's case is under international scrutiny may offer some protection and save the victim from a worse fate. Non-urgent cases are sent to the government by letter, generally with a request for an explanation of the case and information on measures the government has taken to address the concerns.[38] The annual report of each mechanism to the Commission on Human Rights focuses attention on violations by a wide range of governments. The cumulative political impact of a government being identified as a human rights violator year after year, or of appearing simultaneously in several different reports, should not be underestimated.

Amnesty faxes cases almost daily to one or other of these mechanisms. These include cases of torture and flogging and severe cases of cruel, inhuman or degrading treatment, 'disappearances', suspicious deaths in custody, persons who have received death threats from paramilitary groups or government-sanctioned 'death squads', prisoners on death row in imminent danger of execution, prisoners of conscience held for their beliefs or peaceful political activities, and cases of unfair trial or other instances of arbitrary detention. Many of Amnesty's 500 or more submissions a year involve groups of people, so that the individuals brought to the UN's attention in this way number well into the thousands.

Most of the theme mechanisms have also adopted the practice of carrying out field missions to conduct a more in-depth investigation into the situation in a particular country and to make recommendations to the government concerned about steps to be taken to address violations. Amnesty routinely submits its country reports to the mechanisms, both to highlight those countries where a field mission is warranted and to assist in briefing the mechanisms before such a mission. Its own recommendations to a government or to the Commission also often include a call for one or more of the thematic mechanisms to be invited to carry out such a field mission.

In its lobbying work, its statements and its informal consultations with governments at the Commission on Human Rights, Amnesty frequently puts forward proposals that would make these mechanisms more effective and reinforce their authority and impact. A number were also included in Amnesty's report on UN reform submitted to the World Conference on Human Rights,[39] although the World Conference paid very little attention to the theme mechanisms in its final recommendations. Amnesty has repeatedly drawn attention to their derisory financial resources and understaffing and has also urged the Commission to exert greater pressure on countries to allow access to the theme mechanisms. It has called on the Commission to provide the resources and political support for joint visits by several mechanisms and to focus more directly on the individual countries which feature in the theme reports.

The treaty-monitoring bodies

There is no formal role envisaged for NGOs in connection with the interpretation, implementation or monitoring of the international human rights treaties. These tasks are reserved for the specialist committees of experts set up under the terms of these treaties. Their core function is to review periodic reports by states indicating how they are implementing the treaty. Some also investigate complaints by individuals, where the treaty incorporates a complaints procedure, and adopt authoritative interpretations of treaty provisions which are published in the form of 'General Comments'. Initially the committees tended to be wary of NGO involvement in their work and, until recently, it was left very much to NGOs like Amnesty to carve out a role for themselves in this process.

NGOs can play an important role in providing these committees with additional information about state practice to flesh out what states themselves choose to report. NGO information will be even more crucial now that some of the committees are considering examining the implementation record of states which persistently fail to submit any reports. To avoid such states being exempted from the committee's scrutiny by default, the committees may go ahead on the basis of other reliable information and, in such situations, NGO information may be all that is available.

Although the treaty bodies have proved to be very open to receiving NGO information, they have been reluctant to formalise procedures for this. It is generally left to the committee to 'invite' input rather than giving NGOs and others any right of initiative.[40] Over time, however, informal practices established by NGOs themselves in regularly transmitting information to the committees have become a more accepted and regular aspect of their work.

Although Amnesty provides information to a range of treaty bodies from time to time, the two committees which it regularly addresses are the Human Rights Committee, monitoring the International Covenant on Civil and Political Rights, and the Committee against Torture, monitoring the Convention against Torture. Five times a year, before each committee session, Amnesty sends up-to-date information on the group of countries whose periodic reports the committee will be considering. This can give a more comprehensive picture than might be expected from the government's own report and assists committee members in identifying areas for closer questioning of government representatives. The specificity of the questions often indicates that Amnesty's materials have been used and members of the Committee against Torture even raise Amnesty cases and issues quite directly with the government. Amnesty country specialists may also attend the sessions and are available to brief committee members in more detail, if required.

The examination of state reports can be a very effective way of holding governments to account, yet the process attracts little international attention. Amnesty is increasingly using press statements to publicise the procedure and to highlight the findings of a committee in respect of a particular country, such as its recent statements on China, Portugal, Spain, Turkey and the United Kingdom. It tries to stimulate the crucial involvement of domestic NGOs in this review process, informing them about the procedure and when their government's report is up for examination so that they can send information and attend the session. Whenever possible, Amnesty also provides feedback to domestic NGOs on their government's report and the committee's examination to ensure that these issues can be the subject of domestic debate. It has not been possible, however, for Amnesty to undertake this task systematically or comprehensively and more outreach by the committees themselves is essential.

Observers are sometimes surprised that Amnesty does not submit individual cases to the complaints procedures set up under some of these human rights treaties.[41] These procedures generally require NGOs to act as the formal representative of the individual concerned. As a matter of policy, Amnesty has always avoided representing individuals in judicial or quasi-judicial proceedings, whether at the national or the international level. It is anyway practically impossible for Amnesty, as a global organisation dealing with thousands of individual cases in all regions of the world, to take up individual cases in this way. It does, however, play an educative role in informing individuals, lawyers and others about how to use the complaints procedures and joins in efforts at the United

Nations to improve their effectiveness and scope. It also monitors carefully the decisions of the committees in order to track the emerging jurisprudence on the interpretation of the treaty to assist in Amnesty's own work.

There is, however, a unique procedure, under Article 20 of the Convention against Torture, which Amnesty has used. This enables the Committee against Torture to conduct its own examination of the systematic practice of torture in a state party on the basis of 'reliable' information. Amnesty has made a number of submissions under Article 20 in respect of countries such as Turkey and Egypt, although the excessive confidentiality of the procedure is a drawback for NGOs seeking to use it. Although the cooperation of the state concerned must be sought at all stages, the NGO making a submission is not thereafter involved in the process at all and is not even notified whether the Committee is taking any of the steps envisaged under Article 20.[42] Nor is the NGO informed of the state's observations and, although the procedure can take some considerable time, there is no provision for the original submission to be updated at any stage unless the Committee specifically requests this. The procedure is very slow and has been used very little since the Convention came into force in 1987. Amnesty and other NGOs will have to review its effectiveness in due course to determine its usefulness.

Despite Amnesty's longstanding involvement in the work of these treaty bodies and the increasing participation by other NGOs, few NGOs attend their sessions as compared with the Commission on Human Rights, prompting complaints that NGOs do not take their work sufficiently seriously. Yet committee members tend to maintain a distance from NGOs who do attend. They may fear undue influence or interference in the work of an expert body that does not see itself as a target for the kind of lobbying that is more commonly accepted by the governmental bodies. Moreover, most of the committees are much less open to NGO input on organisational and methodological aspects of their work. NGO input on new or revised General Comments, interpreting provisions of the treaties, is not generally sought, with the committees perhaps too jealously holding on to their role as sole guardians of the treaty. The committees have, however, said that NGO information is of major importance in their work[43] and a recent study on the treaty bodies recommended that each committee should 'seek to develop a more open, rational, transparent and balanced approach to dealing with information from non-governmental organisations'.[44] There remains, however, some way to go before this can be achieved.

Peace-keeping and peace-building

UN peace-keeping is not a field in which Amnesty has previously sought to have an input. Since 1988, however, the United Nations has launched more operations than in the previous forty years and the nature and scope of these operations have changed radically. They have developed well beyond the traditional mandate and tasks of the old-style peace-keeping forces, and human rights issues have been more prominent. Linkages have been affirmed between the maintenance of peace and security and respect for human rights. The UN Secretary-General has said, for example, '. . . respect for human rights constitutes a vital, indeed a critical, component among measures to resolve, on a long-term basis, conflicts of this nature, including efforts to promote enduring conditions of peace, national reconciliation and democracy'.[45]

The establishment in 1991 of the UN Observer Mission in El Salvador (ONUSAL) to verify a human rights agreement between the government and the armed opposition was a new departure that attracted the attention of Amnesty and other human rights NGOs. Suddenly human rights appeared to be at the heart of a new area of UN operations. The following year the UN Transitional Authority in Cambodia (UNTAC) included a large human rights monitoring component, with new powers for the UN to intervene and take remedial action in the case of violations. It soon became clear, however, that the UN's attention to human rights in the context of various peace-keeping operations was at best inconsistent and *ad hoc* and, at worst, wholly inadequate.

Amnesty began examining and monitoring these new-style peace-keeping operations much more closely. It takes no position on political negotiations, on whether peace-keeping operations should be established, on military aspects of the operations or on peace-keeping methods in general. Instead, it has concentrated on the human rights situation in the country concerned and the steps which need to be taken in the context of the settlement or peace-keeping operation to address human rights concerns.

It has made specific recommendations in respect of human rights and peace-keeping in Angola, Burundi, Cambodia, El Salvador, Guatemala, Haiti, the Israeli-Occupied Territories, Liberia, Mozambique, Rwanda, Somalia, South Africa, Western Sahara and the former Yugoslavia. Amnesty has a variety of channels to influence those taking the decisions – raising public awareness by publishing reports and recommendations; direct approaches to the UN Secretary-General and other senior UN officials; lobbying and direct approaches to governments, such as members of the Security

Council and others with a special interest or role in a particular operation; and approaches to the parties themselves.

It has not been easy for Amnesty and other human rights NGOs to make an impact in the area of UN peace-keeping. Traditional methods of action are not necessarily effective. The political negotiations proceed in the strictest secrecy. Proposals for UN action are formulated at the highest political levels and are debated and ultimately approved by the Security Council. Peace-keeping operations involve interlinked components – military and civilian – operating in a highly volatile political context. Human rights are too often subordinated to political or military imperatives. The UN's own human rights bodies have been largely excluded from the design, planning and implementation of peace-keeping operations, including those with a full human rights component. So there has been no opportunity for NGOs to influence the process through their normal channels of operation within the human rights sphere. While it may be preferable for NGOs to keep some distance from the political deals, it means that positive influence at an early stage is much more difficult to achieve. Yet, if human rights are not dealt with early on, it is infinitely more difficult to address these issues after the settlement and implementation plans are in place.

In January 1994 Amnesty published its first comprehensive paper on UN peace-keeping and human rights.[46] This included a fifteen-point programme setting out the main issues which ought to be addressed by the international community in the context of peace-keeping operations. Coming at a time when the UN's role in conflict resolution and peace-keeping is being fundamentally questioned, it signals the fact that this is an area that will continue to merit considerable attention by Amnesty.

Conclusions

While Amnesty's activities at the United Nations may not catch the public eye very often, they are part of an active and growing programme and touch on almost every other aspect of Amnesty's work. The profile and recognition that Amnesty has established at the UN have created tremendous scope for action and influence. At the same time this has a price; it leads to heavy demands on the organisation and expectations that it can and will act on every issue, sometimes making it difficult to focus Amnesty's own priorities.

Although Amnesty has, over the years, greatly increased its presence and its impact at the United Nations, this is by no means an easy forum in which to operate. Essentially a governmental club, it operates often in secrecy and by the rules of diplomacy, negotiation and compromise. Amnesty is not party to many informal intergovernmental discussions where crucial decisions are taken and can find it tricky to judge the prevailing political climate. A refusal to compromise on principles can make Amnesty's demands appear naive and to be going against the grain of political realism. Being too outspoken may be counter-productive, serving only to intensify government resistance, particularly by those countries smarting from Amnesty's criticisms of their human rights records. When governments make political compromises to get agreement on an initiative, Amnesty has to decide whether to go along with a weaker initiative which may be better than nothing, or whether to continue to insist on a more far-reaching proposal which may fail altogether.

These tensions between quiet diplomacy and public campaigning are not easy for an NGO to resolve. Some argue that working at the United Nations calls for too many compromises and brings NGOs too close to governments. Others insist that, to be effective, NGOs have to function within the system and play by its rules. This conflict continues to be the subject of intensive debates within the Amnesty movement. What is perhaps most important for Amnesty is always to maintain its independence and never to compromise its *capacity* to criticise and to insist on the highest standards of human rights protection at the UN.

The insistent voices of Amnesty and other NGOs at the United Nations remain as essential as ever. It is clear that the international human rights system would not be as advanced, nor could it function as it does, without their contribution. Yet, while human rights are much more firmly entrenched on the UN's agenda, international consensus on these issues remains extremely fragile. The universal condemnation of grave violations of human rights, such as torture and political killings, may dissolve when action is called for against a particular country. The same governments that have appointed a High Commissioner for Human Rights are allowing the rest of the human rights protection system to grind to a halt through lack of resources. New monitoring mechanisms are set up to address an ever-expanding range of specific concerns, while those that have functioned for over ten years are still not being heard. NGOs like Amnesty have a responsibility to maintain their vigilance over the system they have helped to establish in the legitimate expectation that it can and should be made to serve the cause of human rights and fulfil the aspirations set by the UN Charter.

NOTES

1. Amnesty International, *Annual Report* (1 June 1966 – 31 May 1967), p. 2.
2. A brief overview of Amnesty's role within intergovernmental organisations can be found in Nigel Rodley and Amnesty International – Section Française, 'Le rôle d'une organisation comme Amnesty International au sein des organisations intergouvernmentales' in Mario Bettati and Pierre-Marie Dupuy, *Les O.N.G. et le Droit International* (Paris: Economica, 1986), p. 127. Nigel Rodley served as Amnesty's first Legal Adviser and later head of its Legal and Intergovernmental Organizations Office from 1973 to 1990. He was instrumental in developing a major part of the organization's UN work and represented Amnesty on numerous occasions at the UN and related international meetings.
3. Amnesty's primary concentration on civil and political rights continues to attract criticism from other human rights actors, particularly now when attention is increasingly focused on the neglect of economic and social rights within the international system. See, for example, Philip Alston, 'The Fortieth Anniversary of the Universal Declaration of Human Rights: A Time More for Reflection Than for Celebration' in *Human Rights in a Pluralist World* (UNESCO, 1990), p. 1. There may be some truth to the argument that Amnesty's weight and reputation has exacerbated the relative lack of attention to rights that are not within its core mandate. However, it is also the case that its precise and limited mandate has contributed to Amnesty's achievements and strengths, giving direction, focus and coherence to its work. In addition, much of its work at the UN has an impact beyond the specific cluster of rights in its mandate and is directed towards improving a system which protects the full range of human rights.
4. Annual surveys of Amnesty's on-going work at the UN and other intergovernmental organisations are included in each of the organisation's Annual Reports. These are published mid-year and cover the activities of the previous calendar year.
5. Amnesty International, *Refugee Protection at Risk – Amnesty International's Recommendations to the 44th Session of the Executive Committee of UNHCR*, September 1993, AI Index: POL 33/06/93.
6. Amnesty issues a survey of relevant concerns and recommendations in advance of each annual International Labour Conference. See, for example, Amnesty International, *The 81st International Labour Conference: Amnesty International's concerns relevant to the Committee on Application of Standards*, April 1994, AI Index: IOR 42/01/94.
7. For a short survey of the NGO role at the World Conference, see Fateh Azzam, 'Non-Governmental Organisations and the UN World Conference on Human Rights', *The Review* (International Commission of Jurists), no. 50, 1993, pp. 89–100.
8. Amnesty has played an active role in drafting a large number of UN standards. They include the Convention against Torture and Other Cruel, Inhuman or Degrading Treatment or Punishment; the Code of Conduct for Law Enforcement Officials; the Principles on the Effective Prevention and Investigation of Extra-Legal, Arbitrary and Summary Executions; the Body of Principles for the Protection of All Persons under Any Form of Detention or Imprisonment; the Basic Principles on the Use of Force and Firearms by Law Enforcement Officials; and the Declaration on the Protection of All Persons from Enforced Disappearance.
9. For a detailed account of the evolution of UN action against torture see Nigel

Rodley, *The Treatment of Prisoners Under International Law*, (Oxford: Clarendon Press, 1987), especially Chapter 1.

10. General Assembly Resolution 3059 (XXVIII) of 2 November 1973.
11. Declaration on the Protection of All Persons from Being Subjected to Torture and Other Cruel, Inhuman or Degrading Treatment or Punishment, adopted by General Assembly Resolution 3452 (XXX) of 9 December 1975.
12. General Assembly Resolution 32/62 of 8 December 1977.
13. The text of the Convention is given as an Annex to General Assembly Resolution 39/46 of 10 December 1984.
14. This NGO is now known as the Association for the Prevention of Torture. Its founder, Jean-Jacques Gautier, was the driving force behind this concept of an international system of inspection.
15. For an account of some of the standard-setting activities of the International Commission of Jurists, for example, see Niall MacDermot, 'The Role of NGOs in Human Rights Standard-Setting', *UN Bulletin of Human Rights* vol. 90/1, 1991, pp. 42–9.
16. Theo Van Boven, 'The Role of Non-Governmental Organisations in International Human Rights Standard-Setting: A Prerequisite of Democracy', *California Western International Law Journal*, vol. 20, no. 2, 1989–90, at p. 218.
17. The full title of this text is the Declaration on the Right and Responsibility of Individuals, Groups and Organs of Society to Promote and Protect Universally Recognised Human Rights and Fundamental Freedoms.
18. See Van Boven, *op. cit.*, at p. 220.
19. General Assembly Resolution 47/133 of 18 December 1992.
20. Amnesty International, *Draft Body of Principles for the Protection of All Persons under Any Form of Detention or Imprisonment*, AI Index: IOR 41/05/86.
21. General Assembly Resolution 43/173 of 9 December 1988.
22. Introductory Statement by Tullio Treves (Italy), Chairman of the Working Group, 21 November 1988.
23. General Assembly Resolution 45/155 of 18 December 1990.
24. Amnesty International, *Facing Up To The Failures: Proposals for Improving the Protection of Human Rights by the United Nations*, December 1992, AI Index: IOR 41/16/92.
25. San Jose Declaration on Human Rights of 22 January 1993, UN doc. A/CONF.157/LACRM/12/Add.1.
26. The Vienna Declaration and Programme of Action, June 1993, Part II.A, para 18.
27. See Amnesty International, *A High Commissioner for Human Rights – A Time For Action*, October 1993, AI Index: IOR 41/35/93.
28. General Assembly Resolution 48/141 of 20 December 1993. Mr Ayala Lasso (Ecuador) was appointed as the first High Commissioner for Human Rights in February 1994.
29. See Rodley, *The Treatment of Prisoners Under International Law, op. cit.*, pp. 158–63.
30. Amnesty International, *The Need for Further United Nations Action to Protect Human Rights in Iraq*, July 1991, AI Index: MDE 14/06/91.
31. The International Civilian Mission in Haiti was a joint initiative of the UN and the Organisation of American States. Its task was to promote and protect human rights and included making recommendations to the authorities and verifying their follow-up. Its task was never easy but it was forced to terminate its activities prematurely in October 1993 when the Governors Island Agreement, by which President Aristide was to return to Haiti, collapsed. Attempts

to reinstate its activities in 1994 have not been successful and the human rights situation continues to deteriorate.

32. Diego Garcia-Sayan, 'Non-governmental organisations and the human rights movement in Latin America', *UN Bulletin of Human Rights*, vol. 90/1, 1991, p. 39.
33. Amnesty has published a number of explanatory documents on some of the international procedures. See, for example, Amnesty International, *Summary of Selected International Procedures and Bodies Dealing with Human Rights Matters*, August 1989, AI Index: IOR 30/01/89.
34. Amnesty International, *Amnesty International's Concerns at the 50th Session of the United Nations Commission on Human Rights*, November 1993, AI Index: IOR 41/38/93.
35. As part of its discussions in 1990 on improving the effectiveness of the Commission, ECOSOC agreed, in Resolution 1990/48, to the holding of such special sessions with the agreement of the majority of the Commission members. The first attempt in 1992 to convene a special session on the Israeli-Occupied Territories failed, but two special sessions on the former Yugoslavia were held that year and a third special session on Rwanda was convened in May 1994.
36. Philip Alston, 'The Commission on Human Rights' in Philip Alston (ed.), *The United Nations and Human Rights – A Critical Appraisal* (Oxford University Press, 1992), pp. 145–55.
37. The use of the death penalty is only partially dealt with by the Special Rapporteur on Extrajudicial, Summary or Arbitrary Executions as the use of the death penalty *per se* is not yet absolutely proscribed under international human rights law. While Amnesty International is unconditionally opposed to the death penalty and campaigns against the imposition or carrying out of death sentences in all circumstances, the Special Rapporteur is confined to taking up death penalty cases which involve some other violation of human rights, such as the execution of minors or the mentally-ill or capital punishment imposed after unfair trial or without the possibility of appeal.
38. It should be noted, however, that some governments do not respond at all to the theme mechanisms. Furthermore, although the rate of response has gradually improved, in many cases government responses are wholly inadequate and simply refute the allegations made or state that the case has been investigated and the government is satisfied that the individual is in no danger and his or her rights have not been violated. Although this makes the task of the thematic mechanisms much more difficult and frustrating, the fact that a government knows its actions are under scrutiny can still provide a measure of protection for the individuals concerned.
39. See Amnesty International, 'Facing Up To The Failures', *op. cit.*, pp. 25–30.
40. A more ambitious provision in the draft rules of procedure of the Committee against Torture, which would have given NGOs a form of observer status with the Committee, was rejected. However, the Committee did empower itself to invite NGOs in consultative status to submit information and written statements in any form which it would determine. This Committee monitors implementation of the Convention against Torture and Other Cruel, Inhuman or Degrading Treatment or Punishment. More recently-established treaty bodies dealing with economic, social and cultural rights and with children's rights have proved to be much more enlightened in their approach to NGOs. Recognising them as essential contributors to the monitoring of government compliance, they have made special provision for obtaining NGO information and input.
41. For example, the Optional Protocol to the International Covenant on Civil and Political Rights permits individuals to submit complaints of any violations

of the Covenant to the Human Rights Committee for investigation. The Convention against Torture and Other Cruel, Inhuman or Degrading Treatment also has an individual complaints procedure built into it.

42. If the Committee determines that a submission contains 'well-founded indications' of the systematic practice of torture, it must first invite the observations of the state concerned. It may then undertake a confidential inquiry, which can include a field mission. It transmits its findings and recommendations to the state concerned. In the recent case of the Committee's inquiry into torture in Turkey, it took the unusual step at the end of the process of issuing a press statement which drew attention to its findings of torture.

43. Report of the Third Meeting of Persons Chairing the Human Rights Treaty Bodies, October 1990, UN doc. A/45/636, para. 68.

44. Philip Alston, *Interim Report on study on enhancing the long-term effectiveness of the United Nations human rights treaty regime*, UN doc. A/CONF.157/PC/62/Add.11/Rev.1, April 1993, para. 225.

45. Report to the Security Council on Angola, UN doc. S/25840, May 1993.

46. Amnesty International, *Peace-Keeping and Human Rights*, January 1994, AI Index: IOR 40/01/94.

8

NGOs AND THE RIGHTS OF
THE CHILD

Michael Longford

Historical background

Governments in democratic countries have seldom acted entirely on their own initiative when enacting social welfare legislation. The pioneering work needed to identify social problems and to make proposals for solving them has usually been undertaken either by committed individuals or, more commonly in recent years, by non-governmental organisations (NGOs). If the recommendations of the voluntary sector are accepted by the political party in power and eventually incorporated in national legislation, a department of central or local government is normally given responsibility for providing and paying for a particular social service that had previously only been obtainable from charitable sources.

Many of the great pioneers of social reform in Britain began their work by trying to tackle, at a local level, the social problems which they saw. They usually did this by providing relief, food or shelter directly to those they wanted to help, for example children, refugees, widows and elderly or sick people. However, many of the people who tried to provide a direct service to those in need came to see that the problems were too great for any one individual or voluntary organisation to solve. They therefore concluded that the interests of the people they were trying to help would be better served by mobilising public opinion, and by enlisting the help of political leaders and governments.

The work of NGOs, including their activities as pressure groups, is now an accepted feature of political life in any democratic country, and their contribution in Britain during the last two centuries has been enormous. NGOs also have great influence on international organisations, although the ways in which NGOs operate at international level differ in several respects from the methods appropriate when dealing with national governments.

The UN Convention on the Rights of the Child, and the international instruments which preceded it, provide good examples of the

214

part which NGOs can play in the affairs of the United Nations.

The person whose work began the process which culminated in the Convention on the Rights of the Child was a British teacher, Eglantyne Jebb. She was born in 1876, and had a childhood that was privileged, happy and secure, typical of children of the gentry at that time. After graduating from Oxford, she made what seemed to many a surprising decision and took up training as a teacher. Her work as a teacher did not last very long, but it nevertheless gave her experience of what she herself described as 'the real enemy of the human race: the poverty, squalor, disease, and helpless ignorance which dooms generation after generation of children, East and West, to a subnormal existence'.[1] Although she was often ill, she did not find the life of an unmarried daughter at home fulfilling, and in 1912, when war broke out in the Balkans, Eglantyne Jebb joined the Macedonian Relief Fund. In 1913, she travelled to Southern Serbia to administer relief to suffering children and to report on conditions there. This visit provided her first experience of the horrors of war, and it convinced her that 'every war is a war against the child'.

In 1914 the First World War broke out, and Eglantyne Jebb declared herself a pacifist. A few months after it ended, she launched the Save the Children Fund, making an appeal in the Albert Hall on 19 May 1919. At that time many people in Britain regarded it as ludicrous to give money to provide relief for the children of a defeated enemy, but George Bernard Shaw was an early supporter and answered those who attacked him for being pro-German with the words 'I have no enemies under seven.'

The work of Save the Children was initially concerned with relief, but Eglantyne Jebb soon came to appreciate, as many other social pioneers in Britain had already done, that relief provided by one charitable organisation could never be enough. In 1920, she founded the Save the Children International Union, which was modelled on the International Red Cross. On 24 January 1923, in a letter to her friend Suzanne Ferrière, she wrote:

> Another question which, as you may have heard, has been greatly occupying my attention, is the Children's Charter. The moment appears to me to have come when we can no longer expect to conduct large relief actions. If we wish nevertheless to go on working for the children – whose need is indeed so great that it appears to demand a continuance of effort – the only way to do it seems to be to evoke a co-operative effort of the nations to safeguard their children on constructive rather on (sic) charitable lines. I believe we should claim certain Rights for the children and labour for their universal recognition, so that everybody – not merely the

small number of people who are in a position to contribute to relief funds, but everybody who in any way comes into contact with children, that is to say the majority of mankind – may be in a position to help forward the movement.[2]

From 1919 till her death in 1928, Eglantyne Jebb devoted all her time and energy to her work for The Save the Children Fund. While in Switzerland, she drafted a document known as 'The Declaration of Geneva',[3] and in 1924 the French version of this document was adopted by the League of Nations, the precursor of the United Nations.

The thirty-eight signatories to the Geneva Declaration include Eglantyne Jebb herself and Janusz Korczak (1878–1942), the Polish paediatrician and author of books on children's rights. (Korczak was in charge of an orphanage for Jewish children in Warsaw, and during the German occupation of Poland in the Second World War, he accompanied 200 children to the concentration camp at Treblinka, where he and the children all died.[4]) The Declaration is quite a short document. It calls upon men and women of all nations, recognising that mankind owes to the child the best that it has to give, to accept as their duty the following five principles:

1. The child must be given the means requisite for its normal development, both materially and spiritually.
2. The child that is hungry must be fed, the child that is sick must be nursed, the child that is backward must be helped, and the orphan and the waif must be sheltered and succoured.
3. The child must be the first to receive relief in times of distress.
4. The child must be put in a position to earn a livelihood and must be protected against every form of exploitation.
5. The child must be brought up in the consciousness that its talents must be devoted to the service of its fellow men.

Although Eglantyne Jebb died at the early age of fifty-two, nine years after founding The Save The Children Fund and only four years after drafting the Geneva Declaration, her influence has continued to grow. The Save the Children Fund (UK) is one of twenty-five autonomous SCF organisations around the world which now make up the International Save the Children Alliance.[5]

The Geneva Declaration has also evolved in ways which Eglantyne Jebb herself could hardly have foreseen. The Universal Declaration of Human Rights,[6] which was adopted and proclaimed by the General Assembly of the United Nations on 10 December 1948, refers in Article 25 to the need of childhood for special care and assistance.

In 1950 work began on the preliminary text of a new declaration on the rights of the child. There were long delays, caused partly by the need to complete work on two other international instruments and partly by disagreements on issues of policy. NGOs were able to submit written statements commenting on the draft text and to take part in the debate in the Commission on Human Rights, but very few did so.[7] The most contentious points were whether the declaration should be explicitly against abortion by proclaiming rights 'from the moment of conception',[8] and whether the state as well as the family had responsibility for a child's welfare. In the end consensus was obtained and on 20 November 1959 the General Assembly unanimously adopted the second Declaration of the Rights of the Child.[9]

The preamble of this Declaration includes an assertion of the child's need, 'by reason of his physical and mental immaturity, for special safeguards and care, including appropriate legal protection'. This was essentially the wording from the Commission on Human Rights. As a compromise on the question of abortion, the Assembly added that the protection should be 'before as well as after birth'. The preamble also mentions that the need for such special safeguards has already been stated in the Geneva Declaration of the Rights of the Child of 1924, and recognised in the Universal Declaration of Human Rights.

The 1959 Declaration is longer than that of 1924. It 'calls upon parents, upon men and women as individuals, and upon voluntary organisations, local authorities and national governments to recognize these rights and strive for their observance by legislative and other measures progressively taken in accordance with the following principles'. It then sets out ten principles. These are more detailed than the five principles enunciated by Eglantyne Jebb in 1924. The child is to enjoy all rights without discrimination on account of race, colour, language, religion, or sex (although the English version of the Declaration persistently refers to the child as 'he'). The child is to be given opportunities to enable him to develop in a healthy and normal manner, and in conditions of freedom and dignity. He shall be entitled to a name and a nationality, and to enjoy the benefits of social security. A child who is handicapped is to be given the special treatment required by his particular condition. He shall, wherever possible, grow up in the care of his parents, but special provision shall be made for children without families. He is entitled to receive education. The child shall be among the first to receive protection and relief (this appears to be a weakening of the third article of the 1924 Declaration, which omits the word 'among'). He shall be protected against neglect, cruelty and exploitation, and from practices which may foster discrimination, and he shall be brought up in a spirit of understanding, tolerance, friendship among peoples, peace, and universal brotherhood.

However, neither the 1924 nor the 1959 Declaration had any legally binding force on governments or individuals, and neither document included any procedures aimed at ensuring its implementation. It was not until 20 November 1989, sixty-five years after Églantyne Jebb drafted the Declaration of Geneva and exactly thirty years after the proclamation of the second Declaration on the Rights of the Child, that the UN Convention on the Rights of the Child was passed unanimously by the General Assembly.[10]

The contribution of NGOs to the drafting of the UN Convention on the Rights of the Child

In February 1978, the government of Poland submitted a proposed text to the Commission on Human Rights for a UN Convention on the Rights of the Child. The essential difference between a Declaration and a Convention is that a Convention is legally binding on all countries which ratify it, whereas a Declaration is not. Poland assumed that a Convention based on the 1959 Declaration would constitute a step forward in promoting children's rights. Poland is the country where Janusz Korczak had worked for orphans, and given his life for them in 1942.[11] More than thirty years later, the Polish government felt that the progress already achieved in that country in improving social care for children would establish its credibility in taking this initiative, and that a Convention designed to come into force in 1979, which had already been proclaimed as the International Year of the Child, would be a suitable way to mark the twentieth anniversary of the 1959 Declaration. Although the 1970s continued to be a period of ideological confrontation between East and West, Poland also hoped that a Convention on children's rights would be a humanitarian and non-political matter in which all states would be able to work together constructively. The UN General Assembly considered that during the nineteen years which had elapsed since the adoption of the 1959 Declaration 'conditions to take further steps by adopting a Convention had been created', and it requested the Commission on Human Rights to organise its work in such a way that the draft of the Convention might be ready for adoption, if possible, during the International Year of the Child.[12]

In 1979 an 'open-ended Working Group' was set up by the Commission to draw up a Convention. At a very early stage in their discussions, however, it was agreed that the Convention should not be confined to those matters already covered by the 1959 Declaration, but should also include articles on various matters which had come to light in the intervening years and in the course of the International Year of the Child. In October 1979, the Polish government therefore submitted a new version of the draft Convention.

When the Working Group held its first meetings, the attitude of many Western democracies to a Convention on the Rights of the Child was unenthusiastic. Children were human beings, it was argued, and as such were already sufficiently protected by the various international instruments already in existence. To add a new Convention specifically on the rights of the child would involve a laborious exercise of drafting for very little purpose. If the Convention added little of substance to what was already included in other instruments or in the domestic legislation of member states, then the drafting of a new Convention would be a pointless rigmarole. On the other hand, if the Convention were to impose new requirements on the states which ratified it, then they would be preparing rods for their own backs, both in the field of enacting new legislation, and in having to carry out any requirements the UN might impose to enable compliance to be monitored. Another factor which may have reinforced the scepticism of some Western democracies was that, whatever progress it might claim to have made in the field of child welfare, Poland, the country which seemed to be taking the initiative, did not have an unblemished record in the field of human rights.

Fortunately, the arguments in favour of a Convention specifically for children prevailed. Many of the theoretical reasons for providing special care for children are set out in the Preamble to the Convention, which refers to the statement in the 1959 Declaration that 'the child, by reason of his physical and mental immaturity, needs special safeguards and care'. The facts also speak for themselves. A quarter of a million children die every week, many from diseases which can be prevented at very little cost. Millions more live on with malnutrition and almost permanent ill health. In 1985 a UN seminar estimated that 'over 100 million children – the exact number is not known – are the victims of exploitation of child labour'. More than 100 million children between the ages of six and eleven are deprived of schooling. At least 155 million children under five in the developing countries live in absolute poverty. Children are being killed and mutilated, and are forced to take part in the killing of others, in armed conflicts throughout the world. Sexual abuse of children occurs, not only in the brothels of Asia, but in Britain and many other developed countries as well.[13] The horrifying statistics published every year in the UNICEF annual report

The State of the World's Children provide compelling arguments in favour of stronger measures than mere 'declarations'.

The open-ended composition of the Working Group meant that, in addition to the forty-three member states of the Commission itself, all other states in the United Nations could send delegates to the meetings if they so wished. NGOs with consultative status were also allowed to attend. According to a list compiled in 1987 by Rädda Barnen International, there were forty-one NGOs which attended one or more of the meetings of the Working Group.[14] Of these, only five were Category I NGOs, twenty-seven were in Category II and the other nine were on the Roster. There was no discernible difference in the quality of the input from the different categories of NGO, but there was a difference between the input of those representatives of NGOs with a child care background, and those whose day-to-day involvement with children's rights seemed tenuous.

There are two factors which can cause delay in the UN legislative process. The first is the need for the translation of documents into the six official UN languages. The second is that the UN tries to operate by consensus rather than by majority voting. The task of completing the final draft of the Convention took very much longer than had been anticipated. The Working Group met in Geneva for one week at the end of January each year from 1979 until 1987. In 1988 it had two meetings, each lasting two weeks. During its first years, when the Group was discussing the definition of a child, nationality, non-discrimination, separation from parents, place of residence and similar matters, the United Kingdom was represented by an official from the Home Office. In 1983, however, it was decided that an official from the Department of Health and Social Security should represent the United Kingdom, and I became the British government delegate to the Working Group.

At the beginning of each meeting, the Working Group elected its chairman, and every year it unanimously re-elected the same person, Professor Adam Lopatka, the Minister of Religious Affairs and later the President of the Supreme Court in Warsaw. The official records of the Commission of Human Rights refer to the respect in which Adam Lopatka is held 'for the high offices he held in his own country and for the admirable way in which he conducted the deliberations of the Working Group'.[15] In the opinion of many who took part, the eventual success of the Working Group in producing an acceptable draft Convention is due in no small measure to the personal qualities of Adam Lopatka.

When he presided over meetings, he was fair and polite to each participant, and never refused permission to anyone who wished to speak. There were times at first when he seemed to be too patient, but I later realised that his patience was a major factor in turning what had seemed to be an argumentative rabble into a team who listened to each other's views with respect, and collaborated constructively in a very difficult task. He was knowledgeable about children, and his summing up of arguments and counter-arguments put forward in debate was always masterly. He also had an excellent technique for resolving contentious points that were threatening to delay the proceedings of the Working Group. When two points of view seemed irreconcilable, he would invite the main spokesmen on each side to form a drafting sub-group, together with one or two other delegates to act as 'honest brokers', and to meet in the corridors and report back to the main Working Group at a pre-arranged time, preferably with a compromise wording acceptable to both sides. This method frequently proved successful, possibly because it focused the responsibility for success or failure on a comparatively small number of delegates.

I found the 1983 meeting of the Working Group unpleasant. Children's matters cover the responsibilities of many different ministries, but colleagues in several other Whitehall departments had not yet accepted that the draft Convention was worth bothering about, and the briefing I received before going to Geneva for the first time was very inadequate. In addition to feeling ill-prepared, the atmosphere of the meeting itself was acrimonious. Several delegates were extremely rude to each other. There seemed to be no common aim in the Group. All the NGO spokesmen and many national delegates appeared to be in favour of the Convention, but a small minority of government delegates were very negative, and seemed to hope that if they dragged out the discussions interminably, then the draft Convention would go away. The NGO contribution at the 1983 meeting was not particularly impressive either. The Chairman was scrupulously fair in allowing anyone who wanted to speak to take the floor. However, some of the NGO speakers were inexperienced, and put forward in an unconvincing way points of view which were either irrelevant or impracticable.

Following the 1983 meeting, three NGOs (Defence for Children International, the International Catholic Child Bureau and Rädda Barnen International) took the initiative to call together interested NGOs, which set up an informal NGO Group to coordinate the NGO input to the drafting of the Convention. Some twenty NGOs were active, and the network of interested NGOs grew over the years. Defence for Children International (DCI) agreed to act as the secretariat for the NGO group.[16]

DCI had been set up in 1979, the year designated by the United Nations as the International Year of the Child. That year brought

to light disturbing indications of the suffering of children throughout the world, and it also alerted those concerned with children's
rights issues to the absence, at that time, of any international
organisation with the specific aim of promoting and protecting the
rights of the child. DCI is an international non-governmental
organisation which is both non-confessional and non-political. Its
international secretariat is based in Geneva, conveniently close to the
UN building in Geneva. DCI has members in over sixty countries
throughout the world, and, in about forty of these, DCI sections
have been set up to ensure more effective action at the national
level. Its activities are financed by grants from a wide range of
sources, including governments, foundations, inter-governmental
bodies, private associations, individuals and, of course, from the
subscriptions of its members.[17]

In 1984, there was a very marked improvement in the quality of
the Working Group meeting, and this continued until the drafting
was completed. In Whitehall, the Foreign Office responded to my
request for more thorough briefing by convening each year, before
I went to Geneva, an *ad hoc* meeting attended by representatives
of all the various government departments whose policies have
an impact on children. One national delegate who had been particularly aggressive at the 1983 Geneva meeting was replaced in
1984 by another who had the ability to express her disagreement
in a polite way. But the most striking feature of the 1984 meeting
was the emergence of the NGOs as a really positive force in the
Working Group. At the time I was not aware of the reasons for
this change, but the process and the reasons for it were described
in a speech given in Geneva in 1990 by Nigel Cantwell, the Director
of Programmes of DCI.

Over the ten-year period, though more particularly as of 1984,
the impact of the NGOs on the Convention snow-balled, not just
in terms of drafting itself, but also with regard to the importance
given to the future Convention and its adoption. . . . NGOs have
obviously influenced the content of other international treaties
in the past. There does seem to be general recognition, however,
within the UN, among governments, and in the NGO community itself, that their impact on the Convention on the Rights
of the Child was both quite unprecedented in degree and particularly useful and constructive.

From the start of the drafting process, there had been some
attempt to foster inter-NGO cooperation, and indeed a written
statement co-sponsored by several NGOs was submitted very
early on. It seems that there was a feeling of great frustration

among NGO representatives, however; they knew that they had a potentially major contribution to make, and that they – and children – were somehow losing out because of an inability to 'get the message over' in the right way and at the right time. Very few had had previous experience of working within this kind of context. Individual NGOs were certainly given the floor almost each time they requested it, but all too often they wasted these valuable opportunities by labouring a viewpoint that was clearly not viable or even arguing a point among themselves, rather than putting a reasoned proposal to the government delegates. Many of the latter visibly tended to 'switch off' when it came to an NGO's turn to speak. NGO credibility was not high in the Working Group, and their influence on the draft articles adopted in the first five years was very limited, restricted essentially to the results obtained by a small handful of well-established human rights organisations.

It was in this climate that some of the NGO representatives present at the 1983 meeting of the Working Group decided that a change had to be wrought – or at least sought. With logistical assistance from UNICEF Geneva (and more especially its NGO Liaison Officer) they convened an 'NGO Consultation' in May of that year. Over twenty NGOs were represented there, and the major decision from the meeting was that NGOs interested in the Convention should form themselves into an Ad Hoc Group in order primarily to foster remedies for the two major ills identified in NGO efforts to date: lack of preparedness and lack of a coherent NGO stand. The Group needed a 'focal point', and elected Defence for Children International (DCI) to serve as its Secretariat. A further meeting was called later that year, and the NGO Group came up with joint proposals on a number of articles that were due for consideration at the January 1984 session of the Working Group. These proposals were set out in a very presentable report which was made available to the delegates at the session. The effect was immediate and considerable. The proposals made in the report – which was unofficial in that it had not been submitted through the Centre for Human Rights – were referred to during the debates; the NGOs were asked to explain certain aspects of their proposals; individual delegates came over to discuss such-and-such an issue. In sum, the ground was laid for substantially improving NGO input and impact.

Encouraged by this result, the NGOs again met twice during 1984. In addition to producing a report containing their proposals, they refined their strategies, and, in particular, organised the first of what were to be annual 'briefing meetings' for representatives of Permanent Missions in Geneva, where they explained their view-points so that country delegates could be informed about them prior to the Working Group meeting and could, therefore, have them taken into account when their country's position was being determined.

In fact the NGO Group has tentatively identified some fifteen substantive articles or paragraphs for whose inclusion in the Convention they were primarily responsible, a similar number where they had a significant impact on the formulation, form or content, and two for which the NGO proposal was used as the basic draft text by the Working Group.[18] At the same time, of course, there were also many instances when the NGO Group failed to convince the governmental delegates – the most notorious being the question of permissible participation of children aged 15–17 in armed conflicts.[19]

The above passage is quoted at length because it describes from the inside a process in which I played no part, but whose results I was able to see for myself.

In the same paper, Nigel Cantwell analysed the three major factors that the NGOs felt were behind the success of their work:

1. the clear focus of their aim: it was not a general alliance on children's affairs, but a grouping set up to accomplish a well-defined task;
2. the time-limited nature of its work: once the text of the Convention was adopted, the NGO Group's *raison d'être* would in principle disappear; and
3. the availability of adequate financial support to ensure effective operation, bearing in mind that the nature of the Group's activity meant the level of outside resources required was relatively limited.

He went on to refer to a wide range of other factors which helped the NGO group to achieve its objectives. The members of the NGO group generally had greater professional experience in the field of children's rights than many of the governmental delegates. There was a high degree of motivation and good relationships within the NGO group, which met regularly while work on the Convention was progressing. As the NGO representatives became more familiar with the procedures within the United Nations, they became more skilled negotiators, and they organised themselves to become an effective lobby. The establishment of the NGO group's secretariat served to provide a focal point for those – governments and others – who requested information or advice. The NGOs were able to obtain the cooperation and support of the appropriate specialist body within the UN framework – UNICEF – and the members of the NGO group made the most of the opportunities provided by social events to develop informal contacts with governmental delegates and the Working Group Chairman. The friendships which built up during our weeks in Geneva were certainly an important ingredient in the teamwork which developed in the whole Working Group as drafting progressed.

The governmental delegates themselves came from widely differing backgrounds. Apart from the obvious differences of ideologies and countries of origin, some countries sent very senior people (one sent its former President, another a former Ambassador), while other countries sent very junior officials who seldom opened their mouths. A large number of delegates were legal draftsmen from Ministries of Justice or Departments of External Affairs. I was not the only delegate from a ministry with responsibility for child care policy, but we were in a minority. Whatever our backgrounds, during the period between 1979, when the Working Group was set up, and 1989, when the Convention was finally adopted, all the governmental delegates came to respect the professionalism and dedication of the NGO representatives in matters relating to children and their needs.

The Convention on the Rights of the Child[20] contains a preamble and 54 articles. Part I (Articles 1–41) sets out the rights which the states that ratify the Convention are required to implement. Article 1 defines a child as 'every human being below the age of eighteen years, unless under the law applicable to the child, majority is attained earlier'. Articles 2 to 40 set out a very wide range of political, civil, cultural, economic and social rights. Many of these articles are based broadly on principles which had been accepted long before work on drafting the Convention began, and which were referred to in the 1924 and 1959 Declarations. They include, for example, the articles about a name and nationality (Article 7); non-discrimination (Article 2); freedom of thought, conscience and religion (Article 14); education (Article 28); health care (Article 24); special provisions for physically, mentally or socially handicapped children (Article 23); and protection from exploitation (Articles 34 and 36). Although the principles are unchanged, the Convention gives more detailed guidelines than any previous document about new ways to apply old principles.

There are also some articles which give a completely new right, for example Article 12, on the right of a child to express his or her opinion, and for the child's opinion to be given due weight in all matters affecting the child; Article 33 on drug abuse; and Article 39 about rehabilitative care for children who are victims of abuse. The whole text of Part I, but particularly the innovative paragraphs, owes much to the professional expertise of the members of the NGO forum who attended the meetings of the Working Group.

Part II (Articles 42–45) contains a requirement to 'make the principles and provisions of the Convention widely known, by appropriate and active means, to adults and children alike' (Article 42). Articles 43–45 set out the procedures for monitoring progress made by states in implementing the provisions of the Convention. This task is to be carried out by a Committee consisting of 'ten experts of high moral standing'. States parties are required to submit periodic reports to the Committee, outlining the measures they have adopted to give effect to the rights contained in the Convention. Members of the Committee are elected by secret ballot from a list of persons nominated by states parties, and the membership of the Committee at present includes a number of experts who are closely linked with NGOs, for example Thomas Hammarberg, the former Secretary-General of Rädda Barnen (Swedish Save the Children). The Committee may invite other competent bodies to provide expert advice, and this could include advice from NGOs. It also has the power to transmit, to UNICEF and other competent bodies, reports from states which contain a request, or indicate a need, for technical assistance and advice. Part III (Articles 46–54) sets out procedures for various other matters, including ratification by states, entry into force, the languages of authentic texts of the Convention, and the submission to the Secretary-General of proposals for amendments to the Convention.

In the Working Group discussions where the work was done that actually produced the text of the convention, the attitudes of national delegates and NGOs were fairly predictable. The Eastern bloc were more enthusiastic about economic than political rights, whereas the United States was not keen on any rights that carried suggestions of a 'welfare state'. Roman Catholic countries and Roman Catholic NGOs wanted survival rights applied explicitly to the unborn child. This would have ruled out the possibility of consensus with countries where abortion is legal. Islamic countries rejected out of hand anything which did not conform to Islamic religious law, for example a Chinese proposal regarding the rights of children born out of wedlock. Developing countries made frequent reference to their economic problems, and the need to recognise limitations on their ability to implement any obligations placed on them. This view is reflected in the wording of Article 4, which specifies that the parties to the Convention will undertake measures 'with regard to economic, social and cultural rights . . . to the maximum extent of their available resources'.

Some people may think that Article 4 weakens the whole Convention. It seems to me, however, that the Convention on the Rights of the Child sets realistic standards, and that the NGO delegates showed great wisdom in not pressing too hard for the inclusion of over-ambitious provisions which could have created problems for many countries. Those who draft Conventions often have to make the difficult choice between 'the best' and 'the good'. Instruments which are too ambitious are of much less practical value than more modest and realistic ones, which set targets which can be achieved even by poor countries. It serves little practical purpose for a state to ratify a Convention which it is not able to implement fully, or for a Convention to be ratified only by a tiny number of states.

The NGOs are, on the whole, satisfied with the wording of the Convention, although most of them wish that the article on Children in Armed Conflict (originally numbered as Article 20, but later renumbered as Article 38) had fixed the minimum age for direct participation in hostilities at eighteen rather than fifteen.[21]

Each article was discussed in full before it was adopted, but there were some which were more contentious than others. The discussion about Article 38 was particularly long and difficult. In 1979, when the Polish government submitted a revised version of the draft Convention,[22] there was no article relating to children in armed conflict. In 1980, however, a text prepared by the Friends World Committee for Consultation, a Quaker committee, was put before the Working Group.[23] This drew attention to the provision, set forth in the protocols adopted by the International Diplomatic Conference on Humanitarian Law in 1977, that parties to a conflict should 'take all feasible measures in order that children who have not attained the age of fifteen years do not take a direct part in hostilities and, in particular, they shall refrain from recruiting them into their armed forces'.[24]

In 1981 a further text from the Friends World Committee was tabled.[25] This referred to the fact that children in ten countries had been taking part in civil wars, in resistance movements, wars of liberation from colonial powers and in international conflicts. The text urged that the Convention should include a provision designed to ensure that children should not take a direct part in hostilities, and should not be recruited into the armed forces. The following year, a joint NGO proposal for a new article was submitted to the Working Group by ten NGOs, including the Friends World Committee. This included a provision, from which the Friends World Committee dissociated itself, that in recruiting people between the ages of 15 and 18, priority should be given to the oldest.[26] Further proposals concerning children in armed conflict were submitted: by Algeria in 1983, by Canada in 1984 and also by the Islamic Republic of Iran. In 1985 a joint proposal was submitted by the delegates of the Netherlands, Belgium, Sweden, Finland, Peru and Senegal,[27] and also by the NGO Ad Hoc Group.[28] These texts made no distinction between those below and those above the age of fifteen.

In the end a draft article presented by the Polish delegation was taken as the basis for detailed discussion by the Working Group at its meeting in 1986. This discussion revealed a clear difference of view between those countries, including the United Kingdom, where the minimum age of recruitment into the armed forces was less than 18, and other countries, broadly supported by the NGO group. The briefing of the delegates who came from the countries with a lower age of recruitment seemed to be unambiguous. They did not want to bend to pressure to adopt by consensus a form of words that would require them to modify their existing recruitment policies.

After prolonged discussion by the full Working Group at the 1986 session, the Chairman decided to invite the delegates of Finland, the Soviet Union, the United Kingdom and Venezuela to hold informal consultations with a view to drafting a new text for the contentious paragraph. As a result of those informal consultations, a revised text was produced, and after yet more discussion, this formed the basis of what was adopted towards the end of that session of the Working Group.[29] The adoption of that article in 1986 was not an end of the argument, however. The representatives of several countries continued to express their concern during the sessions in 1987 and 1988 about what they regarded as the undermining of existing standards of humanitarian law,[30] but the article remained in a form which permitted the recruitment of children of as young as fifteen years old.

The discussion on Article 38 illustrates how difficult it can be, and how long it can take, to reach international consensus. If the pressure for the higher minimum age of recruitment into the armed forces had been successful, this would probably have discouraged a number of countries from ratifying the Convention as a whole. That would have been much more damaging to the cause of children's rights than the inclusion in the Convention of one article which many people regard as too weak.

Fortunately, not every article was so contentious. Article 39, for example, was adopted much more quickly. This provides for the rehabilitation of children who have been the victims of exploitation or abuse. The text originated in a proposal by the NGO Group at the 1987 meeting.[31] This proposal was elaborated in consultation with a number of national delegations and the NGO Group, and it was submitted to the Working Group in 1988 by the Norwegian delegation, with acknowledgements to the NGO Group.[32] There was no disagreement about the substance of the article, and the Working Group's discussion on the text was mainly concerned with the linguistic problem of how the English expression 'rehabilitation' should be expressed to give precisely the same meaning in the other official UN languages, in particular French and Spanish.[33] Article 39 was one of more than a dozen articles or paragraphs for which the NGOs were basically responsible. NGOs also had a significant influence on the content of a similar number of articles or paragraphs.[34]

It took more than ten years to complete the drafting of the Convention, and in the years leading up to 1989 the Working Group made special efforts to complete its work in time for the Convention to be ready for adoption on the thirtieth anniversary of the proclamation of the Declaration of the Rights of the Child. This may have been a factor which helped to persuade the representatives both of governments and of NGOs to bring the drafting to a close, so that the Convention could be adopted on the desired target date. In a statement to the 1989 session of the Commission on Human Rights signed by thirty-two NGOs, they summed up their position as follows:

> It is unlikely that any government or NGO could say that it is entirely happy with the draft as it stands . . . (but) . . . if the present draft of the Convention reflects the standards of child welfare and protection that the world's population believe to be just and feasible in 1989, so be it . . . Whilst there will always be some level of discontent, and certain improvements to be made in the quest for perfection, there must be a decision at some point to stop formulation and begin implementation. We believe that time has now come.[35]

In addressing the UN General Assembly on 20 November 1989, when the Convention was adopted unanimously, exactly thirty years after the Declaration on the Rights of the Child had been proclaimed, the Secretary-General, Javier Perez de Cuellar, said:

> The drafting of the Convention was no easy task. In the years since the Declaration of the Rights of the Child was adopted, many perceptions have changed and many concepts have evolved, and the Convention has had to be shaped accordingly. The process of its drafting was a model of how our organisation can and should strive to achieve common goals. Unproductive political confrontations were set aside while delegates from countries with different social and economic systems, representing the various cultural, ethical and religious approaches to life, worked

together with non-governmental organisations in a spirit of harmony and mutual respect and with the best interests of the child as their paramount objective.[36]

Some reflections on UN/NGO consultation arrangements

All the members of the NGO Group which took part in the drafting of the Convention on the Rights of the Child were representatives of organisations that have consultative status with ECOSOC. The arrangements for consultative status which were in operation throughout the years that the Convention on the Rights of the Child was being drafted were based on ECOSOC Resolution 1296, adopted in May 1968.[37] In February 1993, ECOSOC decided to establish, under the auspices of its Committee on NGOs, a review of the participation of NGOs in UN activities and to up-date the resolution presently in force.[38] The decision to carry out such a review was presumably an indication that there was some dissatisfaction about the way in which the system was operating. While writing this chapter, I had discussions with representatives of various NGOs with a particular interest in human rights, social welfare and children, and I was left in no doubt that some NGOs would like to see changes in the existing arrangements, although the organisations which did not have consultative status were not sure how to make their views known.

The Secretary-General of one organisation with consultative status, the International Council on Social Welfare (ICSW), Dr Sirpa Utrainen, commented that it would be in the interests of all NGOs to increase their participation, and did not share the fears expressed by a few organisations that collaboration with the United Nations might compromise their independence. In referring to the need to facilitate the active participation of NGOs from the developing world, Dr Utrainen said that classifying NGOs into 'northern' and 'southern' had acquired some strange features. The main criterion used for designating an international NGO as 'northern' or 'southern' was the location of its secretariat, not the composition of its members. Thus ICSW, for instance, was considered a 'northern NGO' despite having two-thirds of its national members in developing countries. Using the same logic, the UN itself could be categorised as 'northern'. Dr Utrainen also stressed the financial problems for small local NGOs, especially those in developing countries, who wished to send a representative to UN meetings. These may last for up to thirty days, and are generally held in the main UN centres in New York, Geneva or Vienna. In Dr Utrainen's view, any proposals to widen NGO participation in UN affairs must be accompanied by the appropriate concrete financial measures.[39]

My own experience of the issues described by Dr Sirpa Utrainen is based largely on the impressions formed while attending meetings concerned with children, and may therefore be untypical of the work of the United Nations as a whole. However, I formed a positive impression of the ability and knowledge of most of the NGO representatives. Their special experience and professionalism were certainly of value to the UN. While it is conceivable that some other NGOs might have made just as valuable a contribution, it would be absurd to suggest that any of the organisations which contributed so positively to the meetings on children's rights do not deserve consultative status.

Nevertheless, discussions with various child care and human rights NGOs, both national and international, made it plain that they had several concerns they would like the ECOSOC review to consider. The first question related to the machinery for ensuring that all the NGOs which had expertise that could be of value were given the opportunity to take part in consultations on appropriate subjects. The 1968 rules have been interpreted by some national NGOs as excluding them, by definition, from participation in discussions in the UN or its affiliated bodies because they are not organised with an international membership. However, the history of social reform is full of examples of pioneering work done in one country which has then been copied in other countries. It would strengthen the influence of NGOs within the United Nations, and the influence of the UN in the voluntary sector, if national NGOs could play a greater part than they do at present in the affairs of the UN.

A second question concerns the machinery for ensuring that all those NGOs which at present have consultative status really deserve it. Those NGOs which played an active part in the drafting of the Convention on the Rights of the Child included some specialist organisations. It may be a long time before they have another opportunity to make such a useful contribution to the United Nations, on the basis of their own expert knowledge. However, all those who took part in the NGO group during the drafting of the Convention seem to me to have earned their consultative status for many years to come. On the other hand, there are a number of NGOs with consultative status whose activities are also connected with children, but who did not contribute anything to the drafting of the Convention.

Another problem concerns the fact that many NGO spokesmen are very knowledgeable about their own fields of special interest, but less so about UN procedures. Many NGOs are extremely effective in lobbying their own governments, but their techniques may not be appropriate for someone who is negotiating in a body which relies on international consensus rather than majority voting. Nigel Cantwell's comments quoted above refer to the inexperience of some of the NGO representatives attending UN meetings for the first time. Participants at UN meetings would probably benefit from some sort of training seminar about UN procedures, or, failing that, from a published training manual.

Dr Utrainen's comments mentioned above refer particularly to the problem of the non-participation of NGOs from 'southern' countries and the need for procedures to be evolved, and, if necessary, resources to be made available, to encourage more active participation from 'southern' NGOs. Several of the governmental representatives at the Working Group meetings came from developing countries, but it appears from a list compiled in 1987 by Rädda Barnen that none of the NGO representatives did so, although there are many NGOs in developing countries which are active in the field of children's rights. At a UN seminar on the exploitation of child labour in 1985,[40] there were observers from twenty-eight NGOs in consultative status with the UN. Only three of these organisations, the Inter-African Union of Lawyers, the Islamic African Relief Agency and the Indian Council of South America, appeared to be based in developing countries. In spite of the prevalence of child exploitation and child prostitution in some Asian countries, none of the NGO participants at the seminar on child labour came from Asia. The non-participation of NGOs from poorer countries seems to be a serious defect in the present system, but many 'southern' NGOs will not be able to send delegates to UN meetings without financial help. It may also be the case that most of the NGOs which are really representative of the developing countries are too poor to operate in more than one country, and therefore feel themselves excluded by the broad requirement that NGOs should be international or regional in order to qualify for consultative status.

In discussions with senior staff of a number of NGOs in Britain while preparing this paper, I heard several other complaints. The Director of one NGO said that he thought there was something seriously wrong with the UN machinery for consulting with the voluntary sector. His organisation and certain other major British voluntary organisations would have had a great deal more to offer from an informed viewpoint than most of the NGOs with international links. Another expressed the opinion that although Defence for Children International played an outstanding role in the drafting, very few of the other NGOs prominent in Geneva and with UN standing had any real feel for children's rights apart from the basic survival issues. He expressed concern that the UN Committee on the Rights of the Child tended to be surrounded by NGOs committed to human rights, but not necessarily sensitive to children's rights, and in particular not to their civil and political rights.

There are several national NGOs in Britain (and elsewhere) which could make a valuable contribution to the work of the United Nations. If the UN wishes to limit the number of organisations with consultative status, as I think it must, then this will inevitably involve making difficult judgements about the relative merits of different organisations.

Making the Convention work effectively

The response to the adoption of the Convention on the Rights of the Child was quite unexpected. No other human rights treaty has been ratified so quickly by so many countries. It was adopted by the General Assembly on 20 November 1989, opened for signature and ratification on 26 January 1990 and entered into force on 2 September 1990. At the end of 1990, fifty-seven states had ratified or acceded to it. One year later, a further forty-five countries had done so. At the end of 1992, the number of states parties to the Convention was 117 and at the end of 1993 the total reached 154.[41] Less than a year after the Convention was adopted, a World Summit for Children was held in UN Headquarters. Even though it coincided with the Gulf crisis, it was attended by seventy-one heads of state or heads of government, and 88 senior delegations. The Summit attracted a great deal of publicity, and when it ended the participants agreed to a 'World Declaration on the Survival, Protection and Development of Children'. This Declaration states that the Convention on the Rights of the Child 'provides a new opportunity to make respect for children's rights and welfare truly universal'. The signatories made a solemn commitment to give high priority to the rights of children, sought the support of the UN system, as well as other international and regional organisations, in the universal effort to promote the well-being of children, and asked for greater involvement on the part of non-governmental organisations, in complementing national efforts and joint international action in this field. Specific goals were agreed on at the Summit, and the prime ministers and presidents committed themselves to achieving these goals by the end of the decade.[42]

By the beginning of 1994, fewer than thirty countries had still to sign the Convention. These included several members of the former Soviet Union, some very small countries and a few countries involved in civil wars, such as Bosnia and Somalia. Only one major country, the United States of America, had not signed, although many Americans were actively campaigning for children's rights and it was clear that President Clinton's administration was less unsympathetic to welfare rights than its predecessors. Several national professional and humanitarian organisations in the United States have endorsed the Convention. It is also possible for individual states to act more rapidly than the US federal government. In 1992, for example, the General Assembly of the State of South Carolina adopted a resolution affirming its support for the Convention, and calling on all agencies in South Carolina to ensure that their programmes aim to achieve the Convention's goals.[43] (The United States eventually signed the Convention in 1995.)

When the Working Group drafted the Convention's articles relating to the examination of the reports submitted periodically by states parties, it was assumed that a committee of ten members, with its secretariat, would be able to cope with the work-load. There seems now to be a real danger that the Convention may become the victim of its own success, as the number of countries which have ratified the Convention, and are therefore required to submit reports, is far greater than envisaged. As a result the government of Costa Rica proposed an amendment to Article 43 of the Convention to increase the membership of the committee from ten to eighteen experts. No decision had been taken by September 1993.[44] It should be borne in mind, however, that enlarging a committee, far from speeding up its work, may have the effect of delaying it.

The role of NGOs did not come to an end the moment the Convention was adopted. Both for governments and for NGOs, ratification is only the end of the beginning. Unless it leads to improvements in the way the world treats its children, the Convention will be worthless. Governments are required to take the necessary measures to implement every article in Part I of the Convention and the NGOs have a vital task in ensuring that they do so.

A booklet entitled 'NGO Work for the Implementation of the Rights of the Child' was published in Stockholm by Rädda Barnen in 1993. It contains the following paragraphs on the role of non-governmental groups:

NGOs fulfil several functions in the field of human rights:

- monitoring and fact-finding in their own or other countries;
- investigating and reporting on violations;
- informing and educating about human rights matters and the work of international organisations;
- mobilising interest groups and lobbying national governments and international bodies;

– advising on or directly contributing to the implementation of human rights standards.

Which of these functions is performed, and how, vary [*sic*] from country to country and from NGO to NGO. For instance, some organizations emphasise fact-finding and advocacy, while others give direct service. Naturally, national and international groups tend to play different, but often complementary roles.

The Convention on the Rights of the Child is the only human rights treaty which specifically gives NGOs a role in the monitoring procedures. As 'other competent bodies' they can be invited by the Committee on the Rights of the Child to give 'expert advice'. In fact, the Committee has given NGOs an important place in its procedures. It is clear that NGO input will be important for the Committee proceedings.

However, NGOs are important not only in relation to the Committee reporting process. Especially on the national level, they can play a major role in creating awareness about the Convention, its content and mechanisms. They can pressure for ratification and the first legal steps towards implementation. They can request and contribute to a national system of monitoring. Finally, they can advocate and/or undertake themselves the necessary measures to make a reality of the standards of the Convention.[45]

In Britain, several interested organisations have in recent years been seeking to ensure that the Convention is taken seriously. Their concern prompted the Gulbenkian Foundation (UK Branch) to commission a wide consultation in the statutory and voluntary sectors on a proposal to set up a short-term project to encourage the fullest possible implementation of the Convention. As a result, the independent Children's Rights Development Unit (CRDU) was launched in March 1992. The CRDU was planned as a short-term project, with an expected life-span of only three years and to be funded entirely from non-governmental sources. One important source of its funds is the Gulbenkian Foundation, which has taken the Convention as one of its priorities and plans to initiate and support specific projects of benefit to children and young people. The CRDU has the support of all the major British child welfare organisations, but it is a very small organization with just three staff based in London and links in Scotland, Wales and Northern Ireland.[46] Although the CRDU collaborated with the Department of Health in producing a booklet, 'The Rights of the Child – a Guide to the UN Convention',[47] the Unit is independent and receives no financial support from the government.

The work of the Unit falls into two broad fields, monitoring the implementation of the Convention and promoting awareness of the Convention. During the first half of its very short life, its achievements have been impressive. It aims to produce a National Agenda for Children. This Agenda will identify, article by article, where current law, policy and practice in the United Kingdom fails to meet standards embodied in the Convention. It will develop detailed policy proposals to bring Britain into line with those standards. It will work with local authorities, health authorities, voluntary and professional bodies to develop strategies for applying the principles contained in the Convention to their policies and practice. The Unit has already produced a number of guidance documents and policy papers, and organised conferences and seminars. The main task of the Unit will be completed when the National Agenda for Children and all the appropriate guidance documents have been drafted and widely circulated. It is, of course, sensible that there should be a target date for completion of these tasks, and the organisations which are now funding the Unit can not be expected to do so indefinitely. Even so, it would be helpful if the impetus that it has generated were to be preserved. There are many other countries across the world which would also benefit from the establishment of units comparable to the CRDU.

In the speech that he made to the General Assembly on 20 November 1989, quoted above, the UN Secretary-General referred to the way in which governments had worked with NGOs in a spirit of harmony and mutual respect to achieve the drafting of the Convention. No one would disagree with those comments, but they do not go far enough. The same sort of collaboration will always be needed if the Convention is to bring about any real and lasting improvement in the appalling conditions in which too many of the world's children are now living – and dying.

NOTES

1. Quoted in 'The White Flame' by Gillian Wilson, press officer of the Save the Children Fund, published in *The World's Children*, September 1976, on the centenary of Eglantyne Jebb's birth. For further information about Eglantyne Jebb see Save the Children Archives and Records Management leaflets, *Eglantyne Jebb Facts* and *Eglantyne Jebb Quotations*.
2. The Save the Children Fund – Special Collections: the Suzanne Ferrière papers, document SC/SF/17.
3. A copy of the English translation of the Declaration of Geneva was provided by the Archives and Records Department of the Save the Children Fund, London.
4. For further information about Janusz Korczak, see publisher's note in French

editions of Janusz Korczak, *Le Roi Mathias* and *Le Roi Mathias sur une Ile Déserte* (Rouen: Edition Atelier Cauchois, 1986). See also an article by Georges Laurent Tricot, 'Janusz Korczak, pédiatre, pédagogue, héros national et martyr' published as an appendix to *Le Roi Mathias sur une Ile Déserte*.

5. For a 1994 list of the countries with organisations that are members of the International Save the Children Alliance, see Chapter 9, note 1.

6. The Universal Declaration of Human Rights was adopted and proclaimed by the General Assembly of the United Nations on 10 December 1948 (Resolution 217 A (III)). The text of the Declaration is reproduced in *Human Rights: A Compilation of International Instruments* (New York: UN, 1983), pp. 1–3.

7. UN doc. E/3229, Commission on Human Rights, Report to the Economic and Social Council on the 15th session of the Commission, 16 March–10 April 1959. Two NGOs gave written statements and five spoke in the Commission.

8. Amendments proposed by Italy and by Afghanistan in UN docs. A/C.3/L.713 and A/C.3/L.716 respectively.

9. The Declaration of the Rights of the Child was adopted unanimously by the UN General Assembly of 20 November 1959 as Resolution 1386(XIV). Background material on the history of the drafting is based on a brochure in French prepared by the French Committee of UNICEF in about 1985 and on the *Yearbook of the United Nations 1959* (New York: UN Office of Public Information, 1960), pp. 192–99. The text is reproduced in *Human Rights. A Compilation . . ., op. cit.*, pp. 129–30, and in the *Yearbook*, pp. 198–9.

10. The background to the Convention and the full text can be found in 'The United Nations Convention on the Rights of the Child', produced by the Children's Rights Development Unit, 235 Shaftesbury Avenue, London WC2H 8EL. Another booklet, 'Making Reality of the Rights of the Child' by Thomas Hammarberg, published by Rädda Barnen, 107 88 Stockholm, also contains the text of the Convention, together with a commentary and a copy of the general guidelines prepared for governments by the Committee on the Rights of the Child regarding the form and content of reports to be submitted to the Committee under the provisions of Article 44 of the Convention. (Rädda Barnen is the Swedish counterpart of Save the Children.)

11. See note 4 above.

12. UN General Assembly, Official Records 33rd Session Supplement No. 45 (A/33/45), 20 December 1978. This document is reproduced in *Compilation of the On-going Work of the Drafting of the United Nations Convention on the Rights of the Child 1978–1987* (Geneva: Rädda Barnen International, May 1987), p. 360.

13. The facts mentioned here are referred to in a number of publications, including Human Rights Centre, Geneva, Fact Sheet no. 10; The Report of a UN Seminar on the Elimination of the Exploitation of Child Labour, paper ST/HR/SER.A/18, paragraph 109(b) and various publications by UNICEF, for example the 'Summary of Issues' in the 1992 edition of *The State of the World's Children*.

14. *Compilation of the On-going Work . . ., op. cit.*, pp. 377–9. The following organisations were listed as attending one or more meetings of the Working Group between 1978 and 1987: Associated Country Women of the World, Amnesty International, Anti-Slavery Society for the Protection of Human Rights, Baha'i International Community, Defence for Children International, Four Directions Council, Friends World Committee for Consultation, Human Rights Internet, International Association of Democratic Lawyers, International Abolitionist Federation, International Association of Juvenile and Family Court Magistrates, International Association of Penal Law, International Association of Youth Magistrates, International Catholic Child Bureau,

International Commission of Jurists, International Council of Jewish Women, International Committee of the Red Cross, International Council on Social Welfare, International Council of Women, International Federation of Home Economics, International Federation of Women Lawyers, International Federation of Women in Legal Careers, International Humanist and Ethical Union, International Movement ATD-Fourth World, International Movement for Fraternal Union among Races and Peoples, International Social Services, International Union of Judges, International Union of Child Welfare, Minority Rights Group, Rädda Barnen International, Rädda Barnen Riksförbund, Save the Children Fund, Save the Children Fund Alliance, Women's International Democratic Federation, World Association for the School as an Instrument of Peace, World Jewish Congress, World Movement of Mothers, World Organisation for Early Childhood Education, World Union of Catholic Women's Organisations, World Union of Organisations for the Safeguard of Youth, and Zonta International.

15. UN doc. E/CN.4/1985/SR53/Add.1, p. 27, para. 109, reproduced in *Compilation of the On-going Work . . ., op. cit.*, p. 292.

16. Based on information supplied to the author in a letter of 18 October 1993 by Simone Ek of Rädda Barnen in Sweden.

17. 'Defence for Children International – The Worldwide Movement for Children's Rights' published by the DCI International Secretariat, P.O. Box 88, 1211 Geneva 20. DCI sections exist or are being constituted in the following countries: Australia, Argentina, Bangladesh, Belgium, Benin, Bolivia, Brazil, Canada, Chile, Colombia, Costa Rica, Côte d'Ivoire, Croatia, Czech Republic, Denmark, Ecuador, El Salvador, Finland, Gambia, Germany, Guatemala, India, Israel, Italy, Japan, Lebanon, Mali, Mexico, Nepal, the Netherlands, Norway, Pakistan, Palestine, Paraguay, Peru, Philippines, Senegal, Slovakia, Spain, Sri Lanka, Switzerland, Tanzania, the United Kingdom, the United States, Uruguay, Venezuela, Zaïre, Zambia.

18. Nigel Cantwell, 'NGO Involvement in the Convention on the Rights of the Child', *Bulletin of Human Rights*, May 1991. A footnote on p. 9 of this article states that NGOs were basically responsible for the following articles and paragraphs of the Convention: Article 9 paragraphs 3 and 4 (on separation from parents); Article 28 (on education); Article 29 paragraphs 1 (d) and (e) (on aims of education); Article 30 (on children of minorities or indigenous populations); Article 34 (on sexual exploitation); Article 35 (on sale, trafficking and abduction); Article 37 (on torture and deprivation of liberty); Article 38 paragraph 4 (on the protection and care of children affected by an armed conflict); Article 39 (on rehabilitative care); Article 41 (on respect for higher standards in other national or international laws); Article 42 (on the obligation to make the provisions of the Convention widely known to adults and children); Article 44 paragraph 6 (on the obligation on states to give wide publicity to the reports they submit to the committee on the rights of the child).

In addition to these articles, NGOs also had direct impact on the formulation, form, or content of the following articles and paragraphs of the Convention: Article 8 (on the preservation of the child's identity); Article 13 (on freedom of expression); Article 16 (on protection of privacy); Article 19 (on protection from abuse or neglect); Article 20, para.3 (on having regard to the cultural background of the child deprived of a family environment, for whom alternative care has to be provided); Article 23 (on disabled children); Article 25 (on the periodic review of the placement of a child who is in care); Article 27 paragraphs 3 and 4 (on the state's duty to ensure that parents fulfil their responsibilities for their children, and to recover maintenance from those having financial responsibility for the child); Article 32 (on child labour); Article 33 (on drug abuse); Article 40 (on administration of juvenile justice); and Article 45 (on the fostering of effective implementation of the Convention, and the encouragement of international cooperation of bodies recognised as 'competent' (including NGOs with consultative status) in the field covered by the Convention).

19. Nigel Cantwell, 'How NGOs contributed to drafting the Convention on the Rights of the Child', paper presented at a Symposium on 'The Contribution of NGOs to the Formulation and Promotion of International Human Rights Law', 4 May 1990, Palais des Nations, Geneva.

20. The UN General Assembly adopted the Convention on the Rights of the Child by Resolution 44/25 of 20 November 1989. This was the thirtieth anniversary of the adoption of the Declaration on the Rights of the Child on 20 November 1959. See also notes 9 and 10 above.

21. Information contained in a personal letter dated 5 August 1993 to the author from Thomas Hammarberg, former Secretary-General of Rädda Barnen and now a member of the Committee on the Rights of the Child.

22. UN doc. E/CN.4/1349.

23. UN doc. E/CN.4/NGO/265.

24. Article 77(2) of *Protocol I Additional to the Geneva Conventions of 12 August 1949 and Relating to the Protection of Victims of International Armed Conflicts of 8 June 1977*. A similar provision is given in Article 4(3)(c) of *Protocol II Relating to the Protection of Victims of Non-International Armed Conflicts*.

25. UN doc. E/CN.4/NGO/295.

26. UN doc. E/CN.4/1982/WG.1/WP.1. The organisations which submitted the document were: Friends World Committee for Consultation, International Council of Women, International Association of Penal Law, International Catholic Child Bureau, International Catholic Union of the Press, International Commission of Jurists, International Council of Jewish Women, International Federation of Women in Legal Careers, International Federation of Women Lawyers, World Jewish Congress.

27. UN doc. E/CN.4/1985/64 Annex II.

28. UN doc. E/CN.4/1986/WG.1/WP.1, p. 58.

29. UN doc. E/CN.4/1986/39, paras 124–45.

30. UN doc. E/CN.4/1989/48, paras 600–22.

31. UN doc. E/CN.4/1987/25, paras 157–8.

32. UN doc. E/CN.4/1988/WG.1/WP.2.

33. UN doc. E/CN.4/1988/28, paras 66–70.

34. See note 18 above.

35. Patricia Smyke, 'Caught in the Cross Currents', a Review of NGO/UN Action for Children 1979–89, commissioned by the NGO Committee on UNICEF, pp. 9–10.

36. Official Records of the General Assembly, 44th Session, Plenary Meetings, A/44/PV.61.

37. For the text of ECOSOC Resolution 1296(XLIV), see Appendix Two and for a discussion of the workings of the consultative system, see Chapter 2.

38. See Chapter 2 and 'More or less influence for NGOs at the UN System' in *ICSW Information* – News from the International Council on Social Welfare, Vienna, June 1993, p. 1.

39. *Ibid.*

40. 'Report of a Seminar on Ways and Means of achieving the Elimination of the Exploitation of Child Labour in all Parts of the World' UN doc. ST/HR/SER.A/18, 22 January 1986.

41. UN doc. A/49/41, Report of the Committee on the Rights of the Child, 19 May 1994, pp. 107–11.

42. 'World Declaration on the Survival, Protection, and Development of Children and Plan of Action for implementing the World Declaration' (New York: UN, 30 September 1990), from UN doc. A/45/625.
43. Information contained in a letter dated 18 April 1994 to the author from Professor Gary B. Melton of the Center on Children, Families, and the Law, University of Nebraska-Lincoln. A concurrent resolution to support the UN Convention on the Rights of the Child was adopted by the South Carolina General Assembly on 5 May 1992.
44. Information contained in a personal letter dated 23 August 1993 to the author from Mr John Pace, Chief of Legislation and Prevention of Discrimination Branch, United Nations Office at Geneva.
45. 'NGO Work for the Implementation of the Rights of the Child' (Stockholm: Rädda Barnen, 1993), p. 6.
46. 'Children's Rights Development Unit – the First Year', note dated 11 January 1993, and 'Children's Rights Development Unit – using the UN Convention to audit Law Policy, and Practice – a Guide for Voluntary Organisations etc.', note dated June 1992. For further information on particular aspects of the implementation of the Convention, see also CRDU briefing notes and consultation documents on a wide range of subjects, including: a Guide for Local Authorities; Education and Children's Rights; Child Employment; Youth Justice in England and Wales; Civil and Political Liberties; Race and Culture; Immigration, Nationality and Refugees; Day-to-day Care of Children. For information on the CRDU, see note 10 above.
47. 'The Rights of the Child – a Guide to the UN Convention', Booklet CAG 9 (London: Department of Health, February 1993).

9

THE SAVE THE CHILDREN FUND AND NUTRITION FOR REFUGEES

Angela Penrose and John Seaman

'The child should be the first to receive relief in times of distress.'
— Article 3 of the Declaration of the Rights of the Child 1923

'Approximately half of the refugees of the world are children.'
— Report of the United Nations High Commissioner for Refugees, 1993

Introduction

This Chapter explores how one particular non-governmental organisation, The Save the Children Fund in Britain (SCF-UK), became involved in the issue of the provision to refugees of rations that are adequate in quality and quantity. Throughout the 1980s SCF was directly involved in the response to many emergencies that entailed large numbers of refugees. Repeatedly high levels of morbidity and mortality rates due to inadequate rations were experienced in several refugee camps, most, but not all, in Africa. In working with others in attempting to eliminate this problem, SCF had to go on a long voyage of discovery. If it was to have any impact on the system it was dealing with, it had to learn about that system. It was to discover that the mandates of the UN agencies with responsibility for refugees, the internal structures of those agencies, the relationships between different UN agencies and between UN agencies and other organisations engaging with the system, all had an effect on the ability of the system to work effectively.

The origins and history of The Save the Children Fund

The Save the Children Fund is Britain's largest international voluntary agency concerned with child health and welfare. It was founded in 1919 by Eglantyne Jebb who drafted the Declaration of the Rights of the Child in 1923, which still underpins all SCF's work both in the United Kingdom and overseas. This Declaration was endorsed

241

by the League of Nations in 1924 and evolved to become the Convention on the Rights of the Child, as described in Chapter 8.

The Save the Children Fund was founded as a response to the urgent needs of those affected by the 1914–18 war in Europe. Food shortages were widespread and hundreds of thousands of refugees and displaced people were scattered across the continent and beyond. The organisation's earliest beginnings were linked to the Fight the Famine Council, a body set up to campaign against the Allied blockade of Germany and Austria-Hungary. SCF quickly became independent of the Council, raising funds to relieve the misery of children and their families both in the former Allied countries and in Germany, Austria and Eastern Europe. The suffering of these children was the result of a war waged between their own governments and those countries offering assistance. From the start SCF made it clear that aid was to be given to children on all sides, irrespective of nationality or religion. Eglantyne Jebb was unequivocally working on the premise that individuals had rights, including the right to subsistence, which were basic to humanity rather than dependent on their citizenship of a state. Eglantyne Jebb's activities were also an illustration of the growing belief that there were actors other than governments who could become involved. The results of the very successful first appeal – over £400,000 was raised in the first year, equivalent to £8,000,000 today – were distributed in the form of clothing, blankets and food, either through existing agencies such as the Society of Friends and the Salvation Army, or local groups, schools, orphanages and hospitals.

 SCF continued to operate almost exclusively in Europe and was assisted by the establishment of the Save the Children International Union in Geneva, organised by Eglantyne Jebb, in 1920. This was an umbrella body that included Save the Children organisations from around the world including Sweden, France, Ireland and Germany. All the Save the Children organisations were devoted to the cause of children without regard to race, nationality or creed. The connections through the International Union were disrupted by the Second World War and not resumed afterwards. The strong individual organisations, such as SCF in Britain and Rädda Barnen in Sweden, were able to run significant international programmes on their own initiative. It was not until 1979 that they again came together in the International Save the Children Alliance (ISCA), which now has twenty-five members and is based in Geneva.[1] ISCA members continue to have strong links and have frequently worked together both operationally and in their attempts to influence international opinion. This chapter, however, is, unless specified, a description of activities carried out by SCF-UK.

Although the geographical focus of SCF has changed during the seventy five years of its existence, distinctive aspects of its work first emerged in the earliest years: the recognition that the problems of children are universal, requiring a universal approach; the need to consider the long-term, as well as to respond to immediate need; and the importance of bringing influence to bear on public opinion, on governments and others with the power to bring about improvements in the well-being of children. From 1920, SCF began to allocate grants to organisations in the United Kingdom as well as overseas. From 1926 it ran a school for undernourished children from disadvantaged backgrounds and it opened several nursery schools during the 1930s. As the result of an enquiry in 1933 into the condition of children of the unemployed, which concluded that the best method of dealing with undernourishment in children was to provide nutritious meals at school, SCF began to campaign for school meals to be made mandatory in Britain.

SCF quickly developed its experience of responding to refugee and famine crises. Within a month of its launch a grant was made to help Armenian refugees from the former Ottoman Empire, the first of many to Armenia. In October 1920 a grant of £250 was made for famine relief in China. The words of the SCF Treasurer at the time seem the precursor of many since. 'It is a real grief to us that this contribution is no larger but we have heavy demands on our funds ... and we feel that the work which has already been undertaken through our means must be the first charge on our resources'.[2]

In the following year the major operation in Russia brought two significant innovations that have become characteristic of SCF's ways of working. Staff were sent out to run feeding centres instead of just supervising expenditure as had formerly been the case, and the importance of communicating the need and the response was realised. The process of persuading the public to give money for the relief of children in other countries, often former enemies or, in the case of Russia, currently hostile countries, required a high degree of communication skills, and SCF soon learnt the value of good publicity. 'In the first place,' said Eglantyne Jebb, 'we have to devise ways of making known the facts in such a way as to touch the imagination of the world. The world is not ungenerous, but unimaginative and very busy.'[3] A cameraman was sent to film the Russian famine of 1921 and then to film the feeding centres in operation. Showings of the film around Britain helped to explain the issue and raised over £6,000 in the first year, contributing

towards a much greater sum raised through a hard-hitting advertising campaign.[4]

While SCF began life, and is perhaps best known, as a relief
agency, the bulk of its work has always focused on the 'progressive
realisation' of children's basic rights to health, education and
welfare. This began in the 1920s when villages for the settlement
of refugees were built in Bulgaria and Albania.

Towards the end of her life, Eglantyne Jebb became concerned
over the concentration of SCF's work in Europe. 'As there are
undoubtedly children who are suffering more in Asia and Africa
than in Europe, we should prove the sincerity of our claim to
universality by undertaking work in these continents directly we are
able to raise sufficient funds for the purpose.'[5] Two countries in
particular appeared suitable to her at that time, China and Ethiopia
(Abyssinia).

> Abyssinia is very anxious to profit by European Experience in
> making progress towards the establishment of better conditions
> of life, but fears to accept any help from Europe, which might
> entail an encroachment on its independence. It would therefore
> probably welcome the assistance of our Society. Perhaps the
> greatest evil with regard to Child Life is the sale of children into
> slavery, but in my opinion it would be better, before thinking
> of attacking the problem directly to send a delegate to Abyssinia
> to study the situation of Child Life as a whole and initiate work
> in whatever direction appeared to be most suitable as a begin-
> ning. Special attention should be paid to arousing native interest
> and native help, and thus gradually bringing into being a
> national movement for the care and protection of children.[6]

This memorandum again reflects characteristics that have continued
to distinguish SCF's work: the value of the Fund as an organisation
independent of government, the importance of an adequate situa-
tional analysis to determine real needs before undertaking any new
work and the essential requirement of involving local people.

As is often the case with pioneers, Eglantyne Jebb's vision
exceeded the ability of SCF and its supporters to realise it in the
short term. Despite an influential conference entitled 'The role of
European nations in the health; education in terms of preparation
for life; and general working conditions and protection of children
in Africa' in 1931, a decline in income during the 1930s prevented
extensive involvement in Africa until after the Second World War.
An infant feeding and welfare centre was set up in cooperation with
the Association of Ethiopian Women but this work ended following the fall of the country to the Italians. The refugees who fled

to Kenya and Somaliland were helped by SCF.

During the Second World War almost all SCF's income was spent on projects in the United Kingdom. By 1942 the Fund began to anticipate the likely needs of children in occupied Europe once the war was over, and a report, *Children in Bondage*, containing surveys of the nutritional needs of children in European countries was published in 1943. SCF took a leading part in the formation of the Council of British Organisations for Relief Abroad, and before the war had ended SCF teams had gone into formerly occupied territories including Albania, Greece, Italy and France. In the immediate post-war period SCF carried out extensive relief work in various countries. Work on a major scale continued to be carried out in Italy and Greece, but as the need for emergency work in Europe declined, the focus of SCF's work began to shift, as Eglantyne Jebb had suggested that it should many years before, to Asia and Africa.

Involvement was initially restricted to countries under British colonial administration such as the Sudan and Somaliland, but two major events of the 1950s led to the first significant initiatives in countries that had not been under colonial rule. Both the Korean War and the Hungarian refugee crisis of 1956 involved SCF in considerable work and generated increased income for the organisation. During the 1950s the bulk of SCF's income was still spent in Europe and Asia but from 1960 onwards, which marked the beginning of the Freedom from Hunger campaign, the proportion of SCF's income spent in Africa gradually increased. In 1961, for the first time, SCF spent more in Africa than in the United Kingdom; in 1965 expenditure in Africa exceeded that in Europe and finally, in 1970, as the war in Biafra was coming to an end and the first of the major modern famine crises began, Africa became the leading region for SCF expenditure.

Throughout the 1970s and 1980s, SCF's overseas work and income grew steadily, with surges in income occurring during emergencies, such as the serious drought in Ethiopia and other countries in Africa in the mid-1980s. Long-term development work in partnership with governments, other non-governmental organisations and local communities continues in over fifty countries including the United Kingdom. In many others SCF continues to respond to disaster, both natural and man-made. In 1993 SCF received its highest income to date, £112,845,000, the greater part of which is still raised from the general public by a variety of means. More than 750 branches and 150 shops are run by volunteers who raise money within their local communities. Thousands of people make regular donations through their pay packets or covenants, leave legacies or respond to newspaper advertisements and annual fund-raising appeals. Within the last decade support from companies, including corporate member-companies which pledge to raise £100,000 a year, has increased. In addition SCF receives grants from the Overseas Development Administration (ODA) of the British government and from the European Union for both long-term development work and humanitarian assistance. SCF also receives income from the Comic Relief charity for rehabilitation and development work in Africa.

Important support for SCF is provided by the Princess Royal (Princess Anne) who has been the Fund's President for over twenty-five years. She has travelled extensively and come to know and understand both SCF's programmes and the problems it faces.

SCF and its work with refugees

As can be seen throughout its history, SCF has responded to the needs of refugees and displaced people, particularly refugee children. Its work reflects the historical changes that have affected refugee flows since the First World War. The formation of SCF in 1919 was part of a wider response in Europe to the upheavals causing such misery to civilian populations in the aftermath of the war. In the same year, the major Red Cross societies came together to form the League of Red Cross Societies and to encourage the formation of new societies in a wider range of countries. Also in 1919, the famous Norwegian explorer, Fridtjof Nansen, articulated public concern about starvation and disease in parts of the Soviet Union, in an appeal to the Versailles Conference for food supplies to be sent 'for the alleviation of this gigantic misery on purely humanitarian grounds'. Because of the desire to overthrow the Bolsheviks, Nansen's appeal was rejected and most governments refused to contribute either food or financial assistance.[7]

By the summer of 1921 the people of Russia had endured seven years of disaster. A major crop failure, when food reserves were almost exhausted, resulted in widespread famine. Despite the potential enormity of this new disaster – estimates of those facing starvation were as high as twenty million people and it is estimated that at least seven million people eventually died – the League of Nations took no action. The International Committee of the Red Cross and the League of Red Cross Societies convened a meeting in August 1921. At this conference, attended by sixteen governments, twenty-seven Red Cross Societies and twenty-eight other NGOs, including the Save the Children International Union, an International Commission for the Relief of Famine in Russia was set up to coordinate the activities of the various relief organisa-

tions. Nansen was invited to be its High Commissioner to negotiate
with the Russians and organise the relief effort. Eglantyne Jebb
had spoken at the meeting of work already done by the Union and
on 28 August Nansen allocated the most severely hit province in
Russia, Saratov, to the Save the Children International Union of
which the most active element was SCF-UK. The Union, which had
been planning its relief operation, agreed at once and dispatched
its first cargo of 600 tons of aid in a chartered ship on 7 September.
By the height of the famine, Save the Children was feeding 300,000
children and 350,000 adults. Although individual governments,
particularly the United States, gave support, the League of Nations
still rejected Nansen's appeal to its Assembly to fund the Commission's work within the Soviet Union. However, in response to
public sympathies, Nansen was also appointed by the League as a
High Commissioner for Russian Refugees, to assist those who had
fled to neighbouring countries.

   Just as SCF was part of the international NGO action that initiated
the League's work, it continued throughout the inter-war years to
cooperate with the Nansen International Office for Refugees on
refugee crises such as Armenia. In the mid-1930s strong protests
by SCF helped to block moves in the League of Nations to close
down the Nansen International Office. The Fund's Council sent a
resolution to the League to the effect that such a move 'without
the substitution of a Central League of Nations Organisation
affording legal, social, economic, and moral protection to refugees
is extremely detrimental to the refugees themselves and damaging
to the great humanitarian work of the League'.

   In the last two years of the Second World War and in the following years, SCF was part of a massive international effort by the
United Nations and NGOs to provide relief and rehabilitation or
resettlement to families and children affected by the war. Many of
the recipients of SCF assistance were children of refugees and concentration camp survivors in Europe, but from the 1950s involvement in other areas increased. SCF became involved in funding
or direct operational work in refugee crises in Hungary, Korea,
Algeria, Jordan, Gaza and the West Bank, Cambodia, Central
America, Iraq, Laos, Ethiopia, Somalia and Malawi. It is currently
involved in working with Bhutanese refugees in Nepal, Rohinga
refugees in Bangladesh, Vietnamese refugees in Hong Kong and
in many countries in Africa where it works with both refugees
and displaced people.[8]

   The refugee crises of the 1960s, 1970s and 1980s were markedly
different from those that had earlier characterised European refugee movements. Anti-colonial insurgency and rapid decolonisation,

often followed by civil strife, generated vast numbers of refugees in developing countries. The international community came under mounting pressure to adapt its programmes and policies to give greater assistance to refugees fleeing to countries which were themselves very poor. The potential for overseas resettlement which had underpinned the approach to the European refugee problem was extremely limited. Most of those fleeing conflict in Africa fled across borders to stay with closely connected ethnic groups until they could return home. There are many examples of extraordinary generosity and hospitality. In the Ogaden region of Ethiopia, for example, communities harboured Somali refugees, and in Malawi, until recent repatriation moves, a tenth of the population were refugees from Mozambique (the equivalent of Britain admitting 5 million French people). However, the size of the movements, the poverty of many of the host countries and the political and security implications of accepting refugees from adjoining countries made permanent local settlement difficult and in some cases unacceptable to many countries.

The UNHCR and NGOs

When refugee problems arose in the inter-war years, the League of Nations, and Nansen as the responsible High Commissioner, took them up on an *ad hoc* basis. On each occasion there was an assumption that a temporary response for a particular group of people would be sufficient. This approach continued until the creation in 1951 of the Office of the United Nations High Commissioner for Refugees (UNHCR). At that time it was assumed that the UNHCR would only be needed for three years and the Convention Relating to the Status of Refugees was limited in scope to those who became refugees before January 1951. Officially the UNHCR has never become a permanent body, but its mandate has been regularly renewed for five-year periods, so in effect the UNHCR Office is now a permanent operational branch of the main UN Secretariat. In 1967 a Protocol to the Convention abolished the cut-off point for defining a refugee and since then UNHCR's work has gradually expanded to cover wider categories of 'persons of concern'. The office is subject to political control, by an elected Executive Committee of governments having responsibility to oversee policy.[9]

Some thirty NGOs took part in the conference that drafted the 1951 Convention and one of its resolutions paid tribute to the welfare work of NGOs. The Convention is concerned with the definition of refugees and their legal rights. Neither NGOs nor the need of refugees for assistance is mentioned. However, the Statute of

UNHCR, produced in conjunction with the Convention, includes in Article 8 provisions for the High Commissioner 'establishing contact in such manner as he may think best with private organisations [that is NGOs] dealing with refugee questions' and 'facilitating the coordination of the efforts of private organisations concerned with the welfare of refugees'. Unlike most other UN bodies, there is no formal procedure for consultation with NGOs nor a list of recognised NGOs. Some eighty to 100 NGOs attend the annual sessions of the UNHCR Executive Committee each October, of which about half have ECOSOC consultative status. In the debates, the Red Cross and the International Council of Voluntary Agencies (ICVA – a global umbrella organisation of nearly a hundred NGOs) act as the main voices of the NGO community.

The provisions of Article 8 of the Statute allow the Office to receive and disburse funds through governments and NGOs. In the field, any NGO may become an operational partner for UNHCR, provided it can demonstrate financial responsibility, has no religious or political bias and can offer rapid, good quality service to meet a defined need.[10] The relationship has evolved as UNHCR's assistance role has expanded, as a result of its decision to take responsibility under the 'good offices' mechanism for populations displaced by war. In 1993 UNHCR channelled more than a quarter of its budget, that is more than $300 million, directly or indirectly through NGOs. Approximately 300 NGOs work with UNHCR in a diversity of ways: currently this includes five members of ISCA working in eleven countries.[11] The operational partners are responsible for the delivery of food and provision of shelter, water, sanitation, health care, education and skills training programmes. There is also growing recognition of NGOs as advocates of refugee protection, as they become more involved in dialogue with governments, providing information and monitoring the treatment of refugees.

In 1982 a leading UNHCR official, Gilbert Jaeger, wrote: 'It would not be enough to say that the role of non-governmental organisations in the matter of refugees is important: it is vital. ... For some sixty years, international action on behalf of refugees and displaced persons has been characterised by close collaboration between the non-governmental organisations and the intergovernmental organisations – since 1951, the UNHCR.'[12] In 1992 UNHCR officially went much further than acknowledging the value of consultation and collaboration with NGOs. Following a review by ICVA of UNHCR-NGO relations, UNHCR defined the relationship as being one of equality, a 'partnership', with 'full recognition by UNHCR and NGOs of their respective mandated roles' and 'reciprocal respect and understanding' for their 'complementary and supportive roles'. It was also agreed between ICVA and UNHCR that 'partnership does not necessarily mean full identity of views. Any disagreement should lead to constructive dialogue for the benefit of the refugees.'[13] The campaign to improve refugee nutrition did show that, although it may be a long and arduous task, the dialogue can lead to UNHCR responding positively to pressure from NGOs.

Refugee nutrition – the problem

Large refugee movements are typically associated with a health crisis. The common pattern of the movement of a large population and its concentration into a small area with inadequate water supply, sanitation and shelter always leads to some increase in rates of communicable diseases. In developing countries, where immunisation rates are often low and endemic disease rates comparatively high, the result has often been catastrophic. It is quite commonplace to see a rise in the mortality of those under five years of age, at least in the short term, to thirty per 10,000 per day. There have been cases, for example in Wad Kowli in Eastern Sudan in 1985, where losses in the first few months of a camp's existence have approached 10 per cent of the entire population. The techniques for managing such problems are well understood, but much preventable mortality has occurred because of the failure of the system to implement basic techniques quickly. These failings have often been the subject of debate and recrimination between agencies. However, in such cases the truth and therefore responsibility is elusive. In remote areas some disease and increased mortality must always be expected as there are often unavoidable operational difficulties and delays in the procurement of supplies and personnel. For this reason, although SCF has become used to a routine level of public health failure in such situations and has adapted its own approach to anticipate this, it has not generated a wider debate on the problem. Its approach has been to support training, the preparation of guidelines and field support etc. in the belief that improved local information and skills may improve performance. In several situations it has seconded technical staff to support UNHCR country offices where, because of financial constraints, that organisation could not provide these directly.

The health of refugees also depends upon the adequacy of the quantity and quality of food supplies available. Refugees may arrive at a camp malnourished, bringing neither food nor other resources with them. In the short term, most refugees are dependent upon the rations given to them. In the longer term, the situation varies. In some remote areas, the dependence on rations may remain complete, but refugees can often subsist on their own food production or, by finding work, purchase some proportion of their own food. In most, but not all, cases, refugees can exchange donated food stuffs for other foods through the market to diversify their diet.

The main foodstuffs available to African refugees are given by Western governments. Inevitably, most of these foods are obtained from the intervention stocks held in Europe and North America and tend therefore to be restricted to those commodities for which there is an effective agricultural subsidy, i.e. cereals (wheat, sorghum, maize and, less often, rice), legumes (soya and some other beans) and skimmed, i.e. defatted, milk powder. Other necessary commodities such as oil, pulses and salt are supplied in variable and often inadequate amounts, especially where these have to be purchased locally. The ration received by most African refugees, if used as a complete diet, is barely sufficient to provide enough food energy and will usually be deficient in a range of nutrients, including, most importantly, vitamins from the B group and vitamin C.

Through the 1980s refugees increasingly found themselves in a situation where they were completely dependent upon the rations given them. The food they received was often inadequate in quantity so that people, particularly children, starved. It was also frequently inadequate in quality causing vitamin deficiencies, specifically scurvy, pellagra and other deficiency diseases. Somali refugees can sometimes trade seasonally, for example for milk, and in more propitious areas may occasionally grow some food for themselves. Where this is not possible and they are dependent upon the ration, scurvy is the result. The first outbreak recorded among refugees who had crossed from Ethiopia following the 1978 Somali war was in 1981. This was related to the closure of markets and was followed by regular seasonal outbreaks. The worst of these occurred in 1984 and resulted in significant mortality, not least among women in late pregnancy and during childbirth when vitamin C requirements are high. Similar outbreaks, related to the inadequate quality of rations, were observed in refugees in Sudan, Malawi and Ethiopia.

In the summer of 1988, approximately 400,000 refugees from northern Somalia entered remote areas of eastern Ethiopia. The refugees were settled in an outlying area on the Ethiopia/Somali border and in the Ogaden in the camps of Hartisheik, Harshin and Aware. Refugees in the Hartisheik camp, who came largely from Hargeisa and Bura'o, arrived in good condition. The deficiency in the quantity of food supplies was such that the nutritional status of children, routinely estimated by SCF in collaboration with the Ethiopian government and UNHCR, rose from under 10 per cent malnourished on arrival to over 30 per cent in March 1989, conditions normally associated with famine. In one screening in early 1989, 2.1 per cent were found to have symptoms of scurvy, such as bleeding gums and painful swollen joints. For the first twelve months of the camp's existence, death rates were some 46 per 1000 per annum, about double the normal rate for non-refugee populations in Ethiopia and Somalia. Between February and May 1989, when malnutrition and mortality were at their highest, the average daily ration distributed to refugees was only 1,463 kilocalories.[14]

Case by case attempts were made to solve these problems technically through the distribution of specific nutrients, but this was often logistically impossible or socially and culturally unacceptable. Approaches were made directly to UNHCR, the World Food Programme (WFP) and the donors. In one instance, SCF made a substantial direct provision from its own resources. Approaches to the bilateral and multilateral donor agencies to secure better rations for refugees resulted in some improvements in specific cases. They also revealed a surprising confusion in the international system in the strategies of the different government, UN and non-government agencies concerned with refugee welfare. In several cases movement on local problems was only obtained after all normal channels of discussion had been exhausted and the media had become involved. It also became apparent that there were no agreed international standards for refugee rations.

In the attempts to secure adequate rations for refugees in specific cases, it became clear that the problem was not simple and that there were deep ambiguities relating to the responsibilities within the system. While SCF could intervene and improve the situation for some refugees in one place, this did nothing to prevent a recurrence of the problem. SCF staff therefore tried to look beyond each individual occurrence to the deeper causes. Continuity of staff was important to this analysis and SCF was fortunate in having qualified staff who could make linkages between the different experiences and think strategically about how and where the organisation could try to exert pressure. As the methods SCF used to try to raise awareness of the issue are described, it will be seen that developing and effectively exploiting both formal and informal networks helped to form a framework on which to build other activities. It is important to realise that the momentum came not from a detailed plan of action, but from pursuing the organisation's mandate and seeking to tackle a major and recurring humanitarian problem.

While the focus of this chapter is on SCF's concern with the quantity, quality and timing of delivery of refugee rations, this does not mean that SCF is not concerned with other aspects of refugee nutrition and welfare or is unaware of the complex financial and social problems raised by the long-term donor support of refugees in developing countries. Concentrating on a comparatively narrow and clear problem, however, illustrates how a non-governmental organisation pursued a specific objective to which it attached importance. It also reflects a view held by SCF that by focusing on a single aspect of a problem, the case is more easily argued and can be used to illustrate a much more complex and widely relevant problem.

Understanding the problem

SCF has enormous experience of working with refugees. It has contributed to policy and practice at country level, through its own work and through secondments and support provided to UNHCR and others. It has worked on the evaluation of refugee programmes, on the development of operational techniques and guidelines and contributed to the published literature. However, as SCF's experience of relief work in Africa and Asia grew in the 1970s and 1980s, its staff were entirely operational. It had no policy analysts, campaigners or lobbyists conversant with international law or the intricacies of the United Nations system. Its relationships with UNHCR and other UN agencies were at field level, sometimes at national capital city level and less frequently at regional level. Rarely did SCF-UK engage with UN agencies at an international level. Unlike many campaigning organisations or human rights agencies, it had no permanent representatives in New York or Geneva.[15] While SCF had staff qualified in many technical and practical aspects of health, nutrition, the provision of water and sanitation and relief management, it has to be acknowledged that these staff were not experts on the mandates of each UN agency.

As experience of refugee health problems grew, it became clear that case-by-case analysis and solutions were inadequate. Increasingly SCF looked for deeper causes and sought more general solutions. In order to try to make some impact on the system, SCF first had to understand it. This understanding began with attempts to intervene. A simplified, but not untypical, cycle of intervention would be as follows. There would be an approach to a UNHCR country office in anticipation of, or during the emergence of, a nutritional problem. The response would vary. It might be indifference. Frequently, as the people concerned were non-technical and had no field experience, the attitude was sympathetic, but the view was expressed that the problem was essentially medical and a medical response was required. Further pressure might lead to denial of the problem entirely. Approaches to UNHCR, often via technical staff, would be sympathetically received and acted on; but frequently the response would be that they, in turn, had had a similar response from their own line management. Approaches to the donors produced different results. The most typical response was an expression of concern but with the rider that the donor only responded (or did not) to requests from the United Nations, that the donor was not responsible or that no request had been received. The cycle would then be repeated: the parcel being passed from bureaucracy to bureaucracy. The cycle could, we learned, be broken reliably only by adverse publicity.

It was increasingly clear that the crisis was fundamentally one of responsibility. Host governments were responsible for the refugees according to international law, but in an increasing number of cases the countries receiving large influxes were also suffering from severe food shortages themselves and did not have the resources to discharge the responsibility. The UN agencies had poorly defined responsibilities for the material welfare of refugees and no resources other than those given by donors. Donors had the resources but no legal obligations.

Gaining knowledge of the system was a gradual process involving a growing understanding of bureaucracies. It was only repeated experience that allowed the organisation to predict what would occur as the original assumptions of how a hierarchy would and should work were often proved to be false.

UNHCR's mandate

Before SCF began to try to discover why the problem of inadequate rations arose so frequently, it assumed it knew what the mandate of the United Nations High Commissioner for Refugees was. It discovered, however, that UNHCR's mandate imposes no requirement upon it to ensure the physical welfare or even the survival of refugees.

The Office of the UNHCR was established in 1951 with two main functions: providing protection for refugees and seeking durable solutions to their problems. The protection mandate is primarily legal and political, designed to protect individuals or groups whose fundamental rights are threatened. This responsibility is essential. It encompasses the promotion, interpretation and development of the fundamental principles of refugee protection and involves maintaining and strengthening an international framework governing the status and rights of refugees. The UNHCR was established primarily to ensure proper treatment for those fleeing persecution or displaced by the events of the Second World War. When the responsibility for providing assistance to refugees was laid at the door of the government of the country on whose territory they have found asylum, it was assumed that for the most part these would be European governments with the resources to accommodate relatively small numbers of refugees. However, refugees increasingly seek refuge in countries where the host government's services to its own civilians, for example health and welfare services, fall below acceptable minimum standards. Many such countries in Africa have recurring or chronic food crises and economies on the verge of collapse. Yet these countries are expected to provide for massive and unpredictable influxes of people.

The responsibility – or lack of it – for the provision of food supplies to refugees was thus identified as being at the heart of the problem. Compounding this problem, there was a lack of technical skills and relevant information within the system.

UNHCR's internal structure

The historical mandate of UNHCR had an impact upon its institutional structure and the nature of its personnel. In regarding itself as a protection agency, which had sometimes to take on a material role, UNHCR was geared to consider political and legal issues relating to the rights of refugees. The staffing of the organisation reflected these historical priorities. At international headquarters level it was not until the mid-1980s that a health adviser was employed (on secondment from the World Health Organisation (WHO)) and there were no permanent advisory staff with responsibilities for health and nutrition until recently. Through the 1980s it appeared that health staff were not considered part of the mainstream institutional structure; they could be consulted or disregarded by management as it pleased.

This structure, and the fact that UNHCR did not accept ultimate responsibility for material provision, meant that it was not always clear who should take action when outbreaks of disease due to inadequate dietary provision were reported. The central bureaucracy and, in some cases, regional and country representatives did not see themselves as having a technical support role. At a seminar held by SCF in 1987 which included eleven UNHCR country representatives, the proposition was debated that 'It is not possible to protect a dead refugee'. The idea that the concept of protection should include physical protection from preventable disease was regarded as no more than interesting; all the UNHCR representatives regarded material provision as being peripheral to their country programmes or responsibilities.

Blockages to the free flow of information within the system were regularly experienced at three levels: between the UNHCR field representatives and UNHCR in Geneva, UNHCR representatives apparently having no obligation to forward information to the centre; in Geneva between technical and administrative staff; and between UNHCR Geneva and the donors. An attempt to track information about scurvy among Somali refugees to the Overseas Development Administration in London and Food-for-Peace in Washington DC revealed that, even far into the period when seasonal scurvy outbreaks were a regular occurrence, neither donor had been officially informed.

The relationship of UNHCR and WFP

Food for refugees is generally supplied to the host country by the United Nations, the food being provided by the larger donors such as the United States and the European Union (EU). Donors usually provide a package of food assistance, together with cash for transport, storage and distribution. Alternatively, donors provide cash for local purchase and transport, or funding for more complicated exchange arrangements or regional purchase. During the 1980s the channels and mechanisms for supplying both emergency food and longer-term assistance for refugees were arcane and uncertain, reflecting the complexities of international food aid policy. There were also complex bureaucratic relationships among the various UN specialised agencies and between these agencies and the recipient governments.

The World Food Programme, for example, was responsible only for transporting food to the port of the country concerned, regarding the government as taking responsibility within its own borders. WFP was responsible for inland transportation only in negotiated cases. By the late 1980s the one thing that was clear was that WFP regarded its responsibility as limited to the supply of food energy and protein, i.e. the chief commodities which could be reliably obtained from donors. They regarded the supply of foods containing other nutrients as the responsibility of the UNHCR. For those attempting to manage refugee rations on the ground, this was like ordering a meal from two different restaurants, neither in reliable communication with the other, and hoping it would all arrive on the plate at the same time.

Technical ambiguities

For a refugee to receive an adequate ration, it is necessary for that ration to be defined. Until 1988 the working figure most widely used, 1,800 kilocalories (the International Committee of the Red Cross [ICRC] had its own ration levels), was drawn from a WHO manual.[16] The figure given in the UNHCR's *Handbook for Emergencies* was as low as 1,500 kcal. 'for initial survival', though they recommended 2,000 kcal. 'for longer term maintenance'.[17] The absence of an agreed ration level led to repeated debate about the adequacy of any particular ration. Nutritional science is less than an exact discipline. The chief problem is that an adequate ration varies according to a number of factors including the body size of the people concerned, the demographic characteristics of the population, clothing and climate. Without an agreed basis for calculation this could, and did, lead to attempts to 'prove' that the case was in some way an exception and that rations which were manifestly inadequate according to the prevailing norms were in fact not so. For example, the low ration levels given to Somali refugees were justified on the basis that, compared to Western populations, adult Somalis have low body weight. Confronted with poor nutritional status figures for an Ethiopian camp, the UNHCR representative first attempted to discredit these technically, and then repeated the survey in an (unsuccessful) attempt to obtain better results. WFP holds that added fats and oils are not necessary to survival and therefore they are not necessary to a normal ration. Although this may be correct in scientific terms, it is not the basis for a satisfactory diet.

Access to additional foods, income generation, trading and marketing opportunities clearly will have varying impact on the amount of food refugees or displaced populations will require. Careful initial assessment and continuing monitoring of each different situation is necessary to determine what food aid is required. Nevertheless, such assessments can only be based upon, and informed by, agreement on the energy requirements of refugees in a situation where they are totally dependent on food rations.

Resources

To some extent the UNHCR has had to evolve to take account of the changes in the nature of the problems which it has the mandate to resolve. A significant weakness however is its continued dependence on voluntary contributions. Only UNHCR's administrative costs are covered by the UN regular budget; the main costs, for assistance to refugees, are funded by voluntary contributions, mainly from governments. Each year a general programme budget is approved which includes an emergency fund but the UNHCR may be requested to undertake special programmes, including major and unforeseen emergency operations for which additional funds must be found. Between 1971 and 1978 annual expenditure rose from $9 million to $135 million and had reached nearly $500 million by 1980. By 1992 new crises in the former Yugoslavia, the Horn of Africa, Bangladesh and southern Africa pushed expenditure over $1 billion. Despite increased financial support, resources are still insufficient.[18]

A good case could, however, be made that, at least through the 1980s, enough food was supplied by donors to meet the needs of all dependent refugee populations. The shortage of supply experienced in parts of Africa was balanced by the comparative oversupply to more politically prominent refugees elsewhere, such as the Afghan refugees in Pakistan. It is probably a fair statement that a shortage of resources, as such, was insufficient to explain the deprivation suffered by some groups.

Tackling the problem

Having gained some understanding of the system, and a realisation of why the system could not ensure the provision of adequate rations, SCF attempted to try to influence that system. This effort was sustained over many years. SCF learnt that time was needed to have an effect and that no single way of working was effective. Several methods needed to be used simultaneously, involving continuous pressure exerted from working within the system, with a willingness to embarrass the system from without. However, it was first necessary to engage with the system. It was an advantage that SCF worked in several countries and regions and could continuously compare, contrast and update its experience. As a large agency with a permanent technical staff based in its London headquarters, it was able to accumulate information and experience over time.

Action over specific cases

As indicated above, SCF had identified an information gap between the problems experienced by refugees and those who might have the power to resolve them. SCF is extraordinarily well placed to obtain information on a broad front. A high premium is placed on this within the organisation as it is perceived to be the basis of any action that the organisation takes. The nature and style of its operations allows regular contacts with governments in recipient countries, the governments of bilateral donor countries, the United Nations and others. As essential as having regular sources of high quality technical information is the capacity to bring this together into a commonly held position. In arguing the case, it was found that the possession of information and a coherent synthesis and view on this has allowed the organisation confidently to pursue its views both within the system and, where necessary, through the media.

A particular consideration for SCF is that the information it obtains is, in a sense, privileged; it could not be obtained without the tacit understanding, generally of the government of the country concerned, that it would not be used without consent. In a sense there is a mismatch between an operational involvement and public advocacy. In practice the Fund was helped by its close links with the countries concerned and in some instances, its ability to act, if not with the active support of governments, then at least with the knowledge that they had no objection. Indeed it was found that it was precisely where government had no power to act – weak governments do not pick fights with the donors – that SCF enjoyed most support.

Technical collaboration with others

Over time it became clear that, within the international system, information may be used to greater effect by some parts than others. There is an informal network of technical personnel within the United Nations and in other organisations, including the US Centre for Disease Control (which provides technical support to the US government), some academics and other NGOs. This network allows access for unofficial bodies to information from official channels. For example, the Centre has channels for information directly to the US State Department, whereas SCF does not.

Publication in academic literature

Use, by SCF and others, of technical and academic journals provided an intermediate position between public and private information. The letters column of *The Lancet* was used to report the problems of scurvy and anaemia in refugees and the inadequate institutional arrangements for action. More generally, SCF contributed to the documentation of the problems and contributed to literature reviews, for example, the many publications of the US Centre for Disease Control. The development of a substantial published technical literature put the nutritional problem of refugees, which had been ignored or even denied for a long time, beyond question.

Helping to establish technical norms

One clear deficiency in the system was the lack of agreed technical norms. A focal point in the UN system for harmonising many

administrative procedures is the Administrative Committee on
Coordination (ACC), which brings together the executive heads of
all the specialised agencies and the main programmes of the UN.
Under the ACC there is a Sub-Committee on Nutrition which
offered an appropriate forum for discussion of technical norms.
In September 1988 SCF, in collaboration with the London School
of Hygiene and Tropical Medicine, provided a background paper
on the nutritional aspects of emergency food relief[19] to an international conference, *Nutrition in Times of Disaster*, held under the
auspices of the ACC Sub-Committee on Nutrition and the International Nutrition Planners Forum, a group of senior nutrition planners and managers from developing countries, and organised by
WHO and UNHCR at WHO's headquarters in Geneva. The paper
set out recommendations for basic minimum standards of relief
rations. Calculations were based on a sedentary population, with
a demographic composition representative of a developing country,
under no environmental stress and with no other special need. The
resulting figure, 1,900 kilocalories, was meant as an average
minimum daily requirement to be used for planning purposes and
to be followed by an assessment and adjustment as soon as possible. The working groups at the conference accepted this calculation
and issued a statement recommending that 'a minimal standard for
food provision for emergency conditions must be maintained. This
requires the provision of at the very least 1,900 k-cals/person in
the daily diet. Furthermore, such a standard diet should contain
all essential nutrients at levels that have been deemed necessary to
maintain health and sustain life.'[20]

Attempts were also made to find practical, technical solutions to
problems locally. For example, following a serious outbreak of
pellagra among Mozambican refugees in Malawi, SCF installed
the capacity for the nutrient fortification of maize meal. This was
a standard technology, but one which was new to food aid for
refugees.

Publicising the problem

SCF helped to build a wider constituency for the problem among
NGOs and institutions involved with the issue. It was involved in
two international symposia organised with different concerned
groups. The first, in December 1988, was entitled 'Health Care for
Displaced Persons and Refugees' and was held at Georgetown
University. It was co-sponsored by the Centre for Disease Control,
the League of Red Cross and Red Crescent Societies, the Refugee
Policy Group, UNDP, UNHCR and WHO among others. This led to
The Georgetown Declaration on Health Care for Displaced Persons

and Refugees, covering a number of key technical areas relating to
emergency health care efforts. The second symposium, 'Responding
to the Nutrition Crisis among Refugees: the Need for New Approaches' was held in Oxford in early 1991. It was supported by a con-
sortium of NGOs including SCF, Oxfam, Médecins Sans Frontières
(Belgium, France, Netherlands), International Rescue Committee
(USA), the Refugee Studies Programme, UNHCR and WFP. This
also resulted in several strong recommendations.[21]

Engagement with the system at all levels

SCF staff became increasingly familiar with the institutions at all
levels. This involved gaining an understanding of where responsibilities lay. Throughout the mid-1980s SCF experienced numerous
practical difficulties in dealing with an international bureaucracy
which had not been designed to deal with the problems that it was
now facing. This gave SCF considerable insight into how that
bureaucracy worked and how to have an impact.

Some solutions to the problem

It is not true to say that all aspects of the problem have been
resolved, or that the improvements can be attributed to any one
NGO. The progress that has been made is largely due to the
development of a wider constituency for the problem. There has,
however, been a perceptible change in approach, the development
of a consensus that a generic problem exists. We have seen that
children are most likely to be the casualties when malnutrition
occurs among refugees. This means the attempts to improve nutritional standards should be set in the context of the attention given
by UNHCR to children as a distinct group.

Increasing UNHCR's awareness of the needs of children

Until the late 1980s there was little recognition, even among the
NGOs, that policy should be directed to meeting the special needs
of children for assistance with nutrition and health.[22] The problem of unaccompanied refugee children became a major concern
of UNHCR in the early 1980s, but initially the main focus was on
their psychological trauma, their legal position and family reuni-
fication, rather than their physical welfare.[23] Arising from the
original concerns with unaccompanied children and then broaden-
ing into other issues, the NGOs expressed dissatisfaction with the
lack of attention given by UNHCR in Geneva to the specific needs
of all refugee children.

In the mid-1980s the International Council of Voluntary Agencies appealed every year at the UNHCR Executive Committee for a staff member to be appointed to act as a focal point for questions concerning children. Eventually John Williamson of UNHCR felt he could not continue going back to ICVA annual meetings to argue that no response was necessary.[24] The Executive Committee also responded in 1986 and called on the High Commissioner to report on existing and proposed programmes for the benefit of children.[25] As a result a long process of policy development began in 1987. A Working Group on Refugee Children, composed of middle-level technical UN staff, was established with John Williamson in the chair. It surveyed UNHCR field offices, to identify what they felt were the problems. The first Report on Refugee Children was produced[26] and the Executive Committee adopted a set of *Conclusions on Refugee Children*, which highlighted their particular vulnerability.[27]

The *Conclusions* acknowledged that children form more than half the world's refugee population (then estimated to be more than ten million), emphasised the importance of the special psychological needs of children, underlined the fundamental importance of primary education and drew attention to the particular problem of unaccompanied children, disabled children, and those who spend extended periods of time in a refuge camp environment. The nutritional and health risks of children were recognised, but governments, rather than UNHCR itself, were held responsible for providing a balanced and safe diet, immunisation and primary health care. It was recommended that the High Commissioner should produce a set of guidelines to promote the security, well-being and development of refugee children. The first draft of the guidelines was produced by John Williamson and the Working Group drawing together contributions from different sectors of the UNHCR staff. It was widely circulated among UN bodies and NGOs and then debated at a residential seminar with NGOs, including participants from SCF and other ISCA members. In August 1988 UNHCR issued the *Guidelines on Refugee Children*, which represented an attempt to call attention to children's problems, with the intention that it should provide practical guidance for UNHCR activity in the field to meet the full range of children's fundamental needs for protection and assistance.

The Guidelines still gave much attention to the traditional legal and protection questions, but also covered health, nutrition, treatment of disabilities, education and social needs. The section on nutrition recognised the need for high quality rations, that children might not be given all the foods available and that the basic rations might not be appropriate for weaning foods. However, the Guidelines did not specify procedures to ensure the implementation of the sound goals for general food provision. This was in sharp contrast to the section on protection of breast-feeding for infants, which unambiguously asserted that 'milk powder should never be used as a breast-milk substitute', baby bottles should be actively discouraged and in cases of verified lactation problems only a cup and spoon should be used. No doubt the superior specification of policy on breast-feeding was due to the sustained campaign on this question that had been waged by many NGOs since 1973.

Concerned that the first edition of the Guidelines was not having sufficient impact, SCF, in collaboration with ISCA, initiated a review of their implementation in Malawi, to where almost one million Mozambican refugees had fled. The consultancy revealed a wide gap between the theory of the Guidelines and the reality of programmes on the ground. The impetus towards improvement that the development of the Guidelines sought to promote had not materialised within UNHCR, nor among NGOs and host governments. The report, entitled *Refugee Children in Malawi*, concluded that issues related to refugee children lacked a standard bearer in Geneva, and a lack of coherent training and implementation strategies was contributing to the lack of impact of the Guidelines.[28] Partly as a result of this work, Anna Skatvedt was appointed in 1992 as Senior Coordinator for Refugee Children, so that for the first time UNHCR had a focal point for policy on children. One of her first tasks was to respond to the criticisms, from ISCA and others, and to initiate a major review of the Guidelines. The consultations were even more extensive than in 1988 and 2,500 copies of the first draft report were circulated to UNHCR staff, other UN bodies, governments and NGOs. The revised version came out in 1994 as a much more detailed document, in book format, titled *Refugee Children. Guidelines on Protection and Care*. It sought to commit all governments to effective action by putting the needs of refugee children firmly in the context of the Convention on the Rights of the Child which, by March 1994, had been ratified by 155 states (see Chapter 8). In a substantial change from the 1988 edition, the UNHCR accepted responsibility for meeting nutrition standards, monitoring food storage and distribution, and monitoring the occurrence of illnesses that result from malnutrition.[29]

Obtaining endorsement of standards

The conclusions of the WHO/UNHCR Geneva conference, as set out in a *Statement on Nutrition in Times of Disaster* were adopted by the ACC Sub-Committee on Nutrition.[30] The Statement urged 'donor nations to increase their emergency resource allocations and to programme these according to estimates of emergency needs rather than reacting to each situation in an *ad hoc* manner.' This was subsequently endorsed by the full Administrative Committee on Coordination. The figure of 1,900 kcal was also incorporated in a WHO/FAO Recommended Daily Allowance, while UNHCR and WFP used the same standard in a joint *Guidelines for Calculating Food Rations for Refugees*, recommending that the figure should be increased in certain circumstances.[31] These documents were then reaffirmed in the 1994 *Guidelines on Refugee Children*.[32] The widespread recognition of the need of the whole system to shift away from *ad hoc* responses to defined standards of response was in part due to persistence, the constant repetition of the issues until more notice was taken.

Improved information

Another way in which the ACC Sub-Committee on Nutrition has taken up the problem of refugee nutrition is by the regular publication of information on the nutritional status of refugees worldwide. This information is put together from the United Nations and NGOs by an informal working group at which the UN, donors and NGOs are represented. Although it is too early to predict the effect of this reporting system, the initial impression is that it has reduced or even perhaps eliminated the tendency of individual agencies to suppress or deny reports from the field. With support from major donors including the Norwegian Agency for Development Cooperation (NORAD) and USAID, the Sub-Committee on Nutrition now provides information in the form of a regular report based on the Refugee Nutrition Information System. Significantly the report is published by the Secretariat of the ACC Sub-Committee on Nutrition, which is answerable to the ACC. Although it receives funding from UNHCR and WFP, it is not tied to any of the individual specialised agencies.

The right to food: reform or reinterpretation of the mandate of UNHCR

Pressure has been brought on UNHCR to clarify its position on the issue of its responsibilities for the material welfare of refugees. UNHCR has now accepted that it is responsible – not because of the Office's mandate but because, as a UN agency, its mandate is subordinate to the UN Charter and to the Universal Declaration of Human Rights of 1948. Despite taking on the responsibility as a matter of principle, fulfilling it remains problematic. In a paper presented in 1991 to the symposium 'Responding to the Nutrition Crisis Among Refugees', UNHCR and the World Food Programme stated that:

> While UNHCR's protection responsibility is exercised independ-
> ently of a government request, UNHCR provides assistance only
> in response to a government request. When such a request is
> made, UNHCR is the organisation charged by the international
> community with mobilising and coordinating the international
> response to the needs of refugees. How this responsibility is
> exercised depends largely on the wishes of the host government.
> As a rule, UNHCR assistance is delivered through an implemen-
> ting partner, which may be a governmental, non-governmental
> (NGO) or international organisation. Other factors being equal
> UNHCR seeks to work through indigenous organisations.[33]

Such a description suggests how problems arc likely to arise when lines of responsibility are unclear as they often were in the large complex emergencies of the 1980s.

With the publication of the revised *Guidelines on Refugee Children* in 1994, it appears that UNHCR is taking a more authoritative approach. Instead of deferring to governments, it is asserted that 'these Guidelines will help countries of origin and countries of asylum to understand what UNHCR is trying to do for refugee children'.[34] It also accepted a more direct and more central role: 'UNHCR, together with operational partners, is responsible for the adequate distribution and delivery, storage and distribution of food'.[35] Workshops and training programmes on nutrition have been organised and some specialist nutritionists have been appointed to UNHCR staff.[36] It remains to be seen whether in future emergencies, when adequate time and resources are available, UNHCR can actually prevent malnutrition occurring.

Relations between UNHCR and WFP

In December 1989 the Committee on Food Aid Policy (CFA), the governing body of the International Emergency Food Reserve (IEFR), approved a policy change affecting operations which marked the abandonment of WFP's short-term approach to the relief requirements of refugees and displaced persons. These new procedures introduced specific projects for the protracted feeding of refugees and displaced persons. In 1991 WFP and UNHCR defined new terms and areas of collaboration. Finally, in January 1994, they published a *Memorandum of Understanding on the*

Joint Working Arrangements for Refugee, Returnee and Internally Displaced Persons Feeding Operations.

This revised Memorandum of Understanding is intended to improve the emergency response capacity of both organisations by further clarifying the division of programming and operational responsibilities in all jointly assessed refugee, returnee and, more selectively, internally displaced population (IDP) situations, thereby avoiding unnecessary duplication and maximising the respective strengths and comparative advantages of UNHCR and WFP. Additional qualitative measures have been introduced in all phases of the feeding operations in order to make the Memorandum of Understanding more operational, based on clear division of responsibilities and clearly outlining the accountability of both agencies.[37]

Today WFP is recognised as the coordinating body for mobilising basic food commodities, such as cereals, oils, sugar and proteins, in most large refugee feeding programmes. UNHCR is responsible for 'complementary commodities', such as vegetables, fresh meat, spices, dried milk and high protein biscuits. In order to pre-empt micronutrient deficiencies, WFP will ensure that vitamins and essential minerals are added to basic foods, so that 'micronutrient fortified blended foods' are available both for refugees already suffering from malnutrition and for those who are wholly dependent on food aid. Under the 1991 agreement, which is reaffirmed in the Memorandum, WFP progressively assumed responsibility for internal transport of basic foods and blended foods from the ports in developing countries to 'extended delivery points'. From there UNHCR takes responsibility for delivery within the refugee camps. From January 1995 UNHCR took over all aspects of smaller operations covering less than 5,000 refugees. WFP and UNHCR will decide policy jointly in Food Assessment Missions, with WFP providing the team leader and a logistician and UNHCR providing a nutritionist and a specialist in promoting refugee self-reliance. The two organisations will also jointly monitor food distribution, although UNHCR will assess the nutritional status of refugees. In principle the problems of responsibility for food quality, transport and distribution have now been resolved.

Conclusions

Over ten years SCF sustained an attempt to bring about fundamental change by engaging directly with, and at times embarrassing, the system. It is extremely difficult to assess which of the methods it chose to employ was most significant. The most likely interpretation is that the measures were cumulative and contributed to a momentum that eventually effected some change. Although SCF determined to try to bring about change, it must be remembered that there were many others – aid officials, other non-governmental organisations, academics and refugees themselves – who were deeply concerned about the issue and were involved in the attempts to make the system more responsive and accountable.

Some small improvements – which must of course be partially due to the influence of these other actors and events – can be measured: UNHCR's mandate and responsibilities were clarified; the division of responsibilities between WFP and UNHCR was clarified; target standards were raised; and information systems were improved, ensuring that responsibilities were recognised. The structure of UNHCR changed considerably; there was an improvement in technical support and more note was taken of field concerns, enabling staff on the technical side to be involved in decision-making.

Such progress may seem insignificant in the context of the continuing global refugee crisis and the dilemmas UNHCR and its partners face in managing that crisis. It is estimated that there are now twenty million refugees with at least another twenty million displaced persons. UNHCR experiences considerable difficulties in fulfilling its mandate because of the lack of requisite financial resources and personnel. Theoretically, refugees flee to save their lives, whereas migrants move to improve their economic prospects. The distinction has, however, become increasingly difficult to draw as people flee from countries where poverty and violence are direct consequences of the political system. Governments all over the world are becoming less tolerant towards refugees, and the institution of asylum and the concept of protection are themselves threatened. The international community is not meeting its legal and ethical obligations to protect and assist refugees. In such a climate, the role of NGOs becomes even more important. They are ideally placed to monitor the performance of the international community in meeting its obligations and to show constructively how improvements can be made.

NOTES

1. Members of the International Save the Children Alliance are (1994) Australia, Austria, Canada, Denmark, Dominican Republic, Egypt, Faroe Islands, France, Greece, Guatemala, Iceland, Japan, Jordan, Republic of Korea,

268 *Angela Penrose and John Seaman*

Lesotho, Malawi, Mauritius, Mexico, Netherlands, New Zealand, Norway, Sweden, Tunisia, United Kingdom, USA.

2. SCF Archives, Eglantyne Jebb Papers, EJ/2/14. The letter was from H.D. Watson to the Chinese Relief Fund, 28 October 1920.
3. Notes for the English Delegates to the Council Meeting of The Save the Children Fund (Central Union), Geneva, February 1920 (Eglantyne Jebb Papers).
4. R. Breen, 'Saving Enemy Children: Save the Children's Russian Relief Operation, 1921–1923', pp. 221–37 in a special issue to mark the seventy-fifth anniversary of Save the Children (UK) of *Disasters: The Journal of Disaster Studies and Management*, vol. 18, no. 3, September 1994.
5. Memorandum on Relief Policy, SCF Archives, Eglantyne Jebb Papers, CB 3/8.
6. *Ibid.*
7. Letter of 3 April from Fridtjof Nansen to President Wilson, Clemenceau, Lloyd George and Orlando, and reply from the President and the three Prime Ministers, printed in *The Times* of 19 April 1919. Superficially the reply appeared to offer support to Nansen, but it contained such strict conditions, including a complete cease-fire in the civil war, that it amounted to a rejection of Nansen's 'commission of a wholly non-political order'.
8. This is based upon the work of Rodney Breen, SCF archivist, and the SCF archives.
9. For more details about UNHCR, its origins and its work, see UNHCR, *The State of the World's Refugees 1993* (New York and London: Penguin Books, 1993). For more general discussion of refugee politics, see L. Gordenker, *Refugees in International Politics* (London: Croom Helm, 1987) and G. Loescher and L. Monahan (eds), *Refugees and International Relations* (Oxford: Oxford University Press, 1989).
10. See *UNHCR/NGO Partnership. Reference Document on Relationship between UNHCR and NGOs* (Geneva: UNHCR, February 1992), 'Part II Criteria for Selection of a Non-Governmental Organisation as an Operational Partner for UNHCR'. Three essential 'basic conditions' and eleven 'criteria' for consideration are listed.
11. See *UNHCR & NGOs. Directory of Non-Governmental Organisations* (Geneva: UNHCR, October 1992), for lists of the NGOs by country of origin, country of implementation and sector of operational activities.
12. Gilbert Jaeger, 'Participation of Non-Governmental Organisations in the Activities of the United Nations High Commissioner for Refugees' in P. Willetts (ed.), *Pressure Groups in the Global System* (London: Pinter, 1982), quotations from p. 171 and p. 178.
13. See *UNHCR/NGO Partnership . . ., op. cit.*, 'Part I. Partnership. Basic Elements'.
14. Michael Toole, *Case Study: Somali Refugees in Hartisheik A Camp, Eastern Ethiopia, Health and Nutrition Profile, July 1988–June 1989*, 'Responding to the Nutrition Crisis among Refugees: The Need for New Approaches', International Symposium, Oxford, March 1991. Much of the material from this symposium has been edited and published as D. Keen, *Refugees: Rationing the Right to Life* (London: Zed Books for the Oxford University Refugee Studies Programme, 1992).
15. In the 1980s the US and Swedish Save the Children were active at the UN in New York and Geneva, respectively. In 1989 ICSA took over the work in Geneva.
16. C. de Ville de Goyet, J. Seaman and Geijer, 'Management of Nutritional Emergencies in Large Populations' (Geneva: WHO, 1978).
17. *Handbook for Emergencies* (Geneva: UNHCR, December 1982), chapter 8: 'Food and Nutrition', p. 102.

18. For details of UNHCR annual expenditure in 1967–92, see UNHCR, *op. cit.* 1993, p. 177.
19. J.P.W. Rivers and J.A. Seaman, 'Nutritional Aspects of Emergency Food Relief, Nutrition in Times of Disaster', ACC-SCN Symposium Report Series paper no. 1, November 1989.
20. 'Statement on nutrition in times of disaster', in Report on the fifteenth session of the Sub-Committee on Nutrition and its Advisory Group on Nutrition, UN doc. ACC/1989/PG/2.
21. See D. Keen, *op. cit.*, chapter 7.
22. *The Handbook for Emergencies, op. cit*, does recognise the technical problems of micro-nutrient deficiencies and specifies the need for supplementary feeding programmes for malnourished children, but it gives little attention to the social and organisational problems of achieving adequate nutrition and its procedures were not being implemented in the field.
23. A major research project on unaccompanied children, sponsored among others by UNHCR, Redd Barna (Norwegian Save the Children) and Save the Children Federation (USA) was carried out from June 1982 to March 1985. Surprisingly, this project gave no serious attention to the nutrition and health needs of children. See E.M. Ressler, N. Boothby and D.J. Steinbock, *Unaccompanied Children: Care and Protection in Wars, Natural Disasters and Refugee Movements* (Oxford University Press, 1988).
24. Personal communication of 24 September 1994 with John Williamson, who in mid-1980s was in the UNHCR Social Welfare Section.
25. Part of *General Conclusions on International Protection* no. 41(XXXVII) in para. 125 of Report of the 37th Session of the Executive Committee of the High Commissioner's Programme, UN doc. A/AC.96/688 of 15 October 1986.
26. *Report on Refugee Children*, UN doc. EC/SCP/46, 1987.
27. The *Conclusions on Refugee Children* no. 47(XXXVIII) are para. 205 of the Report of the Executive Committee of the Programme of the United Nations High Commissioner for Refugees on the Work of the 38th Session, UN doc. A/42/12/Add.1 of 3 November 1987.
28. David Tolfree, *Refugee Children in Malawi: Consultancy on the UNHCR Guidelines* (London: ISCA, 1992).
29. *Refugee Children. Guidelines on Protection and Care* (Geneva: UNHCR, 1994), pp. 58–9.
30. UN doc. ACC/1989/PG/2, *op. cit.*
31. *Provisional Guidelines for Calculating Food Rations for Refugees*, UNHCR Inter-Office Memorandum no.66/91 and Field Office Memorandum no.68/91 of 20 September 1991, due to be finalised at the end of 1994. This document directly attributes the standard of 1900 kcal per day to the adoption of the proposal from the September 1988 conference. See also 'Rations and food aid requirements', Chapter A6 of *Food Aid in Emergencies, Book A: Policies and Principles* (Rome: World Food Programme, September 1991).
32. UNHCR, *Refugee Children . . ., op. cit.* 1994, p. 58.
33. UNHCR/WFP, *The United Nations' Response to Refugee Food Requirements*, 'Responding to the Nutrition Crisis Among Refugees: The Need for New Approaches', International Symposium, Oxford, March 1991.
34. UNHCR, *Refugee Children . . .*, p. 12.
35. *Ibid.*, p. 59.
36. UN doc. A/AC.96/814 of 30 August 1993, p. 10.
37. UNHCR/WFP, *Memorandum of Understanding on the Joint Working Arrangements for Refugee, Returnee and, Internally Displaced Persons Feeding Operations*, (January 1994), p. 1. The first *Memorandum of Understanding* was agreed in 1985 and 'Revised Working Arrangements' came into effect from January 1992.

10

CONCLUSIONS

John Sankey

This book has broken new ground in combining a general overview of the origins of non-governmental organisations and their role in the United Nations system with a series of case studies of noteworthy achievements in selected areas. *Selected* must be stressed; for example, only a few aspects of the work of NGOs in respect of human rights and refugees have been covered, and whole sectors of the UN system, e.g. health matters and WHO, have hardly been touched on. The aim has been to focus on key areas where the NGO contribution can be regarded as significant and where the reasons for this can be analysed. Another volume, or series of volumes, would be needed to do justice to the entire contribution of NGOs throughout the UN system.

The extent of the NGO contribution over the past fifty years is the more remarkable because the sole mention of NGOs in the UN Charter is a single sentence in Article 71, referring to economic and social work. The authors of the Charter saw the United Nations as an association of sovereign states, and never envisaged that accredited representatives of governments would be willing to accord to NGOs the role and influence they have attained fifty years later. Nevertheless, it is important not to paint too rosy a picture of the present situation. Although this book gives numerous instances of NGOs being accepted as full and equal partners, there is a degree of tension still present in some parts of the UN system and the debate about the relative legitimacy of government delegates, secretariat officials and NGO representatives continues.

The relationship of government representatives with NGOs is both collaborative and competitive. NGOs are often innovators, while governments tend to be absorbed with day-to-day problems and inclined to preserve the *status quo*. NGOs are able to concentrate on universal and timeless values, while governments predominantly respond to events and keep an eye trained on the next election. On paper, the two sides appear not to meet on equal terms – the committees and working groups are composed of government representatives, and the NGOs seem to have a peripheral role. In practice, NGOs have over the years secured access to virtually all UN conferences and committees, and are able to attend and speak in most meetings. Although they do not have the right to vote, this is less important in an era when most important decisions are taken by consensus. Much of the actual work of the UN is done in informal ways, outside the committee meetings and off-the-record, where the NGOs can more readily make their influence felt.

Secretariat officials in the UN and its agencies, like representatives of governments, range from those who have no problem in working with NGOs (and often regard NGOs as their lifeline to the real world outside the committee room) to those who see no good reason why they should spend time listening to the special pleading of NGOs with no formal authority or mandate. Such people, while far fewer than in the early days of the UN, still exist.

Nor is the attitude of NGOs towards the UN system easy to define. Many have acquired a thorough understanding of the complex UN procedures (and even enjoy the warm glow of acceptance as virtual equals in the diplomatic round); while at the other extreme some organisations refuse to 'play the game' and regard governments, and most of the UN, as inherently evil and liable to corrupt those who associate too closely with them.

NGOs usually acknowledge that there are practical limitations to the collaboration and partnership they can expect from national governments. States must have a certain degree of formality and bureaucracy to work efficiently, and they need to take account of the interests of *all* their citizens, not just those of a particular NGO, or group of NGOs, advocating a particular point of view. Moreover, democratically elected governments are directly responsible to their electorates, whereas not all NGOs are as democratically elected, accountable to their membership or representative of public opinion as the governments they criticise.

Another difficult area is that of NGO independence from governments. Bearing in mind the old adage 'if you can't beat them, join them', some 'governmental' NGOs are funded or controlled by governments in order to infiltrate, inform on or otherwise disrupt the work of genuine NGOs, particularly in the field of human rights. The UN Secretary-General drew attention to the problem in a speech on 20 September 1994, when he said '. . . States are sometimes tempted to try to utilize or control non-governmental organizations in order to place them indirectly in the service of their own national policies.' He then urged NGOs to 'secure their independence with regard to all States. This is a basic condition for their credibility . . . NGOs must be beyond reproach in the political field.'

Although this book has devoted much attention to the work of NGOs at UN headquarters (both in New York and Geneva) or at major conferences, the achievements of NGOs in the field are arguably even more important. International agencies and governments rely more and more on NGOs to implement their aid programmes, and indigenous Third World NGOs will play an ever-increasing, and indeed predominant, role. One of the key changes in recent years has been the dramatic growth in the number and professionalism of national and regional NGOs in Asia, Africa and South America. These may not have the resources or experience of their European counterparts; but they are closer to grassroots problems and often have a sharper focus. NGOs from developing countries like Brazil and India have their own particular priorities and methods, and long-established NGOs can often learn from them.

Factors such as operational experience, technical expertise, negotiating skills and precise objectives make all the difference between an effective NGO and one which enjoys less success, however worthy the cause or dedicated its representatives. Collaboration *between* NGOs and concentration of effort pay dividends, whatever the issue.

The lessons of the past few decades have been on the whole encouraging. They show that thousands of individuals are ready to give their time, effort and in some cases their lives working for NGOs to secure a better environment, to promote human rights, to bring relief to refugees and countless other essential tasks. They show that ordinary people in the wealthier areas of the world are prepared to contribute significant sums of money voluntarily to thousands of NGOs. The more serious threat to NGOs is probably not from governmental indifference – because governments need NGO field operations more than ever – but from 'compassion fatigue'. NGOs will need to work even harder to explain what has already been achieved and how much more needs to be done to meet future challenges.

The UN system itself has changed dramatically over the last forty years, particularly in the area of human rights. In UN debates during the 1960s, any attempt to refer, even obliquely, to the political or human rights situation in an individual member state (unless it was one of the two then 'pariahs', Israel or South Africa) was at once ruled out of order. Article 2(7) of the UN Charter was the sacred text forbidding intervention in matters 'essentially within the domestic jurisdiction of any state'. Governments happily voted for broad declarations on human rights without any intention of applying the provisions in their own backyards. Due in part to the slow but steady pressure of NGOs, the screws have steadily tightened – declarations have been replaced by binding conventions, monitoring their implementation has been entrusted to special committees and rapporteurs, and individual governments suddenly find themselves being called to account for cases of torture, arbitrary detention and 'disappearances'. In this situation the human rights NGOs have to be the conscience of the world, as one government will often be reluctant to make accusations against another because of political alliances, commercial interests or fear of the 'pot calling the kettle black'. NGOs must therefore continue to make maximum use of the existing UN human rights machinery to keep governments on their toes and ensure that the Human Rights Commissioner has the necessary support to do his job properly.

The experiences of NGOs in this book illustrate the difference between conference diplomacy and committee diplomacy. Much time, effort and money have been spent in organising massive conferences, such as the UN Conference on Environment and Development at Rio and the second World Conference on Human Rights at Vienna. These have played an important part in focusing the attention of world leaders, public opinion and the media on key topics, as well as enabling NGOs engaged on the particular issues to make common cause. However, when the 'captains and kings' have departed, it is the task of the less glamorous committees to ensure that well-meaning declarations are implemented in practice. This is where patience and persistence are most needed. Perhaps the message to be given to governments by NGOs should be that, after several years of mega-conferences, the next decade should be the time for committee diplomacy. Whatever the formal rights of NGOs in a particular conference or committee, the informal situation is usually more favourable. NGOs often make a more effective contribution when the forum is smaller and less public, and neither governments nor NGOs need to play to the gallery.

NGOs must also practise the virtue of patience. The walls of Jericho may have fallen at the first blast of the trumpets, but the walls of the United Nations are more durable. From Eglantyne Jebb's unofficial Declaration of the Rights of the Child in 1924, it took 35 years before the UN Declaration was adopted and another thirty years before the legally binding UN Convention was finally completed in 1989. William Wilberforce founded the Society for the Abolition of the Slave Trade in 1787, but it was 1834 before the Abolition of Slavery Act was passed by the British Parliament, and the continued existence of the Anti-Slavery Society today reminds us that many injustices still need to be righted. NGOs have to be tough, resolute, well-briefed and adequately funded if they are to be able to pursue a particular cause or crusade through the labyrinthine procedures of the United Nations for so many years.

No study of NGOs can fail to note the importance of individuals with vision, or dedication to an ideal, or dogged determination, or all three, who identify an objective, who refuse to accept discouragement and who have the charisma to inspire followers to continue the fight until the goal is achieved. They include Eglantyne Jebb, who founded The Save the Children Fund in 1919 and drafted the first Declaration of the Rights of the Child in 1924; Eleanor Roosevelt, who pioneered work on human rights; Peter Benenson, who launched his Appeal for Amnesty in 1951 and saw Amnesty International grow to 2,000 branches in thirty-two countries within twenty years; Julian Huxley and Maurice Strong, who in their very different ways, ensured that NGOs played a key role in UNESCO and at the Stockholm and Rio environmental conferences, to mention but a few. There is always a risk that, over the years, NGOs become too successful, too comfortable, too bureaucratic. NGOs should continually review their methods and objectives to ensure that they are true to the spirit which inspired their original founders and possibly to confirm that the need still exists.

This book has identified the important characteristics of an effective NGO as vision, patience and professionalism. The question remains – what are the practical results from all this hard work, dedication and oratory? The following stand out from the preceding chapters as worthwhile achievements:

– persuading the World Bank to involve local populations far more closely in the planning and implementation of development, to take seriously the adverse social and human consequences of structural adjustment programmes, and to recognise the importance of protecting the environment;
– alerting world opinion to the dangers of dumping toxic wastes, to the threat of extinction facing rare species of animal and marine life, to the destruction of tropical rainforests and to the other environmental problems which governments would prefer to ignore;
– placing the human rights of women on the international agenda;
– helping to create effective international machinery in one of the most politically sensitive human rights areas, that of the use of torture by governments;
– playing a crucial role in completing the Convention on the Rights of the Child, the only Convention which makes specific provision for NGOs to give expert advice on its implementation;
– securing a change in the mandate of the UN High Commissioner

for Refugees, so that it covers not only the physical protection of refugees, but also their food, clothing and medical welfare.

Many more tasks of this nature remain to be tackled, and on past form the UN system, left to its own devices, will not have the courage or the persistence to devise solutions – the pressure and expertise of NGOs will still be needed.

Among the challenges facing the United Nations in the next decades, the most urgent seems to many observers to be the need to fill the vacuum in the world security system left by the collapse of the Super Power system. Until the late 1980s the Soviet Union and the United States policed their respective spheres of influence in a rough and ready way, with occasional demarcation disputes and some help from the UN. Now the duty of preserving the peace has passed almost entirely to the UN – and the task is proving a heavy one. Perhaps there is a role for a new Eglantyne Jebb or Peter Benenson to launch a movement which can persuade governments to give greater priority and more resources to preventing small and vulnerable countries from reaching the point where they tear themselves apart and helping to bring to an end the anarchy and carnage seen in Somalia, Rwanda and elsewhere.

In his speech to NGOs on 20 September 1994, the Secretary-General of the United Nations stated that the vast enterprise of the United Nations of building peace presupposes that NGOs will be involved at every stage. He mentioned three areas where he believed NGOs had a key role:

– in preventive diplomacy, because NGOs are familiar with the situation on the ground and are well placed to alert governments to nascent crises and emerging conflicts;
– in peacemaking, where NGOs can give humanitarian and social aid under perilous and difficult conditions; and
– in post-conflict peace-building, where NGOs can help fragile governments and destitute populations to find the confidence and the resources to make peace last.

Mr Boutros-Ghali concluded by noting:

It must be understood that democracy is not a model to be copied from certain states but a goal to be reached by all peoples. NGOs have a crucial role to play in this area. They can help develop effective ways of spreading the ideas of peace and democracy. They can take part in the birth and development of democratic institutions within states. They can also serve as vigilant monitors, helping to guarantee respect for democracy throughout the world.

With such encouragement from the Secretary-General himself, and on the basis of the achievements recorded in this book, let us hope that NGOs will respond wholeheartedly and effectively to this new challenge, and that the decades ahead will see a further development of the cooperation within the UN system between governments and NGOs which has been so painstakingly established over the past fifty years.

NGOs AND THE STRUCTURE OF THE UNITED NATIONS SYSTEM

When the United Nations Charter was approved, it was presumed that NGOs would have access to the Economic and Social Council (ECOSOC) and the specialised agencies, but not to the other parts of the UN system. Since 1945, the UN has become a much more complex organisation than was originally envisaged and NGOs have obtained at least some access to all UN bodies. This Appendix aims to provide the basic information on the structure of the UN system, from the perspective of what is relevant to NGOs.

The principal organs of the UN

The UN Charter specifies that it has six principal organs. The General Assembly can discuss and make recommendations on any subject and is the central focus for general debate on all the main issues in world politics. It is assisted by three smaller specialist Councils. The Security Council has 'primary responsibility for the maintenance of international peace and security',[1] which in practice means that it is usually the first to respond to new crises involving military conflict. The Trusteeship Council was initially intended to have a central role in the decolonisation process, but it only gained responsibility for eleven territories, with the last one, Palau, achieving independence in 1994.[2] The Economic and Social Council (ECOSOC) oversees the work of the UN on economic and social questions; in addition, the UN's work on human rights and on the environment comes under its mandate. The Assembly and the three Councils are serviced by the Secretariat headed by the UN Secretary-General. The Secretariat has two major roles. It provides the administrative services for the decision-making bodies, and is also responsible for UN field operations, including peace-keeping, development projects, training programmes and disaster relief. The International Court of Justice is responsible for giving advisory opinions on interpretation of the UN Charter and other international treaties, and adjudicating on any legal disputes between states, when those states accept its jurisdiction. Although the Trusteeship Council had a routine procedure for receiving petitions from any individual or group, and the International Court has taken evidence from NGOs,[3] both these organs may be considered to have been marginal to the politics of most NGOs. The other four organs are relevant to NGOs' concerns.

The impression given by the Charter is that authority is clearly allocated. The Security Council appears to dominate the UN's response to armed conflicts and potential threats to international peace. The General Assembly seems to be the main authority for all other issues. ECOSOC has a wide range of responsibilities, but all its decisions are subject to approval by the Assembly. The Secretariat is subordinate to the other decision-making bodies and officially has no political role, except for the right of the Secretary-General to bring conflicts to the attention of the Security Council.[4] While attempts may be made at times to assert these legal relationships, in practice there is a more subtle, ever-changing pattern of influence, with each of the four organs having a significant role to play on most questions.

Military conflicts, the Security Council and NGOs

In deciding what steps should be taken in cases of military conflict, the leading role is usually taken by the Security Council. Under Article 12 of the Charter, the General Assembly may not make any recommendation on a conflict when the Security Council is handling it, unless the Council requests it to do so. Practice, however, does not always reflect this strict demarcation of responsibility. Ten of the fifteen Council members are elected by the Assembly, and feel some responsibility towards the regional groups which elected them, while the five permanent members are anxious not to become too distant from the majority in the Assembly, particularly when there is a high degree of consensus on how to respond to the conflict. Therefore, if the Assembly wishes to pass a resolution to put pressure on the Council to change its decisions, Article 12 is ignored.

The members of the Security Council and the General Assembly sitting in New York have to rely on many sources of information – from the media, from their own governments and from the Secretariat – before they can take any decisions. Most peace-keeping operations are authorised in the form of a resolution endorsing plans presented to the Council by the Secretary-General. In some situations journalists, diplomats or UN Secretariat officials may be available on the ground to report back to their headquarters. However, it may be the case that the only people who can provide reliable and impartial information to the media, to governments and to the Secretariat are the local field personnel of NGOs. Once

Table A.1. THE FOUR MAIN 'PRINCIPAL ORGANS' OF THE UNITED NATIONS

	Membership	Responsibilities	Authority	Relations with NGOs
General Assembly	All UN members. One vote each.	All subjects.	Recommendations on policy. Binding decisions on finance and electing other organs.	Informal NGO lobbying of delegates. Written statements and speeches by NGOs at Special Sessions.
Security Council	5 permanent: China, France, Russia, UK, USA. 10 elected by the General Assembly.	International peace and security.	Recommendations to UN members. Binding decisions, when Chapter VII of the Charter is invoked	Occasional hearing of witnesses by the Council or its committees.
Economic and Social Council	54 UN members, elected by the General Assembly	All economic, social, sustainable development, women's rights and human rights questions.	Recommendations to UN members, to specialised agencies and to the General Assembly.	Consultative status: arrangements for submitting agenda items, written statements and speeches.
Secretariat	Secretary-General elected by Assembly and Security Council. Other staff appointed by the Secretary-General.	Administration of all meetings and all tasks authorised by the other principal organ.	Bringing conflicts to the Security Council's attention. Preparing reports. Internal personnel management	NGO Unit administers ECOSOC relations. Department of Public Information and other units co-operate with NGOs.

UN peace-keeping gets under way, there are UN civilian operations and NGO operations to provide relief to refugees and other casualties of the fighting. The media coverage of the crises in Somalia, Bosnia and Rwanda have brought these interrelationships to the public's attention. These problems have shown more dramatic and intense examples of the tensions between peace-keepers and NGO relief workers than have occurred before, but the fundamental moral and practical issues have arisen in most conflicts in modern times.

The Economic and Social Council and its subsidiary bodies

ECOSOC was constituted in 1946 as a relatively small executive council of eighteen governments, elected by the General Assembly. In 1965 it was expanded to twenty-seven members and in 1973 expanded further to fifty-four members. This has made it too large to act as an effective executive. It can review broad policy questions, but it can no longer negotiate the details of policy implementation. Most of its resolutions and decisions repeat the exact texts, or slightly amend the texts, recommended by its subsidiary bodies. There are nine functional commissions, each dealing with a single policy domain and reporting to the Council. In addition, there are five regional commissions, acting as mini-councils mainly on a continental basis. There are also various standing committees and expert committees of a lower status.[5] A few of these bodies also have their own subsidiary bodies, notably the Commission on Human Rights which has a Sub-Commission on Prevention of Discrimination and Protection of Minorities and several specialist Working Groups and Rapporteurs. All the functional and regional commissions, along with the most important committees are listed in Table A.2.

NGOs officially have consultative status with the Economic and Social Council under the authority of Article 71 of the Charter. The recognition of NGOs and the supervision of the arrangements for consultation is carried out by the Committee on NGOs. In practice the relations with the full Council are little used and of little significance. NGO influence on the Council occurs indirectly through its subsidiary bodies and other organisations that report to the Council. Perhaps the greatest influence to date has been upon the Commission on Human Rights, the Commission on the Status of Women and the Population Commission. In these three policy domains, the UN might have taken little or no action were it not for the work of NGOs.

Table A.2. THE MAIN ECOSOC SUBSIDIARY BODIES

The Functional Commissions

Statistical Commission
Population Commission
Commission for Social Development
Commission on Human Rights
Commission on the Status of Women
Commission on Narcotic Drugs
Commission on Science and Technology for Development
Commission on Sustainable Development
Commission on Crime Prevention and Criminal Justice

The Regional Commissions

Economic Commission for Africa
Economic and Social Commission for Asia and the Pacific
Economic Commission for Europe
Economic Commission for Latin America and the Caribbean
Economic and Social Commission for Western Asia

The Main Standing Committees

Committee on Non-Governmental Organisations
Committee for Programme and Co-ordination
Commission on Transnational Corporations
Commission on Human Settlements

UN operational programmes

There is no clear constitutional relationship between ECOSOC and the General Assembly spelling out their respective responsibilities. The Assembly has established a range of programmes that might have been expected to have originated from the Council's mandate. They cover such important activities as general development policy and project funding; the welfare of refugees; the health and nutrition of children; food aid; environmental monitoring, research and policy; population planning; and drug control. These programmes each have their distinct secretariats; although nominally part of the main UN Secretariat, they have their own directors and operate separately. In each case policy is determined by an executive committee, board or council that has been elected by ECOSOC. UNRWA is an exception – its Advisory Commission is chosen by the Assembly. Although the main political initiative for each of these programmes came from the Assembly, they all, except for UNRWA, report to the Assembly via ECOSOC.

The relationships between the secretariats of these programmes

Table A.3. THE MAIN UN OPERATIONAL PROGRAMMES

UNDCP	United Nations International Drug Control Programme
UNDP	United Nations Development Programme
UNEP	United Nations Environment Programme
UNFPA	United Nations Population Fund
UNHCR	Office of the UN High Commissioner for Refugees
UNICEF	United Nations Children's Fund
UNRWA	UN Relief and Works Agency for Palestine Refugees
WFP	World Food Programme

and NGOs concerned with their work is exceptionally close. This is true both at headquarters and in the field. NGOs offer information, experience, advice and opinions in policy-making and policy implementation. Strong working relationships can exist, through NGOs being executive agents or sub-contractors for projects, or simply through the UN and NGOs running projects in parallel with each other in particular areas. The pattern of NGO relations with the intergovernmental executive committees for these programmes is more varied. Generally, the same relationships as for an ECOSOC subsidiary body apply. Some programmes use the list of NGOs recognised by ECOSOC, some have developed their own list, and some have no formal arrangements for the executive to consult NGOs.

Specialised global conferences

Under the UN Charter, the Economic and Social Council has the power to call specialised international conferences.[6] The Assembly does not have this power explicitly, but nevertheless it too has called conferences on its own initiative. One particular variant of this has been when special sessions of the Assembly are called to give consideration to a single policy domain, notably on Palestine, Namibia, disarmament, drugs or international development co-operation. The Assembly has also taken upon itself the right to determine the main terms of reference and the procedures for many of the conferences convened by the Council. Nothing in the Charter gives NGOs the right of access to the specialised conferences, but the ECOSOC consultative arrangements are taken as the starting point for all conferences convened either by the Council or by the Assembly.[7] By an extension of these practices, NGOs now also have limited rights to participate in General Assembly special sessions. NGO influence, both in the major conferences covered by the world's media and in more technical, less publicised conferences, can be substantial.[8]

The specialised agencies

The term 'the UN system' is generally taken to cover both the United Nations itself and some twenty agencies related to it. When the UN was formed there was a desire to bring existing independent global intergovernmental organisations into a close relationship with the UN and to establish new ones to tackle the post-war problems. By 1950 there were ten organisations recognised as UN specialised agencies. They signed agreements with the United Nations, committing themselves to report on their work to ECOSOC, to coordinate with each other and to cooperate with ECOSOC's policy. Since the early days another six organisations have signed agreements and hence become specialised agencies.[9] A further four organisations work closely with the UN in a comparable manner, but each has a somewhat different formal status. Technically the twenty organisations have separate constitutions, different membership from the UN, their own secretariats and their own budgets. Legally, except for UNCTAD, they are independent and are not part of the UN; they have merely agreed to cooperate.[10]

Table A.4 lists the twenty agencies, grouping them into four commonly used categories. In addition to the sixteen specialised agencies, there are four similar organisations. The International Atomic Energy Agency is virtually identical to a specialised agency except that it is supervised by the General Assembly and the Security Council rather than ECOSOC. The General Agreement on Tariffs and Trade (GATT) used to operate from Geneva in close co-operation with the UN. Technically it was a treaty with a secretariat and not a legal organisation. As a result of the Uruguay Round, GATT has now become the World Trade Organisation, which may be expected to become a specialised agency in due course. The United Nations Conference on Trade and Development (UNCTAD) became a permanent UN organ in 1964 when the developing countries wanted to establish a specialised agency to deal with their trade concerns that were being ignored by GATT. They failed to obtain sufficient support to create a full agency, but as a compromise UNCTAD became a permanent UN organ. Nominally, it is a subsidiary body of the General Assembly, but in practice it acts like a separate agency. The International Sea-Bed Authority is being created to manage exploitation of minerals in the oceans beyond each country's Exclusive Economic Zone. It too might become a specialised agency.[11]

Table A.4.   AGENCIES RELATED TO THE UNITED NATIONS

The Major Specialised Agencies

FAO	Food and Agriculture Organisation of the United Nations
ILO	International Labour Organisation
UNESCO	UN Educational, Scientific and Cultural Organisation
WHO	World Health Organisation

The Technical Specialised Agencies

ICAO	International Civil Aviation Organisation
IMO	International Maritime Organisation
IFAD	International Fund for Agricultural Development
ITU	International Telecommunication Union
UNIDO	United Nations Industrial Development Organisation
UPU	Universal Postal Union
WIPO	World Intellectual Property Organisation
WMO	World Meteorological Organisation

The Financial Specialised Agencies

IMF	International Monetary Fund
IBRD	International Bank for Reconstruction and Development
IDA	International Development Association
IFC	International Finance Corporation

Other Agencies Related to the UN

IAEA	International Atomic Energy Agency
ISBA	International Sea-Bed Authority
UNCTAD	United Nations Conference on Trade and Development
WTO	World Trade Organisation (formerly GATT)

The specialised agencies, except for the ISBA which is still being formed, all have strong working relationships with NGOs. They do not follow the ECOSOC consultative status system; NGOs have to develop their relationships separately with each agency. Most agencies have official lists of recognised NGOs. Some differentiate them into three categories like ECOSOC, while others have a single list. The IMF, however, has no formal arrangements.[12]

Co-ordination in the UN system

Although the UN and the various agencies are legally separate entities, there is significant administrative and financial integration. The Administrative Committee on Co-ordination (ACC) brings together the executive heads of the agencies and the operational programmes, with the UN Secretary-General in the chair. The ACC operates by consensus and cannot impose any centralised authority, but it can focus on common problems and stimulate attention to a common policy agenda. Other bodies have promoted standardisation of personnel questions, covering recruitment, salaries, pensions and conditions of service. The UN Environment Programme has acted as a small secretariat that defines its role as being a catalyst to stimulate attention to environmental policy throughout the system. At times major political questions, notably the recognition of the communist government in Beijing rather than the government of Taiwan as the Chinese representatives, have been decided in the UN and followed by the agencies.

Finance has provided important links. The administrative budgets of each specialised agency are separate, but they are relatively small. Specialised agencies derive about 40 per cent of their operational funds from United Nations programmes and funds.[13] Most of this finance comes from the United Nations Development Programme (UNDP) and, as a result, UNDP has been able to exercise a significant co-ordinating role on development policy. The international financial institutions, the IMF and the World Bank, are more independent from the rest of the UN system, because they control large-scale financial flows and are able to fund their administration from the profits.

While there is some administrative and financial integration across the whole UN system, there are also substantial problems due to lack of coordination. At the policy level, UNDP, UNFPA and UNICEF and the operational agencies have major differences with the IMF and the World Bank about their role in promoting development. Moreover, the various bureaucracies act as rivals in claiming responsibility for programmes and raising funds. In the field, different programmes wish to maintain their autonomy and undertake the most newsworthy and prestigious work. Sometimes NGOs will be angry about the loss of efficiency, speed and effectiveness that is caused. At other times NGOs take advantage of the differences, to work with the bureaucracy that is most sympathetic to their own priorities.

NGO access to the UN System

For most purposes each NGO has to decide for itself, when and how it will seek to exercise influence in the UN system. As we have seen, the formal rights of access vary from the established arrangements in ECOSOC, its subsidiary bodies, operational programmes

and the specialised agencies, through the different rules of procedure for UN conferences, to occasional *ad hoc* opportunities in
other bodies. However, the NGOs come together in a joint organisation, the Conference of Non-Governmental Organisations in
Consultative Status with the United Nations Economic and Social
Council (CONGO), to promote and enhance their rights of participation throughout the system. CONGO was formed in May
1948, in order to influence the development of the ECOSOC consultative arrangements in their formative years. It has continued to
act as the guardian of those arrangements. It has also lobbied
unsuccessfully to standardise the procedures for UN conferences
and to gain the right of formal access to the General Assembly.

CONGO operates both in New York and in Geneva, while in
more recent years there has been a branch in Vienna as well. The
main authority lies with a triennial general conference, which elects
twenty NGOs to a Board that meets twice a year. Regular work is
in subject committees: there are CONGO committees on development, disarmament and human rights in New York and Geneva;
committees on women and youth in New York and Vienna; and
a committee on narcotic drugs in Vienna. Even these subject committees are mainly concerned with NGO access to the relevant UN
committees and branches of the UN Secretariat. They do not very
often adopt joint positions on substantive issues. The only thing
that all the NGOs have in common is their support for participation
rights. Otherwise they are jealous of their independence. Indeed,
they protest whenever a diplomat or official suggests one NGO can
represent the whole NGO community.

While most NGOs that relate to the UN can address most of their
concerns through the ECOSOC consultative arrangements, gaining
formal access to the General Assembly has for many years been a
goal for CONGO. The Assembly oversees ECOSOC and can pass
resolutions affecting the mandate of ECOSOC on specific activities. Equally, decisions of many subsidiary bodies come before the
Assembly, primarily via ECOSOC, and affect its decisions. It is
thus a curious anomaly that NGOs officially have involvement
through ECOSOC in some stages of UN decision-making, but officially are excluded from the Assembly, when the same subjects are
discussed. However, the unofficial political processes do not necessarily exclude the NGOs. Those who are registered with ECOSOC
are allowed access to UN buildings. This enables them to sit in on
debates and engage in lobbying in the corridors to affect the
Assembly's decisions on issues of concern to them.

For many years, there were just two focus points in the UN
Secretariat for relations with NGOs. The NGO Unit, currently

Table A.5.   OPERATIONAL ACTIVITIES IN THE UN SYSTEM
(*sources of expenditure, $US millions, in 1992*)

	$USm.	%
United Nations Development Programme (UNDP)	1026.8	22.4
UNDP-administered funds	137.6	3.0
United Nations Population Fund (UNFPA)	128.2	2.8
United Nations Children's Fund (UNICEF)	743.8	16.2
World Food Programme (WFP)	1575.2	34.4
UN Regular Budget	16.6	0.4
Regular Budgets of UN agencies	225.0	4.9
Extrabudgetary Sources of UN agencies	727.2	15.9
Total	4580.4	100.0

located in the Department for Policy Co-ordination and Sustainable Development, operated from 1947 with three professional and three support staff. In 1992 this was increased to four in each category. With such limited resources, they have been able to do little more than service the ECOSOC consultative arrangements and maintain close relations with CONGO. From the beginning the Department of Public Information has also had its own relations with NGOs, both in New York and through UN offices around the world. It does not limit itself to the ECOSOC NGOs and has its own NGO/DPI committee, separate from CONGO, to oversee what is essentially public relations work for the UN.

In 1975 an independent United Nations Non-Governmental Liaison Service was established with support from a variety of UN programmes and specialised agencies. Despite its general name, it is only concerned with development issues, including supporting NGOs from developing countries and North-South NGO networks. It actively promotes NGO participation in UN development debates and negotiations, providing documentation, briefing sessions and fund-raising to assist with the costs of participation. Finally, in addition to the operational programmes, most departments of the UN Secretariat now have their own working relationships with NGOs. The increasing financial pressures on the UN, particularly from the early 1980s, have encouraged UN officials to consider NGOs as a potential supplementary resource on which they can draw.

The UN Secretariat is not supposed to be a political actor. In practice international civil servants usually have their own commitments to particular policies and their own bureaucratic concerns. Through the drafting of reports, the preparation of budgets, the allocation of personnel, the design of programmes, making public speeches in debates and private lobbying of delegates, these officials do exercise political influence. Sometimes strong leadership by the directors of Secretariat units can make a major difference to the success of a programme. It has already been pointed out that NGOs and the Secretariat may have strong working relationships in the field. Another route for NGOs to have influence on policy is for them to work with Secretariat officials at the headquarters, particularly through providing expertise to help with writing reports. The exchange of information and ideas can also be useful. NGOs and officials can at times form strong alliances.

Conclusion

Just as there is no such thing as a typical NGO, there is no standard way by which decisions are produced by the UN. Outcomes may be decided in obscure committees and simply be endorsed at higher levels or there may be serious debate in a major forum open to the public. The content may appear boring and technical to journalists and not be covered in the media or attract widespread interest and passionate public concern. Resolutions may originate from government delegates, from Secretariat officials or from NGO activists.

NOTES

1. Charter of the United Nations, Article 24.
2. A Compact of Free Association between Palau and the United States was approved in a plebiscite on 9 November 1993. The Trusteeship Council by Resolution 2199(LXI) of 25 May 1994 considered it appropriate to terminate the trusteeship agreement in October 1994. The Security Council terminated the agreement by Resolution 956 (1994) on 10 November 1994.
3. The World Court Project, an international NGO, successfully lobbied for World Health Assembly Resolution 46.40 of 12 May 1993, to request an advisory opinion of the ICJ on the legality of nuclear weapons, and on 10 June 1994 had their evidence on the case placed in the Court's archive by the Registrar.
4. Charter of the United Nations, Article 99.
5. It is confusing that some of standing committees, although they are not commissions in terms of the UN Charter, are nevertheless also called commissions.
6. Charter of the United Nations, Article 62(4).
7. Conferences convened by the Council are covered by ECOSOC Resolution 1296(XLIV), paragraph 34, given in Appendix B. There is no general provision for NGOs to attend conferences convened by the General Assembly, but the practice is identical.
8. For a list of the 147 global conferences that took place from 1961 to 1985, see P. Willetts, 'The Pattern of Conferences' in P. Taylor and A.J.R. Groom, *Global Issues in the United Nations' Framework* (London: Macmillan, 1989), pp. 64–72.

9. The term 'specialised agency' is only used within the UN system to describe the sixteen intergovernmental organisations that have signed agreements with the UN, under the terms of Articles 57 and 63 of the UN Charter.
10. For further reading on the specialised agencies, see E. Luard, *International Agencies. The Emerging Framework of Interdependence* (London: Macmillan for the Royal Institute of International Affairs, 1977), and D. Williams, *The Specialized Agencies and the United Nations: The System in Crisis* (London: C. Hurst for the David Davies Memorial Institute, 1987).
11. The United Nations Convention on the Law of the Sea, Article 162(f) provides for the Authority to 'enter into agreements with the United Nations'.
12. GATT was like the IMF. In the whole of its forty-seven years it never had any formal relationship with NGOs. However, this will not be the case for its successor. Article V of the Agreement Establishing the World Trade Organisation provides for 'appropriate arrangements for consultation and co-operation with non-governmental organisations'.
13. *An Agenda for Development*, UN doc. A/48/935 of 6 May 1994, p. 27.
14. *Ibid*. Data in Table A.5 is from Annex II, p. 48. The data excludes costs of administration and peace-keeping. It also excludes concessional and non-concessional financial flows.

DOCUMENTS ON THE FORMAL ARRANGEMENTS FOR CONSULTATIVE STATUS

CONTENTS

Charter of the United Nations
Article 71

The Economic and Social Council may make suitable arrangements
for consultation with non-governmental organisations which are

concerned with matters within its competence. Such arrangements may be made with international organisations and, where appropriate, with national organisations after consultations with the Member of the United Nations concerned.

The UN Economic and Social Council Statute for NGOs
ECOSOC Resolution 1296(XLIV), adopted unanimously on 23 May 1968

The Economic and Social Council,
Having regard to Article 71 of the Charter of the United Nations,
Recognising that arrangements for consultation with non-governmental organisations provide an important means of furthering the purposes and principles of the United Nations,
Considering that consultations between the Council and its subsidiary organs and the non-governmental organisations should be developed to the fullest practicable extent,
Approves the following arrangements, which supersede those set out in its resolution 288 B (X) of 27 February 1950:

ARRANGEMENTS FOR CONSULTATION WITH NON-GOVERNMENTAL ORGANISATIONS

Part I
PRINCIPLES TO BE APPLIED IN THE ESTABLISHMENT OF CONSULTATIVE RELATIONS

The following principles shall be applied in establishing consultative relations with non-governmental organisations:
1. The organisation shall be concerned with matters falling within the competence of the Economic and Social Council with respect to international economic, social, cultural, educational, health, scientific, technological and related matters and to questions of human rights.
2. The aims and purposes of the organisation shall be in conformity with the spirit, purposes and principles of the Charter of the United Nations.
3. The organisation shall undertake to support the work of the United Nations and to promote knowledge of its principles and activities, in accordance with its own aims and purposes and the nature and scope of its competence and activities.
4. The organisation shall be of representative character and of recognised international standing; it shall represent a substantial proportion, and express the views of major sections, of the population or of the organised persons within the particular field of its competence, covering, where possible, a substantial number of countries in different regions of the world. Where there exist a number of organisations with similar objectives, interests and basic views in a given field, they shall, for the purposes of consultation with the Council, form a joint committee or other body authorised to carry on such consultation for the group as a whole. It is understood that when a minority opinion develops on a particular point

within such a committee, it shall be presented along with the opinion of the majority.

5. The organisation shall have an established headquarters, with an executive officer. It shall have a democratically adopted constitution, a copy of which shall be deposited with the Secretary-General of the United Nations, and which shall provide for the determination of policy by a conference, congress or other representative body, and for an executive organ responsible to the policy-making body.

6. The organisation shall have authority to speak for its members through its authorised representatives. Evidence of this authority shall be presented, if requested.

7. Subject to paragraph 9 below, the organisation shall be international in its structure, with members who exercise voting rights in relation to the policies or action of the international organisation. Any international organisation which is not established by inter-governmental agreement shall be considered as a non-governmental organisation for the purpose of these arrangements, including organisations which accept members designated by governmental authorities, provided that such membership does not interfere with the free expression of views of the organisation.

8. The basic resources of the international organisation shall be derived in the main part from contributions of the national affiliates or other components or from individual members. Where voluntary contributions have been received, their amounts and donors shall be faithfully revealed to the Council Committee on Non-Governmental Organisations. Where, however, the above criterion is not fulfilled and an organisation is financed from other sources, it must explain to the satisfaction of the Committee its reasons for not meeting the requirements laid down in this paragraph. Any financial contribution or other support, direct or indirect, from a Government to the international organisation shall be openly declared to the Committee through the Secretary-General and fully recorded in the financial and other records of the organisation and shall be devoted to purposes in accordance with the aims of the United Nations.

9. National organisations shall normally present their views through international non-governmental organisations to which they belong. It would not, save in exceptional cases, be appropriate to admit national organisations which are affiliated to an international non-governmental organisation covering the same subjects on an international basis. National organisations, however, may be admitted after consultation with the Member State concerned in order to help achieve a balanced and effective representation of non-governmental organisations reflecting major interests of all regions and areas of the world, or where they have special experience upon which the Council may wish to draw.

10. Consultative arrangements shall not normally be made with an international organisation which is a member of a committee or group composed of international organisations with which consultative arrangements have been made.

11. In considering the establishment of consultative relations with a non-governmental organisation, the Council will take into account whether the field of activity of the organisation is wholly or mainly within the field

of a specialised agency, and whether or not it could be admitted when it has, or may have, a consultative arrangement with a specialised agency.

Part II
PRINCIPLES GOVERNING THE NATURE OF THE CONSULTATIVE ARRANGEMENTS

12. A clear distinction is drawn in the Charter of the United Nations between participation without vote in the deliberations of the Council and the arrangements for consultation. Under Articles 69 and 70, participation is provided for only in the case of States not members of the Council, and of specialised agencies. Article 71, applying to non-governmental organisations, provides for suitable arrangements for consultation. This distinction, deliberately made in the Charter, is fundamental and the arrangements for consultation should not be such as to accord to non-governmental organisations the same rights of participation as are accorded to States not members of the Council and to the specialised agencies brought into relationship with the United Nations.

13. The arrangements should not be such as to overburden the Council or transform it from a body for coordination of policy and action, as contemplated in the Charter, into a general forum for discussion.

14. Decisions on arrangements for consultation should be guided by the principle that consultative arrangements are to be made, on the one hand, for the purpose of enabling the Council or one of its bodies to secure expert information or advice from organisations having special competence in the subjects for which consultative arrangements are made, and, on the other hand, to enable organisations which represent important elements of public opinion in a large number of countries to express their views. Therefore, the arrangements for consultation made with each organisation should involve only the subjects for which that organisation has a special competence or in which it has a special interest. The organisations given consultative status should be limited to those whose international activities in fields set out in paragraph I above qualify them to make a significant contribution to the work of the Council and should, in sum, as far as possible reflect in a balanced way the major viewpoints or interests in these fields in all areas and regions of the world.

Part III
ESTABLISHMENT OF CONSULTATIVE RELATIONSHIPS

15. In establishing consultative relationships with each organisation, regard shall be had to the nature and scope of its activities and to the assistance it may be expected to give to the Council or its subsidiary bodies in carrying out the functions set out in Chapters IX and X of the Charter of the United Nations.

16. In establishing consultative relations with organisations, the Council will distinguish between:
(a) Organisations which are concerned with most of the activities of the Council and can demonstrate to the satisfaction of the Council that they have marked and sustained contributions to make to the achievement of

the objectives of the United Nations in the fields set out in paragraph I above, and are closely involved with the economic and social life of the peoples of the areas they represent and whose membership, which should be considerable, is broadly representative of major segments of population in a large number of countries (to be known as organisations in general consultative status, Category l);

(b) Organisations which have a special competence in, and are concerned specifically with, only a few of the fields of activity covered by the Council, and which are known internationally within the fields for which they have or seek consultative status (to be known as organisations in special consultative status, Category II).

17. Organisations accorded consultative status in Category II because of their interest in the field of human rights should have a general international concern with this matter, not restricted to the interests of a particular group of persons, a single nationality or the situation in a single State or restricted group of States. Special consideration shall be given to the applications of organisations in this field whose aims place stress on combating colonialism, apartheid, racial intolerance and other gross violations of human rights and fundamental freedoms.

18. Major organisations one of whose primary purposes is to promote the aims, objectives and purposes of the United Nations and a furtherance of the understanding of its work may be accorded consultative status in Category II.

19. Other organisations which do not have general or special consultative status but which the Council, or the Secretary-General of the United Nations, in consultation with the Council or its Committee on Non-Governmental Organisations, considers can make occasional and useful contributions to the work of the Council or its subsidiary bodies or other United Nations bodies within their competence shall be included in a list (to be known as the Roster). This list may also include organisations in consultative status or similar relationship with a specialised agency or a United Nations body. These organisations shall be available for consultation at the request of the Council or its subsidiary bodies. The fact that an organisation is on the Roster shall not in itself be regarded as a qualification for general or special consultative status should an organisation seek such status.

Part IV
CONSULTATION WITH THE COUNCIL

Provisional Agenda
20. The provisional agenda of the Council shall be communicated to organisations in Categories I and II and to those on the Roster.

21. Organisations in Category I may propose to the Council Committee on Non-Governmental Organisations that the Committee request the Secretary-General to place items of special interest to the organisations on the provisional agenda of the Council.

Attendance at Meetings
22. Organisations in Categories I and II may designate authorised

representatives to sit as observers at public meetings of the Council and its subsidiary bodies. Those on the Roster may have representatives present at such meetings concerned with matters within their field of competence.

Written Statements

23. Written statements relevant to the work of the Council may be submitted by organisations in Categories I and II on subjects in which these organisations have a special competence. Such statements shall be circulated by the Secretary-General of the United Nations to the members of the Council, except those statements which have become obsolete, for example, those dealing with matters already disposed of and those which had already been circulated in some other form.

24. The following conditions shall be observed regarding the submission and circulation of such statements:

(a) The written statement shall be submitted in one of the official languages

(b) It shall be submitted in sufficient time for appropriate consultation to take place between the Secretary-General and the organisation before circulation.

(c) The organisation shall give due consideration to any comments which the Secretary-General may make in the course of such consultation before transmitting the statement in final form.

(d) A written statement submitted by an organisation in Category I will be circulated in full if it does not exceed 2,000 words. Where a statement is in excess of 2,000 words, the organisation shall submit a summary which will be circulated or shall supply sufficient copies of the full text in the working languages for distribution. A statement will also be circulated in full, however, upon a specific request of the Council or its Committee on Non-Governmental Organisations.

(e) A written statement submitted by an organisation in Category II or on the Roster will be circulated in full if it does not exceed 500 words. Where a statement is in excess of 500 words, the organisation shall submit a summary which will be circulated; such statements will be circulated in full, however, upon a specific request of the Council or its Committee on Non-Governmental Organisations.

(f) The Secretary-General, in consultation with the President of the Council, or the Council or its Committee on Non-Governmental Organisations, may invite organisations on the Roster to submit written statements. The provisions of sub-paragraphs (a), (b), (c) and (e) above shall apply to such statements.

(g) A written statement or summary, as the case may be, will be circulated by the Secretary-General in the working languages, and, upon the request of a member of the Council, in any of the official, languages.

Hearings

25. (a) The Council Committee on Non-Governmental Organisations shall make recommendations to the Council as to which organisations in Category I should be heard by the Council or by its sessional committees and on which items they should be heard. Such organisations shall be entitled to make one statement to the Council or the appropriate sessional

committee, subject to the approval of the Council or of the sessional committee concerned. In the absence of a subsidiary body of the Council with jurisdiction in a major field of interest to the Council and to an organisation in Category II, the Committee may recommend that an organisation in Category II be heard by the Council on the subject in its field of interest. (*b*) Whenever the Council discusses the substance of an item proposed by a non-governmental organisation in Category I and included in the agenda of the Council, such an organisation shall be entitled to present orally to the Council or a sessional committee of the Council, as appropriate, an introductory statement of an expository nature. Such an organisation may be invited by the President of the Council or the Chairman of the committee, with the consent of the relevant body, to make, in the course of the discussion of the item before the Council or before the committee, an additional statement for purposes of clarification.

Part V
CONSULTATION WITH COMMISSIONS AND OTHER
SUBSIDIARY ORGANS OF THE COUNCIL

Provisional Agenda
26. The provisional agenda of sessions of commissions and other subsidiary organs of the Council shall be communicated to organisations in Categories I and II and those on the Roster.
27. Organisations in Category I may propose items for the provisional agenda of commissions, subject to the following conditions:
(*a*) An organisation which intends to propose such an item shall inform the Secretary-General of the United Nations at least sixty-three days before the commencement of the session and before formally proposing an item shall give due consideration to any comments the Secretary-General may make.
(*b*) The proposal shall be formally submitted with the relevant basic documentation not later than forty-nine days before the commencement of the session. The item shall be included in the agenda of the commission if it is adopted by a two-thirds majority of those present and voting.

Attendance at Meetings
28. Organisations in Categories I and II may designate authorised representatives to sit as observers at public meetings of the commissions and other subsidiary organs of the Council. Organisations on the Roster may have representatives present at such meetings which are concerned with matters within their field of competence.

Written Statements
29. Written statements relevant to the work of the commissions or other subsidiary organs may be submitted by organisations in Categories I and II on subjects for which these organisations have a special competence. Such statements shall be circulated by the Secretary-General to members of the commission or other subsidiary organs, except those Statements which have become obsolete, for example those dealing with matters already disposed of and those which have already been circulated in some other form to members of the commission or other subsidiary organs.

30. The following conditions shall be observed regarding the submission and circulation of such written statements:

(a) The written statement shall be submitted in one of the official languages.

(b) It shall be submitted in sufficient time for appropriate consultation to take place between the Secretary-General and the organisation before circulation.

(c) The organisation shall give due consideration to any comments which the Secretary-General may make in the course of such consultation before transmitting the statement in final form.

(d) A written statement submitted by an organisation in Category I will be circulated in full if it does not exceed 2,000 words. Where a statement is in excess of 2,000 words, the organisation shall submit a summary, which will be circulated, or shall supply sufficient copies of the full text in the working languages for distribution. A statement will also be circulated in full, however, upon the specific request of the commission or other subsidiary organs.

(e) A written statement submitted by an organisation in Category II will be circulated in full if it does not exceed 1,500 words. Where a statement is in excess of 1,500 words, the organisation shall submit a summary which will be circulated, or shall supply sufficient copies of the full text in the working languages for distribution. A statement will also be circulated in full, however, upon the specific request of the commission or other subsidiary organs.

(f) The Secretary-General, in consultation with the Chairman of the relevant commission or other subsidiary organ, or the commission or other subsidiary organ itself, may invite organisations on the Roster to submit written statements. The provisions in sub-paragraphs (a), (b), (c) and (e) above shall apply to such statements.

(g) A written statement or summary, as the case may be, will be circulated by the Secretary-General in the working languages and, upon the request of a member of the commission or other subsidiary organ, in any of the official languages.

Hearings

31. (a) The commission or other subsidiary organs may consult with organisations in Categories I and II either directly or through a committee or committees established for the purpose. In all cases, such consultations may be arranged on the request of the organisation.

(b) On the recommendation of the Secretary-General and at the request of the commission or other subsidiary organs, organisations on the Roster may also be heard by the commission or other subsidiary organs.

Special Studies

32. Subject to the relevant rules of procedure on financial implications, a commission may recommend that an organisation which has special competence in a particular field should undertake specific studies or investigations or prepare specific papers for the commission. The limitations of paragraph 30 (d) and (e) above shall not apply in this case.

Part VI
CONSULTATIONS WITH AD HOC COMMITTEES OF THE COUNCIL

33. The arrangements for consultation between ad hoc committees of the Council authorised to meet between sessions of the Council and organisations in Categories I and II and on the Roster shall follow those approved for commissions of the Council, unless the Council or the committee decides otherwise.

Part VII
CONSULTATION WITH INTERNATIONAL CONFERENCES
CALLED BY THE COUNCIL

34. The Council may invite non-governmental organisations in Categories I and II and on the Roster to take part in conferences called by the Council under Article 62, paragraph 4, of the Charter of the United Nations. The organisations shall be entitled to the same rights and privileges and shall undertake the same responsibilities as at sessions of the Council itself, unless the Council decides otherwise.

Part VIII
SUSPENSION AND WITHDRAWAL OF CONSULTATIVE STATUS

35. Organisations granted consultative status by the Council and those on the Roster shall conform at all times to the principles governing the establishment and nature of their consultative relations with the Council. In periodically reviewing the activities of the non-governmental organisations on the basis of reports submitted under paragraph 40 (b) below and other relevant information, the Council Committee on Non-Governmental Organisations shall determine the extent to which the organisations have complied with the principles governing consultative status and have contributed to the work of the Council, and may recommend to the Council suspension or exclusion from consultative status of organisations which have not met the requirements for consultative status as set forth in the present resolution.
36. The consultative status of non-governmental organisations with the Economic and Social Council and the listing of those on the Roster shall be suspended up to three years or withdrawn in the following cases:
(a) If there exists substantiated evidence of secret governmental financial influence to induce an organisation to undertake acts contrary to the purposes and principles of the Charter of the United Nations;
(b) If the organisation clearly abuses its consultative status by systematically engaging in unsubstantiated or politically motivated acts against States Members of the United Nations contrary to and incompatible with the principles of the Charter;
(c) If within the preceding three years, an organisation had not made any positive or effective contribution to the work of the Council or its commissions or other subsidiary organs.
37. The consultative status of organisations in Categories I and II and the listing of those on the Roster will be suspended or withdrawn by the

decision of the Economic and Social Council on the recommendation of its Committee on Non-Governmental Organisations.

38. An organisation whose consultative status or whose listing on the Roster is withdrawn may be entitled to reapply for consultative status or for inclusion on the Roster not sooner than three years after the effective date of such withdrawal.

Part IX
COUNCIL COMMITTEE ON NON-GOVERNMENTAL
ORGANISATIONS

39. The members of the Council Committee on Non-Governmental Organisations shall be elected at the first session of the Council each year, on the basis of equitable geographical representation, in accordance with Council resolution 1099(XL) of 4 March 1966 and rule 82 of the rules of procedure of the Council. The Committee shall elect its Chairman and other officers as necessary. A member shall serve until the next election unless it ceases to be a member of the Council.

40. The functions of the Committee shall include the following:

(a) The Committee shall hold a session before the first session of the Council each year to consider applications for consultative status in Categories I and II and for listing on the Roster made by non-governmental organisations and requests for changes in status, and to make recommendations thereon to the Council. Organisations shall give due consideration to any comments on technical matters which the Secretary-General of the United Nations may make in receiving such applications for the Committee. The Committee shall consider at each such session applications received by the Secretary-General not later than 1 June of the preceding year, on which sufficient data have been distributed to the members of the Committee not later than six weeks before the applications are to be considered. Reapplication by an organisation for status, or a request for a change in status, shall be considered by the Committee at the earliest at its first session in the second year following the session at which the substance of the previous application or request was considered, unless at the time of such consideration it was decided otherwise.

(b) Organisations in consultative status in Categories I and II shall submit to the Council Committee on Non-Governmental Organisations through the Secretary-General every fourth year a brief report of their activities, specifically as regards the support they have given to the work of the United Nations. Based on findings of the Committee's examination of the report and other relevant information, the Committee may recommend to the Council any reclassification in status of the organisation concerned as it deems appropriate. However, under exceptional circumstances, the Committee may ask for such a report from an individual organisation in Category I or II or on the Roster, between the regular report dates.

(c) The Committee may consult, in connection with sessions of the Council or at such other times as it may decide, with organisations in Categories I and II on matters within their competence, other than items on the agenda of the Council, on which the Council or the Committee or the organisation requests consultation. The Committee shall report to the Council on such consultations.

(*d*) The Committee may consult, in connection with any particular session of the Council, with organisations in Categories I and II on matters within the competence of the organisations concerning specific items already on the provisional agenda of the Council on which the Council or the Committee or the organisation requests consultation, and shall make recommendations as to which organisations, subject to the provisions of paragraph 25(*a*) above, should be heard by the Council or the appropriate committee and regarding which subjects should be heard. The Committee shall report to the Council on such consultations.

(*e*) The Committee shall consider matters concerning non-governmental organisations which may be referred to it by the Council or by commissions.

(*f*) The Committee shall consult with the Secretary-General, as appropriate, on matters affecting the consultative arrangements under Article 71 of the Charter, and arising therefrom.

41. The Committee, in considering a request from a non-governmental organisation in Category I that an item be placed on the agenda of the Council, shall take into account, among other things:

(*a*) The adequacy of the documentation submitted by the organisation;

(*b*) The extent to which it is considered that the item lends itself to early and constructive action by the Council;

(*c*) The possibility that the item might be more appropriately dealt with elsewhere than in the Council.

42. Any decision by the Council Committee on Non-Governmental Organisations not to grant a request submitted by a non-governmental organisation in Category I that an item be placed on the provisional agenda of the Council shall be considered as final unless the Council decides otherwise.

Part X
CONSULTATION WITH THE SECRETARIAT

43. The Secretariat should be so organised as to enable it to carry out the duties assigned to it concerning the consultative arrangements as set forth in the present resolution.

44. All organisations in consultative relationship shall be able to consult with officers of the appropriate sections of the Secretariat on matters in which there is a mutual interest or a mutual concern. Such consultation shall be upon the request of the non-governmental organisation or upon the request of the Secretary-General of the United Nations.

45. The Secretary-General may request organisations in Categories I and II and those on the Roster to carry out specific studies or prepare specific papers, subject to the relevant financial regulations.

46. The Secretary-General shall be authorised, within the means at his disposal, to offer to non-governmental organisations in consultative relationship facilities which include:

(*a*) Prompt and efficient distribution of such documents of the Council and its subsidiary bodies as shall in the judgement of the Secretary-General be appropriate;

(*b*) Access to the press documentation services provided by the United Nations;

(*c*) Arrangement of informal discussions on matters of special interest to groups or organisations;

(*d*) Use of the libraries of the United Nations;

(*e*) Provision of accommodation for conferences or smaller meetings of consultative organisations on the work of the Economic and Social Council.

(*f*) Appropriate seating arrangements and facilities for obtaining documents during public meetings of the General Assembly dealing with matters in the economic and social fields.

Source: Yearbook of the United Nations 1968, pp. 647–52.

List of NGOs with Category I Consultative Status

Assemblée internationale des parlementaires de langue française
CARE International
Greek Orthodox Archdiocesan Council of North and South America
International Alliance of Women – Equal Rights, Equal Responsibilities
International Chamber of Commerce
International Confederation of Free Trade Unions
International Cooperative Alliance
International Council for Adult Education
International Council of Voluntary Agencies
International Council of Women
International Council on Social Welfare
International Federation of Agricultural Producers
International Federation of Associations of the Elderly
International Federation of Business and Professional Women
International Federation of Red Cross and Red Crescent Societies
International Movement ATD Fourth World
International Organisation for Standardisation
International Organisation of Consumers Unions
International Organisation of Employers
International Planned Parenthood Federation
International Social Security Association
International Union of Family Organisations
International Union of Local Authorities
International Youth and Student Movement for the United Nations
Inter-Parliamentary Union
Inter-Press Service International Co-operative
Muslim World League
Organisation of African Trade Union Unity
Rotary International
Society for International Development
Soroptimist International
United Towns Organisation
Women's International Democratic Federation

World Assembly of Youth
World Confederation of Labour
World Federation of Democratic Youth
World Federation of Trade Unions
World Federation of United Nations Associations
World Muslim Congress
World Veterans Federation
Zonta International

Source: UN document E/1994/INF/5 of 13 May 1994.

Decision 1/1 of the Preparatory Committee of the United Nations Conference on Environment and Development
Role of non-governmental organisations in the preparatory process for the United Nations Conference on Environment and Development

1. At its 22nd meeting, on 14 August 1990, the Preparatory Committee for the United Nations Conference on Environment and Development agreed that the effective contributions of non-governmental organisations in the preparatory process were in its interest.
2. There was agreement on broad-based involvement by relevant non-governmental organisations.
3. The Preparatory Committee's policy should be to encourage an equitable representation of non-governmental organisations from developed and developing countries and from all regions and also to ensure a fair balance between non-governmental organisations with an environment focus and those with a development focus. The Preparatory Committee would encourage the participation of scientific and other organisations.
4. The Preparatory Committee decides that, only for the purpose of its first session, the following rules would apply without prejudice to any decision that might be taken by the General Assembly at its forty-fifth session:
(*a*) Non-governmental organisations shall not have any negotiating role in the work of the Preparatory Committee;
(*b*) Relevant non-governmental organisations may, at their own expense, make written presentations in the preparatory process through the Secretariat in the official languages of the United Nations as they deem appropriate. Those written presentations will not be issued as official documents except in accordance with United Nations rules of procedures;
(*c*) Relevant non-governmental organisations in consultative status with the Economic and Social Council may be given an opportunity to briefly address plenary meetings of the Preparatory Committee and meetings of the Working Groups. Other relevant non-governmental organisations may also ask to speak briefly in such meetings. If the number of such requests is too large, the Preparatory Committee shall request the non-governmental organisations to form themselves into constituencies and each constituency to speak through one spokesman. Any oral intervention

by a non-governmental organisation would, in accordance with normal United Nations practice, be at the discretion of the Chairman and with the consent of the Preparatory Committee or the Working Group, as the case may be.

5. The Committee noted with appreciation the initiative taken by the Secretary-General of the Conference to seek extrabudgetary resources, in addition to the voluntary fund established pursuant to General Assembly resolution 44/228 of 22 December 1989, in order to facilitate access in the preparatory process to especially important contributions that would not otherwise be available, particularly through the effective participation of institutions and experts from developing countries in various aspects of the preparatory process. In that context, the Secretary-General was requested to utilise those resources, to enable representatives of relevant non-governmental organisations from developing countries, in particular the least developed among them, to participate in the preparatory process and the Conference, either independently or as members of official delegations if their countries so decide.

6. The Chairman would, with the assistance of the chairmen of the regional groups, other co-ordinating groups and the Secretariat, propose a procedure for determining non-governmental organisations' competence and relevance to the work of the Preparatory Committee.

7. The Preparatory Committee recommended to the General Assembly that it consider at its forty-fifth session the question of the participation of non-governmental organisations in the preparatory process for the Conference taking into account the decision adopted by the Preparatory Committee at its first session.

8. The Preparatory Committee endorsed the proposals made by the Secretary-General of the Conference in his report (A/CONF.151/PC/9) subject to the present decision.

Source: Report of the Preparatory Committee for the United Nations Conference on Environment and Development, First Session 6–31 August 1990, UN document A/45/46 of 25 January 1991, pp. 22–3.

Decision 2/1 of the Preparatory Committee of the United Nations Conference on Environment and Development
Procedure for determining non-governmental organisations' competence and relevance to the work of the Preparatory Committee

At its 28th meeting, on 18 March 1991, the Preparatory Committee for the United Nations Conference on Environment decided on the following procedure for determining non-governmental organisations' competence and relevance to the work of the Preparatory Committee:

1. Non-governmental organisations in consultative status with the Economic and Social Council and others desiring to be accredited for participation in meetings of the Preparatory Committee, in accordance with decision 1/1 of the first session of the Preparatory Committee as endorsed by General Assembly resolution 45/211 of 21 December 1990, may apply

to the Conference secretariat for this purpose.

2. All such applications must be accompanied by information on the organisation's competence and relevance to the work of the Preparatory Committee, indicating the particular areas of the Conference preparations which such competence and relevance pertains and which could include, *inter alia*, the following information:

(*a*) The purposes of the organisation;

(*b*) Information as to the programmes and activities of the organisation in areas relevant to the Conference and its preparatory process, and in which country(ies) they are carried out;

(*c*) Copies of its annual reports with financial statements, and a listing of governing body members and their country of nationality;

(*d*) In respect of membership organisations, a description of its membership, indicating total numbers and their geographical distribution;

(*e*) Non-governmental organisations in consultative status with the Economic and Social Council shall be deemed to have satisfied these requirements to the extent that they have already provided such information to the United Nations.

3. In cases where the Conference secretariat believes, on the basis of the information provided in accordance with paragraph 2 above, that the organisation has established its competence and relevance to the work of the Preparatory Committee, it will recommend to the Preparatory Committee that the organisation be accredited. In cases where the Conference secretariat does not recommend the granting of accreditation, it will make available to the Preparatory Committee the reasons for not doing so. The Conference secretariat should make its recommendations available to the Preparatory Committee at the start of the session.

4. The Preparatory Committee will decide on all cases within 24 hours of the Conference secretariat's recommendations having been made available to its members. In the event of a decision not being taken within this timeframe, interim accreditations shall be accorded until such time as a decision is taken.

5. A non-governmental organisation that has been granted accreditation to attend a session of the Preparatory Committee may attend all its future sessions.

Source: Report of the Preparatory Committee for the United Nations Conference on Environment and Development, Second Session 18 March–5 April 1991, UN document A/46/48 of 21 June 1991, pp. 21–2.

Extracts on NGOs from the United Nations Conference on Environment and Development, Agenda 21

Section III STRENGTHENING THE ROLE OF MAJOR GROUPS
Chapter 23   Preamble

23.1. Critical to the effective implementation of the objectives, policies and mechanisms agreed to by Governments in all programme areas of

Agenda 21 will be the commitment and genuine involvement of all social groups.

23.2. One of the fundamental prerequisites for the achievement of sustainable development is broad public participation in decision-making. Furthermore, in the more specific context of environment and development, the need for new forms of participation has emerged. This includes the need of individuals, groups and organisations to participate in environmental impact assessment procedures and to know about and participate in decisions, particularly those which potentially affect the communities in which they live and work. Individuals, groups and organisations should have access to information relevant to environment and development held by national authorities, including information on products and activities that have or are likely to have a significant impact on the environment, and information on environmental protection measures.

23.3. Any policies, definitions or rules affecting access to and participation by non-governmental organisations in the work of United Nations institutions or agencies associated with the implementation of Agenda 21 must apply equally to all major groups.

23.4. The programme areas set out below address the means for moving towards real social partnership in support of common efforts for sustainable development.

(The nine major groups were then dealt with in the following chapters: 24, Global action for women towards sustainable and equitable development; 25, Children and youth in sustainable development; 26, Recognising and strengthening the role of indigenous people and their communities; 27, Strengthening the role of non-governmental organisations: partners for sustainable development; 28, Local authorities' initiatives in support of Agenda 21; 29, Strengthening the role of workers and their trade unions; 30, Strengthening the role of business and industry; 31, Scientific and technological community; and 32, Strengthening the role of farmers.)

Section IV. MEANS OF IMPLEMENTATION
Chapter 38. International Institutional Arrangements
L. Non-governmental organisations
38.42. Non-governmental organisations and major groups are important partners in the implementation of Agenda 21. Relevant non-governmental organisations, including the scientific community, the private sector and women's groups, should be given opportunities to make their contributions and establish appropriate relationships with the United Nations system. Support should be provided for developing countries' non-governmental organisations and their self-organised networks.

38.43. The United Nations system, including international finance and development agencies, and all intergovernmental organisations and forums should, in consultation with non-governmental organisations, take measures to:

(a) Design open and effective means to achieve the participation of non-governmental organisations, including those related to major groups, in the process established to review and evaluate the implementation of Agenda 21 at all levels and promote their contribution to it;

(*b*) Take into account the findings of review systems and evaluation processes of non-governmental organisations in relevant reports of the Secretary-General to the General Assembly and all pertinent United Nations agencies and intergovernmental organisations and forums concerning implementation of Agenda 21 in accordance with the review process.
38.44. Procedures should be established for an expanded role for non-governmental organisations, including those related to major groups, with accreditation based on the procedures used in the Conference. Such organisations should have access to reports and other information produced by the United Nations system. The General Assembly, at an early stage, should examine ways of enhancing the involvement of non-governmental organisations within the United Nations system in relation to the follow-up process of the Conference.
38.45. The Conference takes note of other institutional initiatives for the implementation of Agenda 21, such as the proposal to establish a non-governmental Earth Council and the proposal to appoint a guardian for future generations, as well as other initiatives taken by local governments and business sectors.

Source: Report of the United Nations Conference on Environment and Development, Rio de Janeiro, 3–14 June 1992, in UN document A/CONF.151/26 of 14 August 1992 (Vol. III)

ECOSOC Decision 1993/215: Procedural arrangements for the Commission on Sustainable Development

At its 3rd plenary meeting, on 12 February 1993, the Council:
(*a*) Decided that, with the following supplementary arrangements, the rules of procedure of the functional commissions of the Economic and Social Council should apply to the Commission on Sustainable Development:

Participation of and consultation with specialised agencies and participation of other intergovernmental organisations
1. While the participation of and consultation with specialised agencies and the participation of other intergovernmental organisations are governed by rules 71–74 of the rules of procedure of the functional commissions of the Economic and Social Council, the Commission on Sustainable Development or a subsidiary organ thereof shall invite relevant intergovernmental organisations within and outside the United Nations system, including multilateral financial institutions, to appoint special representatives to the Commission to serve as focal points for the Commission's members and the Secretariat.

Representation of and consultation with non-governmental organisations
2. Representation of and consultation with the non-governmental organisations in the Commission would be governed by the following arrangements, which would supplement, solely for the purposes of the Commission, rules 75 and 76 of the rules of procedure of the functional commissions of the Economic and Social Council:

(i) Non-governmental organisations in consultative status with the Council, Category I or II, or relevant and competent non-governmental organisations on the Roster may designate authorised representatives to be present at and observe the meetings of the Commission and its subsidiary organs;

(ii) These non-governmental organisations may, at their own expense, make written presentations to the Commission and its subsidiary organs through the Secretariat in the official languages of the United Nations, as they deem appropriate. Such written presentations will not be issued as official documents;

(iii) These non-governmental organisations may be given an opportunity to briefly address the meetings of the Commission and its subsidiary organs. Taking into account the number of non-governmental organisations expressing a desire to be accorded that opportunity, the Chairman of the Commission or its subsidiary organ may request the non-governmental organisations concerned to address the meetings through one or more spokespersons. Any oral intervention by a representative of a non-governmental organisation shall be made at the discretion of the Chairman of the Commission or its subsidiary organ and with the consent of the members of the Commission or its subsidiary organ, as the case may be;

(iv) Non-governmental organisations shall not have any negotiating role in the work of the Commission and its subsidiary organs;

(v) The Commission may consult with and/or hear, as appropriate, non-governmental organisations in consultative status with the Council, Category I or II, or relevant and competent non-governmental organisations on the Roster either directly or through a committee or committees established for that purpose;

(vi) The relevance and competence of non-governmental organisations to be included in the Roster shall be determined by the Council on the recommendation of the Secretary-General;

(b) Requested the Commission to encourage equitable representation of non-governmental organisations from the developed and developing countries and from all regions and also to strive to ensure a fair balance between non-governmental organisations with an environment focus and those with a development focus;

(c) Decided that any non-governmental organisation which was accredited to participate in the work of the Preparatory Committee for the United Nations Conference on Environment and Development by the conclusion of its fourth session could apply for and should be granted Roster status, subject to approval by the Council and bearing in mind the provisions of Article 71 of the Charter of the United Nations;

(d) Invited non-governmental organisations, with a view to enhancing their effective and co-ordinated contribution to the work of the Commission and to the follow-up of the United Nations Conference on Environment and Development in general, to consider, or continue organising themselves in various constituencies and interest groups and to set up non-governmental networks, including electronic networks, for the exchange

of relevant information and documentation;
(e) Decided further, in the light of paragraph 2 above and its decision 1993/207 of 12 February 1993, to make the following changes to the rules of procedure of the functional commissions of the Council:

(i) In footnote 1, add the Commission on Sustainable Development to the enumeration of functional commissions of the Council;
(ii) In footnote 4, add a reference to the Commission on Sustainable Development;
(iii) Add a footnote to rules 75 and 76 reading:
'The terms of representation of and consultations with the non-governmental organisations in the Commission on Sustainable Development have been further determined by the Economic and Social Council in its decision 1993/215 of 12 February 1993.'

Source: UN document E/1993/INF/2 of 4 March 1993.

Letter inviting NGOs to participate in the Commission on Sustainable Development

NOTIFICATION, 3 MARCH 1993
The first session of the Commission on Sustainable Development which was recently formally established by the Economic and Social Council will take place in New York on June 14–25 1993.

Non-governmental organisations in consultative status with ECOSOC
Non-governmental organisations which already have Category I, II or Roster status with the Economic and Social Council are eligible to take part in the work of the Commission, as a functional commission of ECOSOC, in accordance with existing legislation.

Non-governmental organisations accredited with UNCED but not in consultative status with ECOSOC
1. The Council has decided that any non-governmental organisation which was accredited to participate in the work of the United Nations Conference on Environment and Development can apply for and shall be granted Roster status solely for the purpose of the Commission on Sustainable Development, subject to approval of the Council, bearing in mind the provisions of Article 71 of the Charter of the United Nations.
2. Such a status would, in particular, allow competent and relevant non-governmental organisations to be represented at the sessions of the Commission on Sustainable Development in accordance with the procedural arrangements determined for the Commission by ECOSOC in its decision 1993/215.
3. If your organisation was accredited to participate in UNCED and is interested in being represented at the sessions of the Commission on Sustainable Development, the Secretariat of the United Nations will require a communication from your organisation confirming such an interest. The deadline for the receipt of such communication is 15 April 1993. The

Secretariat will then prepare a first list of recommended non-governmental organisations for consideration and approval by ECOSOC at its resumed session to be held later this year and prior to the first session of the Commission on Sustainable Development.

Other non-governmental organisations

1. Other non-governmental organisations, which were not accredited to participate in UNCED but consider themselves to be relevant and competent in the areas pertaining to the work of the Commission on Sustainable Development, may seek such accreditation solely for the purpose of this Commission, subject to approval by ECOSOC. These organisations would have to submit to the United Nations Secretariat the following information:

– copies of the latest annual report and the most recent budget;
– copy of constitution and/or bylaws and information on governing body composition;
– proof of the non-profit nature of the organisation;
– a short statement of how the organisation's activities relate to the Commission on Sustainable Development, a description of membership and location of headquarters (please duly complete the attached form).

2. Due to time constraints the Secretariat will not be in a position to consider any applications from non-governmental organisations seeking accreditation before the first session of the Commission on Sustainable Development received after April 15 1993 to prepare relevant recommendations for the Council at its resumed session mentioned in paragraph 3 above.

Source: Mailing by World Federalist Movement, Amsterdam, and Centre for Development of International Law, Washington DC, on behalf of International NGO Task Group on Legal and Institutional Matters, copying letter from UN Secretariat, NGO Unit.

Commission on Sustainable Development upgrades NGO Participation

The following recommendation was endorsed by ECOSOC Decision 1994/300 of 29 July 1994, 'subject to a final resolution of the issue . . . following the outcome of the review'. Its effect was to add 552 environmental NGOs to the Roster, giving them access to all meetings of ECOSOC and all its subsidiary bodies, rather than just the CSD.

The Commission recommends that the overall access of major groups, including non-governmental organisations, to the Commission's work throughout the year be clarified and enhanced, and, without prejudice to the outcome of the general review of arrangements for consultations with non-governmental organisations to be carried out by the Economic and Social Council, recommends that:

(a) The Economic and Social Council at its substantive session of 1994 place non-governmental organisations accredited to the Commission by Council decision 1993/220 on the Roster, as envisaged in Council decision 1993/215;

(*b*) The Council continue to grant Roster status to those non-governmental organisations that were accredited to the United Nations Conference on Environment and Development and that confirm their interest in being accredited to the Commission.

Source: Report of the Commission on Sustainable Development on its Second Session, 16–27 May 1994, UN document E/1994/33-E/CN.17/1994/20 of 12 July 1994, paragraph 24.

APPENDIX C

STATEMENT BY THE UN SECRETARY-GENERAL, BOUTROS BOUTROS-GHALI

AT THE UN DEPARTMENT OF
PUBLIC INFORMATION
FORTY-SEVENTH ANNUAL CONFERENCE
OF NON-GOVERNMENTAL ORGANIZATIONS,
'WE THE PEOPLES: BUILDING PEACE'

New York, 20 September 1994

Madame President, ladies and gentlemen, dear friends,

On behalf of the United Nations and for myself, I welcome you. I want you to consider this your home.

Until recently, these words might have caused astonishment. The United Nations was considered to be a forum for sovereign States alone.

Within the space of a few short years, this attitude has changed. Non-governmental organizations are now considered full participants in international life. This change is largely due to the quick succession of historical events which we have witnessed in recent years. The fall of the Berlin Wall, the end of the cold war and of East-West antagonism, shattered the ideological screen which concealed the reality of international relations. Political, economic, social and cultural phenomena have been revealed in their true dimensions and in their profound complexity.

Today, we are well aware that the international community must address a human community that is profoundly transnational. For a long time, the international order was regarded as political and firmly established. Now we must now learn to accept and to deal with a world that is both social and mobile. The movement of wealth, people, capital, and ideas is as important today as control of territory was yesterday. We therefore must build a framework which takes into account not only political issues, but economic behaviour and social and cultural aspirations. Non-governmental organizations are a basic form of popular representation in the present-day world. Their participation in international organiza-

311

tions is, in a way, a guarantee of the political legitimacy of those international organizations.

It is therefore not surprising that in a short space of time we have witnessed the emergence of many new non-governmental organizations.

Today, NGOs continue to increase in number on every continent. This is true in developed countries. In France, 54,000 new associations have been established since 1987. In Italy, 40 per cent of the associations have been set up within the last 15 years. This phenomenon is also occurring in developing countries. Within a short space of time 10,000 NGOs have been established in Bangladesh, 21,000 in the Philippines, and 27,000 in Chile. In Eastern Europe, since the fall of communism, non-governmental organizations have been playing an increasingly important role in people's lives. Their development is inseparable from the aspiration for freedom which, in various forms, is today shaking international society.

Ladies and gentlemen,

You have chosen as your topic for this year, the role of non-governmental organizations in peace-building.

This is a particularly ambitious and innovative subject. We are well aware of what non-governmental organizations do in social, cultural and humanitarian fields, as well as their work to protect human rights and to promote development. But we do not often have occasion to think about what these organizations can do for international peace and security.

I, for my part, am convinced that NGOs have an important role to play in the achievement of the ideal established by the Charter of the United Nations: the maintenance and establishment of peace. We all know that States play the preponderant role in this area. We all know that the Charter confers the primary responsibility for the maintenance of peace upon the Security Council. But I have sought, in 'An Agenda for Peace', to emphasize as clearly as possible that 'peace in the largest sense cannot be accomplished by the United Nations system or by Governments alone. Non-governmental organizations, academic institutions, parliamentarians, business and professional communities, the media and the public at large must all be involved'.

This is the point I wish to stress to you. For to paraphrase an old saying: peace is too important to be entrusted to States alone.

Accepting this perspective, non-governmental organizations can, I believe, pursue their activities on three fronts.

In the search for peace, non-governmental organizations must obtain the means – and we must help them do so – to engage in assistance, mobilization and democratization activities, all at the same time. I should like to consider these three types of activity with you for a few minutes.

With regard to assistance, non-governmental organizations have a key role to play – and many are already doing so. In fact, in the area of peace-keeping, NGO activities have to a large extent paralleled the changes which have taken place within the United Nations itself.

Today, the mandates of United Nations operations go far beyond the standard definition of 'peace-keeping' employed in the past.

These operations reflect recent international developments, in that conflicts increasingly are taking place within, rather than between, countries. Every day the United Nations deals with civil wars, secessions, partitions, ethnic clashes and tribal conflicts. It will be understood how difficult the mission of the United Nations then becomes, obliged as it is to respect the fragile balance between the sovereignty of States and a mandate to intervene.

Moreover, the role of these operations is no longer confined to simply deploying a neutral presence between two belligerent parties. The aim of the new operations is the making, and indeed the building, of peace. This can involve electoral assistance, humanitarian aid, administrative activities, the rebuilding of roads and bridges, rural demining operations, the promotion of democracy and the protection of human rights.

In 'An Agenda for Peace' I stated explicitly that 'this wider mission for the world Organization will demand the concerted attention and effort of individual States, of regional and non-governmental organizations, and of all of the United Nations system'.

Indeed, the vast enterprise of building peace pre-supposes that non-governmental organizations will be involved at every stage. In the field of preventive diplomacy, non-governmental organizations, because of their familiarity with the situation on the ground, are well placed to play a part in early warning machinery by drawing the attention of Governments to nascent crises and emerging conflicts.

With regard to peacemaking, there is wide recognition of the humanitarian and social work done by NGOs, generally under perilous and difficult conditions.

Lastly, with regard to post-conflict peace-building, non-governmental organizations can do a good deal to help fragile Governments and destitute populations, find the confidence and resources to make peace last.

But it is essential that the activities of non-governmental organizations and those of the United Nations should complement each other. I am sure that you will reflect at length on how best to coordinate NGO activities with those of the United Nations. We can all recall the difficulties, misunderstandings and differences which have arisen from time to time between the world Organization and certain NGOs in the context of specific operations.

Today it must be stated quite clearly that we must all make an honest and fundamental reappraisal. We want not to lay blame at anyone's door, but to avoid any repetition of events which undermine peace – the objective which together we are pursuing.

Perhaps the United Nations has not yet fully appreciated the importance of the role of NGOs in the field. Perhaps it does not cooperate enough with institutions on the spot which can provide essential support.

But NGOs must also understand the political complexity of any peace-keeping operation. Perhaps in their desire to resolve problems urgently they do not appreciate how much time is needed to settle any conflict. Perhaps their involvement in activities sometimes prevents them from grasping all aspects of a conflict. Perhaps on occasion they are too quick to point the finger, whereas the over-riding aim is to reconcile the belligerents.

I believe that the time has now come to tackle these problems so that together we can act still more effectively to promote peace.

You can rely on me to undertake an in-depth analysis of how to better coordinate our common activities. I am confident that you, for your part, will contribute to this analysis through your deliberations. This is my sincere expectation.

Yet I hope you will do still more. For, as I have said, NGOs must also, in my view, undertake essential mobilization activities.

The mobilization of States and public opinion by NGOs is an essential element in international activities to promote peace.

As you are aware, the end of the cold war has, in some cases, had untoward effects. Certain regions of the world have suddenly lost strategic interest for the great powers. As a result, these powers have been sorely tempted to leave those regions to their own devices, to let them sink into economic underdevelopment, or to founder in political disorder.

As the Secretary-General of the United Nations, I know that it is sometimes difficult to convince States to commit themselves to peace-keeping activities which, nonetheless, are essential. For States to commit personnel, material and money in the service of peace and in the framework of United Nations activities, it is often necessary for national public opinion to lead the way.

It is the non-governmental organizations which, in most cases, have helped to clear this way.

I wish to state it to you as clearly as possible – I need the mobilizing power of non-governmental organizations.

But here again, each of us must consider the matter in depth. Just as the United Nations must constantly strive to transcend partisan differences in order to uphold the higher interests of peace, non-governmental organizations must also secure their independence with regard to all States.

This is a basic condition for their credibility. Non-governmental organizations are infinitely diverse by virtue of their size, statutes, fields of activity, methods, means and objectives. It is understandable that States are sometimes tempted to try to utilize or control non-governmental organizations in order to place them indirectly in the service of their own national policies.

It is quite obvious that in order to be able to carry out fully their role as a stimulus for the international community in promoting peace, NGOs must be beyond reproach in the political field.

I know that this is not an easy task and that it entails constant and continual work. But I also know that I can rely on you to be vigilant. For, let me repeat, your independence is essential for you to be able to be full participants in the international peace process.

Indeed, the mobilization mission that the international community expects of you will be possible only if you really represent the profound aspirations of all the integral parts of international society.

In other words, this mobilization can be truly meaningful only if it is based on a third element: your activities for democratization.

In 'An Agenda for Peace' I had occasion to reflect on the necessary democratization of international relations and of the United Nations. I stressed the fact that, for me, 'democracy at all levels is essential to attain peace'. Yes, democracy must be the guiding principle both in relations between States and within States themselves. And I believe that non-governmental organizations have a major role to play in the democratization process.

As I said at the beginning of my statement, the international order in which we must conduct our work today is radically different from the one in which those who drafted the Charter operated.

We find ourselves today within a world system that has profound doubts about its own structures and, strangely, about the most fundamental of these: the very notion of the State.

Undoubtedly, the twentieth century will not only have been the century of the downfall of empires – the consequences of which we have yet to fully experience or sustain. But the twentieth century will also have been the century in which doubt was cast on the nation State. With tragic uncertainty, certain peoples, seek to reconcile the rational nature of the State with the urges of micro-nationalism. Elsewhere, it is the very substance of the State that is collapsing. Social integration has become more difficult even within Western societies. This decaying of institutions has led to the resurgence or rebirth of primitive ties of solidarity, many of which, alas, seem prone to engender fanaticism and a desire to exclude.

Accordingly, it is necessary to provide the men and women in today's world with a framework that will enable them, amidst the practical challenges of concrete situations, to mobilize themselves in favour of the great ideals of the international community.

It is the NGOs, which, in most cases, make it possible for these complex and often diffuse aspirations to take form, and to flourish. In this way, you are carrying out an essential representational role. You are an essential part of the legitimacy without which no international activity can be meaningful. Often, it is you who, on a day-to-day basis, constitute the link between democracy and peace. Indeed, the democratic imperative is inseparable from the activities that we must carry out to promote peace. In my opinion, diplomacy that consolidates peace and democracy is of the utmost importance at the close of the twentieth century. I will pay close attention to your ideas on how to strengthen the link between peace and democracy.

I am convinced that, just as human rights are universal, democracy can be adapted to all cultures.

I have already said that human rights are the common language of mankind. The same holds true for democracy. Democracy, too, is the political expression of our common heritage. For, it must be understood that democracy is not a model to be copied from certain States but a goal to be reached by all peoples.

Non-governmental organizations have a crucial role to play in this area. They can help develop effective ways of spreading the ideas of peace and democracy. They can take part in the birth and development of democratic institutions within States. They can also serve as vigilant monitors, helping to guarantee respect for democracy, throughout the world.

Madame President, ladies and gentlemen, dear friends, I should like, in conclusion, to carry this line of thought even further.

Today we are all searching for an international order that is acceptable to all. Nevertheless, we also know how profoundly ambiguous the very notion of an international order is. For the concept of an international order – if there is one at all – fulfils various different functions in the lives of States and peoples. It has a political and an ideological dimension, as well as an economic and a cultural one. It can be used by the very powerful to buttress a legal argument, and it can also be used by the very weak in support of a militant speech. In short, what we call the international order is both the expression of the present-day balance of power and an idealization of a society in evolution.

In order for every woman and every man in the world to perceive their true stake in the great ideals of the world Organization, it is necessary to have many more institutions such as yours.

Only thus shall we be faithful to the urgent exhortation with which the preamble to the Charter begins: We the peoples of the United Nations.

INDEX OF NON-GOVERNMENTAL ORGANISATIONS

ABBREVIATIONS USED IN THE INDEXES

Ass.	Association	Dev.	Development
Comm.	Commission	Fed.	Federation
C'ttee	Committee	Intgov.	Intergovernmental
Conf.	Conference	Int.	International
Conv.	Convention	Orgs.	Organisations
Co.	Council	Rapp.	Rapporteur
Decl.	Declaration	W. G.	Working Group
Dept.	Department		

319

SUBJECT INDEX